Arts and Crafts in Waldorf Schools

An Integrated Approach

Arts and Crafts in Waldorf Schools

An Integrated Approach

Edited by Michael Martin

Floris Books

Translated by Carl Hoffmann; ceramics: Harlan Gilbert

First published in German as *Der künstlerisch-handwerkliche Unterricht in der Waldorfschule* by Verlag Freies Geistesleben in 1991

First published in English as *Educating through Arts and Crafts: An integrated approach to craft work in Steiner Waldorf schools* by Steiner Schools Fellowship Publications in 1999
This third edition © Floris Books 2017

The Authors have asserted their right under the Copyright, Designs and Patent Act of 1988 to be identified as the Authors of this Work

All rights reserved. No part of this publication may be reproduced without the prior permission of Floris Books, Edinburgh www.florisbooks.co.uk

British Library CIP data available
ISBN 978-178250-459-7
Printed in Great Britain
by Bell & Bain, Ltd

Table of Contents

Preface 7
Introduction 9

Part One: From Play to Work

1. *From play in learning to joy in work*
   by Ernst Bühler 17
2. *The age of 'work maturity'*
   by Michael Martin 21

Part Two: Crafts in the Middle School

3. *Preface to Part Two*
   by Michael Martin 33
4. *Getting ready for craft lessons* (Class 5)
   by Johannes Geier 35
5. *Shifting emphasis in craft lessons*
   (Class 6) by Michael Martin 41
6. *Crafts in the Middle School*
   (Classes 5–8) by Walter Dielhenn 44
7. *A forestry main-lesson class trip* (Class 7)
   by Liesel Gudrun Gienapp 65

8. *Reflections on moveable toys*
   (Class 7) by Michael Martin 70
9. *Investigating the nature of wood*
   (Classes 6–8) by Klaus Charisius 77
10. *Artistic elements in the crafts*
    by Michael Martin 90
11. *Colour in the craft room*
    by Michael Martin 99

Part Three: Crafts in the Upper School

12. *Arts and crafts and the human being*
    (Class 10) by Michael Martin 103
13. *Form-giving elements and techniques*
    (Classes 9–12) by Michael Martin 106
14. *Pottery lessons* (Classes 9–12)
    by Gerd von Steitencron 126
15. *Pottery workshops and modelling rooms* by Michael Martin 146
16. *The shoemaking block* (Class 9)
    by Gerard Locher 148

17. *Working with metals* (Classes 9 and 10) by Herbert Seufert — 156

18. *Working with iron* by Wolf von Knoblauch — 168

19. *Copper and iron workshops* by Michael Martin — 175

20. *The joinery main-lesson blocks* (Classes 9 and 10) by Friedrich Weidler — 178

21. *Wood and carpentry workshops* by Michael Martin — 189

Part Four: Formative Artistic Lessons in the Upper School

22. *Lessons in modelling and shaded drawing* by Michael Martin — 193

23. *Metamorphosis and modelling lessons* by Anna-Sophia Gross — 217

24. *Working with stone* (Classes 10–12) by Rainer Lechler — 230

25. *Stone carving in the Upper School* (Classes 11 and 12) by Winifred Stuhlmann — 234

26. *Woodcarving and art* (Class 13) by Uwe Bosse — 252

Part Five: Further Thinking

27. *Work and rhythm* by Herbert Seufert — 259

28. *Methods in the formative lessons* by Michael Martin — 264

29. *The influence of work on thinking* by Michael Martin — 271

30. *An integrated approach to craftwork* by Aonghus Gordon — 288

Notes — 295
Index of activities and materials — 299

Preface

This book was written by craft teachers, either still teaching or retired, who have been working for many years in the various areas of arts and crafts in Steiner-Waldorf schools. They tell of their experiences with children in the workshops. But the articles are more than the teachers' experience in the classrooms; they are also an expression of their individuality. And this must be so, as a Steiner-Waldorf teacher is allowed to and, indeed, ought to work from the commitment of their personality. Each teacher will attempt to find their way to an art of education. This common aim provided the basis for this book.

Any individual person could not have done it. It would have meant decades of learning in order to master all the subjects in the arts and crafts taught in Steiner-Waldorf schools. Whilst the specialist in carpentry may be called upon to learn pottery or the craft of the blacksmith should their school demand it, or the fully trained sculptor be asked to learn all about joinery, should this be required, they will, however, feel more secure in their own specialised area and, therefore, probably teach it better. Because of this it seemed to be sensible to ask many specialists to contribute towards the great variety of the arts and craft lessons practised in Steiner-Waldorf schools. This book is the result.

Over and above the many different areas of arts and crafts is the pedagogical task. Why is a certain subject taught during any one year? What are the aims? The search for answers unites the individual teachers. But joy in doing is not enough. The teacher must know the developmental stages engendered by the work and how such stages can be nurtured.

Textbooks and encyclopaedias cannot provide answers. Instead we have the knowledge of the human being given to us by Rudolf Steiner. The many lecture cycles concentrate on the very kernel of all educational efforts: the human being. Intensive work with this knowledge, applying it to day-to-day school events, and getting the confirmation of its truth during lessons all result in a wealth of far-reaching discoveries of new knowledge on which the school's further development rests.

The weekly teachers' meetings, as well as the numerous meetings of specialist teachers, are devoted to the study of Rudolf Steiner's pedagogy. The handwork and craft teachers also frequently meet, study Rudolf Steiner's indications and, through this activity, continue to improve their work. During annual meetings of craft teachers nationwide – always held in a different school –

the teachers exchange experiences. Their efforts are contained in this book. They are meant as stimuli for further work, for transformation, for discovering new ways. They are to serve as examples but do not claim to be general values applicable to all schools, or to be the last word on the subject.

We hope that this book will make it easier for the newcomer. It will allow him or her to build on proven ground and gradually feel encouraged to find an individual approach. It is only through the individual creative element that any educational intention can succeed. What is merely traditional or copied cannot provide the spark that must connect teacher and children.

Every ideal that can be realised in a practical way will ultimately have to transform, to adapt, if it is not to remain tied to a well thought-out but yet abstract heaven. This applies especially to schemes that can provide a kind of thought structure that allows for greater clarity. But they are no more than that – structures that must be translated into life! The teacher's sensitive observation of their students and educational intention can never be replaced by schemes or structures, however excellent they may be.

An experienced teacher of the first Waldorf school in Stuttgart expressed this as follows:

A curriculum has been worked out that does not contain an iota of programming or dogmatism. This applies also to the following indications for the teaching of subjects in the various classes. They should not be taken as dogma or rigid rules. The ideal curriculum must trace the ever-changing picture of the developing human being during the different ages. But, as each ideal, it is confronted by the full reality of life, to which it must adapt.[1]

We wish to thank all those who contributed to this book. But also those who will read it with interest and patience.

MICHAEL MARTIN, 1990

Introduction

The publication of Richard Heinberg's seminal book, *The Party's Over: Oil, War and the Fate of Industrial Societies* and his address to the Hiram Summer Conference in June 2007 gave positive affirmation to the syllabus and curriculum inherent in Rudolf Steiner schools, particularly where classroom activities are supported by a connection to land, farming, gardening and practical craftwork. The premise that cheap oil will be here beyond the next decade is so profoundly challenged that a paradigmic shift is required from society to re-engage schools in a deeper practical and land-based curriculum. Physical and practical work, says Heinberg, will once again become meaningful and dignified.

Rudolf Steiner understood the imperative for children to engage with practical life in such a way that they become inter-connected at the deepest level. The following quote illustrates the point:

Do not omit, even at the beginning, when showing the child the connection between agriculture and human life, to give him a clear idea of the plough, of the harrow, etc. ... and if you could even make little ploughs and let the children cultivate the school garden, if they could be allowed to cut with little sickles, or mow with little scythes, this would establish a good contact with life. Far more important than skills is the psychic intimacy of the child's life with the life of the world. For the actual fact is: a child who has cut grass with a sickle, mown grass with a scythe, drawn a furrow with a little plough, will be a different person from a child who has not done these things.

The soul undergoes a change from doing things. Abstract teaching of manual skill is really no substitute.[2]

Michael Martin's *Educating Through Arts and Crafts*, alongside the innovative work of the Hiram Trust, provides a wealth of experience from accomplished teachers in the practical realm. However, there is an increasing need to link the sourcing of primary materials to the living environment – wool from sheep, wood from trees, clay from earth – in order to cultivate industriousness in the context of workshop experience. This shift generates further innovative capacity building for our children to meet the future.

The emergence of 'transition towns',[3] the systematic reduction of the carbon footprint within a community, invites response by developing 'transition schools'. Can Rudolf Steiner schools work increasingly so that the curriculum, and in particular, the practical skills, resonate within the sense of place, or 'genii loci', in a context of sustainable activity? In other words: how can teachers help developing children to grow into coherence with emergent local and global needs?

The practical skills curriculum and sustainability agenda converge harmoniously through an awakening to biodynamic integrative thinking – between human beings and the earth. Even tinctures of biodynamic practice give radiations of a healing environment for the school and community. In engaging practical skills with the outdoor classroom, new and regenerative experiences are made available to young people.

The intentional movement within the practical skills curriculum has a heightened efficacy. Not only does it offer self-reflective practice, but provides a learning culture based on non-personalised authority. The lawfulness of the natural materials and the social intention of craftwork, in particular, support adolescents through the Upper School. This external and legitimate authority reflecting back into the feeling life of the adolescent generates *emotional intelligence*, the pre-requisite for the continued development of the germinal ego. This germinal ego has the task of bringing coherence to the emergent being of young people. If directed into skilful practical work, an additional opportunity arises for a highly treasured quality to emerge, namely, autonomy in the service of the world.

Research within the field of neuro-cardiology suggests that the linking of brain and heart is best served through intimate, tactile activities of the hand. Evidence shows that the pre-frontal cortex is awakened and informed by the purposeful use of hands. In the words of Dr Frank Wilson:

> *... if the hand and brain learn to speak to each other intimately and harmoniously, something that humans seem to prize greatly, which we call autonomy, begins to take shape ... to learn to do something well with the hands, an extremely complicated process is initiated that endows the work with a powerful emotional charge. People are changed, significantly and irreversibly it seems, when movement, thought, and feeling fuse during the active, long-term pursuit of personal goals.*[4]

The intensification of the practical skills curriculum within our environment and landscape has a further benefit of generating a culture of 'heart-felt knowing'. This 'heart-felt knowing', which Rudolf Steiner described as the birth of the etheric heart, needs to be increasingly cultivated as idealism and love for the earth. The opportunity for pupils to experience biodynamics within the school setting can offer a seedbed for the development of imagination and experience of the living world. If the school can be so bold as to invite biodynamic land culture into its curriculum, as enshrined in Kolisko's prophetic view of the future of Rudolf Steiner education, then something that could be described as startling and enriching begins to happen – the cosmos, earth, and humans re-integrate.

AONGHUS GORDON, 2008

INTRODUCTION

As in every other subject, the teaching of arts and crafts in Steiner-Waldorf schools has its roots in a truly human pedagogy. It cannot, therefore, be directed primarily to the needs of specialised occupations. Neither should it remain as a kind of 'arty-crafty' pre-occupation. Its motivation can be neither *l'art pour l'art* nor *l'art pour la profession*. Rather, the work in arts and crafts is to support the overall educational aims of the school.

This means helping children and adolescents to find themselves. This self-discovery comes about in mysterious ways through the fact that children – particularly by working in practical subjects, by experiencing the shaping of substances, by improving their manual dexterity and by expressing the needs of the artist within each of them – also progress a little in world experience.

With an anthroposophically deepened understanding of the human being, we may see how craftwork helps children develop. This approach recognises that learning directed to systematised structures is not a spiritual activity as such, but merely a subsequent conservation of those predetermined structures. One of Rudolf Steiner's discoveries was that active, living spirit can more often be detected in the wisdom of practical activity than in mere reflection[1]. For the latter, the brain serves as the organ for thinking. In the former, however, it is the limbs themselves that become the actual organs of knowledge. In manual activities we think differently. There is an intelligence in doing that is important, even necessary, for every occupation, and for life itself. This practical intelligence is first acquired through hands and feet during early childhood. Meaningful practice in physical activity is a truly living spiritual activity, whereas so-called spiritual or mental work is often no more than the structuring of programmes whose distance from reality is well known. Only a person who can deal with life in a practical way can be said to work with the living spirit. Anthroposophy therefore introduces a whole new concept of spirit, and is able to make it fruitful for life.

All the manual/practical subjects in Steiner-Waldorf schools can be seen as eminent starting points for the spiritual development of children. First doing – then knowing; first experiencing – afterwards reflecting; first meeting the creative reality – then the distanced reflection, or else even this will remain empty. With this in mind, handwork lessons, gardening, practical experience in agriculture and forestry, as well as the meaningful movements of the limbs in eurythmy and physical education, support the lessons discussed in this book.

WOLFGANG SCHAD, 1991

The natural scientist Galileo Galilei (1564–1642) is supposed to have said the following sentence that expresses the guiding principle for his striving: 'He who wishes to solve natural-scientific questions without the aid of mathematics undertakes something that cannot be done. One has to measure what can be measured, and make measurable what can as yet not be measured.'

Translated into the language of the modern day, we get: 'Only when we have first gained insight into the methods of natural-scientific thinking and an understanding of mathematical structures can we solve the problems confronting us in our modern, rationalised world.'

This quote comes from the decree of the German Minister of Culture (1969) that introduced 'Modern maths' into the lower primary classes. It continues: 'Schools are given the task of mediating a basic knowledge, a foundation that leads to a comprehension of a mathematical understanding of the reality in which we live.'

What was, in the sixteenth century, limited to natural-scientific problems, is today demanded for the quite general and correct 'comprehension of the reality in which we live': the handling of mathematical structures and insights into the natural-scientific modes of thinking.

We can see this view growing ever stronger over the centuries. The German humorist Wilhelm Busch (1832–1906) characterises the situation in this way:

Darwin said, 'Evolution exists'. Let's assume: from minus X via 0 to plus X. The human being would here be our 0, while the monkey is still climbing about on minus X. The progress from minus 1 to 0 is obvious. Is it possible our world might be a mistake?... All right – in the meantime all life that used to be on 0 becomes extinct, is absorbed into plus 1 where, in the light of the new intellect it immediately resumes its ancient inheritance... We are already at plus 10 million – much head, little body... food: vegetables. Procreation as before. The swollen head cannot as yet infuse sense and reason into the thin body. On we go! Plus 10 billion. Food: air. Procreation by means of phlegmatic bud formation. The human being on 0 has long been forgotten. End. Plus X. Nothing but the head remains. Hardly any will. Procreation: none. The intellect, floating about like balloons, understands everything thoroughly. The little bit of will easily negates itself, and everything fades into – in the words of musicians – conciliatory harmonies...

Education here, now including the teaching of information technology, becomes primarily head development that runs the danger of either atrophying feeling and will or, should these be strongly enough present to allow them to unfold uncontrolled in children and turn into primitive instincts that terrorise the individuals themselves, leading to uncontrolled excesses of the will. Will and feeling no longer interweave harmoniously here.

Those lacking the necessary faculties for such a mind-based 'education' may leave school prematurely and enter an apprenticeship. Unfairly, manual work – crafts, a trade – is still looked upon as inferior, as lacking in intelligence.

It is here where Steiner-Waldorf schools intervene. Rudolf Steiner sees the human being as a threefold being with head, heart and hands. He points to the many relations between them, to their reciprocal influences, to the way they engender each other or, if the balance is disturbed, to the way they obstruct development. He traces the gradual development of these three systems during the

INTRODUCTION

years and shows how each of them contributes its part irreplaceably towards the unfolding of the individual.

It is a fatal mistake to believe that an individual's strength develops through a merely intellectual education or simply by itself. We cannot assess the individuality with average good grades or IQs. Only an education that addresses the whole being, that stimulates and permeates, may dare call itself an education. This is the reason why Steiner-Waldorf schools pay so much attention to the development of feeling and will, which allow a healthy and living intelligence to unfold and lead to the awakening and maturing of the individual.

MICHAEL MARTIN, 1990

Part One

From Play to Work

1

From play in learning to joy in work
Ernst Bühler

Our deeply anchored need to free ourselves from the weight of gravity begins to stir soon after birth. During their first year, with increasing effort, children gradually raise themselves from the horizontal to the vertical position. During the weeks immediately after their birth, babies' hands remain closed in little fists, as though enveloped in sleep, but it isn't long before their hands are able to move more freely. Slowly they begin to open; the delicately shaped fingers making their first tentative movements, not yet guided by any purposeful intentions. They move solely from the need for the will to express itself by doing. Only after several months do fingers begin to move in a co-ordinated way in order to grasp objects in their immediate environment.

Driven by an innate urge, children pursue these learning processes by themselves. During this time their hands become ever more skilled 'instruments'. This comes about without any reflection on actual movements; doing and thinking are as one. Only gradually does thinking develop from this oneness – ultimately leading to the duality of doing and thinking, the basis for all adult actions. The gradual awakening of thinking thus appears to express itself quite early, though unconsciously, in the skills of the hands. It may well be the reason why children wish so strongly to touch everything that is touchable and to hold it in their hands. What their hands touch and grasp is, in time, taken in by their hearts and, ultimately, grasped in their thoughts too. In the Basel lecture cycle, Rudolf Steiner said:

The more we take into account ... that intellect develops from the movements of the limbs, from dexterity and skills, the better it will be!

If we occupy the children with the arts and crafts in the right way, we shall do more for the spirit than by teaching those things considered to be spiritual and cultural.[1]

Hands are insatiably hungry for experiences. They are not content with merely touching and grasping objects, they want to become skilled, to develop faculties, to learn to do things with the objects they grasp. Think of the significance of children's joy when they've learnt to hold a spoon correctly, to put it to their mouth, or when they've learnt to raise a cup of milk to their lips, tilting it at just the right angle and coordinating it with breathing and swallowing. It all happens from the intelligence contained in the activity itself, which led Kant to assert that the hand is the 'outer brain' of the human being.

Imitation

The strong union between thinking and doing affects all children's learning processes. It's also active in what we call imitation. Imitation relies on children's intense powers of perception to connect, without any reservation, to their environment and grow with it as part of it, as one. Knowledge is not enough for children. They feel the need to become as one with the objects around them, and in fact they feel it so strongly that they themselves become an object. This is the strongest form of perception – not merely to perceive an object but to become an object. Information becomes identification. The urge to imitate is so powerful that children can do nothing but connect with everything around them and to 'perform' what their senses perceive – absolutely in the way Goethe expressed it: 'To do, to be active is Man's noblest calling.'

This elemental longing for doing rises from the unconscious depths of our will – but it must be stimulated from without, i.e. from our surroundings. If such stimuli are insufficient, the forces of imitation cannot unfold and children won't have strong enough roots in their environment. This in turn obstructs their ability to connect meaningfully and enthusiastically with anything. If, on the other hand, the impressions coming from without are too powerful – as in today's loud and sensation-overloaded world – this too will negatively affect the healthy development of children's natural urge for doing.

From imitation to work

This wonderful urge to imitate extends to children copying grown-ups at work. Since, however, today's work is generally outside children's sphere of experiences, we must endeavour to compensate by introducing work which children can imitate that differs from the excessive mechanisation and threatening passivity prevalent in our time.

The importance of imitating work lies in the fact that this does not allow children to act merely out of spontaneous inclinations. They must occasionally even learn to adapt to movements demanded by a specific activity. This counters the prevalent instability in our culture by lending strength and decisiveness to their soul. And, though the old fashioned activities on farms or in the home have more or less been done away with, they can be brought to children's experiences, wherever they live.

The kitchen comes to mind. Here children may experience the stages that lead to a meal. To participate not only in eating but also in preparing food is of tremendous benefit for them.

As soon as one sees the significance of children's participation, one will also find opportunities, such as cutting up carrots or potatoes on their very own board. Baking a cake will especially delight small children. To begin with, mere watching will provide strong feelings and impressions. Watching their mother or father beat the butter, knead the dough, stills children's hunger for experiences. And if children are allowed to prepare their own little cake, the joy is complete. Helping in the making of an apple cake, slicing the apples and placing them neatly on the dough, starting at the periphery and working in ever diminishing circles towards the centre, can be a delightful learning experience. These concentric circles produce a satisfied feeling of appreciating what results from order and beauty, even though, at first, children may not get it quite right and need help.

Think of children's astonishment and admiration when they watch a parent peel an apple and see the spiral forms of the peel growing in length. These are impressive experiences of form. Equally impressive is the care and skill the parent demonstrates in their work. When they discard the core, children will frequently gather up the pips, put them on the bird table and watch the birds eating them.

Baking for Christmas is an especially happy occasion. Cutting out heart, star, sun and moon shapes, putting the tray into the oven, watching the rising and colouring of the biscuits, smelling them as they bake, the excitement when they're at last taken out, waiting for them to cool, until they are finally allowed to try one – are experiences no child should be allowed to miss.

But even the more prosaic chores, such as washing and drying the dishes, are activities children will delight in if adults empathise with them, and direct their urge for imitation to meaningful smaller jobs. Devastating boredom is prevented and children's urge to be active is directed into healthy channels.

There are numerous activities around the home that provide opportunities for bringing meaningful work to children. These help them to gain confidence, and develop co-ordination and self-control. Order and discipline enter soul and body, countering today's alarming increase of behaviour disturbances, permissiveness and greed.

Our consumer-orientated society ought to look at the value of work for education anew. There is nothing more destructive for children than to merely consume and rely solely on the TV screen and all the excesses of a questionable affluence for satisfying their needs. Children are by nature predestined to activity, to exploration of the world – and not to passivity.

Play

Early on, something begins to stir in children that cannot be satisfied by mere imitation. They no longer wish only to copy but to transform what they copy. Creative energies and imagination come into their own – a wish to permeate the imitated activities and create something from them. Goethe expressed it thus: 'Forming transforming – eternal maintenance of the eternal senses.' As a result of these energies that come into movement through play, children act out of the individual core of their being whilst, at the same time, remaining connected with what is generally held valid.

We can now understand why Schiller was able, in his *Letters on Aesthetics*, to say: 'The human being is only fully human when he plays – and he is playing only when he is fully human.' In other words: The human being really only lives according to his purpose and calling when he transforms what comes to him from without, with all the powers of his formative forces rising from deeply within, transforms them to the point when outer and inner, humans and world, matter and form, combine in a harmonious union.

Children are fascinated by the four elements that attract them with an almost magical force. They cannot resist the delights of water. They hardly feel the cold when they are wet through after splashing about in a river or pool. They especially enjoy the densified water in snow and ice.

Experiencing the earth is just as impressive, be it sand, mud or clay. They never tire of playing in the sand box, where mountains, caves, tunnels and canals can be built, or cakes and puddings shaped.

The child's most precious thing is sand,
No shortage of this substance ever;
It flows on like a powdered river,
So tenderly through the outstretched hand.

RINGELNATZ

Children experience the air by watching the slow or rapid motion of little hand-held propellers, by blowing soap bubbles, by throwing paper birds and flying kites. Blowing the seed-head off a dandelion and watching the tiny white 'parachutes' glide away provides an especially delicate experience of air.

The most fascinating, albeit dangerous playmate among the elements is fire. Caution and safety must, of course, prevail here. The experience of fire begins with the burning candles on the Christmas tree or birthday cake. The celebration of festivals with candle-held processions are occasions that will never be forgotten. When they are older, children might gather enough firewood for a St. John's fire. Here they can experience this element to the full. In the dying ashes, they might cook a pot of soup, bake potatoes, sausages or apples and allow their stomachs to get their fair share.

There is not enough awareness of the significance of play for the development of children's individuality in later life. The memory of a childhood experience of long ago may demonstrate the formative effect of a game that is no longer possible: fifty years ago and earlier when our streets were also playgrounds, children played with hoops taken off dismantled bicycles. Children from more affluent homes were given gaily-coloured wooden versions.

For months on end these hoops became constant companions. The hoop was kept rolling along by giving it the necessary tap with a stick every so often. Great care had to be taken to keep it in the vertical – falling over had to be prevented at all cost because of the silent vow to get the hoop to its destination without any misadventure. But the attentive guiding of a circle, rolling along in the vertical, had a deep and long-lasting effect on children, one that continued into the future to assume an almost symbolic meaning of life. It would be good if such children's games could again be encouraged – in pedestrian zones or parks – for the benefit of our children.

Play as the basis for learning

The work children must apply to the different school subjects also has a decisive influence on their life. Here, the same strength should be developed as during play. Schiller refers to music as play; actors also refer to their art as play. We can now perhaps understand the demand for an artistic structuring of lessons. What this implies is the attempt to overcome matter through form, to connect with the energies active in all objects and to let them shine through during the learning process. Accordingly, Rudolf Steiner asks the teachers to 'conduct all lessons in such a way that the child may everywhere have the feeling that the physical is a manifestation of the spirit.'[2]

Learning must never be limited to an outwardly reflective, merely rational activity. It must become a formative process that works out of the same centre that provides the creative forces in play. We do not here refer to the questionable 'playful learning'. Learning must not be allowed to turn into playing; rather, the energies active in the full earnestness of children's play should become the basis for learning.

2

The age of 'work maturity'
Michael Martin

There can surely be no doubt that the movements set into motion in handwork develop the human will. In dealing with purposeful tasks, with tools and substances, the human being fuses with the everyday world of work outside. Artistic activity also awakens the feeling and heart-forces: it lends an unmistakably individual character to the work in hand. It is well known today that a human-friendly structure in the environment has a healthy effect on people. The teaching of arts and crafts can, therefore, have only one purpose and goal: to help children mature into healthy individuals who are able to shape their environment in a health-giving way.

It is now our task to look at the different arts and crafts subjects taught in specific classes in Steiner-Waldorf schools, to describe their structure, to give reasons for their inclusion and to show their effects. We principally differentiate lessons taught in the Lower School from those in the Upper School (Classes 9–12). Between the two we have a decisive turning point: the class teacher who had led their class for eight years hands the children over to specialist teachers who now care for them differently from the way they had guided them. This incisive point is in the middle of puberty. We shall, to begin with, concentrate on the preceding school years.

Arts and crafts in the Lower School

During the Lower School it is the class teacher who is responsible for the teaching of arts and crafts. As far as possible, he or she incorporates them into the lessons. We correctly assume that there must be a reason for introducing craft lessons *per se* only in Class 5; and for the strongly differentiated artistic and craft disciplines that are experienced throughout the Upper School. There are obviously crucial points to consider, conditioned by children's developmental stages.

This is indeed the case. It does not mean that before this age children should not work with tools. Rudolf Steiner wanted to introduce crafts as early as Class 3,[1] but certainly from different pedagogical aspects. The circumstances at the time did not allow this. What is essential is that a subject should not be taught merely because children are enthusiastic about it or that the work done is beautiful. A new subject is only introduced because children's development demands it. In other words, because the confrontation with a certain activity supports the necessary stage in children's development. This presupposes the teacher's deepened insight into the inner developmental phases of children that express themselves in outer symptoms. Many lectures by Rudolf Steiner deal with this. The curriculum is built on a knowledge of the human being arrived at through spiritual scientific study and the observation of children.

As far as the teaching of crafts is concerned, Rudolf Steiner gave only indications and did not detail a curriculum for specific age levels. He indicated to the craft teacher Max Wolffhügel in a number of conversations what should be done. The craft lessons began in Class 6. Children were introduced to practical work in wood, producing simple, practical objects. The making of moveable toys was added in Classes 7 and 8. There are several indications, in a number of lectures given at different places,[2] from which it can be seen what Rudolf Steiner's aims for these lessons were. He always carried samples from the Stuttgart school's handwork lessons with him and referred to them during his talks. Other references can be found in the meetings (*Konferenzen*) with the Stuttgart teachers.[3]

All these beginnings are essential, but need to be freed from the taste and conditions prevalent at the time; and they have to be further developed and adapted to the various age levels of today's children.

To do this we must have a thorough understanding of the rhythms within which children's development unfolds during their school life. Of special significance is the transition from the second seven-year period to the third, a crucial time, indeed, that is concentrated on the fourteenth year. Commonly referred to as puberty, Rudolf Steiner frequently called it 'earth-maturity'. The sexual maturity children now experience is its most striking symptom. But in actual fact this is no more than a fraction of a comprehensive process that takes hold of the whole being and transforms it.

Rudolf Steiner used quite drastic words when characterising this age. He speaks of the young as being 'thrown out from the world of spirit and soul... thrown out from the cosmic life of soul and spirit and plunged into the external world...'[4]

These words connect with the Old Testament story of the expulsion from paradise. Pictures from the *Oberufer Plays* arise.[5] Both tell of historical events which we meet again in children as they pass through earth maturity. At the same time we are given the opportunity of establishing a direct relation to the arts and crafts taught at that time, which are connected with this stage of development. A detour to the mythical beginnings of history may, perhaps assist in the understanding of the processes of development as well as the educational measures taken in Steiner-Waldorf schools.

The mythical origins of arts and crafts

Through their 'falling into sin', Adam and Eve gained a new relation to the world: they became aware of their own bodies. They perceived their lack of covering, and hid 'during the cold of the day under trees'. They took a further step in this separation process by weaving clothes from the leaves of trees and dressed themselves with them. To clothe oneself means to separate, to draw boundaries. Their bodies have become needy, defenceless. This marks the beginning of the crafts, starting with weaving. Adam and Eve and their descendants, dismissed from their Creator's loving care, now produce their own protective covering in shelter and clothing and, in order to maintain their lives, must employ their very own will-forces and prove themselves. Handwork and craft are the logical consequence of the separation from the sheaths of soul and spirit, of having to settle on an

2. THE AGE OF 'WORK MATURITY'

earth that demands effort and pain of human life. Its positive side is the possibility of an emerging independent individuality: only by separating from the natural environment, by withdrawing into its very own sheaths, can an inner sphere be established; the forming of an inner space demands the forming of protective sheaths – through the medium of the crafts. This is the reason why most of the original crafts are directly or indirectly concerned with providing covering, shelter – sheaths. During their progressive individuation process, Adam and Eve became the first 'craftspeople'. Master Bertram (circa 1355–1415) depicted this impressively on one of the wings of the altar in the Church of Grabow: Eve, spinning on a distaff that, as a result of its own gravity during the turning, points to the centre of the earth. Adam tills the soil that had become too hard and, therefore, unproductive. He, similarly, lets the hoe follow the force of gravity and literally fall into the earth.

Adam and Eve. Woodcut from Mirror of Human Behaviour, *Basel 1476*

Hoe and distaff are true pictures for people's activities on earth. The cultivated field spreading across the earth and the gravity rising from the earth's centre meet in the human being in the form of a cross. The cross symbolises our task on earth: the human being descended from the sphere of paradise in order to bear the cross. Only through this can the individuality develop.

The symbolic power in such representations appealed to the people during the Middle Ages. Many such works of art exist, including the wood-relief in Basel (1476) that is almost identical with Bertram's picture in North Germany.

So far we have discussed the outer physical aspect of this phase in evolution. Hand in glove with this is another process taking place within, strongly affecting and changing the life of the soul: by eating the forbidden apple, Adam and Eve also fill their soul with desire, with the strong instinctive drive for pleasure. In paradise the pure mirror of their soul was turned to God the Father. It contained no egotistical wishes. The experience of tasting, that sets the metabolic processes in motion, now becomes a matter of the heart. The soul, enjoying pleasure, becomes dependent on the body. The life of will is permeated by a desiring, greed-like element that can intensify to passion. The immediately following chapter of Genesis (Book 1, Moses, 4) tells of Cain's unbridled, untamed will-forces that led him to the rage during which he kills his brother Abel.

The 'fall into sin' has shown us two sides: on the one hand, the soul connects with the body through desire that can fill it with passion; this allowed the human being to be able to settle fully on earth. On the other hand, this separation marks the beginning of continuous individuation. In these momentous events we see the causes for the activities in the arts and crafts: the necessary forming of protective sheaths in the widest sense of the word, and the structuring and representation of the individual soul-forces with the help of art.

Earth maturity

There are developmental stages in children that correspond to people's descent to earth. Rudolf Steiner rediscovered this knowledge. He speaks of it in his many lectures on education, in which he describes children's stages of descent to earth. Our own observation can confirm it. A nadir, prepared during the preceding two years, is reached at the age of fourteen and fades away two years later. It is only now that the young person has 'arrived' on earth. They experience themselves within an outer, terrestrial world whose logic they begin to comprehend.[6] They look back to the lost paradise of childhood and gradually discover their connection with the outer facts surrounding them.

At the same time new, germinating energies are beginning to stir within, energies they must live with on earth, their home. This can only come about if it is not merely their head learning about the world, but if they become active in it. Their head by itself is not able to really understand this earth; they can perceive things through the senses, but cannot connect with them inwardly. The appropriate means for this are the will activity of the limbs, of the whole body. In the process of grasping, in work and transforming matter, the human being becomes as one with the world in which they live. In becoming aware of the outer world through perception and thinking, we at first distance ourselves from it. This we overcome only through being active in it. If young people resist such activity, their relation to the world will remain theoretical, conscious but not experienced.

It is decisive for the entire later life how the human being 'pushes himself into the physical world through adapting to the environment, the outer laws, with the organs of his feelings and will.'[7] These organs of feelings and will are, in fact, our hands and feet.

It is because of this that the speciality subjects are introduced between children's twelfth and sixteenth years: in Class 6 the direct work with the soil, gardening, and also the work with wood at the workbench. Finally, spinning and weaving in Class 10, and a wealth of working techniques to stimulate the youngsters in different ways, to unfold and prove their worth during this time of their lives.

Whereas up to Class 8 the subjects of painting, form drawing and drawing were included in the class teacher's lessons and not taught separately by specialists, now, in Class 9, the formative shaping and structuring is practised in the various disciplines. The students are introduced into the world of form and colour they perceive in the environment, in which, however, their inner life also participates at the same time. Their opening, personal, inner world mirrors itself in the world outside in which they find themselves again. Because it is the pictorial, formative world that makes directly visible what now emerges from their souls. It is not the content of imagination that matters, but the extent to which they can form their inner experiences so that they may hold their own also in the eyes of other people. A healthy practising of crafts contains an element that can bridge the imagination-filled ideas emerging from the strong ocean of the soul with their actual realisation in the external world.

What we refer to as 'earth-maturity' is therefore not only the separation from a paradisiacal state of protection, but also the progress of the young from childhood to a stage that bears the characteristic of self-will.

Everything we have touched upon so far – leaving paradise, descending to earth, taking hold of the earth through work – are no more than the outer tracks of inner processes of metamorphosis. Even the appearance of individually coloured inclinations – wishes, joys, needs and pain – in this new soul space, are no more than outer symptoms of deeply penetrating inner events. It is the emergence of a new soul quality of a will nature, as yet unknown to the young, that wishes to transform and claim the body. What was up to now protected, as by the mother's womb, now emerges into daylight like a wild, incredibly excitable, colourfully moving energy field of the soul – frequently dramatically tense, cooled and warmed through by contradictory expressions – from which an individual relation to the world wishes to develop. Because the external world is now perceived in its distance to the individual life, it is judged anew, perhaps more soberly.

We may speak of a renaissance within the soul, an awakening to the world and to oneself. Rudolf Steiner calls it the 'birth of the soul body' in the sense of faculties that enable the individual to develop to the extent that it makes use of these faculties, improves them further and thus realises its own potential.[8]

This means the loss of the previous joy of movement, grace and ease that characterised everything the child did. No longer the magic of childhood: in its place a clumsiness and heaviness; effort is needed to do something with the impulses of movement, to let the body be permeated and moulded by them.

All these efforts and struggles gradually allow the 'I' to emerge during the third seven-year period, the 'I' that is, seed-like, still asleep in the soul. Effort is ego activity; to unfold it is one of the essential tasks during this time. The ego is now still sustained and protected by the soul's will nature. We have here the very special tasks of the arts and crafts subjects.

Before we discuss these subjects we must first take a look at children's development of the organism of movement, because every kind of work is connected with certain movements and it is important to know what kind of movement may be demanded of them at a particular age.

Developing the movement organism

Pre-school children's overall movements are spontaneous expressions of their feelings. Their bodily movements express their inner life. Soul and physical movements are as one. We can read every nuance of the soul in their outer forms of expression as they react to their environment: joy, curiosity, rage, terror, etc.

After the arrival of adult teeth, children's movements depend more on rhythm, such as those of respiration and blood circulation. Children feel good when they can direct their movements to rhythmic speech and play. This tendency is taken up by eurythmy, a subject introduced in Class 1. Eurythmy is visible speech, that is, the structure of the respiratory processes is made visible. It is permeated with life during the process in which breathing affects the circulation of the blood.[9]

Eurythmy is, therefore, taught as a subject because of children's readiness to practise and learn such eurythmic movements. It is implicit in child development. This changes around age nine: the blood begins to work more strongly into the muscles, causing movement to gradually lose something of the ease and lightness characteristic of breathing. Instead, they become heartier, more flowing and flexible. Because of this, physical education is now introduced – a subject in which muscles are strengthened and made more flexible.

A further important stage between eleven and twelve years leads to a closer connection between muscles and bones. This makes the movements heavier and more mechanical, because now the heaviest, hardest and densest system is reached, that allows the human being to stand firmly on the earth.[10]

There are consolidation processes in children leading from airy, light conditions via the watery/stretchable to the ever more hardening, the bony sphere.

They influence children's movements, and their development calls for new subjects. Handwork and the crafts can support and care for this clumsy complex of movements conditioned by the bony system. As the earth forces come into their own, activities corresponding to children's physical development are now called for. By taking material and substances from the environment and working with them, children detach themselves and discover new, outward points of view.

The emergence of the will

Every day we experience the alternation of light and dark. Sleeping and waking closely connect us to them through their rhythm. Everywhere in space and time we may observe their many effects on the environment.

But we do not only experience outer light and darkness. Deep down within us, light and darkness are anchored in the qualities of the soul. A bright person is a clear, bright thinker. What they say makes sense and illumines something in me; I can understand what they say. A lightning (striking) thought can clarify everything, make it as clear as sunlight. A sensitive observer will easily experience thinking as a light process. Words and phrases like 'lucidity', 'elucidate', 'as clear as the light of day' point to this.

By contrast, our will remains vague, indefinite, dark. It pushes upwards from the unconscious regions, i.e. the not clear, the not light. God the Father in Goethe's *Faust* says: 'An upright man, however darkly driven, is well aware of his predestined path,' or 'Man's doomed to err during his striving' – that is, as long as he attempts to find his way without having a clear knowledge of it. And he is even more at the mercy of his will when subjected to a blind rage rising up within him.

If we consider that both these soul-forces – thinking and willing – produce their field of action in the physical organisation, we can understand how human beings' totality was fundamentally formed out of these primal energies or forces. Both thinking and willing develop in several stages, and only gradually make themselves felt. The forces working in intelligence, previously still active within the physical organism, forming and structuring the internal organs, awaken at about the seventh year, ready to be used for the forming and structuring of thoughts. Children are now ready to learn, to go to school.

During the second seven-year period, the will-forces that previously expressed themselves directly in the bodily movements begin to stir, becoming more and more independent, and help children to pursue individual aims. A decisive stage occurs at around their twelfth year. We have already referred to it from another aspect. As children grow into their bony system and experience their bodies as heavy and clumsy, the individually-tinged will-forces awaken into an urge to assert themselves, to become active. We now see a veritable battle taking place between the powers of light and darkness, the bright, clear forces of intelligence and the dark will-forces that now meet, locked in the struggle for a new union.

Light and shadow shown by spheres drawn in charcoal

Children experience this in a subtle way during their lessons on shadows where both eyes and hands, representing light as well as will, are equally participating. They experience themselves placed between light and shadow as they draw a sphere in charcoal, in broad, short strokes. At first it is no more than a delicately produced plain. Only by the intensified darkening of one side does the two-dimensional drawing appear to curve and turn into a sphere. If the background of the light side of the ball is then drawn still darker, it frees itself from its connection to the plain and seems to glide freely in space. Only when the shadow, cast by the ball's physical density on the ground, is added can one see the way the ball actually lies on the ground and connects with it. We can here clearly see the same process reflected in a similar way to that happening at the workbench, which will be described later: on the one hand, the process of becoming independent, of establishing boundaries, of coming into its own in the form of the ball; on the other hand, the interweaving with the outer world, the environment – here achieved by the shadow. The excitement and tensions these processes produce in children may be illustrated by a story a girl in Class 6 wrote at the end of a main-lesson block on shadows:

Once upon a time there was a shadow that decided to disobey the light. The light had teased the shadow by hopping about the ball and forcing it to lie at the right places. This exhausted the shadow to the point of capitulating. It just stayed where it was.

But then Mr D. arrived and said: 'Dear child, this shadow is wrong. Draw it on the other side.' But the shadow refused to be budged. It clung even more strongly to its place. The light then took pity on it and went to another corner. Since then the two have become great and inseparable friends.

Can this struggle between the impish, light intelligence and the dark willfulness be better described? The happy ending is most satisfying. It could only come about because of the stirring of a new faculty that allows these polarities to be overcome by controlling them, by putting them into the service of children: the 'I' that, as yet safe in the soul's womb, is now able to emerge through the work of the limbs. Rudolf Steiner calls it the 'element of gravity' to which the young must now find his or her way.

The following verse, written by another girl in Class 6, indicates, through her subconscious feelings, that it is up to everybody to develop these central forces:

In light and dark we clearly see
Elements that mysteriously
Can create fine paintings.
As light and shadow they are known.
But each one tends to live alone
And to shun a meeting.
Only he who likes to paint
Could perhaps combine
Their polarities so quaint –
Make them intertwine.

These ego-forces are, indeed, especially strong during the twelfth year, but as yet fully connected to the body. As soon as the heaviness makes itself felt in the limbs, a counter force occurs exactly where this heaviness is most concentrated: in the feet. We see a powerful impulse against this heaviness awaken: the limbs grow stronger, beginning in the feet, followed by the calves and, still later, in the thighs. Corresponding to this is the growth of hands and arms. It is the 'I', still body-bound, which stirs in the limbs. The manual work makes it active and the awakening individual will directs it to its activities.

Through our pre-occupation with shadows, which Rudolf Steiner clearly assigns to Class 6, we have once again been made aware of the important step into gravity, the darkness and firmness of the earth. There are no such clear directions for the teaching of crafts. We can, however, work out a curriculum by making use of such indications as those given for the teaching of shadows.

The craft teacher must absorb these processes into their observations, because only by doing so can the inner picture of a twelve-year-old be rounded and completed. They may, if the situation demands it, have to teach the shadow lessons themselves, if the class teacher has not taught this.

Combining curriculum and will

With this inner picture of the awakening will, we now take another look at the teaching of crafts. Whatever children are producing at this age manifests the character of the 'I', active within their body. We can thus understand what Rudolf Steiner means when he says that:

> *the children who are, in our schools, allowed to work so very freely, to be inventive, may express again in plastic forms, in free, creative activity and not by slavishly imitating, the structure of one or the other limb developing in their bodies…*

If the teacher insists on a definite piece of work to be done, children cannot work from their own forces and selves. They cannot take what is living in themselves and wish to assume form into the world outside. They may become good and skilled people who willingly carry out instructions. But their own ego-forces will remain stunted and will find it difficult to develop and assert themselves.

This naturally presents tremendous problems for the teacher. How are they to tease out of children's frequently blocked up or wrongly formed will-forces their healthy, individual will? How far should they go with stimulating, encouraging, helping? Can the teacher succeed in enthusing children with ideas to the point where they no longer simply remain comfortably enclosed in their heads 'as though on a couch'? In the same lecture Rudolf Steiner says: 'These ideas are asleep because they are merely "meaningful"…' And then he points to the educational aim of our striving: to guide children in a way that

2. THE AGE OF 'WORK MATURITY'

they not only have ideas in their heads, but feel them in their hearts, that the heart warms from the enthusiasm for their lessons. The idea then assumes an inner form, becomes a life-filled form children unconsciously produce within – like a sculpture expressing life and movement. If the inner experiences wax extremely powerful, they push children into creative, will-filled doing.

In the workshop children produce something their inner life urges them to do. They are not motivated by a cool, factual picture they have seen somewhere. What they create will not be in an airless, abstract space, but will be intimately related to the forces of form, active and creative within themselves. In this way, the ideas developed by the teacher during a previous lesson assume a creative energy that pours out into the activities in the workshop. 'The children actually learn also to do what they learn to think.' All the craft teacher must do is to give the right directions.

Rudolf Steiner here pointed to a lofty aim. If the teacher makes the effort, they will find the means of helping children express themselves in two- or three-dimensional form without determining the results. It is the individual will – the dark element in the human body – that places the self into the physical organisation. Because of this, help must be given for its development.

Part Two

Crafts in the Middle School

3

Preface to Part Two
Michael Martin

Our essays so far have been intended to provide the basis for an understanding of the following articles in which several experienced craft teachers describe their teaching experiences. Without the effort of studying and observing children's developmental stages, arts and crafts lessons might appear to be no more than gimmicks, arbitrarily chosen extras in the curriculum.

What any teacher decides to do will always depend on his or her individual abilities, on local circumstances and, above all, on the children themselves. There are schools today that, by continuing the practice of the original Waldorf School, introduce craft lessons in Class 6. These lessons should, however, be taught sooner. Circumstances in 1919 did not allow this. It would be good to include woodcarving, clay modelling and other manual activities in Class 5. This would help to strengthen children's hands and make them more subtle and skilled.

All manual dexterity activities – besides handwork – including the making of candles during Advent in Class 1 or the activities connected with the house-building block in Class 3, are taught by the class teacher, supported by craft specialists. A premature experience of the first actual craft lesson in its proper setting, the workshop, is not advisable.

The following essays should be taken as indications only and not as dogma. The work with clay in the pre-craft lessons in a holding class is thus only mentioned. It will be more thoroughly treated in Part Five in connection with the teaching of modelling in general.

It will, in times to come, be ever more important for city children to know where the material they work with is coming from. I do not mean an abstract knowledge, but an experience children can relate to. The ever-increasing offerings of plastic building blocks, such as Lego that can only be joined together, are materials with which children cannot inwardly connect. Even our hobby shops mostly sell pre-cut and shaped pieces of wood or plastic that do not allow for experiencing their connection with nature. The inclusion of a forest main-lesson would give children the opportunity of experiencing different trees in nature and thus provide a strong basis for all the subsequent craft lessons. Sawing and splitting the wood in readiness for carving will then have a different, healthier quality.

Wood is nature's gift to us. Its most important substances are the result of the interaction of light, air and warmth. Shape and other characteristic features of a tree point to its relation to the cosmos. Knowledge of the connections between earth and cosmos, the planetary forces, was still very much alive at the beginning of the modern age. Scientists today are trying to rediscover these connections in quite different ways.

Working with wood stimulates the heart-forces (*Gemüt*). It is in keeping with the children's age that their heart-forces should have a share in the production of practical articles in the workshop. There is as much room for joy, astonishment and wonder as for humour and liveliness. They provide the right mood for work. The following articles bear witness to this.

4

Getting ready for craft lessons (Class 5)
Johannes Geier

The cultivation of the senses as organs of perception has become one of the most important tasks of education in a world where excessive onslaught on our senses is threatening their healthy function. We are, therefore, endeavouring to help children in our schools to discover ever new worlds in which they may take an active, independent part, show initiative and sensitivity, and develop their skills. Every season offers a variety of opportunities for this.

During autumn and winter children in our younger classes produce smaller objects. We do some modelling or make simple humming toys. But, although they are little more than toys, they are serious business for these children. They discover ever new variations on the theme.

Children's ears are the greatest victims of the sensorial overload mentioned above. Attentive listening can no longer be taken for granted; it must be cultivated. In order to learn to hear delicate sounds, in other words, to activate children's faculty of perception, we make humming bones or humming buttons. The rotating humming tops produce soft buzzing and whirring sounds. These first primitive attempts will later be further developed in the workshops.

We ask children to clean the upper thighbones, after a chicken dinner, and to bring them to school. The bones will then be soaked in hydrogen peroxide for a day. Alternatively, they could be left lying outside for a few months so that they are bleached out and brilliantly white. Two holes are then drilled exactly in the centre between the two ends. A thin string is pulled through the holes and tied together. Holding the string in both hands, children stretch it and rotate the bone. The resulting delicate humming sound never fails to astonish them and to induce them to listen most carefully, almost to the point of awe.

The humming button is even easier to make, because of the already existing holes. Different sized buttons produce different sounds and make experimenting really exciting.

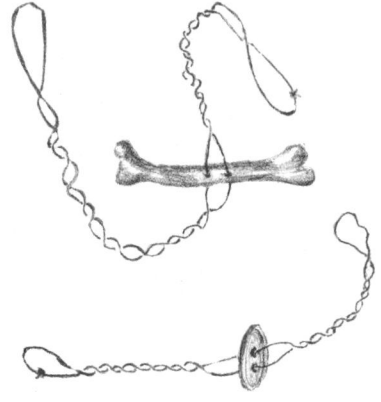

Humming toys

Humming apples or potatoes are made by pushing a 35 cm (14 in) long hazelnut twig through the centre. A wooden ball or disc may be used instead. The two necessary holes will be made by carefully grinding or filing the top and bottom ends of a large hazelnut or walnut. Grinding the opposite sides will result in a wide enough opening for the kernel to be removed. A short rod or stick is then pushed length-wise through the nut. A length of string is tied to the rod inside the nut and wound up.

Putting the rod vertically on the table and holding the nut firmly in one hand, the children then pull the string with a fast movement. The apple (potato, wooden ball or disc) starts rotating like a top, and produces a humming sound. The string rewinds itself inside the nut, ready to be pulled out again.

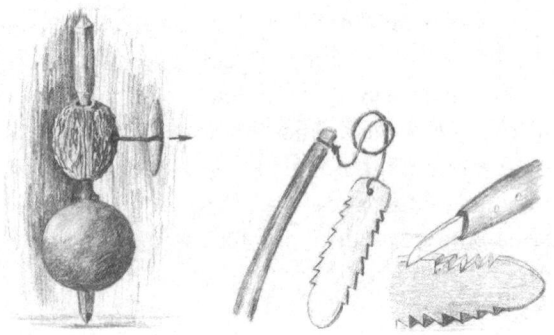

More humming toys, also known as bull-roarers

The next project is the making of wooden humming objects. An archaeological discovery tells us that this was known as far back as the thirteenth century. It consists of an approximately 20 cm (8 in) long oblong or oval shaped piece of hard wood. The sides are occasionally notched. A hole is drilled at one end and a length of string fastened to it. Rotating the wood around an axis produces rough, howling sounds. Pitch and volume depend on the size of the object and the speed of rotation. The humming wood belongs to the family of aerophones. It was widely carried by shepherds in Czechoslovakia who used it as magical protection against the possible ravages created by thunderstorms. Its name was *Ide burka, voztacajmy descice* – 'A thunderstorm is close, let's get the humming wood going'.

Human beings can also produce sounds through exhaling. A single breath can result in a variety of sounds, be it the singing of a song or the giving of a signal. Only a little effort and skill are required for the making of a simple, yet effective musical 'instrument'. The following are but a few suggestions suitable for spring and summer and open-air activities. A simple shepherd's pipe made from soft, hollow reeds or bamboo; blowing on the tops of acorns, across a blade of grass or the stem of a dandelion.

The reed flute is a single length instrument. Hard, dry reeds are best. The reed is cut off just beneath one of its knots. Immediately above the knot the reed is cut off at an acute angle; a clear-cut notch is essential. The top end of the cut is flattened out and slightly rounded. Should there be no knot, the finger can be used to cover it. This allows the sound to be varied. The sounds that can be produced in different ways demand great sensitivity as well as skilled fingers from children in the lower classes. During walks across fields, or through a wood, they will discover all sorts of things capable of producing sounds.

4. GETTING READY FOR CRAFT LESSONS (CLASS 5)

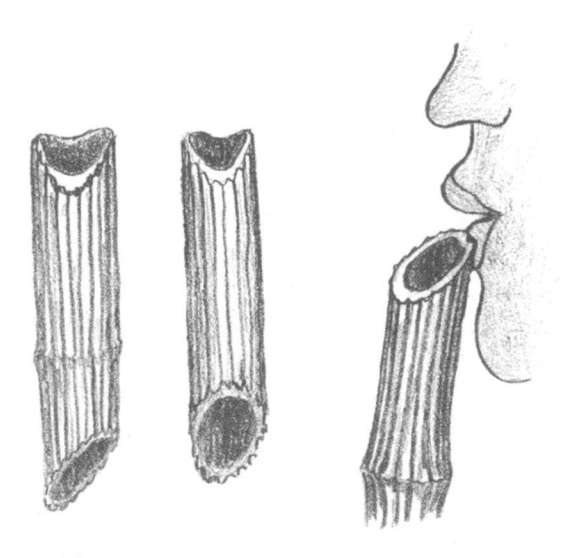

Reed flutes

When the formal teaching of crafts, i.e. manual dexterity, begins in Class 5, these earlier experiences are taken further. Flutes made of willow reeds are just one example. They are more complicated and precise than the earlier reed pipes.

First craft lesson activities

Well prepared for their first day in the workshop, the children are waiting outside the closed door. Their stiffly starched aprons look like knights' armour. The name of each child is brightly imprinted on their apron.

The door is opened and they are at last allowed to enter the room. Their senses are given free play; they touch, feel, smell; they look at the variety of wood, read their names and place of origin. They admire the sculptures of the older children, let their hands glide over the carved animals and deeply breathe in the rich resin scent of the wood.

Sawing and splitting wood

We leave the room and go outside into a little forest of willow trees; recently felled trees are waiting to be sawn and split. An old-fashioned handsaw is used, with a child at each end: pull, let go – pull, let go! The saw sways, like a boat, and must be kept as steady as possible. The shoulders adapt to the harmonious movements. The sawdust drops rhythmically to the dark ground. Every child gets a turn. No questions are asked about the purpose of the work – the movements during the work completely occupy and satisfy children.

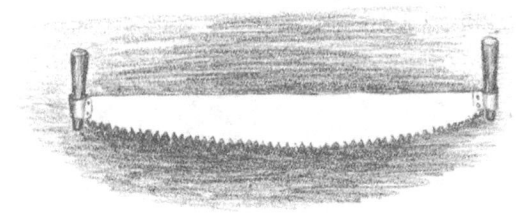

Two-handed saw

The next task is the splitting of the metre-long logs. The wedge drives out the sap, which children taste: some bitter, some sweet. The axe has to be carefully guided in order to hit the right spot. There is a crackling sound as the split widens until the log falls apart. Fresh scent rises from the inner part of the wood, which is now exposed to the light of day.

During the following deserved short break, children are told about the meaning and purpose of their activity, i.e. that the wood must now be neatly stacked and allowed to dry slowly so that, later, precious things may be made from it. This process could take years; the wood might not be ready for use by the time they leave school. They learn about the forester's care of the trees, in spite of the fact that he or she may not be able to sell any of them to a violin maker during their lifetime. And that

PART TWO: CRAFTS IN THE MIDDLE SCHOOL

Splitting logs for shingles

Frow

Mallet

Carving tools

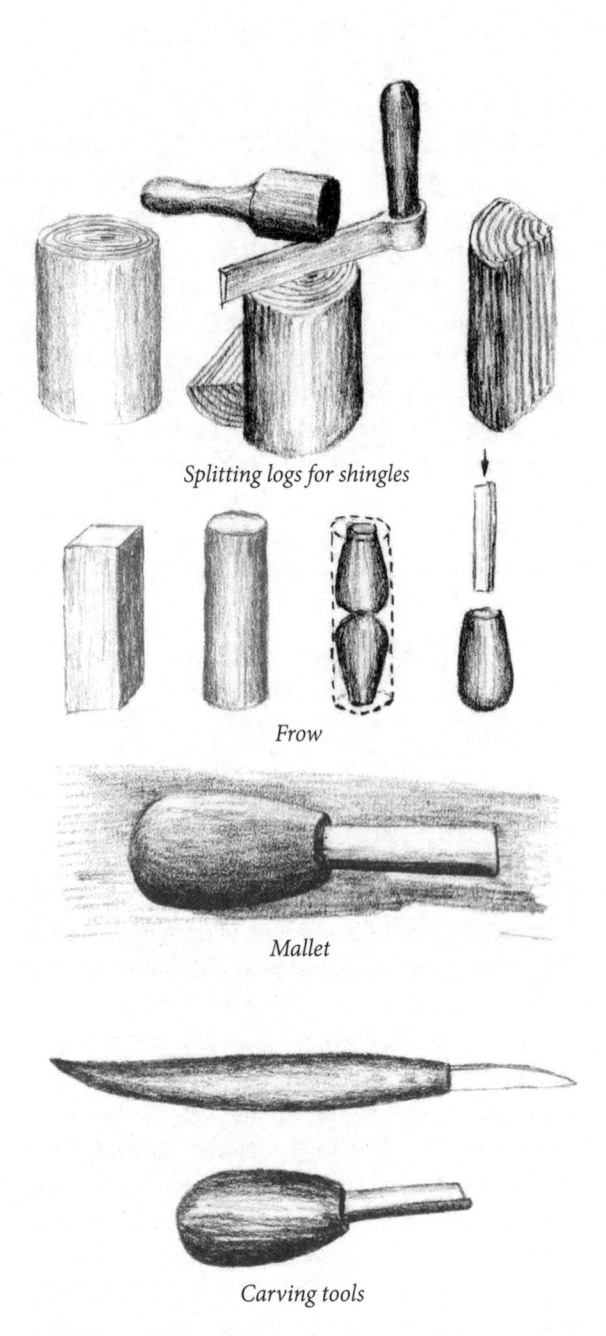

the violin maker themselves would have to prepare the wood carefully to be used by, perhaps, their grandchildren.

The split logs are then stacked neatly with their bark always turned to the earth. The stack is protected from the rain with a suitable cover. Our little forest proves to be an ideal place for the drying and stacking of wood. The nearby creek allows for the necessary moisture, because the drying process must neither be too fast nor too slow.

At the end of the first lesson the tools must be tidied away, each to its allotted place. The children line up to be dismissed with a handshake. A moment of necessary silence precedes this – in which one can hear a pin drop.

Tools

For the subsequent lessons, children are asked to bring their pocket knives.[1] They are told to cut a 20 cm (8 in) length from a lime tree branch, using a special tool for cutting shingle.[2] Children's fascination, as they watch the curling shavings (angels' curls), reaches a point where complete silence ensues. All one hears are the cutting noises and the shavings dropping to the floor. Before this exercise, children are taught the handling of both knife and wood.

Nothing else is done to begin with besides this exercise. The shavings produced by the children are as different as their handwriting. They discover that the shavings cut off edges are the easiest to produce.

Long practice results in the shaping of a small oval handle with a slot at one end into which a steel blade is inserted. This will be used for carving.

4. GETTING READY FOR CRAFT LESSONS (CLASS 5)

The crowning stage is the sharpening of the blade done by the teacher at the grinding machine. Each child may keep this – their first self-made tool. Protected by a piece of garden hose, the knives can be safely put away in satchels. A pocket knife and this simple carving tool are children's first tools in Class 5. With them they make their first basic experiments in woodwork.

Boats and flutes

The next project is a small boat made from lime wood. The rough shape is cut from a branch with one of the tools. The inside is then hollowed out.

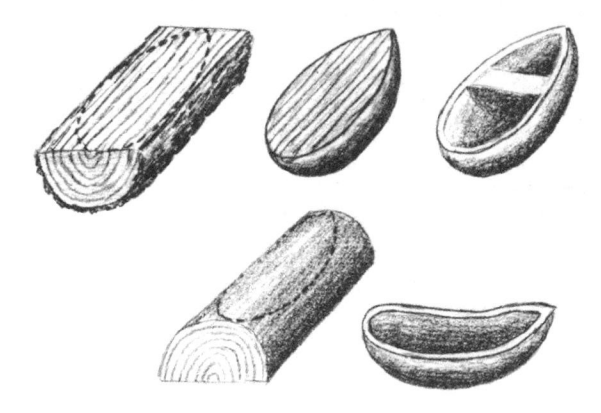

Small boat carved from lime wood

At the time when the sap is at the height of its activity, children learn to make flutes from willow branches. On these instruments – a progression from the simpler reed flutes – real tunes with a range of up to two octaves can be played. A considerable amount of skill is needed in blowing, as every tone is produced by the accurate moving of the core piece.

Lime wood is the most suitable because its bark is easily removed and the cut off branch quickly grows again. The children look for an approximately 20–25 cm (8–10 in) length, free of knots. They then cut a semicircular notch into the bark 10–20 cm (4–8 in) away from the upper end, while 3–4 cm (1–1½ in) from below the bark is cut around the stem. The whole of the bark is then carefully tapped with the handle of the knife. Careful tapping is essential to avoid the splitting of the bark. The bark must then be slid off in its entirety.

Country children used to sing a little rhyme – the 'loosening of the bark' verse – said to facilitate the process:

> *The willow's sap is rising, see –*
> *The flute is made and ready now,*
> *Let's cut a flute for you and me.*
> *Let's jump for joy and dance and bow.*
>
> *Tap, tap, peel its bark and hear*
> *Tap, tap, peel its bark and hear*
> *How my flute is singing.*
> *How my flute is singing.*
>
> *I now can play a merry tune*
> *As I cross field and vale and dune.*
> *Tap, tap, peel its bark and hear*
> *How my flute is singing.*

Provided everything has gone according to plan, the rod can be cut off the rest of the stick and flattened vertically, at a width of about 1–2 cm (½–1 in). This is again cut off, providing the mouthpiece in the tubular bark. The remaining part of the little rod can now be used for producing either a single sound or, with long practice, in the correctly controlled up and down sliding movements the playing of a tune. These 'May flutes' can only be played as long as they are still damp. This activity is especially suitable outdoors. However, should children happen to be dismissed before the end of school, the lessons in other classrooms will be made impossible. The cacophony produced by the flutes in the corridors of buildings penetrates everything.

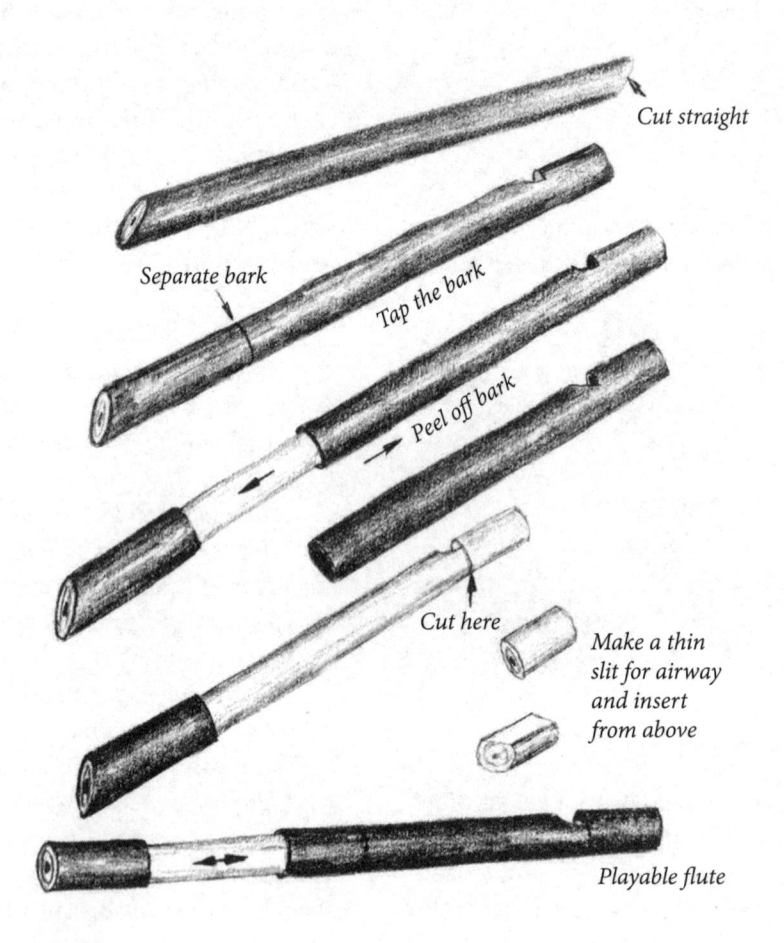

Cut straight

Separate bark

Tap the bark

Peel off bark

Cut here

Make a thin slit for airway and insert from above

Playable flute

May flutes

5

Shifting emphasis in craft lessons (Class 6)
Michael Martin

In the first part of this book we discussed the steps children must take in their development that justify such subjects as gardening and woodwork and assign to them their special tasks. The following will deal with some of the more general phenomena that characterise both subjects.

Mechanics and connection

In both subjects, many purely mechanical processes can be found, such as digging, hoeing, pushing wheelbarrows, sawing, splitting and hammering – work that could be done by machines. Rudolf Steiner tells us that there is no difference between what a human being does with its bony system and that carried out by a machine. Both have the same result. 'Mechanics, dynamics, independent of the human being, enter the skeleton. We must get used to thinking of the skeleton as though it were objective, as though it were not part of the human being...'[1] By working mechanically we become as one with the world around us, absorbing something from it. Other types of work will depend on the sensitivity and dexterity of the hands – such as working with plants or carving with knives. In these activities, something from our hands streams out into the world. Children experience this interaction through these subjects.

Posture is significant in gardening – the body is bent towards the earth. This is necessary for much of the work; the earth demands this bending, kneeling down to the plants. The most important work for preparing the soil is done with the body's strength. The placement of the feet plays a decisive role in it. Unconsciously, children experience the onset of this force in the earth's resistance under their feet. There could, also unconsciously, be the feeling that only loving effort will engender growth, blossoming and fruiting in the earth. This delicate feeling meets with little understanding in our time where forests are dying and nature forces are weakening. Last, but not least, children may also unconsciously have the consoling realisation that, although the paradise of childhood must be left behind, the human being has the possibility of creating a new paradise from seemingly insignificant seeds if they invoke the help of soil, sun, warmth and rain and guide the growth processes with care and protection.

Work in the workshop adds new and different impulses. The material used is taken from its natural connections. Wood is elevated to a position where the hands – within the sphere of feelings – may now work with it. There is a more direct relation between the human being and the material than in gardening. The human being is preoccupied with a particular project. Gardening is group work. In the workshop our working energy meets the resistance of the floor that, in contrast to the earth, is an absolutely horizontal plane. We can see a separation from what is natural. Children now begin to have an 'inwardly experienced understanding of cause and effect, of strength, and of what is felt as vertical and horizontal.'[2]

Movement and rhythm

It is essential for children to have a firm stance, not only when sawing and splitting wood, but also during the delicate processes in carving if the cuts are to be accurate. The teacher must make children aware of the fact that such work cannot be carried out without the firm support of the earth. This was not so earlier on: a sock could be knitted, a piece of wood whittled while sitting on a swing, unconnected with the earth.

The whole relation to work is different before children reach their twelfth year. Until this point, children live entirely within the rhythm of breathing. Muscles, and therefore movements, are clearly linked to the rhythmic system. When children begin, through their skeleton, to adapt to the world outside, their breathing and circulation systems 'become complete in themselves… like a closed off world, a real microcosm.'[3]

Young children can relate to everything of a moving, plastic nature. Modelling meets this predisposition. The handmade forms are still fully embedded in this self-enclosed rhythmic system: both hands enclose and shape the clay, establishing a heart-felt inner space between body and arms. It is only when the clay is put on the firm surface of a board, to be worked with, that a new up/down relation, determined from without, comes about.

Simple carving also fully corresponds to children's constitutions before their twelfth year, especially if the delicate movements are made towards the body. This gesture indicates the taking in of the outer world that gave us the material for our work. Cutting away from the body is a quite different experience. The will here braces itself against the material.

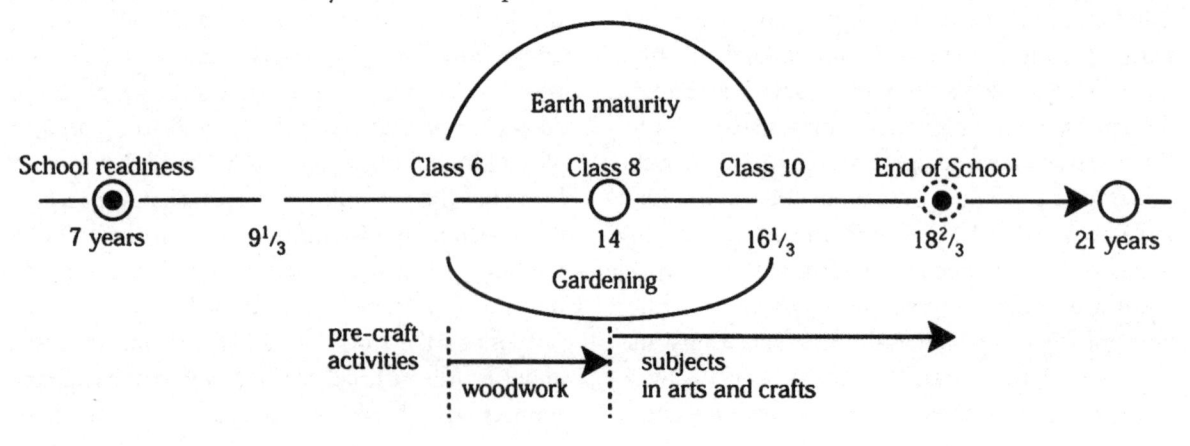

Woodcarving allows us to observe a new element connected with this stage of development: the wood resists the hand. None of the material used before was as hard and unyielding to the knife. The amount of strength exerted by the right hand must be met by the left holding the wood. This produces a complete symmetry within the forces in the muscles that must, however, now be evoked through the use of the opposing employment of energies – else the work cannot be carried out. The hands are working asymmetrically, each has a task diametrically opposed to the other: one holds back, binds, determines; the other presses, urges, moves. Children connect with these processes in an intensive way.

Other subjects correspond to this experience, as, for example, the teaching of the active and passive voice in a grammar block.

Finding balance and 'oneness'

This asymmetrical element, predominant in the craft lessons, is also characteristic of the human form. For example, the skull bones in the head are symmetrically shaped; the right side of the face corresponds to the left. Arms and hands, however, are absolutely unsymmetrical in that they can move independently of each other. They are sustained by the chest and spine, which, through their well-balanced symmetry, provide the support for this freedom of movement. In the growth and lengthening of the limbs we clearly see the strong impact of the will during children's twelfth year: the hands are crying out for movement, for action. The asymmetrical work processes force children to find a balance between them. These processes are characteristic of puberty, which begins at this time.

Children are now given either larger pieces of wood or wood so hard that it can no longer be carved with a knife. The hands by themselves are not strong enough, but people created the necessary 'helpers' – just as the blade for the earlier stage of whittling can be seen as a stronger, sharper fingernail, so, now, there are further tools: the vice that holds the wood in place and the chisel and mallet that allow greater force to be exerted. When driving the chisel through the wood children feel: my whole self is in my right hand! I am experiencing the whole process going on between myself and the workbench that has become part of me. Workbench and I are melting into one another; into the active, transforming, creating process on the one hand and into the passively holding part on the other. The power relation between the left and right sides within the domain of the human being during hand carving now undergoes a decisive change – the power symmetry between active and passive now includes the workbench. The worker here becomes united with the world, becomes one with it. Their own activity, the employment of their physical energies, is supported and sustained by the resistance of the earth; the workbench and the vice that holds the piece of wood are also supported by the floor representing the earth. Earth, bench, working material and I myself combine in a unit, a oneness.

6

Crafts in the Middle School (Classes 5–8)
Walter Dielhenn

Rudolf Steiner frequently referred to the advantages of the kind of school where every child knows all the teachers, and every teacher all the children. This is difficult to achieve in large schools. Craft teachers have, however, many ways of achieving this.

Crafts before the Middle School

Children in the Kindergarten often accompany their teacher to the workshop when a broken toy needs to be mended. And at least once a year they pay us a visit to watch the planing of a rough piece of board. They soon become familiar with the woodwork teacher and the place in which he or she works. Such visits are for me very special events because of the youngsters' ability to show genuine wonder and amazement. They almost jump for joy when the shavings drop like curls to the floor. Each child picks up a handful and takes it home to show their parents.

During Advent, children of the lower three classes make beeswax candles in the workshop. This has become a tradition in our school. The entire school community collects the wax during the year and deposits it in the workshop. In this way children are already very much at home in the workshop long before the actual woodwork lessons begin in Class 5. They frequently visit during break, look at everything and dream about the things they will one day make there. They gaze in awe at the many tools neatly arranged on shelves behind the glass doors of the cabinets. They see the older children's work on the tables: a lion in a cave watched by a giraffe, horses feeding on acorns, gnomes in front of a cave, little dwarfs and their homes, the working model of a crane, a real functioning crane, a complete town with medieval half-timbered houses. And along the shelves many beautiful pieces of wood with their great variety of colour and grains, and branches with their characteristic curved shapes. At the other end of the room are railways and an articulated six wheeler! Most beautiful of all, however, is the large cabinet holding such treasures as bits of bark and roots, little men that move when they are poked, spoons, bowls, wooden fruit and cones, nutcrackers and all sorts of nuts, a donkey cart and real scales, all made of wood – far too much to be taken in all at once. And everything was made by the 'big' boys and girls. One day, they too will learn to make them.

6. CRAFTS IN THE MIDDLE SCHOOL (CLASSES 5–8)

Tools and mould for making bricks

Brick making

The Class 3 curriculum includes the 'house building' main-lesson block. Children make their own bricks that will actually be baked. Children in Class 10 make the required wooden moulds and tools during a carpentry block. Based on the model of ancient Egyptian craftsmanship they make them in a size that corresponds to modern building practice. Great care is taken by the youngsters to get the right amount of moisture, the correct proportion of sand and clay. The bricks have to be firmly pounded – there must be no air bubbles – edges and corners must be clean. The joy of the children is contagious when finally, after cutting off the excess clay, the brick is lifted from its mould with a wire noose. With flushed cheeks and hands covered in clay, they work with enthusiasm. The bricks, stacked on drying racks, are finally stamped with the logo of the class.

The bricks can afterwards be baked in the woodburning kilns made by pupils of Class 10, a delight shared equally by the teacher and children.

The finished bricks can then be used for building a wall, for the foundation for garden seats or even for making a bread oven. Supervised and directed by the craft teachers, all these achievements will have a 'professional' touch.

PART TWO: CRAFTS IN THE MIDDLE SCHOOL

Introduction to wood

The stories told in Class 4, at least in European schools, include the *Nibelung Saga* in which Mimir forges Siegfried's sword. The sword's blade was so sharp that it split a thread of wool that was thrown into a river. Now children can use an equally sharp knife, not unlike a pocket knife, but with a short blade and a simple handle. With it they can easily cut through a vertically held page from a newspaper. It is not all that easy to introduce children to the handling of such sharp tools. They are sitting in a circle, the benches pushed against the walls. The knife is drawn with a sharp, yet careful, movement.

Simple carving knife

Snail and snake drill bits

It all begins in Class 5

There is thus great joy and expectation amongst children when at last the word 'WOODWORK' is included in the timetable. Finally they will not merely visit, but actually work on a regular basis in the room and with the teacher they already know so well.

Elbows at the body, the left hand holding a length of pine branch previously cut to exactly 30 cm (1 ft), we begin carving carefully towards the body – cut after cut. The wood gradually becomes clean, the hands gaining in skill. The fresh scent of resin wafts through the room. Complete, utter silence. After a while we put the knives away and take a good look at the wood. We see its rings. The teacher tells how trees grow, how every year an additional ring appears. Counting the rings we discover that the branches we are holding are older than the children.

The amazement at this discovery is as great as that years ago when they marvelled at the 'curls', the shavings they saw dropping to the ground. This amazement continues into the following lessons, when the carving gains in skilfulness and the children hear wonderful things about this beautiful material: its great variety of colour, smell, hardness and rate of growth; the strong scent of pine; the delicate grains of juniper; the beautiful dark brown wood of the nut tree; the strong, bright shining colour of the plum tree; the wood of the lilac almost as purple as its blossoms... And the difference in weight between two identical sizes of different woods! Between that of balsa and oak – the former light as cork, the latter so dense that it sinks in water.

Tools

During the subsequent lessons, children learn about the different tools – saws, drills, axes and mallets – knowledge needed for becoming real woodworkers. And this children intend to be. They must, therefore, learn to differentiate between a coarsely toothed big saw used for cutting firewood and a delicate saw that can produce the necessary and exact cuts in carpentry. They must learn to differentiate between different drills, the one that looks like a snail's house and that which reminds them of a snake. Again, children are amazed at the way human beings can produce such different tools, each one for a specific task.

First projects

Our first projects are rungs for a rope ladder made from pine branches. The rungs must be of the same length, their holes drilled in exactly similar places, pointing in the same direction. Mutual help is essential here: one child does the drilling, watched by another who makes sure the drill is held absolutely vertical – this can be better determined from a distance. The finished rope ladders are very popular items at our Christmas bazaar. Children are justifiably proud of their work and are allowed to carve their names on their rungs.

The next project takes their experience further. A piece of poplar wood is split, its edges rounded and some parts hollowed out. Out of this transformed piece, children may carve an animal, a human form, perhaps a shepherd.[1] They already think of the recipient of their creation: a younger brother or sister, mother or father, maybe a neighbour's child. It is important for them to know that their work is useful, that their hard and diligent efforts are worthwhile.

We try to make children use both their hands at this time. They complement each other: one holds, the other carves. Will is added to feeling – the countering force of the hand holding the wood is essential for loosening the shavings. The entire work is still carried out within the sphere of the heart and breathing. Muscles and rhythm complement each other.

The transition into Class 6

A new – different – child meets us in Class 6. The ease and grace of movement, still occasionally noticeable in Class 5, now succumbs to the earth's forces of gravity. The muscles, aligning themselves to the bones, are losing their previous rhythm and grace.[2]

Class 6 projects

The project made at the joiner's bench will serve as an example for the introduction of the curved chisel. A wooden spoon is to be carved from a maple branch. Clear thinking precedes the work: Why maple? Well, its wood is hard, has few pores and neither taste nor smell. Its colour is light. All the properties of the material used are fully discussed with children before the actual work begins.

I then demonstrate the required stages of work at the bench: Careful! The protective covering of the plane must be attached. Stop! If I start at the wrong end the wood will split. Which of you has paid attention; who can now do it? Practical demonstration rather than a lot of explaining. We do without drawings. Children are to discover for themselves the appropriate shape from their doing. Every beat of the mallet forces them to observe the effect of the blade. The wooden spoon must not be too cumbersome and yet strong enough to stir even the firmest of doughs. Handle and hollowed out end should be beautifully balanced. The hand with which we knead the bread dough serves as a model. Slowly, cautiously the right form is found, eyes and hands sensitively guiding the tool. The rough parts are carefully evened out, first with a rasp, and then finally with emery paper. The surface must be smooth and perfect.

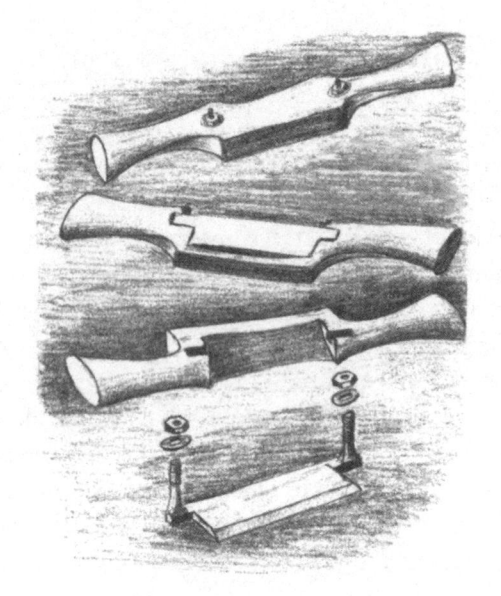

6. CRAFTS IN THE MIDDLE SCHOOL (CLASSES 5–8)

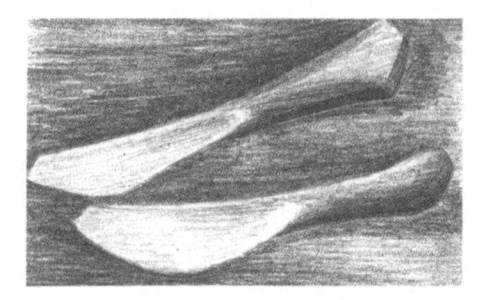

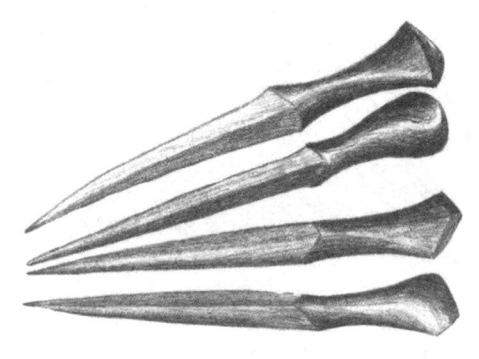

Think of the joy when children's mothers or fathers tell them: 'This is my favourite wooden spoon. It is far better than all the others!' Many a parent must be encouraged to use the wooden spoon. They are so proud of their children's achievement that they keep it along with other treasures on a shelf. They show it to their friends: 'Just look – our Sophie made this at school!'

The spoon is merely one example.

Another, related project might be a mallet they will use in all the subsequent carving projects. The method employed is similar to that of making the wooden spoon. But the mallet is heavier and more rounded and demands greater strength and perseverance. The ideal material is beech wood. All our mallets were made in this way, big and smaller ones. Mallets that have deteriorated from much use are smoothed down to a smaller size and used for more delicate work. The most important feature of these mallets is the shaped handle allowing for just the right grip.

Even a student in Class 11 or 12 will always look for their very own mallet during a woodcarving block. Years of constant use have left their mark, and they smile warmly at the 'younger generation' who handled their mallets during all these years.

Class 6 skills

The different skills of children must be taken into account. Some finish their project long before the slower ones and should be given additional, similar tasks to do before a new technique is introduced to the whole class. Another ladle may be suggested, which they can now make without further help from the teacher. Butter knives and letter openers made of special, hard wood have all proved themselves as useful articles.

The next exercise is both educational and fun. Up to now, they used the chisel as a means of preparing the shape of an object. This was then evened and smoothed out with rasps, files, planes and emery paper. We now look at the bits of wood we have collected during the year, wood that would otherwise have been used for firewood.

They present a wonderful opportunity for learning new skills: shaping and neatly carving surfaces, a skill that is necessary for artistic, sculptural work later on. From these offcuts we carve traditional Nuremberg houses. During their work children can use their imagination to the full. The piece of wood will itself suggest size and shape of the little house, each different but of the same style.

One house may be beautiful, but it takes a number of them to make a toy town for children to play with. We keep supplying Steiner-Waldorf Kindergartens all over the world with such toy towns. Naturally, our Class 6 children do not find it easy to part with them. However, the many letters of appreciation and gratitude soon compensate for their loss:

Dear Children of Class 6,
Thank you so much for your gift. You should have heard the shouts of joy as our children took the houses from the box, all different! We have a longish table along the windows and we put your houses on it, a whole town. The children got me to make lots of people from beeswax who are now walking about on

the streets. A girl called Freya wanted a bride and bridegroom for the church. And Nicole didn't wish to join us for snack – she couldn't tear herself away from the town.

Other exercises may include the hollowing out of the split logs into caves or houses for dwarfs. The latter necessitates the gluing together of two parts after each of them has been neatly finished. Door and lock are important for the comfort and safety of the residents. The hinges are made from strips of leather. The actually working latch is already a forerunner of our subsequent project: moveable toys in Class 7.

Related to our working methods during the making of caves is the production of scoops of flour, sugar and salt. Again, our hand is the model for them. The final shape of the scoop determines the selection of a suitable piece of wood.

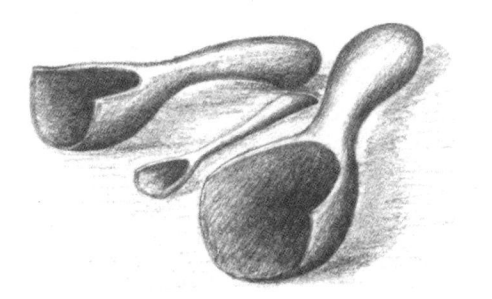

Class 7: the concave form

Let us now take a look at Class 7. Rhythm and grace of movement are noticeably waning. Children withdraw more and more into themselves. 'Inner space' becomes important. We try to produce such an inner space that is, however, still open to the top: a bowl. We carve such bowls in Class 7 from different wood and in different sizes, but all of them for a specific purpose and use.

'What will be put into my bowl?' At the very beginning, before the first cut is made, children know the recipient of their gift. They may have discussed with their parents what kind of bowl was still needed in the house. Here, too, we use only split wood and not finished boards. Wood that still contains the nature of the original tree. Each piece, therefore, looks different; none are identical. The creative work begins at the point of selection: Which is the piece I can connect with? Can I already 'see' the finished product in it?

Inner and outer form

To begin, we fasten a piece of semi-round wood into the vice, curved side uppermost, and without any previous drawing begin our tentative carving towards the centre. We pay attention to the shape, gradually enlarging and deepening the prototype. Children must be fully awake, and carefully guide the chisel. Each new cut must leave the shape beautiful and harmonious.

When given the choice between softer and harder wood children will opt for the former. They always prefer darker to lighter wood. Indeed, heartwood is especially suited to the carving of bowls; its rich range of colouring, from the light sapwood to the darker heartwood at the centre, is far more attractive than bowls made from wood of one colour only. The pattern of the concentric annual rings and the light edge – the result of working from the outside in – is especially striking. In my experience I have only rarely known children in Class 7 who were able to give an individual character to a bowl. The actual artistic forces have not as yet come into their own. A bowl made from a board will always show its origin. The shape of the stem, if used in the way described, will almost by itself determine the harmonious curves of the bowl's rim.

The rim is especially important: its task is to relate the inner to the outer form, to unite the two and not to separate them. I always give children a choice of three possibilities: to round off on both sides, to round off on the outside, to round off the inside. In the two latter instances the result will always be an edge between in- and outside. All these exercises in shaping different rims can easily be carried out by all children in Class 7.

During my reflections on this project – bowls, for which the human hand serves as prime model – I remembered a saying by the Chinese sage, Lao-tse (third or fourth century B.C.): 'Pots are made from clay. And yet it is the empty space that is essential for them.'

Because of this I always make children begin with the inner form, the essential. This has to be smoothly carved and finished. Working from the rim, the shape is formed – because of the rim's dual role of defining the beginning and end of the inner space. Once this inner space has been formed and neatly finished (we had practised this perceiving, sensing by touch and delicate carving during our work on the Nuremberg houses and dwarfs' cottages in Class 6) the outer form will be shaped in correspondence with the inner form. Finally, the rim will be finished in the way described.

We complete our project, a useful article that gives joy again and again because of its beauty and usefulness. The effort was well worth it even though the initial enthusiasm may have occasionally ebbed a little. Hard wood makes tremendous demands! But the teacher was quite right when they jokingly said in encouragement: 'There is no such thing as hard wood, only too large shavings!' The success at the end lets us forget all our troubles and pains. This, the teacher thought, will be a frequent experience of life.

Moveable toys

Rudolf Steiner frequently mentioned the value of moveable toys in his lectures to teachers. It is included in the Class 7 curriculum. Clear thinking in planning and the application of simple mechanics are essential. Rudolf Steiner always meant movements of people and animals. Because of its humorous aspects it is admirably suited to children of that age. But it is not at all easy to translate such characteristic movements into wood and string. We can use the many traditional toys as examples and stimulation. There are simple mechanical laws that can be applied in the process.

Mechanics

The use of levers plays an important part in the making of hammering or sawing men, or in fighting animals as they approach and move away from each other. The lever action in scissors opens up a variety of possibilities, especially suited to group work. A shepherdess, for example, who drives a flock of geese before her; the Three Kings of Orient with their retinue and camels going to the manger. Then there is the simple turning technique by which a great variety of to-and-fro movements can be produced, such as 'cat and mouse' in which the mouse always just gets away from the cat. Movements between two people, between human and animal or between two animals can be produced in this way. Especially effective are movements that are horizontal to the vertically turning wheels such as dancing dolls turning around their own axis.

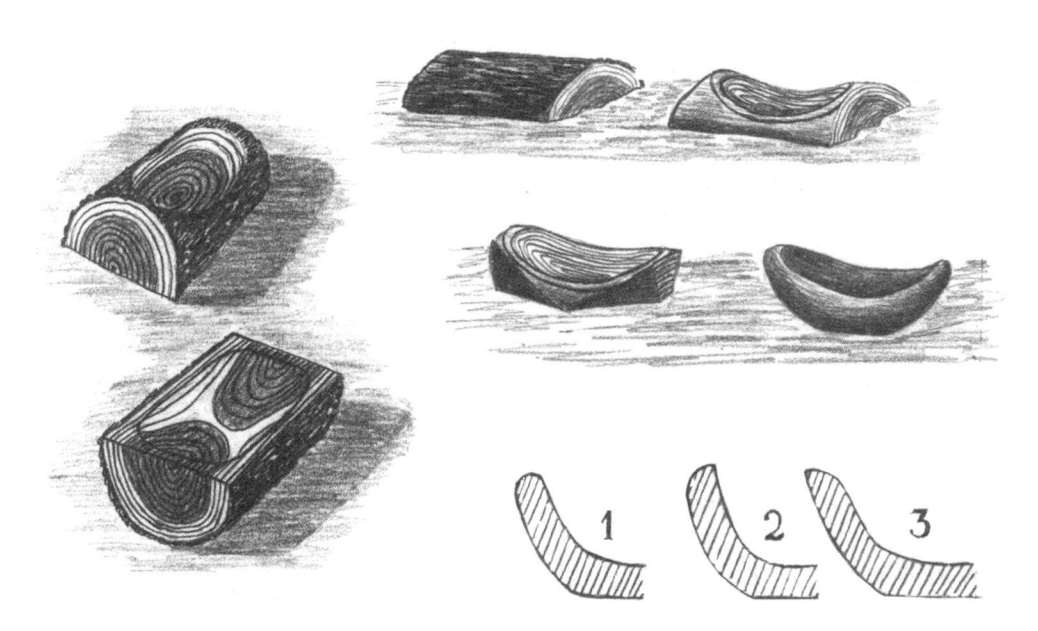

Carving bowls, working from the rim

The use of the pendulum offers other possibilities, be it an animal balancing on the edge of a shelf or a bird moving its head and tail in alternating movements.

The tautening and loosening of a string results in a little man climbing as high as to the ceiling.

Simple mechanics can be applied to the making of more sophisticated toys in Class 8. A train, for example, demands the precise drilling of parallel holes for the axles, something we had already practised when we made rope ladders.

Children especially enjoy building a fully functioning crane. A great variety of models are suggested by the nature of branches and branch forks used for the project, because of our remaining faithful to our principle not to work with 'ready-made' boards. The beautiful results seem to justify this – they could never have been created from boards! There is no base for a turning crane, however beautiful, that can compare with that made from the root of a fir tree, and no ready made hook can be as beautiful and as strong as that carved from the natural fork of a branch from a birch.

Such work allows children to take a good look at the nature processes and experience how their creative forces in roots, branches and twigs can also adapt to technological tasks. By attempting the production of mechanical objects in this original way, we combine technology with beauty: we prepare children for the understanding of simple, basic mechanical principles of which they are made aware in Class 7 and which will later lead to an understanding of machines.

Projects for the community

As we have already said, children are not allowed to keep all the things they make. The rope ladder and the toy town are the result of group work and either sold or given away. In Class 8, also, children will not work for themselves when, shortly before the end of the school year, time does not allow for a new project to be started. In this way we accumulate a great number of cranes, castles, animals and other things for the school community and our workshop, as suggestions for further work. It is just as important, however, that children choose to give some of their work away. The precious things they do keep they often treasure throughout their lives.

Working for the annual Advent bazaar is especially important. Real group work is practised here. Everybody participates in making it a success. The craft teachers not only work extra hours, but extra days! During the four weeks preceding

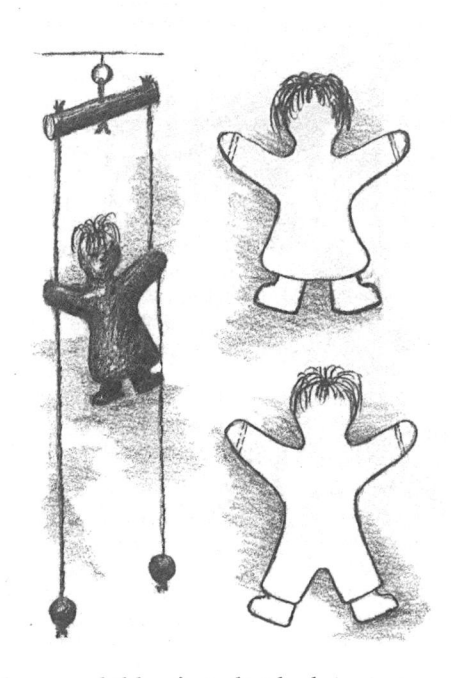

6. CRAFTS IN THE MIDDLE SCHOOL (CLASSES 5–8)

the bazaar children's individual projects are put away in boxes and we concentrate on moveable toys, on train sets made from hazelnut branches, on climbing men or balancing animals, on Nuremberg houses, on jumping jacks or on actually working scales, with weights made from baked clay, for a toy grocery shop.

Contrary to our usual principle, the craft teachers have already prepared the basis on the machine. The single parts for the articles are on the benches, with the corresponding tools next to them. The teacher distributes the work, explains the methods to be employed – often quite new for children. And then the work begins – 'mass-produced' articles, repetitive individual work, each child responsible for a part for the benefit of the whole.

For example, children take an already roughly cut out object and add the finer touches. This is done at the expense of the individuality of the work that characterised the previous projects. However, it is amply compensated by children's selfless devotion to the common good, seeing that more things can be produced in this way and the school community benefit from it.

Indeed, children enjoy it. They become masters of the particular detail they contribute. In the production of an animal and cart set, one might be carving the cart, another an ox, another a donkey and still another a horse. Joining them together is the task of yet another one in the group.

In the production of the jumping jack that proves to be especially popular at the bazaar, children in Class 5 supply the frame, children in Class 6 the arms, Class 7 the legs and Class 8 the bodies – quite a new experience for all of them, because all the single parts have to fit. They also have to be completed at the same time to avoid delay. Everything depends on the commitment, skills and diligence of each one.

PART TWO: CRAFTS IN THE MIDDLE SCHOOL

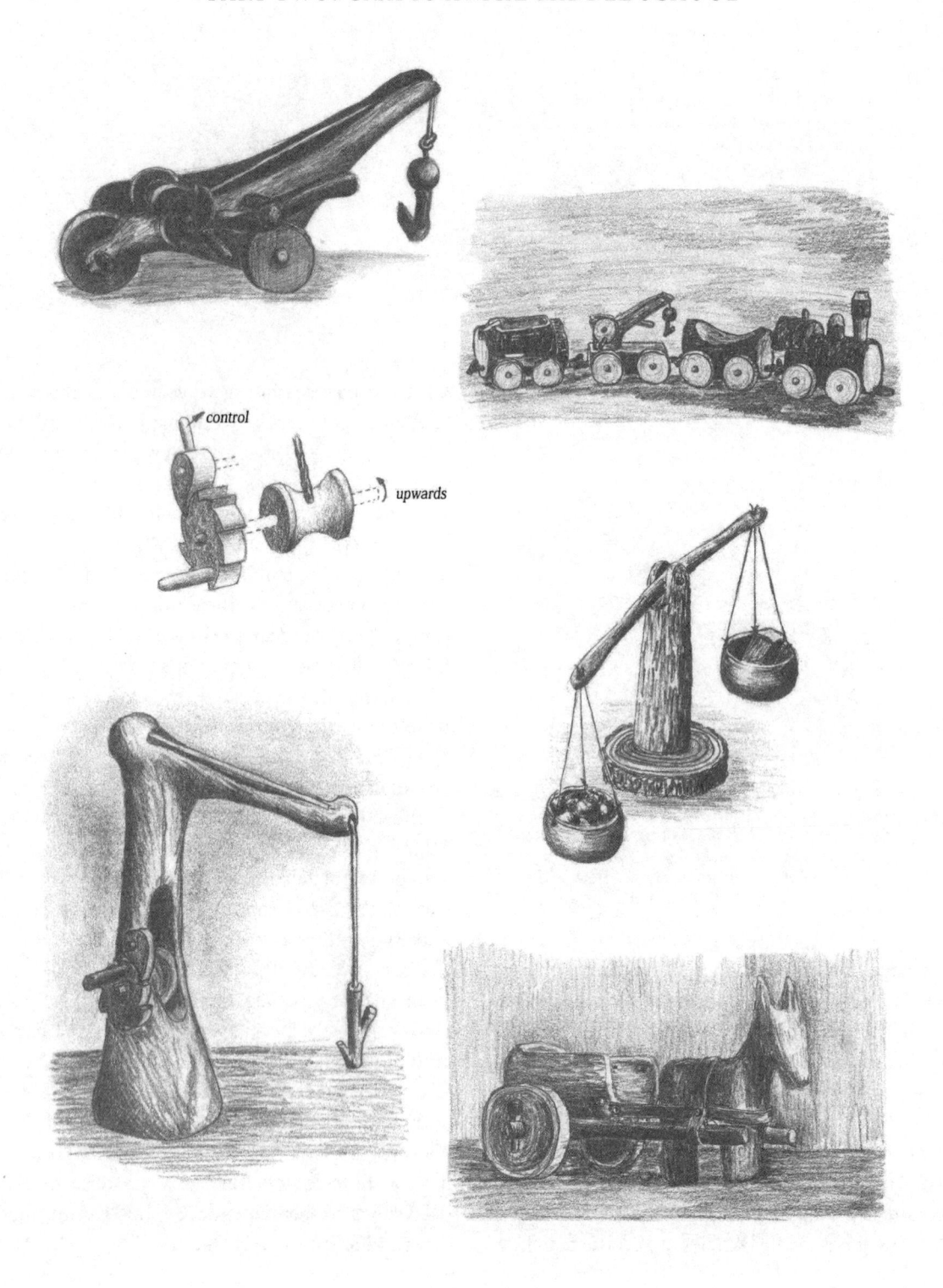

control

upwards

56

6. CRAFTS IN THE MIDDLE SCHOOL (CLASSES 5–8)

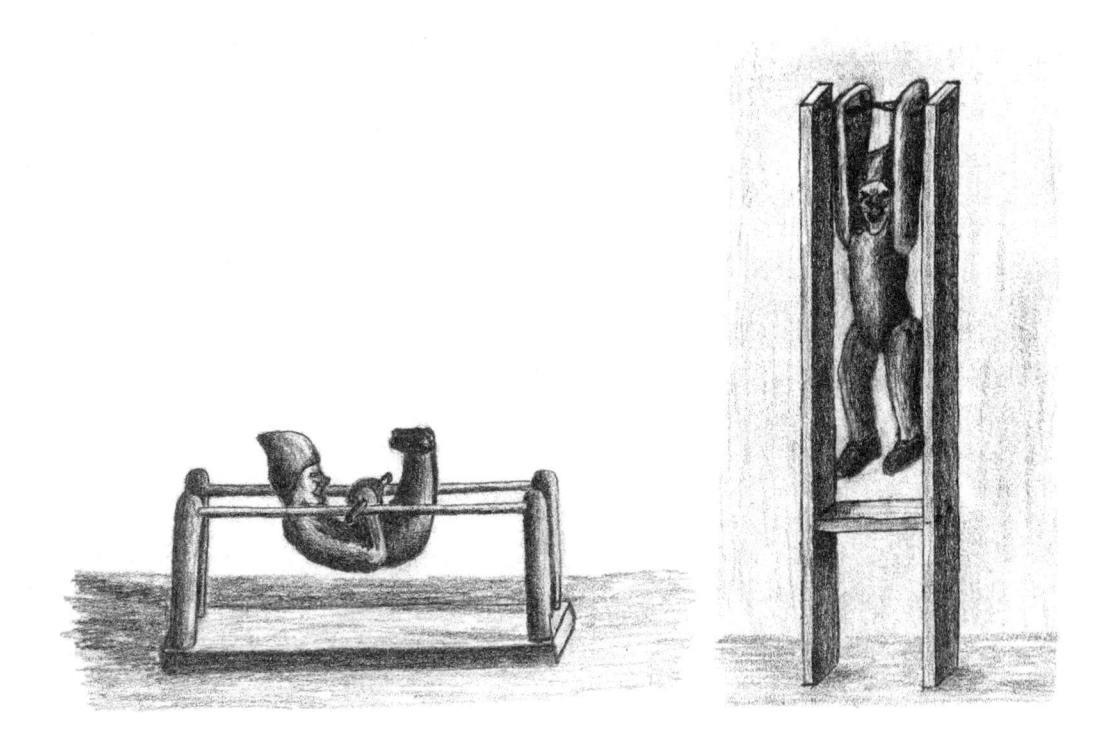

The same applies to the making of a train set. The single parts include the carriages, the engine and wheels. So that they fit, children use templates made by the teacher.

Children are always justifiably proud of their work. At the bazaar they watch the buyers as they examine, try the mechanism, select and, finally satisfied and happy, buy the chosen article and take it away. They are aware of the fact that such beautiful, hand-crafted toys are not available anywhere else. Children themselves know this, too. They become aware of the difference between mass-produced animals, made by machines, and their own hand-crafted products. The teacher occasionally showed them toys sold in shops, and they judiciously studied them and perceived the difference in quality and originality.

They experience how a common, comprehensive project can be realised through combined commitment. At the same time they learn to appreciate the hardship and problems of the millions of people earning their living in this way. Our community work for the bazaar served its purpose if, apart from their direct practical experiences, children will look at their watches, shoes or books with different eyes. All the many objects in our daily use were made by numerous people working in a similar way, each responsible for one part only.

After this interlude children resume their own individual work with even greater joy and enthusiasm – an ever-astonishing experience for the teacher.

Using the right 'skin': wax and oil

Every usable object that is held by the hand – is 'handled' – will need a surface protection in order to be, and remain, useful. This applies especially to wooden toys. They need protection, a kind of 'skin', which, however, does not separate children's hands from the beautiful, warm substance of wood. Varnish is therefore not advisable.

The most suitable material is probably beeswax. Natural beeswax has, however, the disadvantage of remaining sticky and sensitive to moisture. The silky quality we like so much soon fades. We overcame this problem by experimenting with various beeswax ointments until we found the right one which we have now successfully used over a long period.

Its main ingredients are clear beeswax, hardened by adding precious carnauba wax, a natural wax taken from the leaves of the carnauba palm in Brazil. Durability is achieved by the addition of gum from larches, and flexibility through raw linseed oil. All of these ingredients are mixed in a particular proportion. Balsam turpentine oil is added and everything is melted together in a hot water bath. Children and visitors respond by saying, 'It always smells so good in the workshop!'

This, our 'Nuremberg wax', has proved itself not only in the making of toys but in many other useful articles, such as candlesticks, bowls, letter openers, even clay sculptures. The latter regain their original shine – which they lose in the drying process – when, after drying, they are generously rubbed with this substance and the excess moisture later wiped off with a soft cloth. They are then polished to a fine finish.

The wooden spoon is the exception. The wax would melt in hot liquid and taint the food. It is finished with the 'magic wand', a rounded piece of hardwood that is rubbed across the smoothed surface, producing a really magical, delicate shine that fascinates children. Unfortunately, this gets lost after its first use.

Salad servers are rubbed with cooking linseed oil. Larger articles, especially those with a rough surface, are treated with a semi oil – a linseed oil varnish and balsam turpentine oil, 1:1, mixed cold. Only the boats need covering with a waterproof varnish.

Every article thus receives its appropriate skin – and we know from our warm bodies how important this is for our life and health.

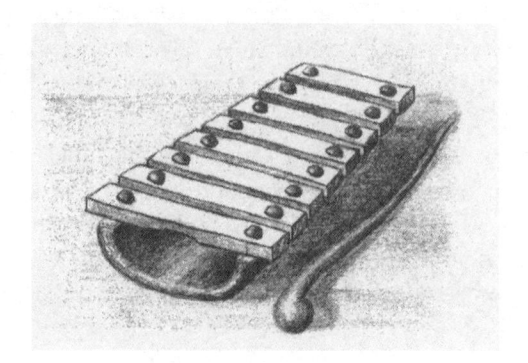

Class 8: beauty and function

Children in Class 8 are given a choice from a variety of projects. Musically gifted students often decide to produce a xylophone and they make the best use of the latent musical quality in the available types of wood. To begin with, the sounding slats are cut off the prepared bits of hardwood in different lengths and finely tuned by ear. Our experimenting tells us that the fullest sound is produced by a piece of wood placed on a hollowed-out sound box with a strip of felt between. Further experiments with different wood lead us to the selection of the best material for the hammer, which is then carved into the appropriate shape. Finally, corresponding to the sounding slats, the open-ended, bowl-shaped sound box is carved.

Nutcrackers are another favourite. Especially those made from a log and carved in the shape of a gnome who cracks the nuts in his mouth. Or a bowl-shaped nutcracker where the work of the previous year is repeated in a more exacting way.

The making of a candlestick needs practical consideration: a firm base is essential. The shape is directed upwards, to the candle. A copper tray with a screwed-in spike for holding the candle and catching the drips of wax is needed. The spike is filed from a brass screw that harmonises well with the finely carved wood. Other students choose to make salad servers made from precious wood. This work is a progression from the wooden spoon in Class 6 – it requires great skill and perseverance.

Making a complicated castle appeals to quite a number of students. The skills they acquired during their work on the Nuremberg houses are now further developed: towers, bowers, oriels, battlements, even a working drawbridge are included in this ambitious undertaking.

The shepherds and animals of Class 5 are now carved again, but in greater detail, as preparation for artistic woodwork in Class 11.

Students now have the knowledge and experience to design and create their own projects. I believe choice to be important at this age, because of the marked individual differences, the different inclinations and rejections that may find expression in the workshop. This results in a stimulating variety of work and demands of the teacher great flexibility and versatility if they wish to do justice to all of the students and their projects.

It is not only the students who, in the face of the magnitude of their tasks, are covered in perspiration: the teacher, too, must set an example with their never waning enthusiasm and joy in the act of creating, in order to lift their students' spirits should they become lazy or lax. They are, however, richly rewarded as they watch children's progress and, if they succeed in reaching them with a sense of humour, enthusiasm and praise, the joyous working mood will be restored and maintained.

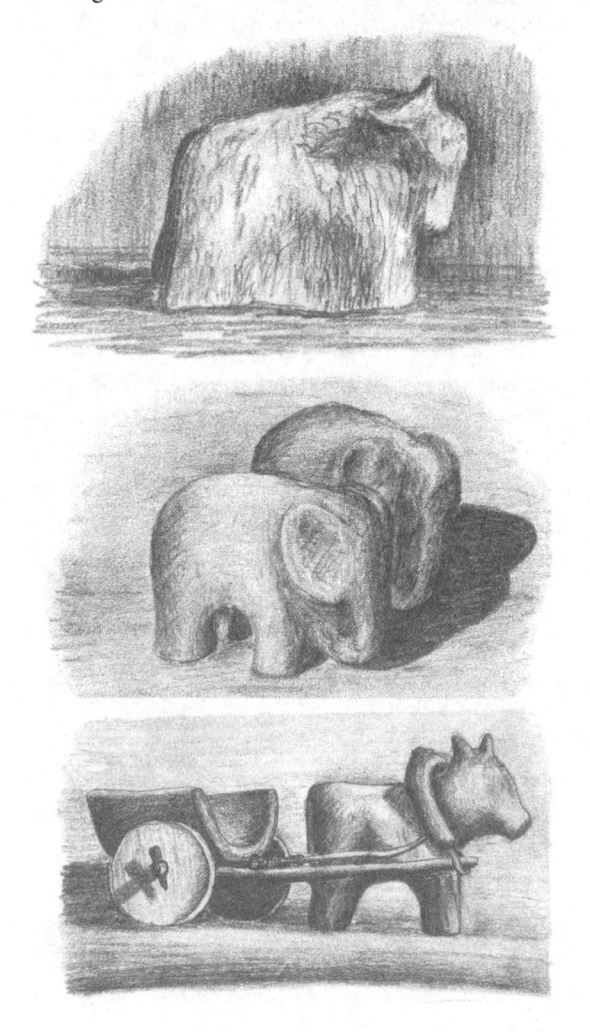

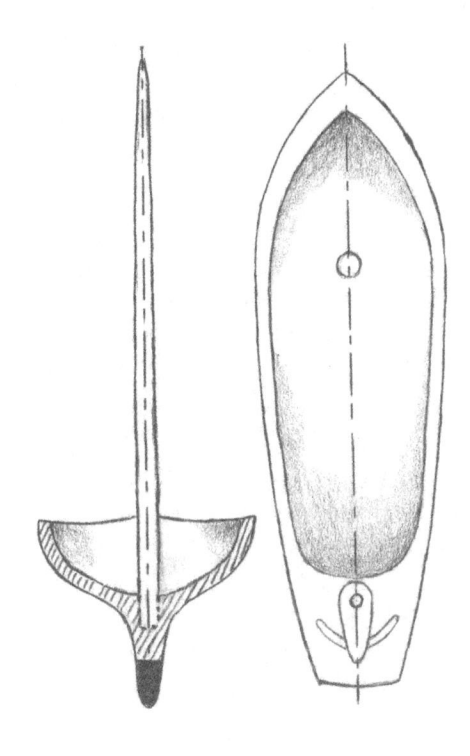

Transitional projects

Making a boat is, I believe, the best project at this age. Think of a boy or girl in Class 8, claimed by the earth's gravity, lounging about, always looking for a prop – a stage through which they sooner or later pass. A boat with its symmetrical shape demands constant attention to the vertical, to the accurate comparison between left and right in order to achieve the required balance. The mast must be inserted vertically towards the top and the keel vertically to the bottom. The students must place themselves into a right angle axis if they wish to succeed in this. Only by standing in the vertical can one see if a picture is hanging straight. As soon as the head is even only slightly inclined, one will lose one's horizontal and vertical orientation.

Drilling the hole for the mast is, therefore, always a tense time: the deck must be absolutely horizontal. Another student watches intently as the hole is drilled, correcting the angle if necessary. Finding their orientation in space through the necessity of overcoming the heaviness of their body – to which the teenager so easily succumbs – is of immense benefit for the young.

The boat's seaworthiness is the test of success. It goes without saying that the leaden keel, poured into a plaster of Paris mould made by the students, must be proportionate to the size of the boat. The body of the boat is carved from a piece of log and the horizontal deck is given graceful, curved lines that blend in nicely with the water. The symmetry is then determined: broader boats float more securely! Speed will depend on the shape of

61

the deck; the wall between bow and stern curves tautly to the centre. Exactly underneath the deck's centre line is the keel. The height of the mast (and thus the size of the sail) and the length and weight of the keel complement each other. Should mast and sail be too big for the keel, the boat will capsize. Too small a mast in relation to the keel will slow the speed. The keel is the model for the point of gravity which the teenagers must discover in themselves. Lightness and heaviness must be well balanced. We are everywhere called upon to find the right balance, the right relation to delicate balancing situations. The rudder also plays an important part and making it demands great care and precision. Most of the boats we make are sailing ships and the rigging has to be professionally added. Our students often know more about this than their teacher.

The finished boat, usually 1m (3 ft) in length, is an achievement of which the fourteen-year old can be justifiably proud.

Especially skilled students like the challenge of building a catamaran. If perfectly built, the teacher will not object to its owner adding such technological extras as remote control or similar things in their spare time. Its negative aspect is the loss of the delicate feeling for wind and waves, and the necessary experimenting with rudder and sail that take the boat to the opposite bank.

All these projects in Class 8, that must be both beautiful and functional – i.e. prove themselves when applied and used – are already transitions to the teaching of applied arts in the Upper School.

The joinery period will then bring a new element to woodwork and take it further.

Thoughts from the workshop

Education in the crafts is education of the will. The students must continuously tame their will as they carve the inner shape of a boat or bowl. I frequently tell my classes about my childhood when I had to help with the ploughing. The oxen did the hard work of pulling the plough but the farmer had to give the directions. He had to stand firmly and move on the earth if he wished to control and tame the strength of the animals. In the same way, the hand guiding the chisel must hold it firmly so that the strength of the other hand is controlled. Children understand the analogy – a picture that helps them to achieve co-ordination.

Encouraging use of the senses

Handwork, woodwork and craft lessons are also a cultivation of the senses. The eyes must learn to differentiate the delicate nuances of form in order to avoid an interruption of the graceful flow of the rim through either a wrong fall or rise of the wood. The inner form is best perceived by the hand gliding gently across the delicately chiselled surface: it can feel even the smallest unevenness. Such skills and faculties should here be developed. Already during the making of spoons the sense of touch is cultivated, every wrong protuberance in the handle is felt, the more so the further the work proceeds. The delicate pressure of the fingertips here becomes more important than the eye. The students are encouraged to trust their own faculties, to find their way to perfection. 'Can you still feel a bump – all right you may now start with the polishing.'

6. CRAFTS IN THE MIDDLE SCHOOL (CLASSES 5–8)

Students make their own decisions and don't merely do what the teacher tells them to.

In weighing up symmetry (as in the making of a boat) the sense of balance comes into its own: together with eye and hands – as well as our sense of touch – we can see if left and right complement each other. If the outer form is wrong, the inner will also suffer and the boat will not float well. The sense of balance is also essential in the fitting of mast and keel. And the sense of movement accompanies everything children observe and do.

Even the sense of hearing is evident. It tells us something about the quality of the wood, about the differences between healthily grown firewood, a piece of soft lime – very different from the clear sound of a piece of hard maple. When making a xylophone the different sounds of a shorter or longer piece are made full use of. Children even notice the vibrations of a piece of wood not properly fastened in the vice. Even the incorrect use of a tool can actually be heard. Children should continually be encouraged to use their senses in order to become more independent in their activities. This is another reason why we don't draw diagrams. Shape and form should be allowed to develop during the actual work, through children's alertness and their own observations.

Working in the workshop is also education for social interaction. There are innumerable opportunities for mutual help – be it in the selection of suitable material in the storeroom or during the sawing and splitting of logs. A stronger student can assist a weaker one, more skilled children will feel good when they patiently teach their less-able friends a few tricks. This development of social feelings is a necessity in our busy and understocked workshops. Consideration is essential: there is no room for selfishness. Clumsier children must be given the better benches and tools, the skilled ones can more easily handle less ideal situations. Mutual understanding and help are the golden rule in the workshop.

Teaching in the workshop

I regard it as absolutely necessary for the teacher to handle every one of the children's articles after school. They must have the picture of each child before them. This will determine the success of the following lesson.

Order in the lessons is essential. Children are used to being greeted by their teacher. They shake hands and sit down, facing the teacher. This quiet minute is necessary; it allows children to calm down after their wild games in the playground and the creation of the right mood for work. They listen to the teacher's remarks about the previous lesson or about the next stage of the work before moving to their assigned places and continuing with their projects.

The teacher must be aware of everything, must praise, reprove, correct if necessary, lend a hand and pay attention to students with special needs. Occasionally the work is interrupted, in order to draw attention to some discovery a student may have made during their work. Through the observation of each other's work new skills are learnt.

A talkative group may be told to work silently for a few minutes. This is more effective when the teacher joins in too. Children, becoming more conscious of their work, frequently feel almost liberated from their inclination to constant talking and are, at the same time, amazed at how quickly their work progresses when they concentrate on it. As talking is prohibited, the teacher communicates through a sign language, often very funny and much appreciated by all. Tidying up ends the lesson. Everybody is called upon to do their part. The workpieces are taken to their assigned places, the benches are cleaned – corners included – the vices closed and the tools returned to the shelves.

The students then take their seats and remain silent. A receptive mood is created for the teacher to say whatever might be useful or necessary. It is important that the lively activity during the lesson is calmed. The names of the four students on cleaning duty are then called out. The remainder are dismissed with a handshake, an opportunity for a possible personal remark.

I hardly ever delegate specific duties, such as tidying the shelves. Every single student is called upon to return their tools to the right place. This is, of course, only possible if the teacher is also tidy and the room is neat at the beginning of the lesson. This serves as example and helps the students in feeling inwardly supported and disciplined. This is particularly important at a time when people find it so difficult to bring order into their lives. Deep down, children long for order. This does not mean that the room has to be prosaic and barren; our description of it will confirm this. Order and *Gemüt* (heart-forces) are not mutually exclusive; children's souls need the right feelings for their nourishment.

Life in the workshop has many aspects. Working within a group awakens many faculties. It is a necessary complement to the other subjects. But it is also a help for life itself, for the purpose of learning is to understand the world, so that one day, we take our place in it, work in it. Henry Ford was surely right when he said: 'There is something really grand in our daily work! Work is the corner stone on which the world rests, it is the root for our self esteem!'

7

A forestry main-lesson class trip (Class 7)
Liesel Gudrun Gienapp

It's easy to cut down a tree –
A chainsaw does it instantly.
To grow a tree to reach its prime
Will take considerable time.

Baron von F., owner of several large forests in Sauerland, had invited us to spend two weeks on his estate in May. It was not the usual class trip: we were to observe the whole cycle of timber production from start to finish – saw mills, thinning, re-planting, germinating, seedlings. A comprehensive overview that could be summed up as: 'From wood to workshop'.

Much of what we use in our daily lives escapes our understanding. Technology has seen to this. Children know well enough that the iron gets hot when plugged in, that the fridge makes a humming sound, that the telephone rings and that calculators are reliable. But they don't know how they work. Without fully realising it, we are surrounded by a world of magic, believing we are in control – as long as everything is in working order – but often at a loss when something goes wrong.

Learning through experience

Our very young children are trying to come to grips with the world around them by asking 'why?' Their questions assume a new urgency at the beginning of puberty. Around age twelve the faculty of reasoning and judgement makes itself felt. It allows children to understand the world through thinking, preparing for the next step into adolescence, during which the young man or woman carefully examines the world around themselves. Children this age look to probe deeply into moral issue and truths behind the phenomena, because they wish to understand their world, find a useful place where they can employ their skills and energies and feel 'at home'. Because of this it is essential for the young to experience the world at this age in a way that they can feel: understanding and insight are possible, connections can be found. The head alone cannot gain such assurance. It must take hold of the whole being, must be felt in every part of the body. It is because of this that experience and doing take priority in the curriculum at this time.

Our class trip was aimed at strengthening awareness, this standing-firmly-in-life by following the processes of timber production from forest to workshop. Its success is not measured merely by how much the students have 'learnt' or by their enjoyment, but by how much they have experienced, and whether this often unconscious experience may help them to stand more securely in life and strengthen their confidence, e.g. I can see the connections, my own activities fit into the world.

Every stage of the wood's progress from forest to workshop provides children with the opportunity of not only intellectually understanding the course of events, but experiencing it with their hearts and senses. During the pre-puberty stage, children are still primarily related to the world through their feelings – friendships and enmities, pleasure and displeasure are important. Gradually, thinking takes over, the students become more awake, their questions about the reality of things become more precise. Much of later life depends on the nature of the environment in which the young people now finds themselves.

The forest as a living community, dependent on the care and cultivation of people, is a picture of interrelationships in which youngsters can learn how to deal with living things. The researcher of the lifeless, the mechanical, must separate the object from the totality. Those who wish to understand and care for living things must discover the relations and connections, and must perceive them and take them into account. When the forester tells us about the numerous functions of the forest, about the refreshing air, the right amount of moisture, the significance of birds and the life of the deer, children's thinking is directed to comprehend the inter-relationships in life. This is a pre-condition for today's demands for ecological thinking.

But this main-lesson block in forestry offers more than the hearing of stories and the observation of things. It allows children to be active themselves. Not only in their thinking – their feelings and will are also addressed, meeting the needs of this age admirably.

I began our first craft lesson in Class 6 with the sentence: 'There is nobody, however small, who cannot be a helper.' Before I could continue, Florian interjected: 'This is true. The grown-ups don't trust us to do anything. When the bridge was being built in our neighbourhood I wanted to watch, but the workers always chased us away – except once, when one of them gave me a broom and asked me to sweep the sand away. This was real fun!'

What did the boy actually say? Work gives joy; to be useful makes one feel strong, useful, wanted and makes one part of a group, makes one belong. We can see the transition from play to work.

The task of education consists of accompanying this stage of development – a real threshold that may determine adult life – with the greatest care and attention. Our two weeks in the forest, during which we assisted the forester, were dedicated to this task.

The trip

Why Class 7?

Our previous experiences made us decide on a forestry main-lesson block for Class 7. The children are thirteen years old and about to grow into adolescence. Not yet fascinated by their own subjective world, they are, however, already intelligent and strong enough to lend a meaningful hand in some projects. They are at the threshold to adult life and yet still open to the magic of the world of elementals. The forest to them means more than the usefulness of timber. These gates will soon close – a Class 8 student perceives the world very differently.

The forest as a classroom

There is much to be done in a forest. Our concern is to provide such tasks that are educationally sound and fruitful. What are they?

They must be meaningful: children must immediately see that their work is important, worthwhile.

And there must be enough room for play. The strength needed in doing one's duty at the expense of self interest must be given time to develop. In their play, little children imitate the grown-ups' work. Activity is the important thing here, not the result. Beginning and end of play is determined by an inner impulse, by the joy and pleasure the activity provides.

Later in life we must meet the demands coming from without. Can we think of tasks that make for a smooth transition from the one to the other, that can give children an inkling of the nature of duty, of responsibility and yet leave enough space for the element of play?

Children should have an opportunity also of experiencing the strengthening effect of community life. How everything combines, interacts, interweaves for the benefit of the whole, the common aim. Strength and gentleness, courage and reflectiveness, direct action and clear planning, eagerness and patience, fun and earnestness. Things happen as long as everybody contributes their best.

In a forest there are many possibilities for the children of this particular age to experience these things. The following are but a few examples:

Go and pick up all the dead wood along the edge of the forest. There mustn't be any giveaway crackling of twigs when the forester goes on her rounds at dusk. The deer are timid and easily scared.

Go to the place we were yesterday. You'll find it by yourselves today. Stay at the spot where the paths fork. Remember the large rock? Wait for the workers. The area covered with fir trees must be thinned out; the weak and sick trees must be removed to give more light and space for the good ones. The woodman will tell you which trees have to be chopped down and how to do it. Take three axes and three saws with you. Remember how to carry them safely? When the trees are down you must stack them neatly at the edge of the forest and get them ready for the truck. Off you go!

I have a special task for you today. It's a fair distance away. There, at the top of that hill where a lot of trees were recently felled, the smaller branches have to be cleared away and burnt. Here are some matches. I wonder if you can get them to burn. Take good care and watch for the direction of the wind. Don't loiter on the way, you'll need all the time you have.

You really did work hard yesterday. But I am sorry I have to disappoint you. The stile you made will not last, the beech wood you used is not suitable, it rots too quickly. You should have used pine. Its gum gives strength and endurance. Would you mind doing it again? Now that you know how to do it, it shouldn't take you long.

Could you repair the bridge behind the main building? The hikers who had their picnic there last Sunday broke the railing. There might be some other damage as well. Let's go and see. You can then get the necessary tools from the shed.

Every morning brings new tasks; and delegated groups, led by an adult, see to them. The children experience a different relationship with the forest than a person who merely strolls through it. The forest speaks a different language to those who work there.

Wind, fog, warmth, rain – the weather is important for those who work outside. Children experience deeply the various moods in nature: the delicate early morning mist, the soft drizzle, a hail shower, the clear sky, the fresh breeze. A bird of prey circling in the air, a deer looking at us from a safe distance and bounding away; frogs in a pond; horses tame enough to allow themselves to be stroked.

We meet the dangers of this age – the isolation of the newly awakening energies, the inclination of the sparkling intelligence towards a cold intellectuality, the physical maturity overpowering the adolescent and making them a victim of primitive instincts – by countering them with activities directed by feelings and thinking, where thinking is founded in feelings and doing.

It is our aim to reach and enthuse the young through intensive experiences, because it is through these that they will be protected from falling victim to intellectuality and brutality. What they experience will affect their future lives. They learn to connect reflection with doing in a healthy, practical way.

Our work in the forest continually connects thinking, feeling and doing: those who act rashly will make things difficult for themselves; those who only reflect, plan and prepare will not get anything done. Those who spend all their time enjoying the open air and the sun will dream their life away.

Consider: before a tree is chopped down, the direction of the fall must be determined. Where is the greatest weight of the crown? Where is the most space for the fallen tree? How should it drop in order to cause the least damage to the other trees? All this is 'professionally' discussed until a consensus is reached. And then the work begins! The whole tree vibrates as the well directed axe bites into the stem. At the right time the saw is employed. The tree begins to bend, gently at first, then faster until it crashes to the ground.

Thinking is needed before the tree is dragged from the creek into which it has fallen: the *how* is as important as the physical strength.

We have thus a healthy interweaving of planning, doing and experiencing in all the things we do in the forest. Experience – reflection – activity; the burning of rubbish needs to be watched, guarded and kept going.

The individual way the students apply themselves to their work offers the teacher opportunities for studying their temperaments. The sanguines are always ahead of everybody else, discovering beehives and feeding troughs for the deer; they quickly make friends with the workers, splash about in the stream during breaks and always have to be called back to work.

The cholerics make a beeline for the axe, feeling their strength as they chop away. They love competing against the others. 'See how much we got done today!'

The phlegmatics do the planning and try their best to succeed with the least physical effort. Yet, in this way they occasionally get more done than the others.

7. A FORESTRY MAIN-LESSON CLASS TRIP (CLASS 7)

The melancholics are given the task of sealing the 'wounds' where branches were cut off. Loving care and exactitude are here more important than physical strength.

Then there are those who prefer to work by themselves. They organise their day's project, are independent, and at the end of the day can show what they had achieved. Most of them, however, like working together as a team. Things get done more quickly and efficiently if done together, and talking seems to put zest into the work. But there are occasions when communal work may prove to be counterproductive. Differences of opinion can slow the work down, for example in the case of two students carrying a tree trunk. 'Stop pushing so hard!' 'I am not – it's you who is pulling too hard!' Such experiences are important for the pupil who wishes to find their place in the world. The children learn to value each other's skills: Eliza's help is always asked when the tree to be carried away is especially heavy. Matthew is the one whose advice on felling a tree is listened to. Evelyn never refuses an appeal for help, and Frank always brings life into the group with his cheerfulness. Mary plods quietly on, unperturbed and never complaining. Each of them could be characterised in the way he or she is trying to find their place in the group, and the way they are helped by their friends, sometimes gently, sometimes a little roughly.

Nobody can opt out of the process. There are transformations in the children during this time. Working in the forest is at the same time working on oneself. I sometimes wonder if the children's parents notice these changes in their sons and daughters after their stay in the forest – the way they have grown.

The two weeks in the forest seemed like a long time because of the wealth of events: dealing with nature, the interaction with one another, with the teacher, the work itself, the occasional homesickness but, most of all, the coming to grips with oneself.

During our subsequent woodwork lessons memories arise: 'Do you remember…?' The students look at the wood from which they are carving a boat or a simple stool with different eyes than previously. It has its own history. Wind, mist, warmth and rain are still present in the children's memories. The circling bird of prey, the deer, the swarm of bees, the call of the cuckoo – they all are part of it and help the children to treat the substance entrusted to them with understanding care and with reverence. They wish to transform it into beautiful and practical objects.

8

Reflections on moveable toys (Class 7)
Michael Martin

The human being and movement

During a visit to Freiburg (Breisgau) in 1919, Rudolf Steiner saw a moveable toy on the top of a wardrobe in a child's room. It was a simple toy, a man sawing wood. He asked for it to be taken down, examined it carefully and said, 'Such toys ought to be made.'[1]

Max Wolffhügel, who was responsible for organising the 'artistic handwork lessons'[2] in the first Waldorf School – supervised by Rudolf Steiner – described this moment as the birth of the moveable toys that have since then been made by children in Class 7. The idea was born before the school opened! It shows the importance Rudolf Steiner attached to it. In subsequent lectures he referred to it repeatedly, and he gave numerous suggestions for it.[3] We must remember that toys at that time tended to be rigid and mechanical, threatening not only children's inner life of imagination, but also the healthy development of their delicate, flexible organs.

The next question to be addressed is the following. Why did Rudolf Steiner consider it so important that children in Class 7 and beyond should themselves invent and make such moveable wooden toys? The process itself obviously corresponds to this age and positively affects children's development, quite independent of the influence the toys might afterwards have on those playing with them. Rudolf Steiner referred to this in different ways: on one occasion he asserted that the making of moveable toys would give children pleasure and make them more skilled.[4]

On another occasion, he emphasised the 'inner mobility', and the 'connection of the soul between the child's life and the life in the world outside'.[5] Here the humorous, hearty and happy nature of the quaint movements of animals and people, brought about by turning, pulling and pushing, the use of gravity etc. plays an important part.

All these suggestions cannot, however, fully satisfy the serious teacher. Pleasure, skills, connection with life etc., may be derived just as well from the knitting of socks, from carving a boat or from potting plants in gardening. There must be something else that makes the production of moveable toys, i.e. mechanical toys, pedagogically so desirable.

8. REFLECTIONS ON MOVEABLE TOYS (CLASS 7)

Unconscious mechanics

In Class 7 children are taught the basic principles of mechanics. The year before, other essential aspects of physics connected to children's sense experiences – seeing, hearing, touching etc. – were discussed. Mechanics is lifeless, dead. It is implicit in our movements that are, if not carried out, supported and sustained by our skeleton. These are unconscious processes – we don't worry about our bones when we move – and yet they provide the basis for the way we control our bodies in standing, sitting or moving about.

Children's relation to their bony system is now undergoing a decisive change. Be it on the playground, in the gymnasium or the gardening lesson, we can observe the increasing heaviness in their movements: they become clumsier, bonier. The earlier graceful movements have gone. Think of a class of eight doing eurythmy: heavy movements, as though directed from without, clumsy legs carrying the body in a circle. It reminds one of marionettes, purely mechanical figures held, controlled and moved from outside. The idea of marionettes is sometimes associated with 'manipulation of people'. Consider, by contrast, the light and graceful movements of a puppet in the hands of a skilful puppeteer.

The German poet Heinrich von Kleist pondered deeply on this subject and he indicated and suggested ways of dealing with this problem. It is essential for the threads moving the lifeless mechanism to be fastened to the correct points of gravity of the corresponding limbs. If, by doing so, the thread is moved forward in a straight line, a graceful movement of the marionette is assured. Success here is conditioned by the full connection of the puppeteer with the process. The path of the thread is identical with the path of the puppeteer's soul that fully places itself into the marionette's point of gravity, in other words, it must move itself.

It is not easy for a grown-up to submerge themselves consciously into their movements. What children unconsciously demonstrate in their natural grace and lightness of touch are, when an adult attempts to imitate them, contrived movements which are all too easily tinged with vanity and offend the beholder. With the growing awakening of the soul, vanity, attention seeking and every kind of self-consciousness are present in the movements. The marionette here has an advantage: being of a purely mechanical nature it cannot be self-conscious or coy.

Harro Siegel: Mephisto

Development in children's twelfth year

We may now move from the marionette to the obviously identical situation of thirteen or fourteen-year-old children. Their natural graceful movements have gone, because of the muscles' growing dependence on the skeleton. 'Later, after their twelfth year, the bony system, placing itself into the outer world, dominates the muscles and, through them, the soul and spirit.'[6] Our task now consists of connecting the newly awakening soul correctly with its own corresponding 'bodily mechanism'.

The young man or woman becomes more awake, more aware of the environment and of their relationship to their body. Coquetry, even arrogance, frequently characterises this age. One is reminded of the time in evolution when the soul united itself strongly with the body. It provided the impetus to progress by filling the soul with desires and wishes it could satisfy through the body. Soul and body became as one, but this progress was paid for with the loss of innocence in paradise. Applied to our subjects this means: the graceful movements of younger children are gone, replaced with mechanical working movements instead.

If we now direct children of this age to produce wooden moveable toys, all their interest, intelligence and reason are occupied in inventing mechanical movements outside their bodies. They must, as it were, slip into the objective mechanism of movements with their souls if the toys are to function well. There is no room for either vanity or attention seeking. Factual thinking and experimenting rule the day, followed by satisfaction if the toy happens to work. The soul connects objectively with the unconsciously experienced mechanism of its own body. If, during puberty, the soul can develop in a way that it can connect itself with the points of gravity in the organism of movement, that is, right into the bones, this will then result in graceful and natural physical movements.

Hand in glove with these dramatic changes in the development of will around age twelve, that show themselves in the movements brought about through the dominant bony system, is the opposite pole of the life of the soul: thinking. Here, too, development occurs. This is, however, a much more difficult problem. Although the exact processes can be practically addressed during lessons, they cannot be easily detected. But they provide help for understanding children at this stage of their development.

Thinking does not only consist of picture elements, but also of will that begins to come into its own at this time. Thinking now connects itself more deeply with the organism, right down as far as the bones. It lights up, as it were, in the densest and most solid system and, through it, becomes capable of understanding the solid elements and processes of our world.

As we enter the twelfth year we acquire a thinking that, in keeping with its will nature, runs its course along with the processes in the bones, in the dynamics of the skeleton. We pass from the soft to the very hard system of the human being – an important transition – that, let me say, places itself into the world like an objective lever system.[7]

As each single bone, complete in itself, borders on the next, so also are the single thoughts now built up, developed in clear and logical sequences: thought on thought, progressing, structured.

Here lie the seeds for thinking in cause and effect. Children have become mature enough for it. Students of anthroposophy have become used to speaking of different 'kinds' of thinking – not, of course, the content of thinking. We cannot understand the utterings of very young children if we apply the factual reasoning of an adult. Children do not simply progress in quantitative thinking, but around their twelfth year, they learn to understand the world of the physical material in a new way, to regard it as their property, accompanied by a feeling of delight. Previously this would have been no more than something they had accepted from outside, learnt about and retained in their heart. Thus, physical and psychological development progress hand in glove.

These developmental stages are of the greatest significance for children's entire future life. Rudolf Steiner repeatedly stressed the importance of craft, hand and field-work during the Middle School years for the unfolding of a living, imaginative thinking, because of the correspondence between the efforts of will through the muscles and those of the thinking process.

Our instincts, urges, desires and wishes are tied to flesh and blood, they are subjective in nature. In past times, the pleasures of the flesh were considered to be contemptible; they had to be fought and conquered. Nobody has as yet spoken of the 'pleasures of the bones'. Bones have neither urges nor desires, they are hidden from sight, serving us selflessly, unnoticed, quietly. It is exactly because of this that they provide the body with secure and decisive support and firmness. If we wish to step out into the world in freedom, without being influenced by our desires and instincts, we must, as it were, submerge ourselves into our skeleton and, from it, set our body in motion. We must put aside 'flesh and blood' and become skeleton or 'truly earth-like', in order to step into the world as free beings.

If we succeed in permeating our thoughts with crystal clear logic and yet with the life-filled dynamics of the skeleton, we liberate our subjective will, that must first evoke these thoughts, from its limiting emotional elements.

If we further succeed in forming our movements from the mechanics of our skeleton, in placing our soul into the points of gravity of our physical mechanism, we can move our bodies freely in the world, without vanity and desire to please. Both thinking and movement permeate themselves in children's twelfth year and beyond with the will that must, because of its strong ties to the skeleton, first be liberated from the excessive elements of instincts and desires that make themselves especially strongly felt during puberty. Thus we lay the foundation for freedom in thinking and doing by connecting the human being with its most lifeless system: its bones. In experiencing the lifeless – death – we have the seeds of a new freedom the young man or woman may acquire. As strange as it may sound, mineralogy, mechanics and, yes, the making of moveable toys will help this development, if they are introduced at the right age.

Movement and mechanics

The structure of our skeleton determines the ways we can move. Beginning with the head, we see its spherical shape that can turn in universally spherical movements. It rests on the uppermost vertebrae of the spine. The human being makes use of spherical and circular forms wherever it is necessary to overcome gravity and friction. In the case of the carriage of a train, its wheels touch the track at a tiny point on which the entire weight rests. This lessens

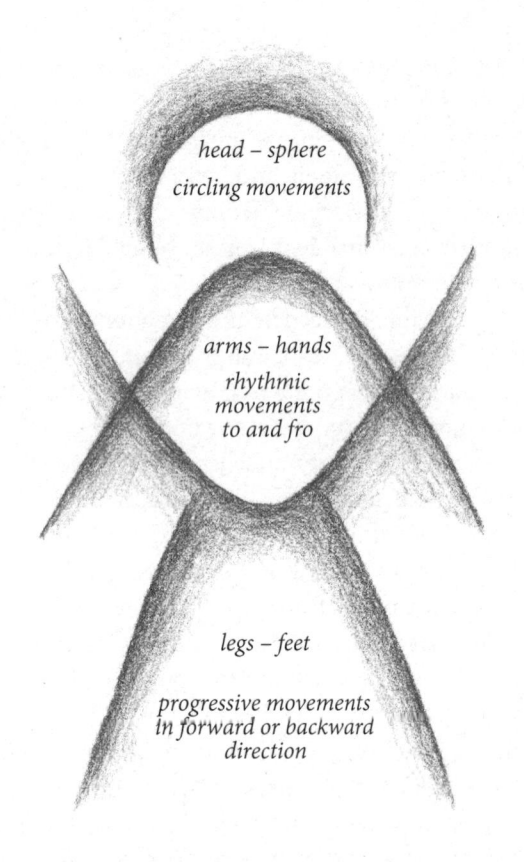

*head – sphere
circling movements*

*arms – hands
rhythmic
movements
to and fro*

legs – feet

*progressive movements
in forward or backward
direction*

towards the front, their movements straight, linear. The joints in the toes make possible only very limited up and down movements; the knees, through their hinge-like joints are fully embedded in a forward movement. The degree of circular or side movements of our legs is made possible through the spherical form of the hips. The linear alignment of legs and feet are in polar opposition to the circling movements of the head. From there they pass in diminishing possibilities in arms and legs into the straight movements of fingers and toes, where the simple up and down movements dominate absolutely. Thus the 'straightness' and 'roundness' of the skeletal structure determine the possible bodily movements. Legs and feet are, through the way they are constructed, in a position to carry the entire body forward. The forward movement is added to the circular one.

Our arms and hands – apart from the similar basic organisation of the legs, the circular movement in the shoulder joints and the dominant up and down movements of the fingers – have an exceptional position. The ulna and radius can turn around an invisible axis between them, making it possible for the lower arm and hand to move – in connection with the shoulder point – freely in all directions. By consciously observing the movements of our hands we have the most beautiful and pertinent picture of freedom.

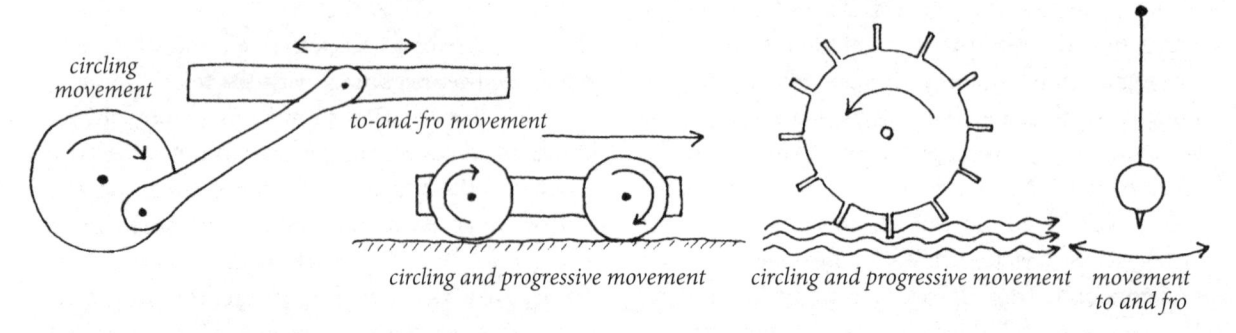

friction to the degree that allows a little amount of energy to move heavy loads. The same principle applies to the use of ball bearings. Spherical forms that overcome the force of gravity by their circling movements are also present in the planets.

Our feet, on the other hand, are directed

*circling
movement*

to-and-fro movement

circling and progressive movement

circling and progressive movement

*movement
to and fro*

8. REFLECTIONS ON MOVEABLE TOYS (CLASS 7)

Apparently unaffected by gravity, they selflessly submerge their bony structure in the unconscious regions. The rhythmical to-and-fro movements are characteristic of arms and hands. We may perhaps now understand why our legs serve us in our forward movements, taking turns. The one supplements the other. A counter movement would inhibit progress.

A great deal of our work depends on the rhythmical movements of our arms. We can therefore speak of three fundamental tendencies:

1. Head: spherical movements, physical basis of thinking.
2. Arms and hands: rhythmical movements, physical basis of feeling.
3. Legs and feet: progressive movements, physical basis of willing.

H. von Baravalle writes about mechanical movements, outside the human being, in the area of the purely physical.

A machine, quite independently of our knowledge of its uses or technological details, becomes an object of our thinking, of our observation.

We begin by ascertaining which of its parts are moving and which remain static, as supports. We then observe the different types of movements. We shall differentiate them in three large groups. The most frequent of them are turning movements, carried out by wheels, cogs, gears etc. Then there are the rhythmical, ever repetitive movements as, for example, by a knife that first raises, then lowers itself in order to cut something, or the various movements of grabbers and excavators depositing or carrying loads. The third type of movement is progressive: these are carried out by a part of the process, enter the machine, run their course and leave it again.[8]

Thus we discover the various movements of the human organisation also in the machine, separated from and independent of the human being. Baravalle connects them with natural phenomena. We find the turning movements again in the movements of the stars, the rhythmical movements in all the life processes in humans and animals, but also, very much slowed down, in plants. Baravalle sees the progressive movements realised most dramatically in the distinctive movements of wind and water.

Let's take a look at one of the oldest moveable toys made in the first Waldorf School, in Stuttgart, the almost legendary 'Waldorf Duck'. It is moved forward by pulling, transforming the turning movement of the wheels into a rhythmical one: the to-and-fro movement of head and beak. It thus contains all three systems of movement. It connects the student who invented it with the basic mechanical systems of movements in our world. Did they work with enthusiasm? We very much hope so, because they would then have united their growing soul-forces intensively and intimately with the mechanism of their work and, at the same time, taken hold of the mechanism within their own skeleton – without vanity and attention seeking that would have impeded clear thinking and the execution of the functioning of movements and the correct shape of the duck.

We are tempted to say: the making of moveable toys at the beginning of puberty facilitates children's descent to earth and helps them to overcome the problems that arise.

PART TWO: CRAFTS IN THE MIDDLE SCHOOL

The handling of mechanics demands – soberingly and inexorably, but also, due to the material used (wood), warmly and invitingly – the objective, rational immersion into its laws. It liberates children through clear thinking and exact doing from their excessive life of feelings that may now harmlessly participate and express itself in the humorous shape and movements of the toys.

The 'Waldorf Duck'

9

Investigating the nature of wood (Classes 6–8)
Klaus Charisius

A walk through a wood can only be fully appreciated at the end. Initially the track is safe and well marked – then suddenly it stops. Puzzled, perhaps annoyed, my first reaction is to turn and go back. But the gently swaying leaves of the trees are too persuasive and inviting. I continue, without a path, and am amply rewarded by one adventure after another in this magical world of trees.

Happy the teacher who is familiar with this life in a forest and who has the opportunity to discover its wonders with children in Class 6, which serves as preparation for their first woodwork lesson. The teacher is indebted to the trees that have been silent friends all these years. They will now become the children's friends too, who will experience them as the primal mothers of all life, as symbols for everything that grows and strives upwards. The trees give us their bodies, their bones, so that we can shape them and build with them. Twelve-year-old children love this material and work with it with enthusiasm and eagerness.

Introduction to woodwork

The first woodwork lesson should be carefully prepared and conducted. A piece of wood has been selected beforehand for its suitability for splitting. Working with it will allow children to get to know its properties. It could be the trunk of a plum tree, with its plain, dry grey bark: children look at its crooked shape, full of branches, lying on the ground. How could they possibly carve a wooden spoon or a mallet from this? They turn it carefully from side to side until they find the best position for splitting it. They try its weight, watch their teacher place the wedge in the right place and see it split lengthwise from end to end. Should something go wrong and the split be uneven, well, children will understand and forgive.

I find it good to line children up along each side of the log. They take turns in hitting the wedge (in which the girls are frequently more skilled). Standing astride the log they do the best they can. Care must be taken to keep the area before and behind the children clear. When every child has had their turn, the time has come to discuss the task ahead and the purpose of splitting the wood.

Too much talking should, however, be discouraged. Children are always raring to do things. One after the other raises the axe and drives in the wedge, some boldly, some timidly. The wedge is biting deep into the wood – what a clear sound when it is hit! At last, the log starts to crack;

the crack grows wider, runs along the entire length, not unlike a lizard running along a furrow. The wedge has sunk into the log. What now? A second wedge is inserted further down the log, widening the crack, and the first wedge drops out. The procedure is repeated. Just before the log falls apart it is good to stop and listen to the wood's groaning and complaining. And then the surprise when a child (perhaps one of the weaker ones) gives the wedge its final blow. The two sides fall apart, still connected by a few fibres that tauten like the strings of a violin. The children, with hardly any exception, give vent to their amazement at seeing the dark red, luminous colour of the wood that had been enclosed by the grey-green bark.

We bend down to inhale the fresh scent. Children are allowed to taste, even eat one of the fibres – except in the case of laburnum or yew. A happy group of chewing or tasting children surround the teacher. They are now ready to admire the clear, strong flow of wood fibres and to touch them with their hands. The branches with their vortex-like, wavy veining are especially beautiful. And if an especially large branch at the end of the trunk is exposed, the amazement is complete. Nobody before us has seen it! In a triumphant mood children now carry or cart their pieces of wood to the workshop and fasten them between the hooks of the planing benches. It is now the turn of the big saw that must be handled by two people. This has to be learnt: each wrong move either bends or jams the blade. Gradually the movements improve, the saw glides rhythmically along and the sawdust drops to the floor. The other children watch intently for the end piece to drop, some of them eager to catch it – this is a good time to get to know their temperaments.

The deep and lasting impressions of the first woodwork lesson often surface when our alumni revisit the workshop. They tell of experiences the teacher would not have dared to plan for. Some recall a monstrously large birch log that used up all the available wedges to no avail. At last, with combined effort, the children forced the log apart, landing on the floor in the process. When they inspected the inner surfaces they saw, so they said, a tiny tree complete with short branches. They were happy to think of the big tree having grown from such a small beginning. The little tree inside the big one was put on a table in their classroom and left there for quite a long time.

Such events are high points of the craft lessons, gifts from the nature beings to children. The teachers also participate in this. Lasting enthusiasm can here be engendered if one meets this age in the right way.

Working with wood

The first adventures on the path to working with wood are thus dramatic ones. Slowly they become gentler and steadier, suitable for the more delicate tools. But every new task follows the same pattern, from the forceful splitting of the log to the final, careful polish. Each temperament finds its appropriate, favourite activity and plenty of opportunities for effort in practical exercises.

Why is wood used exclusively as material during the Middle School? Why not clay, stone, metal, cardboard or even paper? All of these are substances that demand less effort and are, in part, even easier to shape. What are the special effects of wood on children's will? What are the feelings evoked, the consciousness developed from it?

In every working process we can see a basic reciprocal effect: I give the material I work with shape, but I must obey the inherent laws.

9. INVESTIGATING THE NATURE OF WOOD (CLASSES 6–8)

The material thus has its effect on me and the philosopher-craftsman may agree with Novalis when he says: 'To arrange things according to one's wishes or to adapt to them is one and the same.'

When children are working with wood, the life-filled growing element (the children) meets the life-filled element that has grown (wood). Such a meeting does not allow for boredom; it is full of adventure and contains many possibilities for self-education.

During the process, the 'things' by which children educate themselves assume life, be it the wood itself or the tools they use. Here are a few examples that might illustrate this: the task is to make a wooden spoon or a flour scoop. Children and teacher consider the required strength of the object, as well as its user's needs. This gives children a clear picture of the outer form and the necessary degree of hardness of the wood. If then children are shown two roughly shaped spoons made from a plum tree and a mahogany or pear tree in order to examine their differences, they recognise with amazement the difference between short and long fibred wood despite their having the same degree of hardness.

Experimenting with splitting the different woods also reveals their important differences in quality. It will become obvious that a thin handle can only be made from wood with symmetrical, even fibres that remain in place when split or chiselled.

Branches may either be a disturbing or form-directing element. We must take them into account and perceive their possibilities if something beautiful and useful is to be made. The rays of the markings are especially important. They radiate from the centre of the log to the bark and indicate where the piece of wood can be split most easily, because these rays are not unlike tiny channels into which the sap can flow from the periphery.

Cross section of a trunk with irregular radial markings

There is no firm connection between the two walls of the channels. This allows the wood to split cleanly where the water had evaporated or when it is forcibly split with a wedge. Such markings are especially prominent in oaks, but also in some of the beeches and alder trees. When split along the rays of the markings, the walls of the channels become visible. They are approximately 30% harder than the outer areas of the annual rings. They also follow a mysterious law in their interplay with the annual rings: crossing them at right angles. Since the heart of the wood is only found exactly in the centre of the cross section, there are only a few marking rays that are absolutely straight: most of them are curved, and in some woods even quite haphazardly so. When at all possible, the woodsmen insert the wedge into the straight rays and split the log quite easily.

The places below the bark where straight rays may be expected will depend on the spot where the tree has grown and on its immediate surroundings (direction of the light, the slope, and weatherside). Once the cut is cleaned the rays can be discovered emanating from the centre (the position of the 'heart'). Children should be told short stories and shown such properties and qualities of wood through demonstrations. They should be told how people work with them.

They are especially receptive to stories about Stradivarius, the famous violin maker. His contemporaries admired his ability to split wood. He was known as the Wood-splitting Master. In examining his instruments the secret of the extremely thin vibrating parts was discovered. In all the curved parts bearing the greatest strain the markings ran parallel to the curve. And since the area of the marking rays is much harder than the rest of the wood, its thickness could be reduced. In splitting off the sounding board he had to consider the curved direction of the marking rays. It is interesting to know that the best violin bows (used by master performers) are made from thin pernambuco stems, split in such a way that the two sides of the tiny heads are enclosed by two marking rays.

During the years the splitting of wood will be accepted as the right method, and as appropriate to the material. Children soon take to it – it is quick and efficient. They learn to accurately identify with the material, as courage and presence of mind are essential when they hit the wedge and drive the log apart.

Splitting wood is also a matter of consciousness. We do it in order to get the material for the making of practical objects that serve people's needs: spoons, shafts, tubs, backs of chairs, spokes, hammer and axe handles. Long, thin, feathery-light – the split wood serves human beings.

Class 7

Working with wood is especially beneficial to children during puberty. Its resistance challenges the will, but it also shows the result of meaningful work in the beauty of form – the radiant colours and life-filled structures. This is especially the case in Class 7 when children are working a long time on producing inner spaces (bowls). On concave forms, the friendly, beautiful piece of wood shows itself to be a blessing. Even the roughest of children derives pleasure from seeing the elegantly curved shavings they cut from the wood; they repeat this immediately with another cut before feeling the result with their fingertips: 'Is it deep enough? Or must it be made hollower still? In which direction should I make the next cut, so that the shape is just right and the surface smooth?' At best, children enter the process of self education, and unconsciously experience the phases of their own development in their work. Just as in a bowl, layer upon layer must be cut off in order to get the right shape, so must children create their inner path by chipping away and freeing the inner form. The pieces that are removed can be beautiful in themselves or, metaphorically speaking, turn into valued habits.

When children, in carving or planing, produce well-formed shavings we may be sure that they have fully connected themselves with the activity. The teacher can leave them to it, but should nevertheless praise their work.

The noise coming from an adjacent bench tells a different story: uneven, harsh hammer blows, cracking and splintering, angry exclamations. A critical situation that calls for intervention before it is too late. The teacher either takes over by repairing the mishap, or points to a successful part of the work and allows children to discover

9. INVESTIGATING THE NATURE OF WOOD (CLASSES 6–8)

their mistake themselves. Children may have to be reminded of the bowl's usefulness before continuing with their work. The teacher must make every effort to avoid a possible breakdown. Children may well experience a hole in the bottom of the bowl as a catastrophe: they grow quite pale as they stare at it, as though they had cut into themselves. Even when they put on a brave face and shrug it off, this does not hide their real feelings. The teacher must here use all their skills in order to rescue whatever may still be rectified. Getting angry or critical would be as destructive as it would be for a doctor to blame their patient during the mending of a broken leg or the stitching up of a wound.

The children have fully identified with their work, have aligned themselves to the properties of the wood and, on the other hand, left their mark on it. They are fully immersed in it and experience themselves through the work. This can go so far that, when asked whose bowl it is, they do not answer: 'It is mine,' but, 'It's me!'

Class 8

Children in Class 8 have an especially strong connection to wood when they decide to make musical instruments. Take the case of Knut who arrived after the holidays with two curved, 4 m (13 ft) long fir trunks. His father had to enlarge the roof rack on the car to get them home. Knut gets to work on them with a will: sawing, planing, carving them into an alpenhorn. Getting the right outer shape from the natural growth of the trunk was difficult enough. In the process he learnt to handle the largest of our planing benches, an especially long plane of 60 cm (2 ft), used for large objects. He smoothed away all the roughness caused by the branches, split the trunk neatly in two halves and hollowed them out carefully. The resulting channels are not unlike two riverbeds, growing wider towards the outlet. The air is supposed to flow uninterruptedly, to vibrate rhythmically through the whole length in order to produce the required sounds.

Knut removed all the obstacles, kept measuring the thickness of the wood and patiently persevered in his work with his partner – the wood itself. And when, at last, the two parts are fitted together the great moment has arrived for trying it out. A quiet hour should be chosen for this, with only a few people present. The hopes, joys and fears of the past few weeks are reflected in the face of the 'creator'. If the teacher reads a few runes from the *Kalevala*, how Väinämoinen made his kantele from the birch tree, a circle is closed in the child's life, in which he himself took part. He has gained in self-confidence, in sureness and joy in creating, ready for more work. His relation to the working material has become one of love for it. During the work with wood, the initial 'maker' became a 'formative artist'.

When making the wooden soundboard of a musical instrument, children must pay even greater attention and care to the material. Even in the relatively simple flat zither, the space has to be formed into the wood, space that can receive and deliver sounds. In guitars and, especially, in violins and cellos, every fibre vibrates along with the sounds. The bowl here becomes a body, alive with numerous interacting processes and conditions. The children, intent on making such an instrument for their year's project, must immerse themselves deeply into the properties of the wood and keep on practising the use of tools and measures. Surprisingly, the thirteen to fifteen-year-old children seem to have an innate gift, an aptitude for this. It is as though they are able to immediately translate the many life processes that take them to earth maturity, into formative, space-creating structures. They are developing an almost ingenious dexterity in their fingers, acquiring the most delicate flair for dealing with the feathery light and fragile material that has become almost de-materialised in order to make the inaudible audible.

The other students, watching the efforts of their classmates, deeply participate in the successes and failures. A loving empathy for their work awakens in them. This quality can be extended to a loving understanding of, and interest in, both their own work and that of their contemporaries. Rudolf Steiner formulates this as follows:

> *We must take the young man or woman to the point where he or she can develop in clear thoughtfulness beyond puberty, following their own path: then the love for what he or she is doing will develop. This love must develop freely on the basis of everything else: love for work, for what one oneself does. At the moment when the understanding for someone else's activities awakens, the conscious attitude to the love of work, of doing, must develop as complement. Then the child's play is correctly transformed into an understanding of work. This is what we must strive for the sake of our social life.*[1]

If, among other things, we can prepare children in the Middle School during the craft lessons for their inner readiness to develop their love of work, we have achieved a great deal.

Whatever kind of wood we give them to work with, it will prove to be a living and patient partner, opponent, enthuser and an essential co-educator. A material with which children feel connected, by which they learn to know themselves, a material they respect and might even love.

The Upper School

During the Upper School years, work with wood continues, together with other natural and man-made materials. In the joinery block it determines the work processes, helping the students to allow their thinking to be influenced by their hands. In artistic work the wood will respond to the students' ideas of form and feelings. Wood allows itself to be shaped, and in turn affects the shaper, so that, in this co-operation of all the energies a splendid result can come about.

Choosing the right wood

As class teachers we are responsible to find the suitable wood for each child entrusted to us, as well as the kind of work corresponding to his or her development. To do this, we must not only know the static properties, such as long and short fibres, homogeneity and toughness, but also colour, surface quality and even scent. An especially difficult and important aspect is the grasping of forms implicit in each type of wood, in order not to demand the impossible, i.e. to work against the wood's characteristic properties.

Birch

What this means may easily be observed when carving a flat, rectangular bowl from birch wood, with its sharply edged, exact rim; or working at an oval, gently curved bowl with a rim that makes in its curving and rounding only visible – or, rather, tangible – where the hollow passes into the curvature. Comparing the forms, we immediately experience the fact that the delicately veined, bright shine of birch is not suitable for the rectangular shape.

Fruit trees

Sensitive sculptors connect fruit trees to the four temperaments:

The pear tree

This tree is phlegmatic, round, has smooth leaves and fat, short-stemmed clumps of blossoms with heavy fruit pulling downwards, which tends to become doughy and runny. The wood itself is honey-coloured with short fibres. Almost boring with its lack of structure, it is especially suited to woodcuts. This wood was used in the making of the letter types during the early days of printing. Round, placid, circular or oval shapes bring out the best in the pear tree.

The cherry tree

The blossoms and fruit of cherry trees have longish stems, and the leaves are serrated and mobile. The wood has long fibres, and its cross section reveals many shiny points; it is permeated by olive-green to bright yellow-orange colour structures. The sanguine temperament comes to mind – light, living, ever changing. Its wood is most effective when given strained planes, or when curious/cheekily rounded corners are carved out and unexpected dents are elegantly incorporated. Cherry wood lends itself to the innumerable hollow forms of a carved surface with their lively light reflexes.

The apple tree

Concentration characterises the apple tree. Its rose-coloured, delicately tinged blossoms open quickly, not unlike an explosion. Its plump fruit seems almost about to burst. The wood itself is ingrown, hard and resists every attempt to crack it. It dislikes round, pleasing forms and demands clear and strong structure. But its effect is noble, with its golden-yellow, reddish and white colouring.

The plum tree

The most insignificant among the fruit trees must surely be the plum. It frequently grows to the height of a bush, remaining small, thin and lean even as a tree. Its green-white blossoms hardly extend through the leaves and for a considerable time, its longish fruit hang almost invisibly on their often thorny branches behind the leaves. But there is sweetness gathering behind the shimmering blue skin. The reddish brown wood shines strongly, framed by the white-yellow sapwood. However, care must be taken: there are frequently whitish-rotten spots in the centre. Not unlike the melancholic, it can rot deeply into itself, but allowing enough healthy wood to be found for the making of elegantly curved sets of salad servers, as thin as a leaf. And yet, the plum tree persists unchallenged as the favourite wood for many children who love its beautiful colours, its reliable toughness (due to the long fibres), and the shine of its carved and polished surface. They enjoy making longish receptacles for their pens and pencils, letter openers, different types of spoons and tool-handles from it. They treat it almost like precious stones when they make jewellery boxes and candle holders, polishing them lovingly and patiently to a fine finish.

Whatever the wood, it is necessary to know its individual inclinations to form, and to investigate the branches and their neighbouring structures. This makes the gradual densification and hardening processes from the liquid, flowing elements in the wood visible. Characteristic of the different trees is the way their substances have flown, how they passed obstacles (branches); this can be taken into account when forming and shaping an object.

But it is the trees themselves that can best teach us about their formative laws. The shape of their crowns, the angles of the branches to the trunk, the branch forms; in fact, the overall shape of the tree can become a picture for us to examine, according to which we shape its wood. We may also watch the form changes of bud to fruit during the years. Another pointer could be the way a tree looks in sun and moonlight, how it defends itself against a thunderstorm or, in winter, bears the weight of the snow.

The structural elements naturally also influence the shape of the objects. All woods whose pores have grown haphazardly, such as the lime, birch, maple, alder, nut, beech and fruit trees, are especially suited to curved, rounded and hollowed out forms that please the eye because of the shape's correspondence to the nature of the material. Woods with concentrically grown pores (ash, robinia, oak, elm) really demand taut, stretched, tightened forms.

Robinia: pores grown concentrically

Maple: pores grown haphazardly

Summer oak

Piece of wood from a serrated oak

Oak

The oak occupies a special position. Its radial markings are so strong that it frequently transforms its annual rings into circular segment arches – reminiscent of blossom leaves – that become visible in a cross section. This indicates tremendous forces working from the centre to the periphery. We can discover the same laws active in the in-and-out curving forms of the leaves, albeit in a softer, gentler interflowing. Even the shape of the branches – gnarled, sharp-edged curves – shows the alternation of retarding and forward urging forces in their growth that ultimately structure the crown of the tree with the same dynamics. It is in this interplay of damming up and urging ahead that the oak realises its shape. Its visible sign for this is the taproot that anchors itself vertically into the soil. In the circular pores the liquid-loosening nature of the early stages can be seen, as well as the solidifying, hard wood later on. The tree appears to be constantly placed within the struggle of opposing forces. This is the reason why the oak used to be seen as a symbol of the fighting spirit: whenever opposites clash, Mars reigns. The rhythmical movements of Mars opposite the sun also progress in retarding and urging ahead movements. This can be seen not only in old pictures, but also in the planetary seals of Rudolf Steiner that show a metamorphosis of peripheral and centric forces, affecting each other. Rudolf Steiner refers to them as 'planetary developmental stages'. The centre seal (Mars seal) shows both forces at the stage of greatest tension through which it can develop its true, independent form in opposition to the other seals. What comes to expression in the drawing can be discovered in the characteristic growth forms of the oak. The oak is thus an example for the way the craft teacher may, through the observation of the shape of a tree, tentatively find forces active in it.

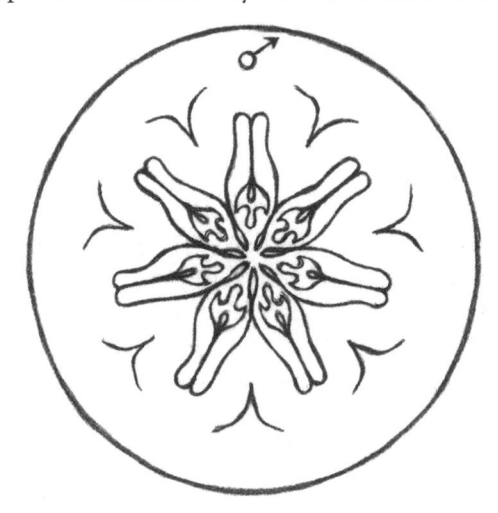

Mars: planetary seal by Rudolf Steiner

The sequence of metamorphoses in the seals designed by Rudolf Steiner can be of invaluable help.

During our investigation of roots we shall find that nearly all the available botanical literature limits itself to descriptions of the upper organs and more or less ignores the finer tangle of roots deeper down. However, much can be learnt from the way a tree interacts with water and soil. An important formative pole of the tree can there be found: the pole of movement can be experienced in the gestures of leaves and blossoms.

Rudolf Steiner advised the makers of musical instruments to investigate the way trees interact with the watery element. This would help them to select the suitable wood for the various instruments. His indications were taken up during his lifetime and string instruments made from unusual wood were built.

Franz Thomastik made his instruments for the 'Planetary Quartet' from maple, cherry, birch and ash. This changed the quality of the sounds produced (together with a new and different construction of the bridge); it is larger and warmer. It is instructive for the students to experience new ways of deriving tonal qualities from different kinds of wood.

Maple and pine

Since nearly all musical instruments used to be made from wood, it may be justified to take a good look at the 'classical' wood of our string instruments – maple and pine. The first violin for the 'Planetary Quartet' was wholly fashioned from maple. Its wood produces a bright, fresh sound; its colour is radiating, clear, and white. Of middle-hard and elastic quality it especially allows the overtones to be heard and the sounds to spread out more widely in the air around them.

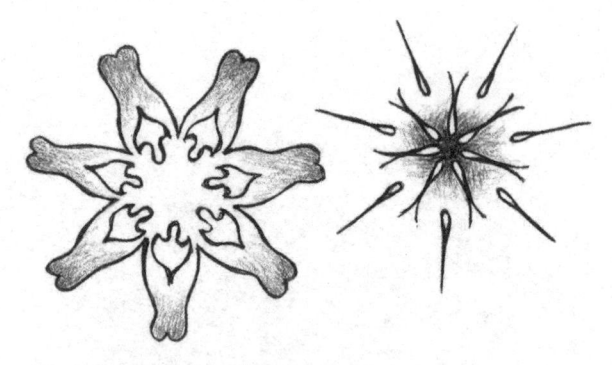

Structure of maple and pine

The bodies of traditional violins, violas and cellos are made from maple, the soundboard from pine. Pine has different growth processes from maple. There is no such sweet sap beneath its bark; it is almost dry. Comparing its needle-like leaf organs with a wide, spread out maple leaf, we can feel the whole economy, almost parsimony of this tree. And yet the pine is fully immersed in the course of the seasons. Its soft, brightly grown early wood tells of the dampness of spring when much of the wood grew with its large, spongy cell structures, permeated by important hollow channels where sap once flowed and, later, much air kept circulating. On the other hand, the dark wood grown during summer and autumn envelops the soft layers with a thin, exceptionally hard and dense ring of cells that not only supports, but is able to vibrate powerfully, almost like a spring. This makes the wood very light, yet strong and elastic. When its thickness is evenly reduced to 2–2½ mm (1/16 in), its effect on the instrument is that of a very sensitive membrane, especially capable of transmitting the various sound colours.

Pine has such a clear, unequivocal structure that it has a strong ordering, concentrating effect on the pupils working with it, not only when they are making musical instruments, but also in the many projects in carpentry and joinery where this wood is used.

Although we must not expect children to produce works of art as such, we as teachers and educators must at least have an idea of the suitability of this material for certain, definite articles and their correct shape.

In looking at the forms and structures the wood has to endure during the natural course of events, we shall quickly see the many hollow forms exposed through rotting, decaying, burning or splitting. The electronic microscope reveals below the smooth, shining surface, a catacomb-like maze of hollow channels, holes and cavities. The mysterious warm darkness in the hollow, inner spaces attracts the heart of the onlooker. Hence the deep effect of the surviving old wood sculptures with their concave, grooving and hollow forms. In Tilman Riemenschneider's magnificent late-Gothic altar carvings, each figure and filigree leaf is composed and embedded into its deep, dark surrounding.

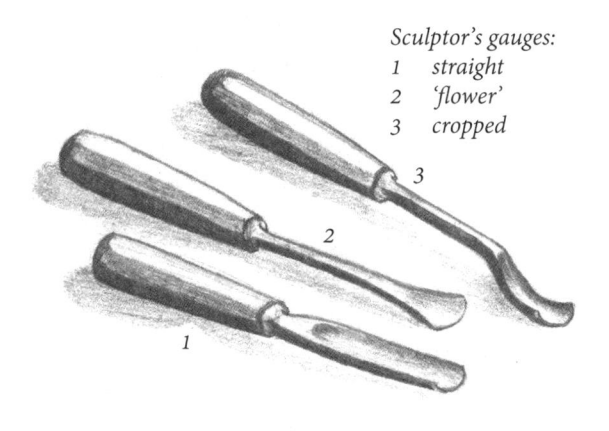

Sculptor's gauges:
1   straight
2   'flower'
3   cropped

Choosing the right tools

The tools of the woodcarver and sculptor conform to this tendency of form. They hollow out, drill, notch and split. The strongly arched shape of the gauge is therefore always produced from many hollow layers during the carving process, the flowing element formed from what is inhibiting, consumptive.

Because of this, the chisel is the wood sculptor's most used tool. It is also mainly employed in our schools. In working with chisel and mallet, the wood is, as it were, slowly consumed. If guided by rough hands, the consuming is intensified to destroying, the necessary reduction of the wood becomes ruinous exploitation of the material. It is only the sensitive, controlled work that leads to form: transforming rough strength into soul-permeated forces, a pre-condition for success.

Riemenschneider's sculptures demonstrate how the wood, through hollowing out, is forced back to an extreme in order to bring out the forms in edges, curves, archings and grooves from the darkness of the wood. Every cut, every detail was carefully, lovingly done, the entire work breathes the artist's submission and devotion to the greatness of the universe, to the divine, spiritual world. Rudolf Steiner, speaking about the wooden Goetheanum building, emphasised that the human being

> ... *must, out of real devotion to the greatness of the universe form, what allows to be formed, when one hollows out such forms in the soft wood, that can live in the concavity. It is only possible to carve concave forms into the wood if one does so out of love for the universe...*[2]

We can see that the work with the chisel demands in an intensified way the quality already earlier referred to as 'love of doing'.

What we can learn from wood

We are indebted to Rudolf Steiner for undoubtedly the most significant wooden art work of our time: the first Goetheanum.³ And although its large rooms with their formed wood areas can only be studied in reproductions and models, one can spend all one's life learning from them. The only completed sculpture by Rudolf Steiner, the 9 m (29 ft) high elm sculpture, survived the fire; it can now be seen in the second Goetheanum building. When we are able to perceive the polarities of the natural retarding and forward urging energies in the oak, so now, in this wooden sculpture, we may now see these polarities artistically structured in a quite different way.

In its centre is the 'human being', overcoming, through inner strength, the expanding forms to the top and the contracting forms below. It steps forward freely between the dissolving and hardening figures, retaining the living centre in itself.

We can discover something of this equalising strength in the elm. Its leaves, for example, are growing in an obviously irregular way; the side facing the branch spreading downwards, the other side, meagrely established, striving upwards. The branch itself, as it meanders along between the leaves, harmonises and gives life to the whole. In the oak two polar opposite forces are at work. In the elm a third – the mediating force – is added. Its wood is as hard and durable as that of the oak, but its annual rings show a free rhythm and, despite its hardness, its surface has a delicately shining appearance – the colours are richer, ranging from a dark, warm brown to the brightest of gold. The forces of light penetrate right into the wood, but the earth forces also are borne upwards and make themselves unpleasantly known by blunting the gauge as it attempts to cut through the mineral substances embedded in the wood.

Branch of a field elm

In this connection we may be justified in inserting a poem by Albert Steffen, as one of the many and various lovingly written poetic expressions regarding trees and wood:

Come, let us love the trees,
The trees, so good and true,
In their green shoots and leaves
God's lifeblood floweth through.

Lasst uns die Bäume lieben,
die Bäume sind uns gut,
in ihren grünen Trieben
strömt Gottes Lebensblut.

Nigh death was the wood once hardened,
When Christ upon it hung;

9. INVESTIGATING THE NATURE OF WOOD (CLASSES 6–8)

That we thereby be nourished,
Eternal blossoming has begun.

Einst wollt das Holz verhärten,
da hing sich Christ daran,
dass wir uns neu ernährten
ein ewiges Blühn began.

Such thoughts and poems cannot be directly used in the lessons. They can, however, live in the teacher and create the appropriate inner mood that allows them to do the right thing at the right time. Children will always be receptive for the descriptions of the mysterious ways a tree builds up its substances from the invisible, how it lives in unison with light, air, water and earth, building its body or, in other words, lets everything flow together. Children, although unconsciously, feel their own growth and life processes, and they take to the wood as something that is living and related to them. They happily pass through a phase in their development together with this most living of all working materials, and their craft teachers have the pleasant responsibility of correctly preparing and accompanying them on this path through the forest.

Student's work, Class 10

10

Artistic elements in the crafts
Michael Martin

Of all the parts of my car, I especially appreciate the bonnet. It takes a backseat in brochures, does not generate power and guzzle fuel – like the things hidden under it. Not of great interest itself, unobtrusively it places itself between the mudguards. Yes – it does protect against rain and it reduces the resistance to air; but then, the engine underneath is exposed to weather and, I am fairly certain, the matter of resistance to air (streamlining) is not all that important. And yet, if my bonnet weren't there, an essential part of the car would be missing! And here is the strange thing: its apparent uselessness makes it especially important, in that its purpose is to provide a part of the covering which, although it is no more than tin and varnish, encloses the whole of the car – in this respect, it's not unlike my skin. Think of all the things that would become visible without it! The whole jungle of engine parts, hoses, screws, plugs – incomprehensible for most drivers, yet details known to be vital for the functioning of the car. Though the things concealed underneath this skin are decisive for function, they aren't attractive to our eyes and ears, nor to our sense of touch, all of which long for harmony and beauty in life.

The engine takes its whirring sounds from another source than the musician their melodies. Why do we experience the slamming of a door differently from a song sung by a human being? The former belongs to the inorganic and lifeless world, the latter wells forth from soul-filled life. The engine, serving our needs and contributing to our modern standard of living, as does all technology, is the product of human intelligence – a useful helper in our daily lives, serving our needs. The sounds thus made also come from this lifeless, mechanical word – unavoidable noises, be they whirring, rattling, purring, roaring or booming. We must accept them as part of our payment for technology's invaluable help.

Beauty and function

Our 'hunger for beauty' has its roots in the soul and spirit and cannot be satisfied with screws, hoses and gears, however well designed their shapes may be. The architect Hans Poelzig (1869–1936) writes from this experience:

All merely technical considerations are a horror for the artist. And even when he knows that technology cannot be avoided, that it must be controlled, he nevertheless also knows and strongly feels that technology

10. ARTISTIC ELEMENTS IN THE CRAFTS

in our time has become far too powerful and that he is called upon to fight its domination. Technology and art remain sharp polarities.

It would certainly neither be necessary nor sensible to give beautiful forms to the wires, levers and all the other mechanical parts of a car.

I am quite happy and satisfied with the polished cover – as representative of my need for beauty – that hides and encloses the mechanism and serves a useful purpose besides. I, too, am enclosed within a skin that both separates me from and connects me with my surroundings, for through it I perceive very important impressions through the sense organism it incorporates, especially through touch and warmth.

In our houses and apartments, the pipes and wires also are hidden. Whenever one or the other is exposed we don't like it. Although technology, i.e. the utilitarian aspect of our life, is essentially helpful and necessary, it is often also ugly, noisy, dangerous and often hostile to life. Whilst acknowledging that it provides for our comforts, we have to admit that it also produces new worries and discomforts. Because of this it is kept hidden from sight. The containers enclosing it protect us from it, but they also protect the machinery within from harmful interference from outside. A line is drawn between us and the working parts of technology to keep it out of sight because it has been developed from the lifeless kingdom. And the attempt is made to bring beauty – in colour and form – into it, an effort that has met with considerable success. Purpose and beauty in technology are not identical. They meet best whenever the shape adapts to the elemental world, such as in the case of a sailing boat or glider. But here there is no need for an engine to be enclosed or protected!

There are, of course, many useful articles without such a mechanism, where these problems of inner and outer, of technology and beauty do not exist: age-old tools such as the axe, spoon and saw amongst others. They are not merely useful but, at the same time, beautiful. By giving them beauty of form, the craftsman raised them above the merely functional to a sphere of a higher perfection of which Michelangelo said:

There is nothing that makes the soul as pious and pure as the effort of creating, of producing something close to perfection: for God is perfection and he who strives towards it strives towards the divine. Art belongs to no country on earth, it comes from heaven.

This applies also to the artistically shaped articles discussed in this book. As soon as form becomes subservient to mere necessity, to mere purpose, beauty takes second place or is lost altogether. Because 'purpose' and 'expediency' do not come from heaven, they are subjected to the necessity of earth-bound, terrestrial laws.

As elsewhere, here, too, we can experience the tragedy of the primal polarities our world has to deal with at its present evolutionary stage. Their tensions produce intensifications and ideas for quite new creative possibilities for the human being.

Form and function in the workshop

Let's return to the workshop to see the consequences our reflections have for practical work.

How, for example, can purpose and beauty be combined in a wooden spoon? What are the forms that may be developed from such a combination?

PART TWO: CRAFTS IN THE MIDDLE SCHOOL

pot   wooden spoon   human being

Independent forms

according to purpose

more than necessary and according to purpose

'beautiful'

Stirring = rhythmical process

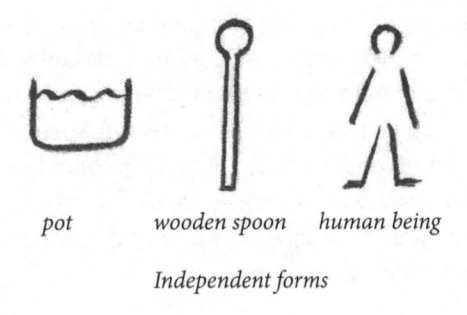

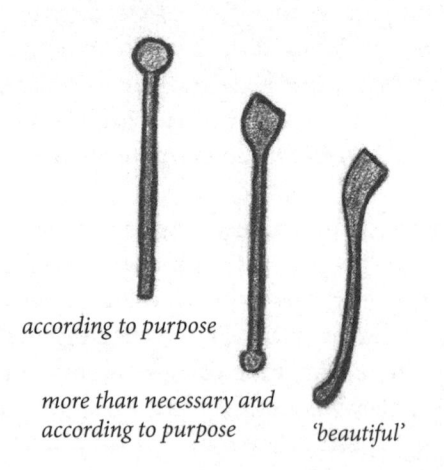

The flat bottom of a cooking pot corresponds to expediency: the nature of the electric element demands it for the sake of efficiency and economy. In the past, the open fire called for rounded shapes of pots that made it easier for the flames to engulf them. Our modern pots are not as beautiful, are not suited to the movements of currents of the heated liquids inside them. Everything has become abstract. The wooden stirring spoon, too, can be an abstraction, if its form is limited to merely the barest essentials: the straight handle, the curved end.

It looks like a concept translated into a visible form, doing its job. But it neither relates to the pot, nor to the person using it – as far as its shape is concerned. Because of this, its function is limited to the bare necessity of what it is meant to do, but it is as yet not realising its full purpose.

This will come about only when its form is adapted to the flat area of the pot's bottom, when we take into account the heat rising to the top. We shall then give the handle an inclined form; make its end, perhaps, a little thicker for a firmer grip.

We could go further and try to give the spoon something of the nature of stirring: the motion in the turning, the flowing element of the liquid. The shape would here once again have to change. During the stirring, hand, spoon and pot, previously independent of each other, are now combined and are fusing into each other. From the state of being spatially related, from lying side by side, we get a temporary process of togetherness. Seen accurately we shall see in the wooden spoon the lengthened hand, impervious to the heat rising from the pot.

When stirring liquid in a pot or bucket with our hand we might discover something we had not expected: a developing rhythmical process. Involuntarily, our hand wishes to open when the arm directs circling movements to the periphery. The opposite movement towards the centre results

10. ARTISTIC ELEMENTS IN THE CRAFTS

in the tendency to close the hand. During the turning, simultaneously, the wrist also participates in the in-out movements. We can make our experience stronger when, during the stirring, we keep our arm in a still position and our hand rigidly stretched out. We shall find this to be abstract, not in keeping with life – similar to the spoon made of a straight handle and curved end. From the alternating of the spreading and contracting, rhythm is born, rhythm that overcomes the merely spatial in the activity of stirring.

Over and above these reflections we enter the world of rhythmical processes that include our respiration, blood circulation, the alternation of waking and sleeping, and of the seasons. Rhythmical processes lie at the base of all living things. As the world we live in consists on the one hand of lifeless objects lying side by side in space so, in the living sphere, does form develop from form in an ever ongoing process of dying and becoming. In this living sphere the energies and forces can only be perceived in their results, in the changing forms. Energies and forces are invisible, but they are active in all rhythmical processes, either reducing or building up. They can be grasped in time, as everything else subject to change.[1]

Thus will an object made from natural material appear artistically shaped if its form assumes something of the rhythmical processes from which it derives: it is 'beautiful'. It widens, stretches, contracts, streams out, dams up at the end… as our trivial wooden spoon that started our discussion.

We may wish to choose the shape we want it to have:
1. The necessary shape; the absolute minimum of effort, in order to serve a specific purpose;
2. A shape in accordance with its purpose – this already implies a relation to the surroundings in which it belongs;
3. The artistic shape that embodies the processes involved, without ignoring the two other principles.

Each of these conditions leads to different, specific ways of working. What happens when we wish to make a cooking spoon corresponding only to the first category?

Here we can take a board with a suitable thickness, preferably maple or birch, free of knots. We make an accurate drawing, using a pair of compasses and a ruler, trace this on the board and, after fastening the board vertically into a vice, start sawing it out. We follow the lines, making sure they remain visible on the cut-out shape. We then rasp, file or sandpaper, smoothing out the unevenness made by the saw until the shape is identical with the drawing. This is followed by chiselling out a slight hollow at the wider end and by octagonally rasping the handle, which makes the rounding of it easier. The whole is then neatly polished, twice submersed in water and each time again smoothed. There it lies in front of us, handle and end perfect, indistinguishable from the other cooking spoons made in this way. The form was objectively determined from without and had been there in the drawing before the hand was able to begin its work.

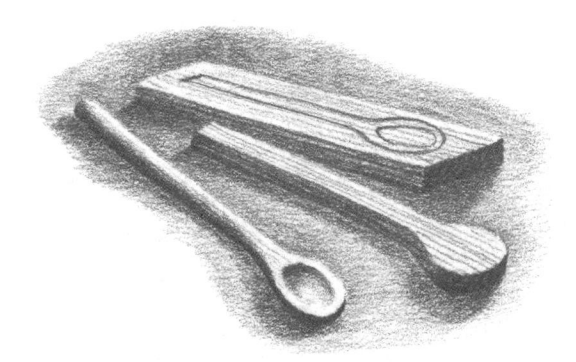

Cooking spoon made from a board

If we allow our children to work in this way they will learn to control tools and hands and to work in an exact way that cannot be faulted. They will be introduced to objective work processes consistent with the nature of pure craftsmanship. Every working sequence follows the other in a logical way; every deviation can spoil it. They can work in this way with enthusiasm – experiencing support and structure. And yet, the soul feels cheated: it is not allowed to participate in the process, the shape produced is foreign to it and remains outside its sphere.

If we wish to proceed with the third possibility we must take a quite different starting point. The differently shaped cooking pots invite us to try out the lengths of wood we split off the maple – to 'get the feel of them' as we stir. Every piece of wood is different, both in shape and size. Which of them is best suited to the pot – the slightly curved one or the one with the lightly wavy or the smooth fibres? We also examine the two ends to determine the one that is best suited to the spoon part.

Only then does the work begin. The handle is carved with the chisel, its thickness gradually reduced to its required size. Our hand's width and the thickness of the fingers indicate the shape of the spoon. The eye alone guides our activity; there is no diagram – the form of the spoon develops during the doing.

Projects in geometricised forms

There is a noticeable tension and excitement in the student as he or she sees the actual form taking shape. The teacher makes sure tools and vice are handled professionally. Impulsiveness is counter productive. Craftsmanship lends strength and support in the free handling of the material.

Finally, the spoon is carefully smoothed down. Every spoon made in this way will be different from all the others. Every one of them corresponds to its purpose, while still bearing the imprint of its creator. The flow contained in the act of stirring is reflected in the spoon's flow and form – characteristic features of the artistic.

Will-forces in arts and crafts

Rudolf Steiner clearly stipulated the correct conduct in craft lessons. He demanded an eye for exactitude from the teacher; children were to learn to work correctly and accurately. On the other hand, the lessons had to be permeated by the artistic element, borne by the 'artistic spirit' of the teacher.[2] Max Wolffhügel, whom Rudolf Steiner entrusted with the artistic craft lessons, wrote in an article:

Cooking spoons made from pieces of wood split from a log

10. ARTISTIC ELEMENTS IN THE CRAFTS

It was Rudolf Steiner's deeply felt wish that the teachers of the artistic craft lessons should not only be fully trained in their work, fully at home in all areas of woodwork, but should also be freely creative artists, able to combine their knowledge with pedagogical enthusiasm. I believe that it is only this constitution that makes it possible, by aiming at the laws in objectivity, to affect the children in a creative, stimulating way.[3]

The article also contains pointers for our woodwork lessons. 'It began with small, harmoniously geometricising forms, and continued with asymmetrical yet carefully balanced larger pieces.' We already mentioned the ever larger role of asymmetry during puberty and beyond: we shall refer to this in greater detail later on.

There is, however, no such reference in Rudolf Steiner's lectures on education; we assume it to have been made in a conversation. Wolffhügel's remarks led to the cultivation of a method after the re-opening of new schools post-Second World War, and was practised in the Middle School:

a method we characterised as 'expedient', i.e. directed to purpose. The work had to proceed from a drawing so that the 'geometricising forms' could be brought about in an exact and professional way.

And yet, Rudolf Steiner emphasised in his lectures that the practical work in the workshop ought to bear the stamp of freedom and independence, and that it should have artistic form. Children should – as we have stressed several times – act out of their will-forces. The teacher must not 'prescribe', but merely direct, guide and suggest in order that children's intentions can be realised. Children's will contains what it has brought with them. This leads us to the basic aims in our working methods, characterised by Rudolf Steiner as follows:

Because of the artistic handling of the lessons, the children have been inwardly gripped by what they were doing. It entered their will, not only their thoughts and heads. And we can, therefore, see, as they concentrate on their work, that this continues to live in their hands. The forms change according

The 'correct horse' in a book on anatomy

to the content in our lessons. It lives itself out in forms. We can see in the forms the children produce what they experienced in the previous main-lesson, because their lessons ought to enter and grasp the whole of the human being.[4]

A year later, this idea of synthesis of the polarities of thinking and willing in the human being as a totality, penetrating each other in the centre, culminates in the following words:

These two things can only be brought together if knowledge by itself passes into ability and if the ability to do is at the same time handled in a way that it is everywhere permeated by thinking, by the soul grasping it, by the spirit participating in and experiencing it.[5]

In order for the knowledge to pass 'by itself' into children's doing, they must be allowed to work freely and be able to let what is living in themselves stream into the activity of their limbs. If I guide them towards using their tools in the correct way, towards a fine attitude of craftsmanship, I give them assurance in the free shaping and forming of whatever they are making, an attitude arising from the appropriate task at their age.

We began by selecting an article that is used in daily life, in order to show the variety of artistic and technical conceptions of the same object. This will become even clearer during the making of a wooden toy animal in Class 7.

How should the teacher prepare for this? Should they go to the zoo, in order to study shape and movement? Should they draw sketches, make clay models or look at illustrations in a book?

Yes, they may do all of this. The romantic descriptions in Brehm's *Life of Animals* will also be a help. If the teacher is looking for what we referred to as 'the purely technical', mere craftsmanship, this could suffice to grasp the form to the extent that they can draw the side view of the animal on a thick board. This can then be cut out by following the lines of the drawing as exactly as possible. Chisel, rasp, file and emery paper will give it the required finish.

Animal images from Ice Age art

10. ARTISTIC ELEMENTS IN THE CRAFTS

Carved from half of a split log

But an artistic approach demands more. The attempt must again be made to transform the static form into a dynamic one; the spatial form must be translated into movement. I must try to slip into the way this specific animal moves, into the rhythms of its movements. Only then can I understand its shape. In practising dynamic drawings I was able to experience it in following the line of the spine, discovering the right curve – the animal with its characteristic movement suddenly stands before me. Body and legs are no more than 'appendages', they merely hang there. What is essential is the flow of the spine, how, starting from the head and ending at the tail, it stretches, dams up, contracts, curves, stretches again etc. Is it really so difficult to see from this linear form of the spine that the horse is, in fact, galloping? That the lion is stalking, the kangaroo hopping?

The animal's movement is engraved in its form. From this we may discover its movement. It begins already with the bones. We deepen this further by making the effort to identify with the animal's instinctive nature, for it is instinct that determines the animal's movements and informs them. We can observe the changes in the animal's posture as it instinctively listens, scents, trembles and, finally, spurts into movement. Or how calmness, undisturbed by urges and instinct, lives in the form, determining it. Here, too, we enter the rhythmical processes – as we did when shaping the cooking spoon – and in this way we shall be able to guide children, even though the form they give to the animals may, to begin with, be only modest expressions of their feelings.

These inner experiences of animal nature will induce us to approach our work differently from merely copying the outer, lifeless form. We must first shape the back, from head to tail. Half the side of a split log will be best for this. We put it horizontally on the bench and carve the back and neck of the animal. In order to get some guidance we could, of course, make a drawing of the intended shape of the back on the straight side of the wood; but this would not be of much use as it would disappear with the first shavings. What must be done is to work from the plastic form itself and not according to the bordering, limiting line. The result should not be a side view with its contours, but the arch of back and neck.

The one-sided arch of the wood makes for a gentle, lateral turn of the animal's form that can be further emphasised, so that the rigid axis – front/back – is overcome. Finally, the legs are carved and the finished shape sawn off the block of wood.

Are children really able to do this, to shape artistically? Only through the guidance or 'artistic spirit' of their teacher. Free, individual artistic work is only possible when, through earth maturity, the imagination has awakened and enters into the formative processes with its very own will. Before this happens, children are inwardly more pliant and not subject to the coercion of concepts. It is because of this that they can accept this mode of working. Their creative strength is still embedded in their bodies and their processes of movements. And this makes every formative expression of children *art*!

11

Colour in the craft room
Michael Martin

Rudolf Steiner suggested different colour sequences for the classroom walls in the three Waldorf Schools existing at that time – Stuttgart, Hamburg and London. There is only one known suggestion for the wall colours of craft rooms: 'Handwork: orange' (Stuttgart, 1922/23). Since this written statement has not been further qualified it has been left to us to investigate the colour quality of orange in order to discover the objective justification of Rudolf Steiner's suggestion and, proceeding from there, to choose the correct colour nuances for the different craft rooms.[1]

My own very strong colour experiences as a young man completely convinced me of the fact that the human being has as much need of colour as of food and drink. I spent several years as a prisoner of war in Russia. Every day followed the same monotonous schedule: the way to work, the stark, bleak buildings, the desert-like surroundings – with no hope for escape. Cool colours – grey, umber, green, blue, white – dominated, changing little in the atmospheric phenomena that were unable to produce the 'warm', 'sympathetic' colour tones.

After the night shift, I secretly picked the bright orange blossoms of the marigold from a small flowerbed between two of the buildings. I deeply inhaled their scent and colour, becoming conscious of the daily lack of colour nourishment.

I had a similar experience when I saw the fiery red bricks that were unloaded at one of the building sites. It was only later that I realised the life-affirming, radiating power of orange that gives strength and encouragement to a temporarily depressed person in a seemingly hopeless situation, strength and encouragement streaming from it and mediating them to the world around it, filling it with the joy of living.

The power of orange

Orange, like yellow, has a radiating quality, but differs from it in the substance of its radiation; it is heavier, more earthy, much warmer and denser. Orange is, therefore, not merely communicating: its side meaning or significance lies in its intimating, imparting, warming quality, expressing the need to participate. We must imagine warmth as a picture in which the spreading, radiating power of yellow meets the primal autonomous power of red, so that, as it were, the power of red can be carried away – on the wings of the airy yellow.

Because warmth always radiates to us, a warm colour seems to come closer to us.

The sense for the musical, but also for the crafts, is reflected in orange – this is how H. Frieling characterises the experience of orange. He sees in it a motivating force, the extroverted, the warmth of feeling. Such knowledge and experiences in colour psychology have long been made of practical use. Orange is not often found in nature. This is why we notice its lively freshness immediately. It is given its right place everywhere where one stage passes into another (traffic lights, direction indicators) when something moves, stirs and must be especially heeded (forked levers, shovel loaders, protective clothing of road workers).

Orange is the natural colour of fire, of the flame. Fire is not at all red, as its symbol (red = fire) leads us to believe. Moving orange-coloured bits of paper give a far more convincing impression of fire than red ones. It is only the glow of fire that is red – the flame here has, as it were, already become as one with the material it has burnt. We can see the path from the airy, the purely fiery to the earthy in the colour sequence as colour intensification. Connected to the intensification of red we have, at the same time, a higher densification.[2]

This description of the progression from the airy, via the fiery, to the earthy can help us experience the inclination of orange to what is active on earth. A radiating – but neither a glossy poster-like nor a dull-lazy orange – as basic mood in a room can stimulate and enliven children's energies in work.

Rudolf Steiner was able to go even more deeply into colour experiences and, from his knowledge, tell us how to practise them. He points to…

…a still more intensified togetherness with the outer world, a unity strong enough to include not only the outer impression of colour, sound and form, but also that which one can experience behind the sounds, behind the colours and behind the forms, what manifests in colours, sounds and form.[3]

Of this more or less meditative immersion into the nature of orange, he says that it had something…

…that wishes to provide us with an inner strength. As we enter the world and become as one with an orange-coloured surface, we move in such a way that, in every step we take we have the following experience: through this experience in orange, through this life in the forces of orange we shall engage ourselves into the world with such strength that we will become ever stronger… Through living in orange we gain the knowledge, or the longing for the knowledge, of the inner nature of the things around us.[4]

Anyone who has at some time shaped a piece of wood, of clay, or perhaps only spun some wool into yarn, and has done any of these things in full devotion to the work, can experience it as an inner urge to immerse themselves so strongly into the depth of a process, or of a material, that they connect with its nature. The experience a craftsman gains from such processes is the result of this 'longing for the knowledge of the inner nature of things'. This can then lead to mastery in any one of the crafts. Expressed in colour, the soul element behind it is orange.

From the above, we may understand how orange is ideal for kindling the basic mood of soul that should prevail in the life of the craft room.

Part Three

Crafts in the Upper School

12

Arts and crafts and the human being (Class 10)
Michael Martin

Intensive study of Rudolf Steiner's investigations of the developmental stages of the human being, and practical experience in teaching, will lead to an understanding of the quite new impulses arising during adolescence – impulses that must affect adolescents because of the strong development of their limbs. They can make use of their limbs in quite new ways, as helpers for carrying out will impulses. The limbs grow in length; the hands get bigger and become earth-bound, due to the bones gradually growing closer together and providing the basis for sturdy manual work. These processes urgently call for the involvement of the limbs in practical work.

Before this time, especially during the first seven years, children live predominantly in their sense organs. They are themselves a sense organ, a sense being. The eye, as an example, imitates the whole of the environment within itself, reflects it, copies it. Very young children receive their environment like the eye and copy whatever comes to them from without. The senses are as much organs of 'internalising' as the hands are of 'externalising'. The eye's retina and the palm of the hand have in their opposite character much in common. Both are organs turned and open to the outside. Both receive what comes to them. The eye, however, makes it still more inward, while the hand, true to its nature, transforms the human being and returns him or her, changed, to the outer world.

The spherical shape of the eye accurately corresponds to the function of receiving and internalising. The shape of the hand, in its many single parts, rays out the impulses it receives from within. The sphere characterises the enclosure of forces directed to the inside; rays characterise the directing of forces towards the world outside. We would never do any work if we had spherically shaped hands and arms! The hand becomes the mediator between our inner and outer world. It can only achieve this by becoming the organ which comes out of the deeds directed by an independent inner world. And this only awakens during puberty. The awakening of the new soul-forces within adolescents is thus directly related to the development of the hand. Young children are determined from without; adolescents are searching for the man or woman they wish to emulate: this person becomes the model they admire. A complete transformation has occurred.

The master craftsman, too, will be such a model: they are familiar with the properties of the materials, efficient in the handling of tools, and they know all the working stages that lead to the finished product. They can give clear directions; they know how to deal with physical matter. If the young man or woman obeys the rules and applies them to their work, they will imprint forms into their newly developed will-organism that will give support and structure to their activities. They are proving themselves, and this gives them a sense of confidence. The correctly directed blow with the hammer on the blacksmith's anvil, the successful use of the plane, or the right pressure in pottery connects adolescents with the material taken from the outer world.

Such activity affects young people formatively and, at the same time, gives the necessary support to their burgeoning will-forces, badly needed at this time when feelings are chaotic and directions vague and aimless.

Knowledge of the earth can be developed in the head; whereas experience is the domain of the limbs. What is only 'momentary' need not as yet be true and appearance can be deceptive. In other words, something is only real once its reality has been investigated more comprehensively – perhaps through touch. Those who wish to stand firmly on the earth must be active on it, must move and do; not remain static at this level of spectator or TV viewer, or be only like the head that needs distance and calm in order to perceive.

The third seven-year period, especially the last stages of puberty (Classes 9 and 10), is thus the time for activity, for work. It is not accidental that in past ages this used to be the time for the beginning of apprenticeship. The will, emancipating itself from the body, receives direction, firmness and measure through work in the crafts, so that it may develop in a healthy way and transform into inner mobility.

Class 10: an important turning point

Class 10 marks the end of puberty – the young man or woman has 'arrived'. The last signs of the verve, the vitality so noticeable in the Middle School and still in Class 9 have vanished. What we now see are the stirrings of new energies that have to be directed and used. This includes a different relationship between student and teacher. And, although many a student would prefer to continue the old, child-like connection with their teacher, it is right and healthy to begin this new phase by addressing the student in a more formal, adult way. In German speaking countries the intimate '*du*' is replaced by the formal '*Sie*'. It reflects the teacher's respect for the student, treating them as an equal. It also strengthens the student if the teacher can now develop a new relationship of trust between them.

Rudolf Steiner emphatically wished to draw attention to this important boundary between Classes 9 and 10. Before the opening of Class 10 (autumn 1921) he repeatedly spoke to the teachers about this 'important moment when we ought to find the right way to children's souls at a most definite and important age'. He drew attention to the fact that 'we were facing the very important task of adding Class 10 to the primary school.'[1]

'It is a matter of summarising all our pedagogy and didactics in an elementary feeling that allows you to experience in your souls the importance and impact of your task: to place human beings into the world.'

This task is now essential, because the subjective element of soul and spirit has now embedded itself in the physical/corporeal organism, and has become fused with it. Up to now their connection was different: not binding, looser. This change will be especially considered in our discussions on craft lessons. In Class 9 the echoes of paradisal childhood had to be done away with; the students in Class 10 are fully turning towards the elements of the earth.

Curriculum questions

All the aims of the Upper School curriculum are directed to encompassing within each lesson a 'knowledge of life!' (Lebenskunde). In the Lower School it was a matter of doing justice to the demands of the human being, 'we are to educate hygienically, healthily and to conduct our lessons with regard to body, soul and spirit'.[2] The task of the lesson content is to correspond to children's developmental processes.

This changes in the Upper School. The students are to grow into the situations life provides. They are to develop their energies in a way 'that [their] work may have meaning for the community and human life'.[3] Rudolf Steiner frequently referred to this subject, mentioning specific lessons, such as spinning, weaving, surveying, practical mechanics, the making of soap, paper and much more.

The lecture cycle in Ilkley (England) contains important general directions. Rudolf Steiner shows how children's play should be guided into artistic structuring, which is, after all, already present in play. This still free structuring and shaping should then continue into the crafts, through the making of simple tools and household articles that already demand a deeper commitment. He might have been thinking of cooking spoons, bowls and candleholders, made in the Stuttgart school at the time.

This utility-orientated work in wood was to find its further progression in the actual joinery and carpentry work. He called it 'practical structuring'.

These are clear indications. Other techniques in the crafts were not yet mentioned. Rudolf Steiner's conversations with Wolffhügel – whom he appointed as craft teacher – resulted in an outline of a curriculum that does not, however, mention a single craft block in the Upper School. But it does speak of 'the plastic shaping of clay, wood and stone', illustrated with numerous photographs. It was only in 1952 that Wolffhügel addressed himself to the 'plastic lesson blocks' in the upper classes, adding: 'According to his (Rudolf Steiner's) indications, joinery and woodcraft were introduced in Class 9 and continued as far as the making of small pieces of furniture.'[4]

Although Rudolf Steiner allowed much space for freedom, he was, on the other hand, a master of connecting specific lesson contents with the corresponding age of the students. He was very much aware, to take an example, of the importance of bookbinding (Class 12), 'especially if it is done at the right age, at the correct time that can be read in human nature itself.'

On another occasion he referred to the surveying block in Class 10:

Oh yes, it does make a difference for the entire life if one has done something at the age of fifteen or later, at nineteen or twenty. At nineteen or twenty it is impressed more from the outside. If done at the age of fifteen it fuses with the human spirit to the extent that it becomes personal property, not merely professional skill.[5]

Much depends, therefore, on our finding the correct correlation between a specific craft and the age when it is taught if we wish to point to a path leading through the Upper School, a path that meets these demands and challenges.

13

Form-giving elements and techniques (Classes 9–12)
Michael Martin

It is purpose and material, but also beauty, that determine form and shape of any craft product. No greater contrast can be imagined than that between the shape of a clay jug and a joined wooden box. Round and rectangular objects belong to different worlds; the curved and straight plane are primal polarities.

During the following reflections we shall concentrate on these phenomena of form in order to discover the consequences this might have for our questions about education. We shall include the activities of the hands, as well as the nature of the different materials in our deliberations. The resulting 'overview' will show that the several techniques employed in the crafts can, when studied in this way, appear to be concretely connected with the age of the students at which they are presented in the Upper School.

Our discussions of the basic principles will be followed by material from specialist teachers.

Preparatory stages

In wishing to find a starting point for our theme, we are taken back to the very first lesson in Class 1. Every child draws a straight and curved line on the blackboard; these are the primal elements and polarity we discover everywhere, e.g. in the basic shapes of head and limbs. In the house-building main-lesson in Class 3, the shaping of bricks and the baking of bread draw our attention to two streams in which children are living on their descent to the earth. The polarities of form here assume an almost palpable reality. Take the following composition by a girl at the end of her house-building block in Class 3, during which real clay bricks were made:

Dear Mr D.,
I really liked it. What I enjoyed most of all was the washing, and pushing of the clay into the moulds. I was really dirty afterwards, especially my hands; when I put them into the water they were really yucky. Johann and I made two bricks, not much, but then they were quite beautiful, and that's worth something. I hope they'll dry well, so that they can be used.

We can see from this how a nine-year-old child is still quite naturally living within the stream of beauty in which she feels itself fully enclosed. At the same time, she is concerned about the result of her work, i.e. whether its purpose is met.

13. FORM-GIVING ELEMENTS AND TECHNIQUES (CLASSES 9–12)

Beauty and purpose meet in children's activity. Children's play in the sandbox, 'baking mud pies', or whatever, with its ever changing forms, now transforms into purposeful work where shape and form is also required – it is a first and significant step into the working world of the right angle.

It is an exciting experience to press the formless, soft clay into the rectangular mould. The damp, cold and heavy clay is put as though into a coffin by which it can become useful. And yet children feel happy when the clay sticks to their hands and firmly connects with their whole being.

When baking bread, the wheat, ripened in the warmth and light of the sun, must be ground and changed during the baking process in order to serve as nourishment. It is a descent from cosmic heights, a transformation into useable substance, into the service of earth life. But think of the way children experience the heavenly elements of light, air and warmth! In breadmaking it is the round, spirally constructed straw basket into which the dough is put. The clay, on the other hand, has long been removed from these life processes; its appropriate form is rectangular if we wish to build a house from it. But, in spite of the fact that they assume quite opposite forms, both bread and bricks come about through related work processes: their substances must be kneaded in a moist condition. The children's hands feel the soft mass until the correct elasticity is reached. Both – the clay only after a long time of drying out – are entrusted to the fire, guarded and guided by the human being, in order to become useful. The round and rectangular meet in the baking of bread and the making of bricks; the former clearly demonstrates its connection with the cosmos, the latter its connection with the earth.

Children are borne into life on the stream of beauty; it is the guarantee against succumbing to the 'merely useful' on earth. But the human being must enter the other stream, coming from the earth itself, must connect with the necessities and demands of life. In children we can already get an inkling of what can become the main theme for the Upper School student: my work will have meaning for the social life; I shall make every effort to achieve this.

Transformation of wheat to bread

Gardening

Unlike the craft lessons with their caesura at the end of Class 8 and their replacement in Class 9 by different arts and crafts subjects, the gardening lessons continue from pre-puberty age uninterruptedly until Class 10. Their purpose is to make children familiar with the preparation of seeds, plants and soil, with the cultivation and care of the plant world, and to lead to an understanding of larger connections (composting, agriculture and meteorology). They also learn about the human being's manipulation of and participation in natural growth processes through such things as grafting, sprays and pest control. The gardening lessons are now frequently supplemented by practical work on farms and in forests where an understanding of our modern ecological problems can be prepared.

Anyone who has had to dig the hard ground of a garden, who has gathered potatoes with their back bent to the earth, who has, perhaps in the heat of the day, tied sheaves of wheat, might have thought of the Angel's words to Adam: 'Adam, thou in fear and dread/with thy brow's sweat shalt win thy bread!' He predicted the worry, thorns and thistles that the earth would hold in store for him. The paradise of old was lost and with it the receiving of protection and food without effort. 'We may say this without exaggeration, because it is true: the human being is, at puberty, thrown out from the cosmic life of soul and spirit and plunged into the outer world,' said Rudolf Steiner.[1] And yet, this event contains also the great hope, a kind of legacy, a paradise of sorts on earth – the plants, to which we are indebted for the sustenance of our lives – even today grow out of their own forces and in connection with the cosmos. It is not we who produce the plants. We can watch their germination, their unfolding, dying and becoming if, by learning to know their laws of development, we prepare the soil and provide the right conditions – moisture, warmth and air. Children experience these things in their gardening lessons more or less subconsciously. As we collaborate with the elements of earth, water, air and light through the way we care for and cultivate the plants, we participate in the unfolding of a new paradise that supports and maintains our lives.

But we also connect ourselves with the cosmos in a different way during our work with the plants: through their formative forces. Even superficial observation shows us how the petals of many blossoms open to the light. Looking closer, we discover that the green leaves also turn towards the light of the sun. Every single leaf can be seen as an organ that longs for the light and stretches towards it.

Our astonishment reaches a climax when we discover that the branches, too, reach towards the light with, as it were, open arms, forming the shape of an upwardly opening bowl. We had been used to seeing the trees' crowns as spherical shapes – and this correctly so. But the branches, as though in a counter movement, are bowl-like, striving upwards. This can be especially beautifully observed in the young shoots of fir and pine tops that only at a later stage, due to their growing weight, turn towards the earth. In view of their tendency to form bowls turned towards the cosmos, the plants appear as parabolic forms with their centre in the sun. These 'bowls' unfold from the seed resting in the earth. At first we have a vertically stretched, supporting

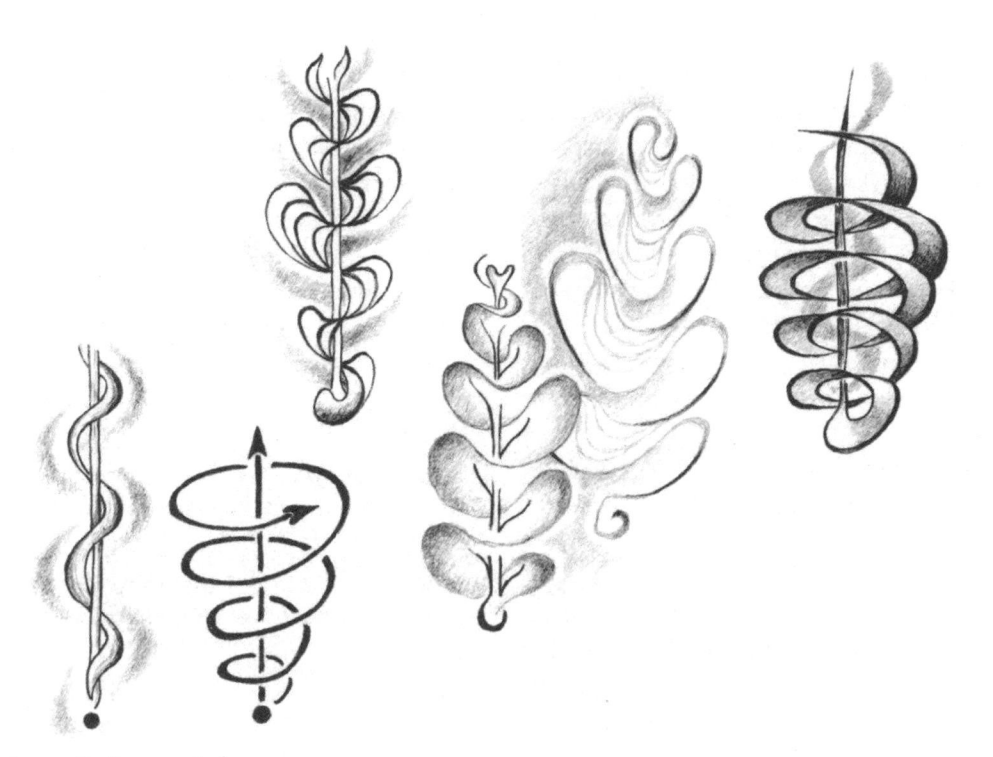

Metamorphoses of a theme: spiral

form: the stem. The leaves grow on it in a spiral sequence and, depending on the species, unfold ever further into their surroundings. The untiring observer, Goethe, drew our attention to these formative forces:

> *The two main tendencies or, if you will, the two living systems by which the life of the plant grows and completes its cycle, are the vertical and spiral systems; the one cannot be thought of as being separated from the other, because the life of each depends on the other.*[2]

There are thus two aspects in the gardening lessons: the one connects children, through the forms of the plants, with cosmic laws; the other connects them with the earth through their actual work. It is because of their connecting cosmos and earth that the gardening lessons continue into the whole of puberty.

Pottery

In keeping with our basic theme, especially that of formative work, the subject of coiled pottery as the first technique of craft is taught immediately after the gardening block in Class 9. We leave the garden and descend the steps to the pottery workshop. We are given a handful of clay and feel its coolness and weight. Its moisture makes it elastic enough to be shaped into a ball. Keeping it in our hands we press deeply into it with our thumbs and, rotating the clay ball carefully, we enlarge this hollowed out space until a near perfect shape is attained. During the process our thumbs are pressing from within, outwards towards the palms; through the continuing rotation and the spirally increasing pressure from within, a hollow space is gradually established: a bowl opens itself upwards. It is put on the bench; this gives it a base to rest on. A ring-like thicker coil is fastened to the rim and, again through rotation and the spiral-like pressure from within, is properly shaped. The bowl grows in size. We must now inwardly experience the up/down direction like an invisible vertical axis, so that the hollow space around may be enlarged without losing its orientation and support, or else the bowl will turn out to be crooked.

We recognise in this technique the same formative elements working in the plants. The human being perceives them and translates them into the way they handle the quite different material – clay. Such considerations certainly put in question the theories of chance or accidental happenings that people apply to technical discoveries in the past. The ancients' innermost connection with nature is well known today. It is clear that they also experienced nature's formative forces and made use of them.

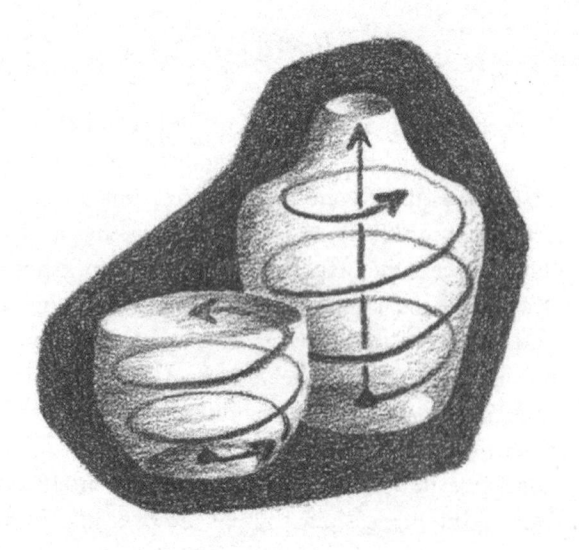

We have a quite extraordinary phase during the making of such a bowl when its opening is to be narrowed or almost closed. It is here where the actual structuring of the hollow, the inner space begins. Quite a few students find this difficult; they need all the concentration they can muster: concentration on the inside, which ignoring all the outer influences, is essential for this work.

The whole of this formative process depends on the right preparation of the clay: on its mixture of different and complementing types of clay, on the correct moisture. And even after the work is completed, the elements of air and warmth are decisive during the drying and firing processes. While it is the potter themselves who shapes the various articles, the completion of their efforts depends on interacting with the elements of earth, water, air and fire in a delicate and professional way. The first distinguishes them essentially from the gardener who does not cultivate the plants entrusted to them out of their own creative power. But both must, in their characteristic way, be familiar with the elements, must enter their nature and be able to handle them: the gardener by immersing themselves fully into their living qualities, the potter by controlling and mastering their mineral-chemical properties.

Basketmaking

The basketmaker also makes use of the spiral, starting from a point and continuing in a spiral to the rim. The starting point is, however, made by the crossing of several willow wands. No longer the flexible clay that allows itself to be shaped according to the sculptor's wishes: in its place we have a number of single, long wands that are placed in layers at right angles to each other, held in

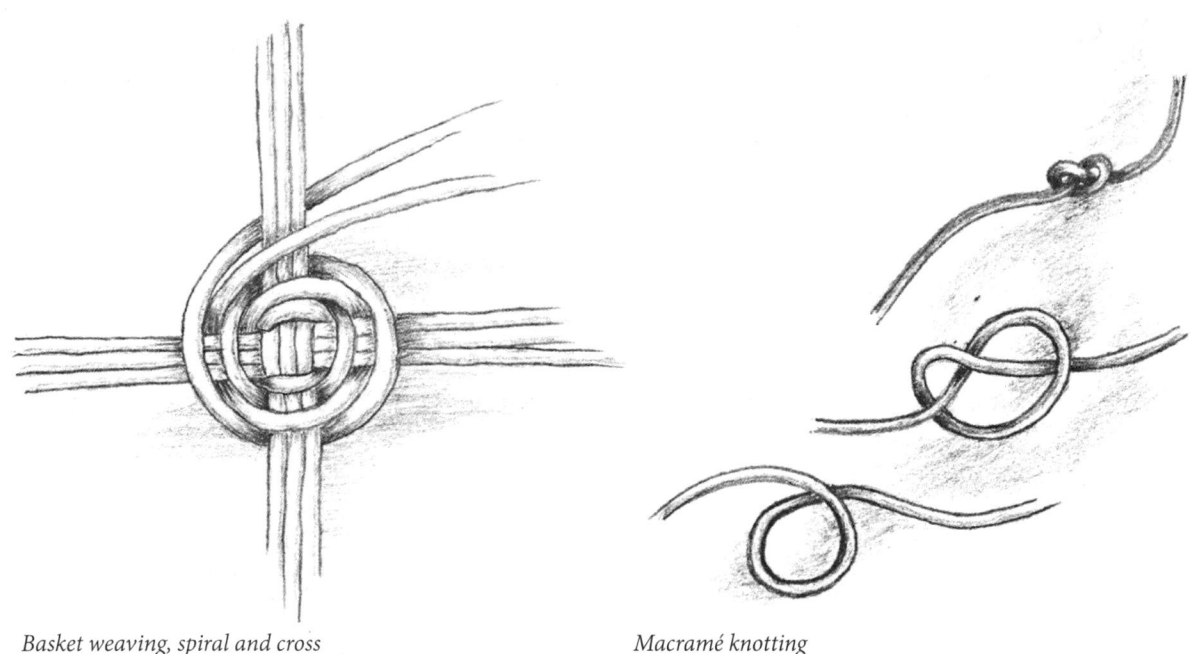

13. FORM-GIVING ELEMENTS AND TECHNIQUES (CLASSES 9–12)

Basket weaving, spiral and cross

Macramé knotting

place by skilled fingers, and through the spiral-like insertion of further wands, interwoven with each other. Before this is done, the cross-like placed twigs are bent away from each other to allow a radiating star to arise. Basket weaving can be seen as a forerunner of traditional weaving. We could speak of the basket as a woven spherical form that is built on a cross in a spiral movement. The crossing of two straight lines at right angles to each other is a form element that contains tremendous strength in whatever is to be fastened, tied and linked. No longer a spherical swinging and vibrating, only compelling inexorability.

It is unfortunately not possible in all Steiner-Waldorf schools to do this, namely to secure willows, and do all the necessary preparatory work of keeping them immersed in water until the optimum flexibility is reached for plaiting. As soon as the basket is finished, the influence of the elements – in this case only water – ceases.

Macramé

The crossing method is again taken up in this subject in Class 9 and intensified. As in basketmaking we again have a definite starting point, but now it is not the loosely formed cross made by layers of willow wands, but the firm knot of thread. It begins in a circular movement and comes to rest in the crossing of the thread – tightening, holding itself together. Adding identical knots, the necessary repetition of the identical movements make this work almost mechanical, in contrast to pottery and basketmaking where the work consists of alternate widening and narrowing.

Remember the way children learnt knotting and looping when they tied their shoes? To get it right, to keep the same distance between the knots, takes a certain degree of wakefulness if the result is to be worthwhile. Be it a knotted net or a hammock, its production demands some previous thinking because of the linear nature of the thread from which the intended object is to come about – very different from the sculpting of a clay pot which is shaped directly by the sensitivity of the hands. Old cultures, e.g. the Incas, used knotted string as 'data banks'. It was an excellent and most original memotechnical aid.

With the help of such knotted strings significant events were stored away, statistics established about everything and anything connected with numbers. Even today, we make a knot in the handkerchief to serve as a memory aid – to bind what wishes to fly away.

this imparting of the earth's heaviness into work processes again and again.

A climax is reached when we progress to the making of a metal box whose accurately fitting lid encloses the consistently made inner space. This takes us to Class 10, and is only fully experienced when we recall the life of the plants as they unfold in living spatial forms towards the light under the influence of their natural environment, processes that lie at the basis of the formative work in the craft techniques discussed so far. Space closes ever more, gaining its centre, its point of gravity within itself.

Metalwork

The step away from the immediate connection with the hand's movement by touch is even greater when the hardness of the material resists it. Help must be found in a tool that takes on this task by complementing the shortcomings of the hand. In the metalwork block in Class 9, as it were, a 'lifeless' or 'dead' connecting link pushes itself between work and hand – the chasing hammer. It becomes the fingertip that must accurately put pressure beside pressure, so that a small object may result from the work.

The hammer, loosely lying in the hand and yet surely guided, pounds on the metal, point after point, always at the correct place. At every blow the weight of the hammer is as though sucked in by the weight of the earth's force of gravity. The weight of the hammer is included in the strength of the beating. The shape of the object, a small bowl, will again open out in a spiral form during the work. What is new is that the weight of the earth, through the hammer, plays a decisive part in the formative process. We shall meet with

Shoemaking

Shoemaking awakens a strong consciousness of our connection with the earth and of the nature of inner space. The theme is already taken during pre-puberty, in the handwork lessons in Class 6. Earlier on, the children crocheted hats, knitted gloves and socks – from head to feet! Our feet are the only organs of our body that are immediately adapted to the earth and to the burden they must carry across it. Without their connection with the earth they appear to be unfinished, merely fragments of a larger connection. This is why, when seen from below, they really look rather strange. Other organs, such as our stomach and lungs, are also directed towards the substances of the earth, but differently; they transform them and do not, as the feet, experience the earth through pressure and counter pressure. This gives our feet their great significance for the energies needed in our vertical posture and, through it, for the ego development. We are not usually aware of this.

We have already spoken of the importance of the pressure of our bodies and the counter

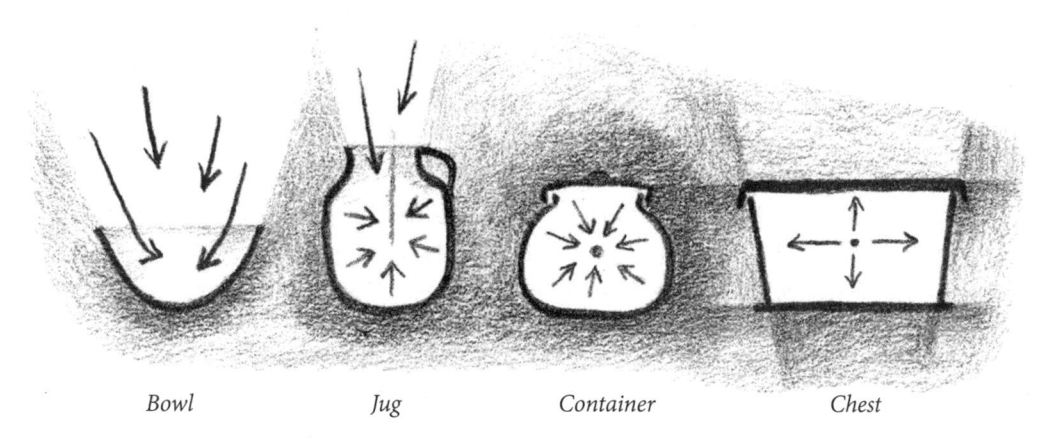

13. FORM-GIVING ELEMENTS AND TECHNIQUES (CLASSES 9–12)

Bowl   Jug   Container   Chest

Relation between inner and outer space

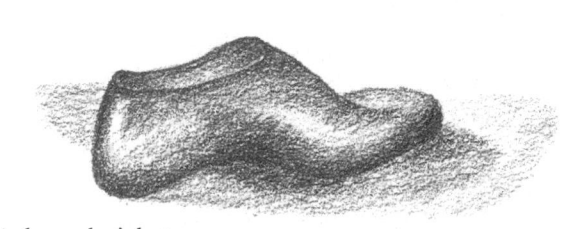

A shoemaker's last

pressure of the earth during work – especially from the beginning of puberty and continuing into the Upper School. And this pertains most directly to our feet. Rudolf Steiner's wish was to have a shoemaker among the staff, but this was not possible at the time.³ His indications were incorporated in the handwork lessons in Class 6. They were to be proper shoes, i.e. the left and right shoe were to complement each other in their symmetry.

Looked at from the aspect of giving shape to something, we have here an excellent example of the transition to the earthly world of forms. The flat area of the sole is connected to the upper leather that, through its curved form, is adapted to the curves and ankle joints of the foot. Only the careful and professional joining of these two parts into an organic unit allows us to stand and move well on the earth. The important role played by sensitively measuring the foot and by carefully selecting the corresponding last (the foot's substitute that is 'clothed' with the leather) relates to tailoring in Class 10. The shaping of an inner space also takes us to Class 10. During metal work and pottery the inner space arose outside the human being: box and lid had to fit. The shoe, shaped on the last, assumes the living form of the foot – an inner space in which the foot must feel comfortable.

Spinning

A decisive new step is taken in Class 10 when spinning is introduced. What is happening when the spiral does not open out from a point towards the top, but from the distance, as though following a downward suction, ever contracting and densifying? We are familiar with the impressive phenomenon of the vortex, e.g. in the bath when the water is drained. This formative process is present in the making of threads. We can observe it during the original hand-spinning process: from the loose, airily picked ball of wool a small part is pulled downwards and twisted, by means of the distaff or spindle, weighted down with a clay or stone weight, into an ever denser and tighter continuous spiral thread. The 'suction into heaviness' here becomes graspable reality. As with the hammer, the earth's force of gravity plays a decisive role. In Class 10, the upwards opening tendency of form is definitely reversed; we have an emphatic orientation to the centre of the earth as centre of gravity. Immediately we can see the significance, the symbolic character, of those processes for the educational task arising from them: the heaviness of the body of the adolescent, expressing itself all too easily and unpleasantly in posture and movement, is here used and translated into formative work processes. The result is a meaningful treatment of controlled heaviness, which is put into the service of people. It is a process that does not negate, but that takes hold and transforms what is present and, indeed, necessary, i.e. heaviness.

We could see the same principle apply to basketmaking, i.e. by adding a number of parts, to be able to lengthen something. In spinning, this idea becomes ingenious reality. A multitude of short fibres is (at least in theory) twisted into an infinitely long thread.

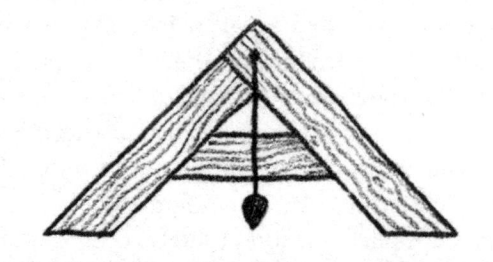

Egyptian levelling instrument, Thebes, circa 1100 B.C.

It took ages before the distaff (hand spindle) was replaced by the spinning wheel, invented in 1530 A.D. In the spinning wheel, the spindle is inserted horizontally – the vertical is replaced by the horizontal. It is obvious that the experience of the vertical must have preceded the learning of accurately handling the horizontal. The exact fixation of the horizontal with the help of the vertical, determined by the plumbline, can be found in ancient Egypt. A geometrical deduction, arising from the experience of the vertical, led to this ingenious discovery: the hypotenuse of a right-angled isosceles triangle will be horizontal if it is exactly halved through the plumbline pointing to the centre of the earth.

Let us reconsider the spinning wheel. It is a mechanism able to produce absolutely dense and indefinitely long spirals. With both hands and feet, the spinner is fully immersed in the process. The foot presses down, the hand guides the thread into the horizontally turning spindle. If we include the wheel's position in space we can discover how the essential parts of this 'machine' were constructed into the three dimensions of outer space. The attentive eye observes and guides the processes in spinning but the regular, smooth movements of the wheel, the regular feeding into the spindle and the quality of the thread depend on the delicate interplay of the hands and the action of the foot. Eyes, hands, feet – the whole human being participates in harmonious interaction.

Technology: screw, weight and density

During our reflections on spinning we were unexpectedly led to the thread form of the screw. In handspinning, the weight of the spindle adds to the connection to the centre of the earth. Screw and weight are basic elements in mechanics. According to Rudolf Steiner the teaching of mechanics should emanate from 'the characteristic nature of matter, of what is dense. Only at a later stage should dynamics be introduced.'[4]

This indication is very important for our teachers of technology in Class 10. In Class 9 we learnt about spiral forms in the growth of plants. Plants grow against the forces of gravity in living, moving forms. In technology the spiral is as though paralysed in the screw and becomes a technical device.

It was Archimedes (died 212 B.C.) who discovered both the screw and gravity. In 200 B.C. the Greek mathematician Apollonius of Perga developed the geometry of the spiral, i.e. its rigid, constructed form. During this time, the Greeks underwent a decisive change of consciousness. They preoccupied themselves especially with the laws of the physical world. And, although their world was still inhabited by gods, they loved their life on earth so much that the post mortem existence seemed shadow-like by comparison. They preferred the prospect of 'being a beggar on earth to a king in the realm of shades.'

Screws made from iron – by which things can be fastened together – were invented as late as the fifteenth century. During this century also a significant change of consciousness took place. Intelligence and will connected more strongly than ever before with earthly substances and energies. The fastening screw is symbolic for holding fast, for clinging, for standing still.

Let's look at a wood screw. We notice the spiral thread, solidified in iron, like a frozen turning movement bound to matter. Its progress gradually narrows towards the point, like an inward and at the same time downward led spiral that finds its point of rest in the tip of the screw. The hand-spun thread is formed according to the same principle.

The screw in technology leads to mechanics. Gravity and density as earth-related principles will be especially strongly experienced during the iron-forging block in Class 10.

Iron forging

In Class 10 the motif of the hammer is intensified to almost brute strength. The hammer is no longer loosely held and guided, as in copper work. Like a stronger-made fist, its cross shape is used to tame the hardness of iron. This is possible only with the help of fire in which the iron becomes malleable enough to be shaped. The clenched fist contains will-forces, expressing itself through warmth. Warmth is engendered when force or energy must be used against an obstacle. Little wonder, therefore, that fire is called upon to help. In essence, it is related to the smith's inner processes during his work. While all the cosmic stars stream out their warmth and light to all sides, the flames of fire on earth, directed upwards, triumph over gravity. Earth-fire allies itself to the will-forces that are present in the will of human beings, effectively directed towards a specific aim.

We have already met with the theme of resistance when discussing the gardening and craft lessons during pre-puberty in Class 6. There it was the earth (the floor) against which strength could be exerted. Now, during the ebbing of puberty, when every action strongly demonstrates our connection with the telluric forces, iron is shaped on the anvil with the hammer. The glowing iron is, as it were, kneaded between them. Strength and fire must co-operate. Presence of mind and a sense of purpose are essential before the iron grows too cold.

Forming a thread

Wood screw

Gimlet

Forging (sledge) hammer — *Pressure* — *Stress-expansion*

Counter pressure — *Anvil*

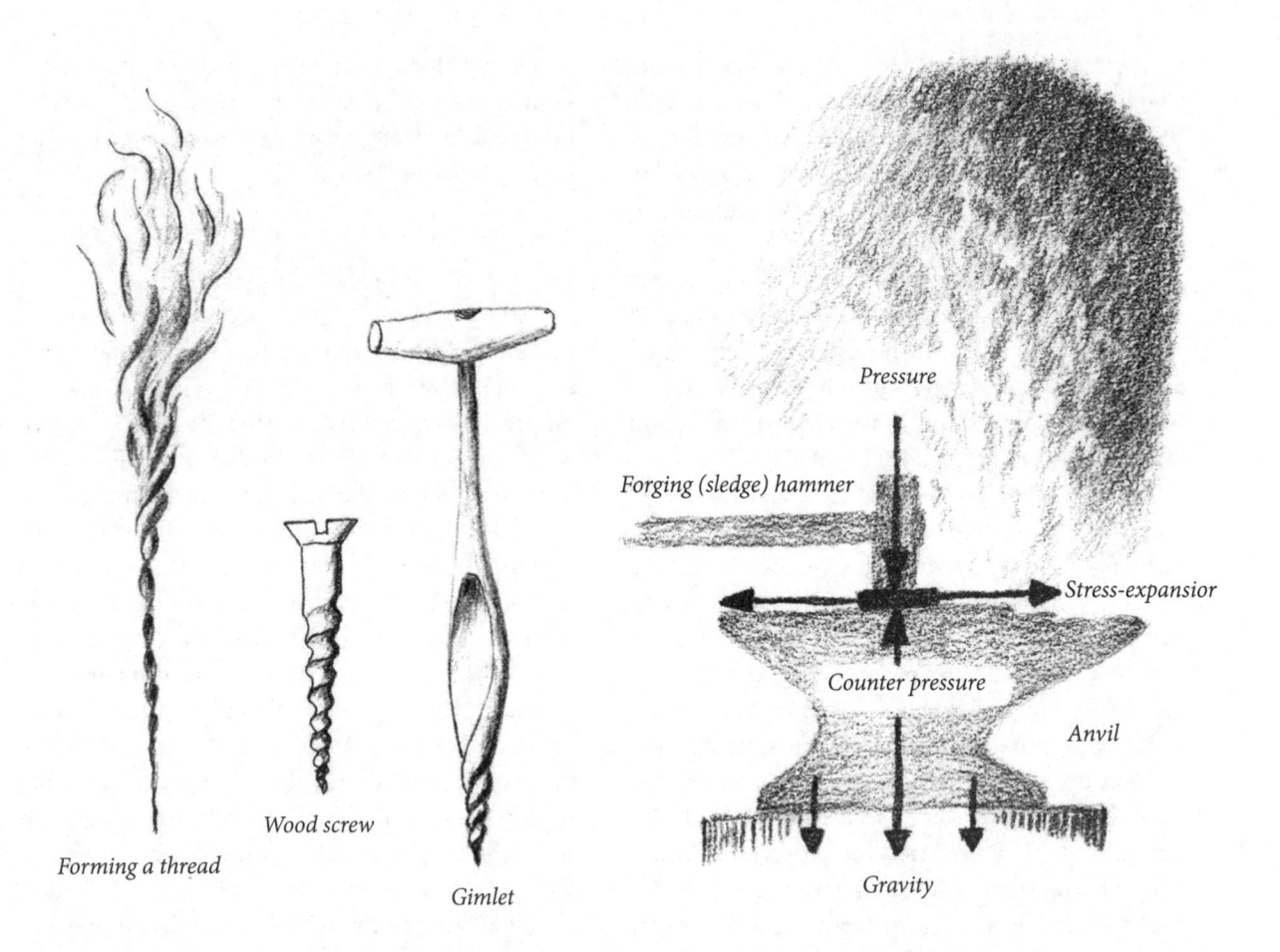

Gravity

Rudolf Steiner characterises what we experience in the process. During pressure and counter-pressure the ego kindles and activates itself, the ego that can always turn active and mobile wherever it meets resistance.

We arrived at the hammer via the spiral and the screw; each of them expresses its relation to the earth in different ways. We shall now return to the thread. It provides the basic element for a quite different form structure we have so far only seen in the sole, in our shoemaking block: the flat area. It will dominate the techniques used in the crafts taught in Classes 11 and 12.

Weaving

In weaving, cloth is produced that, today, can be very wide and, again in theory, infinitely long. In olden times, the natural 'large size' was understood to be the size of an animal's pelt or skin, which was made use of in many practical ways.

It took much abstract knowledge to produce cloth through thin, linear elements interwoven at right angles to each other. All modern woven material, just as in the distant past, is still based on the principle of a dense spiral and the crossing at right angles of warp and weft.

13. FORM-GIVING ELEMENTS AND TECHNIQUES (CLASSES 9–12)

The beauty of a piece of material is due not so much to the actual weaving itself, which must always follow the same routine of crossing the weft and warp threads, but to the different coloured threads chosen. Weaving, as such, is partly a mechanical operation. It is no longer the head that is important but the mechanism, be it ever so simple, which the weaver 'serves'.

The weaving loom has a similar history as the spinning wheel. In ancient times, the weaving was done by weights that pulled down and stretched the warp. The process was orientated downwards. This type of weaving loom was used in Europe as late as the tenth century. Records of the treadle loom are no older than six hundred years. Here the woven cloth lies horizontal to the ground. The working processes penetrate each other cross-like; this makes for a strong tie to three directions: the change of shed occurs vertically through the foot action (up/down), the shuttle is guided horizontally through the changing sheds (right/left) and the enclosed thread is then beaten by the batten (front/back). The immediate connection to the earth's centre, present through the weights pulling the warp, is apparently removed – exactly the same development that led from the distaff to the treadle spinning wheel.

This touches on a deep mystery already mentioned during our reflections on spinning. We do not know whether the human being was first conscious of his vertical position, standing upright on the earth, or of the horizontal plane they perceived in the stillness of the surface of a pond but we may imagine early humans experienced, unconsciously, the upward striving forces which are connected to the delicate balancing relation between scalp and sole, head and feet. In this they could comprehend themselves as beings between heaven and the centre of the earth, and they then abstracted this experience in the vertical line. Goethe referred to it as the 'spiritual rod' in the growth process of plants; and we discovered this also in the centre axis of a clay or copper vessel and in a basket.

The consciousness of distance across the earth's surface came later. Straight lines and flat planes are late phenomena in our cultural creations. They resulted from the experience of the vertical in relation to the horizontal. Le Corbusier, the pioneer of cubistic architecture, said:

The man or woman, drawing a straight line, proves by this that he has taken hold of himself, has become a rational and disciplined being. The rectangle is a symbol for the disposition of culture. We find our way to the straight line when we feel confident and strong enough… In the history of form, the straight line is a late product.

This architecture draws us into a dead world of flat surfaces, straight edges and right angles, all worked out according to the harmonious proportions of the golden mean.

Is an exactly flat plane or a perfectly straight line to be found anywhere in nature? Both are 'discoveries' of our mind; we can imagine them in their perfection, but would find it difficult to apply them to the reality of the physical world. Due to the curved surface of the earth, a straight board lying horizontally on the ground would, if long enough, after a while no longer touch the ground. And the still water in the pond? Its surface would become spherical if it were to expand far enough in all directions. It is only in smaller areas where the illusion of straight lines and planes can apply.

The spherical earth, of which the surface of our pond is but a segment, has its point of gravity at the centre. We use the spirit (water) level to determine the correct horizontal lines, e.g. in building; we relate this to the centre of the earth. A large building project would, as a consequence, be standing on a curved foundation. In this roundabout way, we are again led to see the small flat and horizontal planes, which human beings created, in their connection with the centre of the earth, the centre of gravity. Were our woven cloth to expand in all directions it would ultimately assume a spherical form. We can see in the three spatial directions of the spinning wheel and the weaving loom the basic forms that dominate our entire culture; but the delicate structure of the woven material resulting from the innumerable right angled crossings of equally innumerable straight lines also gives cause for reflection.

Could it, then, not be more than mere 'chance' that these form elements – through Rudolf Steiner's clear and exact indications for spinning and weaving – are such key elements in the lessons in Class 10?

Dressmaking and tailoring

As long as it is a matter of woven articles used in our immediate environment – be they cushion covers, blankets, rugs, carpets or curtains – the original, rectangular form, the necessary product of weaving, can be retained. As soon as the cloth is to be made into a garment it must be adapted to the human shape. And yet, people who still had a natural feeling for the things and processes around them were loath to cut arbitrarily into the logical structure of a length of woven cloth. They preferred to wrap themselves in square or rectangular cloths (e.g. the toga); this is still practised in many countries today. Indian women take a piece of cloth and wrap it in a spiral fashion around their body. The sarong is used by Indonesians: the two opposite ends of a cloth are sewn together, with the excess material being firmly fastened to the body. The word itself means 'container'. In our culture, too, the rectangular cloth – headscarf, shawl, table/altar cloth etc. – has retained its use and significance.

But, increasingly, the fabric is being adapted to the shape of our body. The garment demands the cloth to be divided and cut up, regardless of its right-angled structure. This must surely have been experienced with considerable pain, but also as an important step. In the cutting, the dividing of the cloth is certainly as important as the sewing. Whereas the spherical/round form principle in the previously discussed crafts (pottery, basketmaking, metalwork) was put to practical use within our surroundings, it is we ourselves who become the centre of the article during the making of a garment.

In this way, adolescents in Classes 9 and 10 direct their consciousness ever more strongly and objectively towards themselves, to their physical, bodily shape.

The design of the garment constitutes the first stage. However freely adapted the cut may be to the body's shape – according to the current fashion – its disposition is the right angle. From there the desired single parts follow, correctly transferred from the pattern to the material. The correct quantitative measuring is essential if the garment is to fit. Success is assured only if correct thinking, drawing and measuring precedes the work, for example, if the garment can be seen in full within this form of a pattern. Only then can the hands begin to carry out what had been thought out – we might be tempted to say: to carry out thoughtlessly. Never before was there such a contrast between design and execution – a picture of our modern division of work.

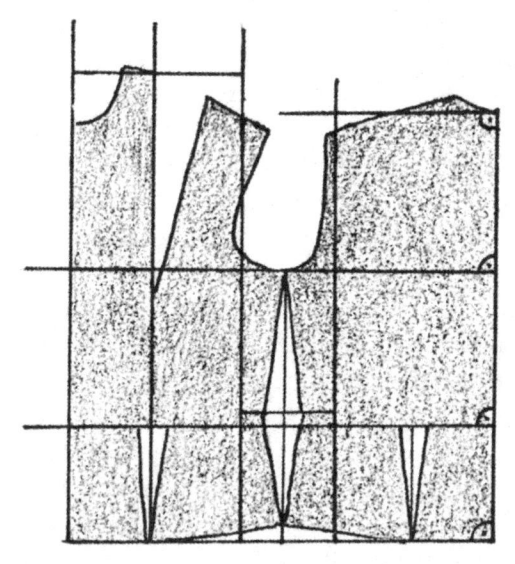

13. FORM-GIVING ELEMENTS AND TECHNIQUES (CLASSES 9–12)

Pattern of a blouse

The cloth is now cut into single parts and, with the important help of the sewing machine, rejoined. The exact correspondence between correct thinking and skilful doing is the happy result of the successful work.

Soap manufacture – hygiene

It is not enough that the activities in our immediate environment are now directed to the physical form itself, giving it, in dressmaking, its covering. When Rudolf Steiner refers to the knowledge of soap production in Class 10, he does not do so from merely theoretical considerations, but from immediate practical life: the care of the important organ of the skin.[5] The skin separates us from our environment, provides us with a 'cover'. This being enclosed within themselves can give adolescents a premonition of their burgeoning individuality coming into its own within their body. Not only the clothing, their individually formed body becomes important to them. This should, however, not lead to vanity, but to its reasonable care, to keeping it healthy. This must be learnt like a craft, a technique in the art sphere of life. The skin, by virtue of its pervious 'breathing' nature, is the physical mediator for a healthy relation to our surroundings. Anyone who, for lack of soap and water, has had to go without a wash for some time, knows the dangers to health resulting from it, and knows that their innate wish to be fully human is diminished by it. In the story of *Bearskin* or *The Devil's Sooty Brother* such a person is shunned by his fellow men as someone who has signed a pact with the devil and is not allowed to wash himself, cut his nails or comb his hair.

The lessons of First Aid and Hygiene are the climax; the crowning touches to this sphere in which adolescents become more aware of their body, learn to treat it in a reasonable way and to recognise it as a precious gift for life.

Joinery and carpentry

In our modern production of clothes we can clearly see that the design, i.e. the thinking activity, precedes the physical work from head to hand. In carpentry, as practised today, the turning away from nature and the use of abstract thinking and attitudes is even more noticeable. In their woodcarving lessons, children up to Class 8 are made familiar with wood in its natural state – branches, bark, logs, etc. found in the garden or forest and brought to the workshop. There are no flat surfaces; the shape of the wood, the living stream in the graining, determines the object made from it.

Only in Class 10 do children experience the nature of a board, its flat surface being sawn at right angles and made into a box, a shelf or the seat of a chair. The living qualities of wood must here be ignored or, we could say, 'tricked'. Such a trick would be the clamping together of the boards for a table top, in order to prevent warping. Warping is really nothing else but the wood's natural tendency to curved, rounded forms. This, the carpenter must not allow to happen. What used to be curved is now objected to and considered to be wrong.

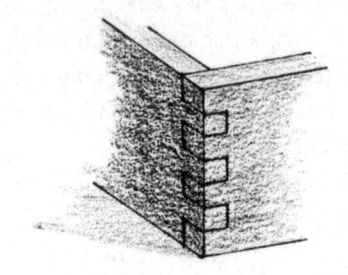

Dovetail joints

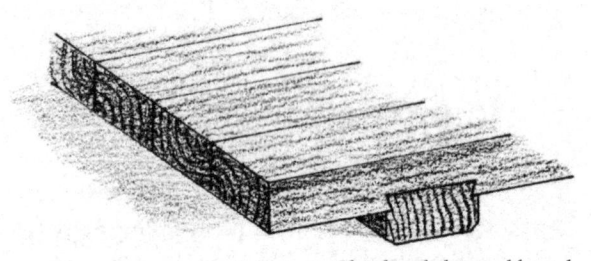

Glued and clamped boards

There is only one living aspect of the wood that persists and cannot be avoided: the expanding and contracting of the boards in-keeping with the natural breathing processes of the air moisture. We know this well enough from those wooden doors and drawers that get stuck in the wet season. We don't particularly like to be reminded of the original living quality of wood!

New techniques have made possible the widening of the natural width of boards through planing, joining and gluing. It is difficult to see in such a product the origin of the wood: the tree trunk. This is especially so in a plywood panel. A (theoretically) infinitely large panel results from very thin layers (literally peeled from the trunk) and glued together, always in successive layers at right angles to each other. The wood is deprived of all its living breathing processes – it has become separated from all life processes.

The basic features in the wood's progress from its natural origin to the board, which allow the students to become familiar with the basic technical elements of joinery, are identical with those in dressmaking. In both a piece of furniture and a garment, the idea, thinking and design come first. Exact measuring, knowledge of special tools, and the use of machines (some of them out of reach for the students because of danger) are essential. There is hardly a part of the work that can be done without the help of a tool. We can see the same basic features in dressmaking and carpentry, but also their specialised individual characteristics.

Surveying

Surveying the exact distances of a given area leads to the drawing of a map according to scale. It is the same process we saw in dressmaking, with the exception that, in dressmaking, we are measuring the body and do not stop at the design (the drawing).

It is interesting to note that, in surveying, we have the same form structure we met in most of the crafts in Class 10: the right angle. The reality of the right angle in the three dimensions of space is absolutely determining. We can find this, in diminished proportions, in the form of a box or drawer. In the larger situation it uncovers

13. FORM-GIVING ELEMENTS AND TECHNIQUES (CLASSES 9–12)

a hidden structure in the landscape that can be objectively grasped and put into a drawing. This happens during surveying where the lifeless space is measured with the help of a plumb line, spirit level, protractor, rods and battens, and the exact ratio determined. The surveyor becomes conscious of the unalterable state of outer space, in contrast to the living phenomena in it that cannot directly be measured. The beauty of the landscape has no part in this. The gentle rise of a hill is divided into rigid angles, the curves of a path, harmoniously embedded in a field, are determined through the right-angled co-ordinates from without.

In dressmaking, the exact measures of the body determine the artistically pleasing pattern; in surveying, in measuring the body of the earth, all life has been taken away from it, giving way to sober objectivity. And it is precisely this that allows the resulting map to be used by everybody, whereas a dress or garment belongs to one person only, its wearer.

Dressmaking and surveying are complementary in their polarities: the one points us directly to the human being, the other leads us into the distance. Both demand great care in measuring what is measurable on our and the earth's body. The technology of surveying is a bridge between the crafts and those subjects that are concerned with the attainment of knowledge.

Working with paper, cardboard and bookbinding

Think of a chest or a cabinet and imagine it shrinking to the size of an outstretched hand. We can make such a little box from cardboard and use it as a receptacle for our stationery. This leads us to the making of paper goods in Class 11 and to its continuation in the bookbinding lessons in Class 12.

Even here it is a matter of producing a covering, the forming of a sheath, but now for the written and printed word. The spiritual and cultural creations of the human being are thus included in the totality of the craft subjects.

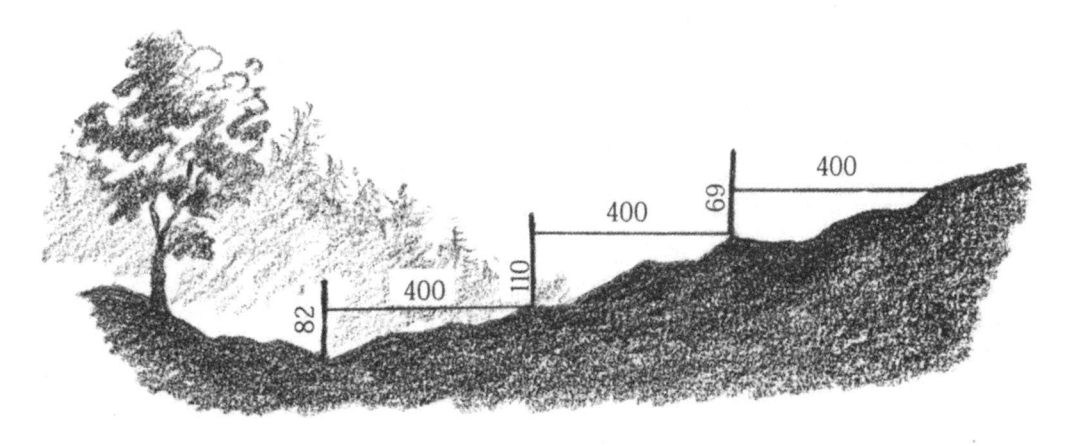

Surveying

PART THREE: CRAFTS IN THE UPPER SCHOOL

Rudolf Steiner wanted Class 11 students to learn about the manufacture of paper.[6] The date of the invention of paper is not known. The oldest known paper was in China, as far back as the reign of Emperor Wuti (141–86 B.C.). Germany's first paper mill was constructed by Ulman Stromer in the Hadermühle on the edge of the Wührder common in Nürnberg in 1390. In spite of its long history and ancient methods of production, *Haarfilz* – hairfelt – is now a very modern material. It is fundamentally different from woven textures, however thinly they may have been made: the short paper fibres are mixed in a watery solution, haphazardly; the more haphazard the better, because this engenders the felting process during the further stages of production, making the paper stronger. Out of this 'atomising' we get a material whose origin can no longer be visibly detected. We could almost regard it as man-made, as synthetic, artificial material that has been further developed in many different ways – such as hardboard, insulation and other building materials – pressed from broken up tiny substances and rebonded.

With paper we also have flat surfaces of any size cut at right angles to each other. The prototype of the book that developed in the monasteries in the Middle Ages has retained its rectangular shape, but its earlier form was the spiral: the papyrus scrolls in Ancient Egypt, Ancient Greece and Rome were rolled up strips of paper that were rewound, after reading, by the other hand around the second rod.

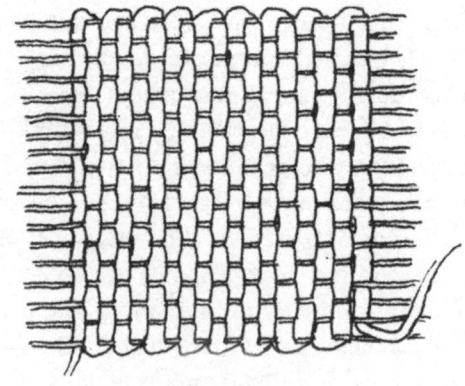

Woven texture

Paper fibres

Bookbinding demands a delicate flair and great manual skill and dexterity – together with an artistic feeling and clear, logical thinking in order to do full justice to the several stages of work. Rudolf Steiner spoke emphatically about the necessity of this subject. Because of its importance we quote verbatim from his lecture of April 21, 1923:

13. FORM-GIVING ELEMENTS AND TECHNIQUES (CLASSES 9–12)

The quite special human activity employed in bookbinding also does something quite special for the most intimate life of spirit and soul, provided it is done at the right age. This applies especially to the practical work. I would, therefore, consider it to be a sin against the human being if we do not introduce bookbinding, the work with paper and cardboard at the appropriate age in our Waldorf schools as part of the craft lessons. These skills are essential if one wishes to become a complete human being. It is not the finished product – be it a cardboard box or a nicely bound book – that is important, but the doing itself, all the various stages of work that are part of the process, including the corresponding thinking and the feelings engendered by it.[7]

The 'right age' is Class 11 and 12, according to Rudolf Steiner's indications reported in the *Conferences*.[8]

If we study Rudolf Steiner's words attentively, we may sense their meaning. Our daily thoughts are restless, changeable, inconsistent, frequently fanciful, unreal and difficult to control. They come and go, distracted by outer impressions. The logical sequence in craftwork can educate them to calm down, to connect with reality, to be consequential, to become objective, without the loss of their liveliness.

Summary

We attempted to show how, during the sequence of the craft lessons, thinking became ever more important. It is still possible in Class 9 to be spontaneously creative in pottery. No previous concept is necessary, the little bowl can change its form during the work. In Class 10, thinking takes over, determining the work in every detail, be it in carpentry, dressmaking or weaving. The work itself clearly consists of two parts: planning and execution.

At the same time the activities separate more and more from the body and, ultimately, from the direct contact with the hand. Specialised tools insert themselves, as it were, between hand and work. Machines take over, simple enough to allow the worker's participation, e.g. spinning wheel, weaving loom and sewing machine. In gardening, the whole of the worker with their strength and movement is still physically employed; in pottery, this is reduced to the palm of the hand; in basketmaking and knotting, it is merely a matter of the strength and dexterity of the fingers; in metalwork, the fingertips have become the hammer.

The work material itself shows an interesting progression: the garden with its nature elements, the life-filled plant world is the creative practising ground for the pupils; in pottery it is a specially prepared and improved (by the human being) piece of earth, made usable through the help of the elements. In basketmaking, the linear branches, already more highly organised by nature itself, are used. The influence of the elements on the actual working process diminishes ever more. In the crafts mentioned so far, the origin of the material can still be recognised. This is no longer so easy when we consider the thread used in knotting. The piece of copper has undergone several transformations: neither its shape nor its substance indicate its connection with the raw material from which it originated. Tin is already a very 'abstract' material. The same applies, at least in part, to the timber used in carpentry that can be essentially estranged from its origin – as veneer or through the way it is handled. We are not conscious of its connection with the tree.

It is similar with the woven cloth, and certainly so with paper that can already be seen as an artificial substance. We can observe the path from the natural material, where the elements earth, water, air and warmth are actively participating in the work, strongly at first but diminishing, until the fire, controlled and mastered by the blacksmith opens up new possibilities. Finally, we have such substances created by human beings themselves or further developed by them.

We have not spoken of the artistic aspects, only of the form principles effective in the course of education. At first the echoes of the second seven-year period resound in the bowl with its opening to the top, followed by the formation of an inner space, both following the spirally-round formative laws. Then the spiral contracts, experiencing the force of gravity. The emergence of the cross takes us to the flat plane, to the linear form and the right angle. The round, inner space becomes the box, cabinet or wardrobe. The influence of the telluric forces waxes ever more strongly and brings about the decisive change in Class 10. The young man or woman who comprehends and controls their inner life is now grounded by the earth's point of gravity (which they unconsciously experience). It is their task to take hold of the earth without falling victim to it, by recreating it out of their very own spiritual, psychological and also physical energies. A beginning must be sought in the top classes in bookbinding, perhaps in an artistically shaped piece of furniture, in the design of a hand-woven carpet or a wrought iron candlestick. In such work we have the unison between the techniques discovered by human wit and intelligence, which the hand has learnt to control during much practice; and the personal, individual imagination engendered by the delight in colour, form and

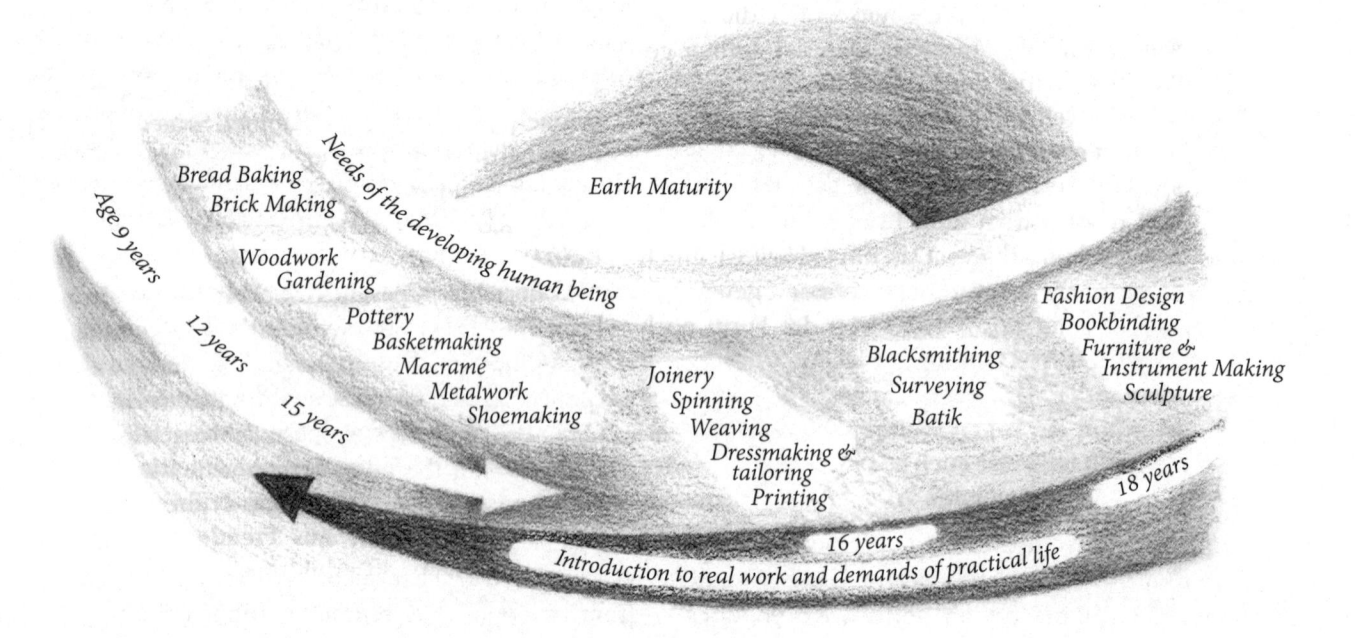

13. FORM-GIVING ELEMENTS AND TECHNIQUES (CLASSES 9–12)

the material used. Only this is true 'culture' and this cannot come about without the formed objects the student has produced in the crafts.

The sequence of the craft subjects in the way here outlined cannot easily be incorporated into a school timetable, if only because of the necessary splitting up of classes into smaller working groups. It is important, however, to know the threads in development that make possible an inner structure of the work processes, of the material used and, especially, the creation of organic forms. This can provide the teacher with a basic orientation from which he can draw whatever may be realisable in his school.

We have been able to see that the craft lessons gain enormously by becoming the outer picture of developmental processes taking place in the students. This is not to belittle other craftwork: for to simply encourage 'creativity' is important; and to do things out of joy and pleasure is refreshing and enlivening. However, Steiner-Waldorf education wishes to go still further by using the work done in the crafts to support and nurture the overall unfolding of the young man and woman.

Explanatory note

This chapter is based on the curriculum by C. von Heydebrand and E. A. Karl Stockmeyer, both of whom were pioneering teachers in the Stuttgart Waldorf School.[9] The views put forward should be taken as stimuli for further research and for finding solutions for other intentions in education. Rudolf Steiner allotted the subjects discussed (and actually related to the special headings of crafts, handwork and technology) to definite age groups, the respective classes being:

- 6–10: Gardening
- 9–10: Basketmaking, Macramé, Dressmaking
- 10: Spinning, Weaving, Surveying, Technical Mechanics (engineering), Hygiene, First Aid
- 11–12: Paper, Cardboard, Bookbinding

14

Pottery Lessons (Classes 9–12)
Gerd von Steitencron

Hand-built ceramics

Everyone is born with innate aptitudes and talents.

> *The sooner that each of us discovers that art or craft which can assist the systematic development of our natural gifts, the happier we will be. What we take in from our environment cannot harm our innate individuality. Our human organs ... are capable of uniting ... that which is acquired from the environment with that which is innate in us.*
>
> GOETHE, LETTER TO WILHELM VON HUMBOLDT, MARCH 17, 1832.

Pottery was not yet included as an independent subject in the curriculum indications in Rudolf Steiner's day. Clay sculpture was to begin in Class 9, yet even here only a few open-ended suggestions were made.[1] Craft and practical activities were not strongly developed in Steiner-Waldorf schools before the 1950s, at which time pottery found a firm place in the curriculum as well.

Pottery signifies the making of pots or vessels. Today it is regarded as just one aspect of ceramics; the latter signifies everything that is shaped and baked using various clay-based materials. Originally, however, pottery was the principle branch of ceramics. It arose to meet the simplest and most primitive necessities of life. This was where art and culture began to develop to meet the human need for decoration and beauty. Even in the most ancient water jars, vases, storage jars and urns, it is evident that the potters were not merely serving bodily needs. Intuition, imagination and a joyful experience of form and colour arose out of their own creative being, their experience of the clay medium, from earth, water and air. Their hands shaped what was needed with loving dedication; even today we are still moved by the immediacy, simplicity and expressiveness of these ancient vessels or works of art when we see them in museums or exhibitions.

How can we make the ancient potter's joy of life and creativity come alive for Class 9 pupils?

Clearly, the pupils must first acquire a certain dexterity through practice before they can give free rein to their imagination and their desire to be creative. They are rank beginners; thus we should not expect too much from them, nor they from themselves. As a material, clay will not be unfamiliar to them, of course. Ideally, they will

14. POTTERY LESSONS (CLASSES 9–12)

have made bricks with their class teacher during Class 3's building main-lesson. These came back from the kiln fresh-baked, hard as stones and completely changed in colour to be built into a wall using mortar. In Class 4 they will have done some modelling in clay, perhaps having formed simple rounded and angular geometric shapes, perhaps even having done some simple pottery, e.g. a dish. In connection with the 'Man and Animal' lesson animal figures were modelled freely, playfully and yet with great concentration and seriousness of purpose.

Now, however, they enter the craft room quite differently. Their spontaneity and uninhibited, fresh approach to life has been lost. They have become more thoughtful, critical and reserved, some somewhat shy, some apparently a bit cheeky. What they will now make with the clay can no longer be merely playful. It must become constructive work, craftsmanship, artistic activity. Only in this way can new, increasingly accessible strength flowing into their hands be properly focused and developed. For this reason, pottery should not be brought as an independent discipline before Class 9.

Our pupils are waking up to their environment. Their experience of our times shows an attitude toward life heavily influenced by the material surfeit of our western-oriented, post-industrial society. We have lost much of our respect for articles of daily use as well as for the natural environment. Running water now means a tap in our homes; we no longer see its source. Everything which gathers this living element is also readily at hand: washbasins, saucepans, teapots, cups, jugs and mugs – we hardly ask ourselves where all these come from any more.

We re-awaken to the original context when we arrive at a stream after a long walk; the precious liquid bubbles out of the cool earth as we cup our hands together to catch it and refresh ourselves. Indeed, our cupped hands are an image of the archetype underlying every vessel.

It is vital to awaken a new feeling in these pupils who have reached an age when the teacher should no longer exercise a natural authority: a feeling that they can accomplish something on their own, take their lives into their own hands, take on and realise an idea. Perhaps this is especially important in our times, for the future can appear to young people today as a great question mark, at least subconsciously.

Listen to an old, experienced potter describing how to shape a small pinch-pot by hand:

A hollow is pressed into a little clay ball using the thumb. Then the thick walls are raised evenly using a slow spiralling movement; the walls grow thinner thereby. Soon a vessel has come into being. After a few minutes, a thick-walled bowl approximately 8 cm (3 in) in diameter has been formed. Now we begin the process again from the middle of the base, this time with a somewhat closer, flatter grip to smooth the surface. The walls of the lower part of the bowl should already have their final thickness. To avoid sagging, the bowl should now no longer be set down; it should be held obliquely in the hollow of the left hand and the walls squeezed up bit by bit with a shaping movement of the fingers. With a little practice, pots the size and shape of a half-coconut, but slightly thicker walled, can be modelled in five to ten minutes without anything being scraped or cut away. Working the clay any longer makes it dry out through the heat of the hands, the top edge cracking; the clay also loses its freshness through being over-worked, becoming tired.[2]

Though it all sounds quite simple, patience, calm and composure are vital. These are, of course, qualities which are worth acquiring anyway should we do not yet have them; they are helpful throughout our lives. Also necessary, however is the ability to concentrate completely on the matter at hand, painstakingly observing every pressure of the fingers and its effect. While shaping our first piece in this way it's good to experience the whole process as a unity, accomplishing it from beginning to end without interruption. Both the inner and outer curves should be kept taut everywhere, the base remaining somewhat rounded. The interior is as important as the exterior; they should not be viewed independently of one another. A synthesis of the polar qualities of concavity and convexity should be sought for. The top edge, which might undulate a bit, should also be incorporated; it should clearly and incisively round off one wall's surface while forming a transition to the other wall. If the edge becomes too irregular it can be sliced away with a delicate knife or a needle and then thoroughly reworked. It should never appear to have been cut off but rather should form the culmination above as naturally as a pendulum which has reached its turning point and begins to swing back again.

While working on and evaluating the form there is often a tendency to be aware of the outline alone, to view the piece two-dimensionally, linearly. For sculptural forms it is more important to achieve a feel for and insight into how volumes and surfaces advance and retreat: Which spatial gesture does the form make towards you, away from you and, simultaneously, in the periphery? How does it approach, retreat from or garner the light, casting shadows?

We can speak about all these questions over the work, during short breaks or (as appropriate) before we start working. We can discuss them, raise or answer questions, above all explain why we are doing it this particular way and not another as well as the effects of what we do and don't do. Examples should be given whenever possible. For example, our bowl would have a tendency to become broader and flatter if we worked with both thumbs inside. It is easier to raise up the walls when we work with one thumb inside while the whole bowl rests in the other hand. In this way it will not so readily warp out of shape, which is to be avoided at all costs. The bowl's shape should be changed slowly and regularly; otherwise it easily becomes structurally unstable and begins to develop cracks.

Some pupils may not be entirely happy with this approach to modelling (the pinch-pot technique). Perhaps one or the other has already seen how a bowl can be 'more easily' built up out of rings or a spiral of clay. Perhaps they have even already practised this common method.

The pupils can be put at ease. We'll not restrict ourselves to the pinch-pot technique. It offers, however, the possibility of acquiring an ever securer feel for the thickness and stability of the walls and for the form of especially the interior without confronting us with other problems (such as those of positioning the clay, adding new clay, the dish sagging when we set it down on a table, etc.). In addition, it is possible to acquire a good feel for how clay moves and reacts in and through the work of our hands, i.e. the constituency that allows it to be worked easily, and how it begins to dry and harden as we work it. The latter happens especially quickly in wintertime in dry, heated rooms.

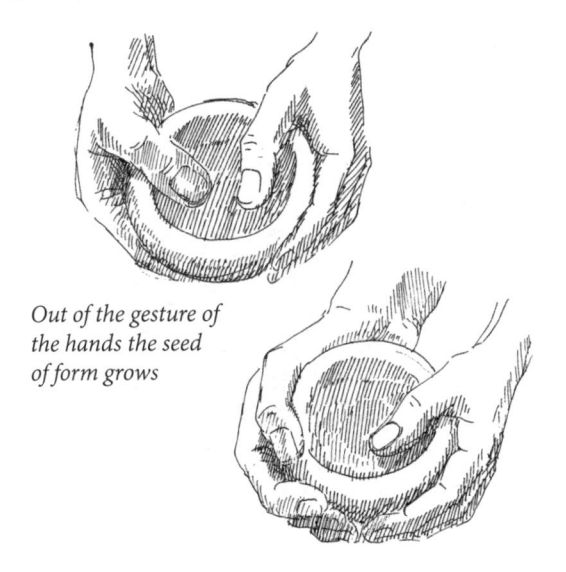

Out of the gesture of the hands the seed of form grows

Another of the pupils' questions will be about the rounded base: 'this thing won't stand up properly', perhaps with the feeling that 'it's sure to tip over'. It is a beautiful experience to see afterwards how the bowl establishes its own balance like a roly-poly man. If we have worked well, the middle axis is upright and the top edge lies horizontally. If not, the pot will tilt, and we can adjust it accordingly.

Originally, all pots had rounded bases. This was not just a question of aesthetics or the ease of firing, but above all of durability. We will return to this when we look at how the clay dries, fires and cools.

It is an open question whether pupils should always be quiet and focussed or be left free to chat amongst themselves. This is fine as long as it remains within an appropriate context.

We can guide them, to ensure that the path is not abandoned, the goal not lost sight of. We can discuss stable and unstable states of balance. We can collect meanings of the word 'cup' or 'shell'[3]; it is always indicative of the covering as opposed to the actual kernel or fruit or content.

If we want to construct larger pots we'll have to begin to add clay. The so far thumb-high pot is planted upside-down on a moist cloth between times, so that the base can dry out a bit and become firmer while the edges remain moist. Clay coils are then firmly pressed onto the top inside edge using similar hand movements as with the pinch-pot.

To do this kind of pottery we must know well and work with the clay's nature and behaviour.

It is important to work on a board, e.g. a piece of absorbent cardboard.

To add clay the following is necessary:

1. Air pockets must be absolutely avoided.
2. New clay must be firmly joined onto old. Since a sort of skin forms during the drying process, this is not so easy.
3. Water does not bond surfaces. It is thus insufficient merely to wet the clay and then press new clay on top of this. There is also a danger that the water can drip down and soften the base of the pot, just the place that should be growing firmer. It is better if the clay is kept moist and thus never forms a skin where the juncture will take place. (Occasionally moisten your hands!)
4. The join must be thoroughly worked. This is only possible if both the edge and the added coil are a good bit thicker than the walls of the pot.
5. The base must be all one piece. A rough ball can first be rolled out into a sort of lens shape, then pressed totally flat, simultaneously raising the edge up about a finger's width.

Apply clay inside and out

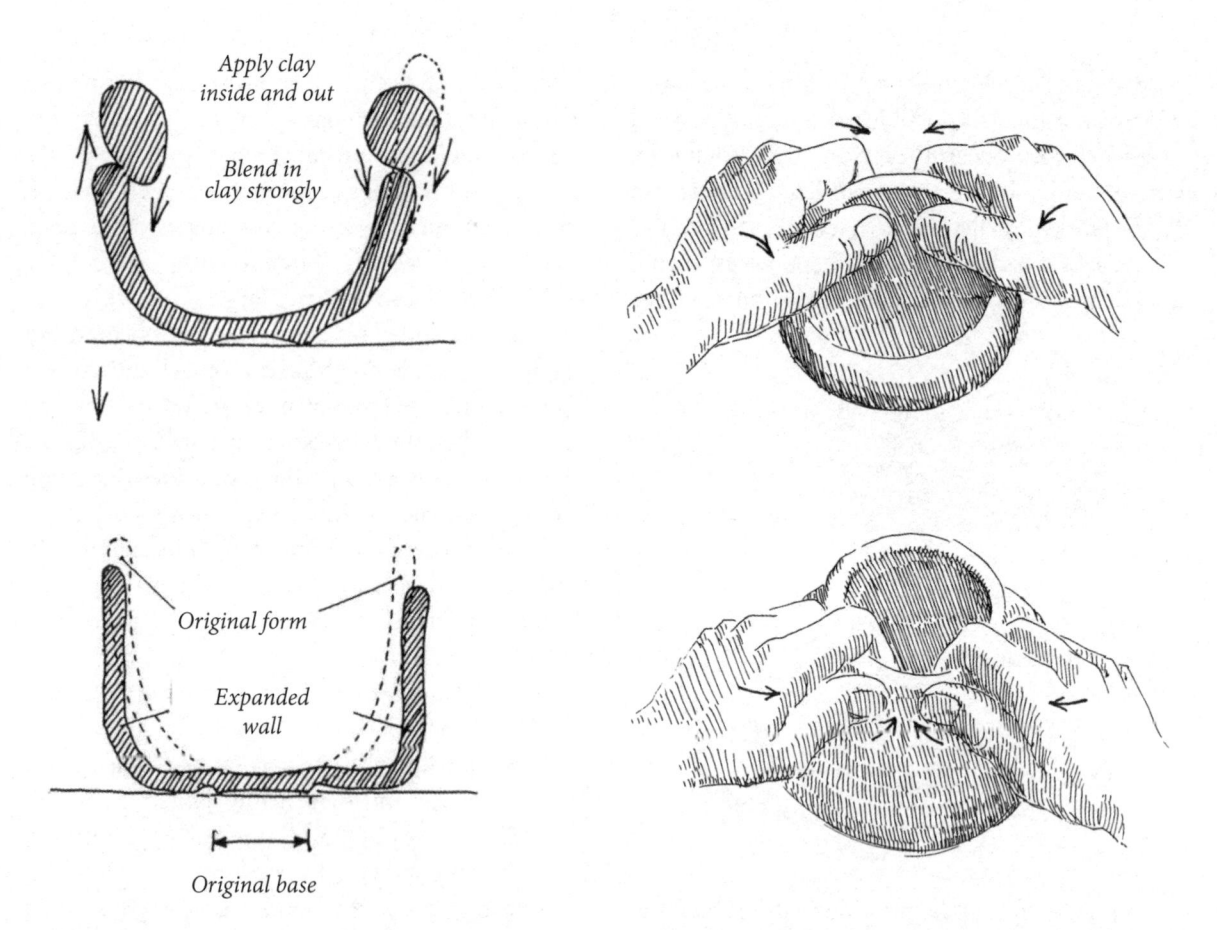

Blend in clay strongly

Original form

Expanded wall

Original base

The pupils will run into difficulties in shaping the clay: every time that the wall is pressed thinner it expands outwards, thus increasing the surface area – this is a simple physical law of the distribution of matter. If I want to bring the wall up more steeply, I have to simultaneously create a constant inward pressure to force the mass of clay upwards. The resulting compression (opposed only slightly by the pressure of the thumbs inside the pot) tends to induce folds in the wall, especially if it is thin. This can easily lead to uncontrolled spreading, beginning already at the base. If the wall is a bit moister, with increasing pressure above due to the weight of the clay the wall begins to sag just above the base. As soon as this danger becomes noticeable we must stop adding on above, correct the situation below, and set the partly finished pot to rest bottom up so that it can dry out and firm up.

If a pot with a narrower neck is desired, a similar difficulty arises in attempting to bring the neck in at the top. Even if a coil of clay is added on the inside edge, the attempt will fail without a special compressive grip which needs to be learned.

If the pupils are attentive, they will learn all this quickly, especially if the teacher unflaggingly demonstrates it over and over, helping them at critical points until they can do it on their own.

The first exercises should be set for the pupils according to the difficulties that have already

14. POTTERY LESSONS (CLASSES 9–12)

arisen. Each teacher must find their own way with this. For example:

1. A pinch-pot
2. A mug (this requires steeper walls)
3. A small vase, either round in form or narrowing as it rises (using one or two added rings). A foot ring can also be added afterwards using slip.

After these exercises the pupils can try modelling whatever they like, gaining ever more freedom. Their ideas must be discussed first, however, the teacher perhaps even developing them together with the pupils, sketching them roughly on the blackboard and considering them carefully. In this way the teacher knows what the pupil wants to try and can help him or her to realise it. How far the pupils can be given a free hand will depend very much on the individuals, the group as a whole and the mood that is present.

As a matter of principle, pots should be made which are to be used (this could include lamps, for instance). The teacher can also give a choice of exercises. He or she can demonstrate possibilities, show successfully completed work (or photos), or even when necessary set a particular task for all to do. A common exercise can result in individual solutions by each pupil. In this case it is a matter of providing a framework so that the pupils are not totally at sea, yet leaving play within the framework for the individual will. The pupil must feel connected with the working process and must be able to experience successfully creating a piece while clarifying the idea of what this should be like and how it might be made in the process.

The teacher should not have a rigid, pre-defined idea of how the pupils' work should turn out. The pupils should not be merely a means to accomplishing the teacher's own ends. No true co-operation would be possible if this were the case; this can only result from pursuing the matter at hand without any personal coloration whatsoever entering in. In the Upper School this is necessary if we want to avoid a sort of 'glass wall' arising between pupils and teacher. The work does not have to turn out exactly as it was originally conceived – especially attractive and beautiful work often comes about as if of its own accord. Sometimes, of course, something goes wrong, which should not be taken too tragically; perhaps we can even make a virtue of necessity!

The pupils need to be acquiring an ever surer and better-defined feeling for form and for what speaks in the form as an expression of life, style and characteristic qualities. Earlier cultures have always had this feeling for form; elements which come to expression in Gothic architecture, for example, are found in the pottery of that time as well.

What are nature's organic forms like in this respect? What are two-dimensional forms such as leaves or three-dimensional forms such as fruits like? What about animal forms, what about the human form? The pupils should be being continually stimulated to observe all the world, including the mineral kingdom (stones, crystal forms and colours). Everything can stimulate our creativity and differentiated perceptions.

If we now look at the terms for the various parts of a vessel, we are immediately confronted with a relationship to the human being – or now and again to animals or, as in the case of the chalice, to flowers (calyx). We have the foot, belly, shoulder and neck of a pot. The jug has a lip (in German this is the 'snout' while the longer spout is a 'beak', the opening is the 'mouth' and the rim is the 'lip'). When a dish has a foot ring the transition from the foot to the body is called the waist; this transition gives the dish its interest. A vessel can have a posture, a gesture. A vase can be narrow or wide, simple or elegant, rough or fine, noble or awkward. It can enthuse us or leave us cold. Its actual purpose is first fulfilled when it is filled with flowers.

Naturally, a coffee pot must look different than a teapot or a watering can. It is not a matter of indifference which shape we give to the things we make. The intended content significantly determines the form. A container 'contains': holds and protects its contents. The latter are generally something needed to sustain life.

A flat dish, e.g. for serving sandwiches, is somewhat like a miniature tabletop; a tray, like a little table. The contents will not stay there for long; they're meant for immediate consumption and to be freely partaken of. A flat breakfast plate on which we butter slices of bread is similar, as is the normal dinner plate; both have only a slightly raised edge to retain what is on them (and for ease of grip). Soups and round fruits that could roll about need somewhat higher perimeter walls. All of these flattish utensils receive and give of their contents readily, holding onto nothing firmly. This gesture, which our hands can also make, can be expressed in the form of our utensils; we can accentuate and articulate it further. Then there are utensils that enclose their contents more firmly and hold them more securely: goblets and cereal bowls, as well as cups, mugs and all deep bowls; the dominant gesture remains that of offering. The pot which gave our activity its name usually has steeper and more enclosing sturdy outer walls. It occupies the middle ground between receiving, protecting and offering. The name 'pot' itself is a collective term which reveals its ancient origin amongst simple peasant folk.

Now we come to forms which narrow at the top: jugs and vases, which include a shoulder or a collar and a neck. Finally we arrive at tea and coffee pots, which are lidded, and the stoppered flask. All these have a circumscribed interior space; they fully enclose, more or less protect and keep warm their contents. A relationship to the human bodily form can be seen in all these forms. Human gestures and postures having an underlying connection with the vowels done in eurythmy can also be seen: there is the opening out of 'A', the enclosing 'O', the upwardly striving 'U'. These are archetypal forms born out of the feeling soul, creative of a rich, perpetually metamorphosing and varied language of form.

Though there are endless creative possibilities, in pottery even more than elsewhere, simplicity marks the master. This applies primarily to the shape, but also to a certain extent to the decoration and coloration of a piece. The simpler, clearer and more unified the shape of a piece appears, the better and more convincing it usually is. The pure geometric forms of the sphere, ellipsoid and cylinder shall not serve as our models here, however. The forms of skins and sheaths, as we find in nature around every sort of fruit, have always been found to be more stimulating for us. Living forms are more appealing!

Pieces with fat, round bellies have something stolid about them; they can express contentment and peace or weightiness and gravity. Amphora shapes, opening up to their widest above the middle height, seem to stand tall, bear upwards. Tall, slender shapes have an air of upward striving and seem lighter, more free of the earth. Our pieces can be given more a feminine or a masculine character. They can be firm or soft, gentle or powerful. In any case they should stand stably.

14. POTTERY LESSONS (CLASSES 9–12)

Since we want our pots and vessels to be readily usable, they'll need some sort of handles and spouts. After the shaped pot has firmed up enough that it is no longer warped out of shape by every little pressure, the parts to be added can be pressed home and worked in using some slip (a mud of clay and water). The handle is initially attached above, then given its final shape and pressed into place and worked in below, again using slip. It must then be wrapped up so that it does not dry out faster than the rest of the vessel.

In shaping a jug we abandon pure symmetry. With hand-made pots we are not, as in the case of the potter's wheel, bound to the vertical axis of symmetry and thereby to round forms as seen from above. We can build up, modify or beat out various kinds of rounded, angular and diverse shapes. We need not make a principle of creating asymmetrical, crooked and hard-edged shapes simply because this is 'in vogue'. Many an arbitrary experiment can be forgone when the pottery is not shaped primarily for the shape's own sake but rather so that the vessel can serve us in a particular manner. This task establishes the potential shape and form. We must not lose sight of this point of view, the potential utility, which is a result of the utensil being readily manipulable, not too heavy, stable and easily cleaned.

Flat plates, fruit bowls and bird baths offer the best possibilities for free form. Vases run the greatest danger of becoming abstract. Consider that everything which is full of life has a tendency towards rounded forms, the form of a water droplet. This is simultaneously the most stable and durable form and allows for the thinnest wall (the egg!).

A vase should not be imagined to be a self-sufficient object; together with the flowers it should beautify the house, complementing the house's atmosphere and the vase's surroundings. Branches of blossoms demand a strongly shaped, securely standing heavy vase or a large jug.

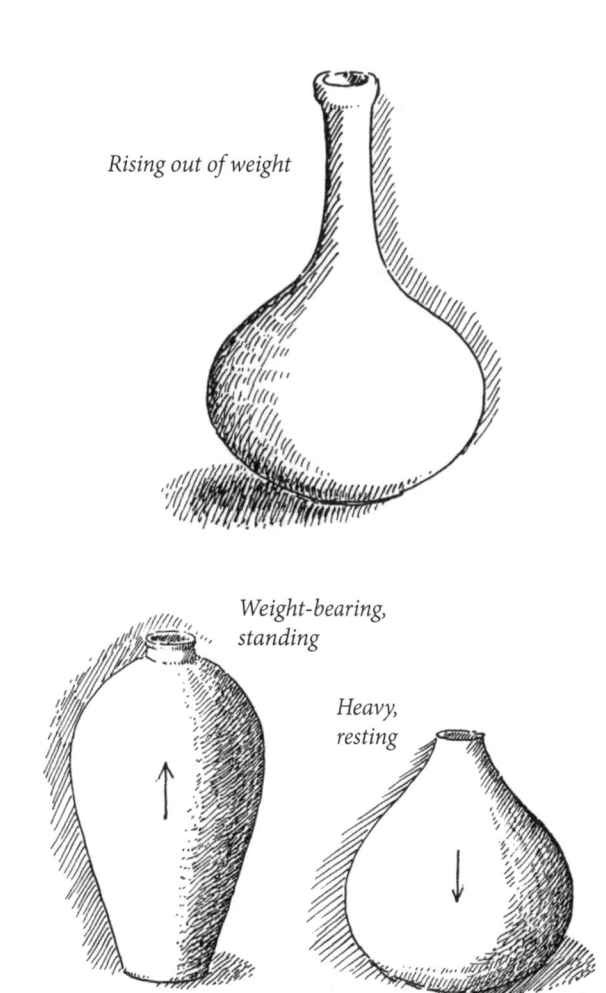

Rising out of weight

Weight-bearing, standing

Heavy, resting

PART THREE: CRAFTS IN THE UPPER SCHOOL

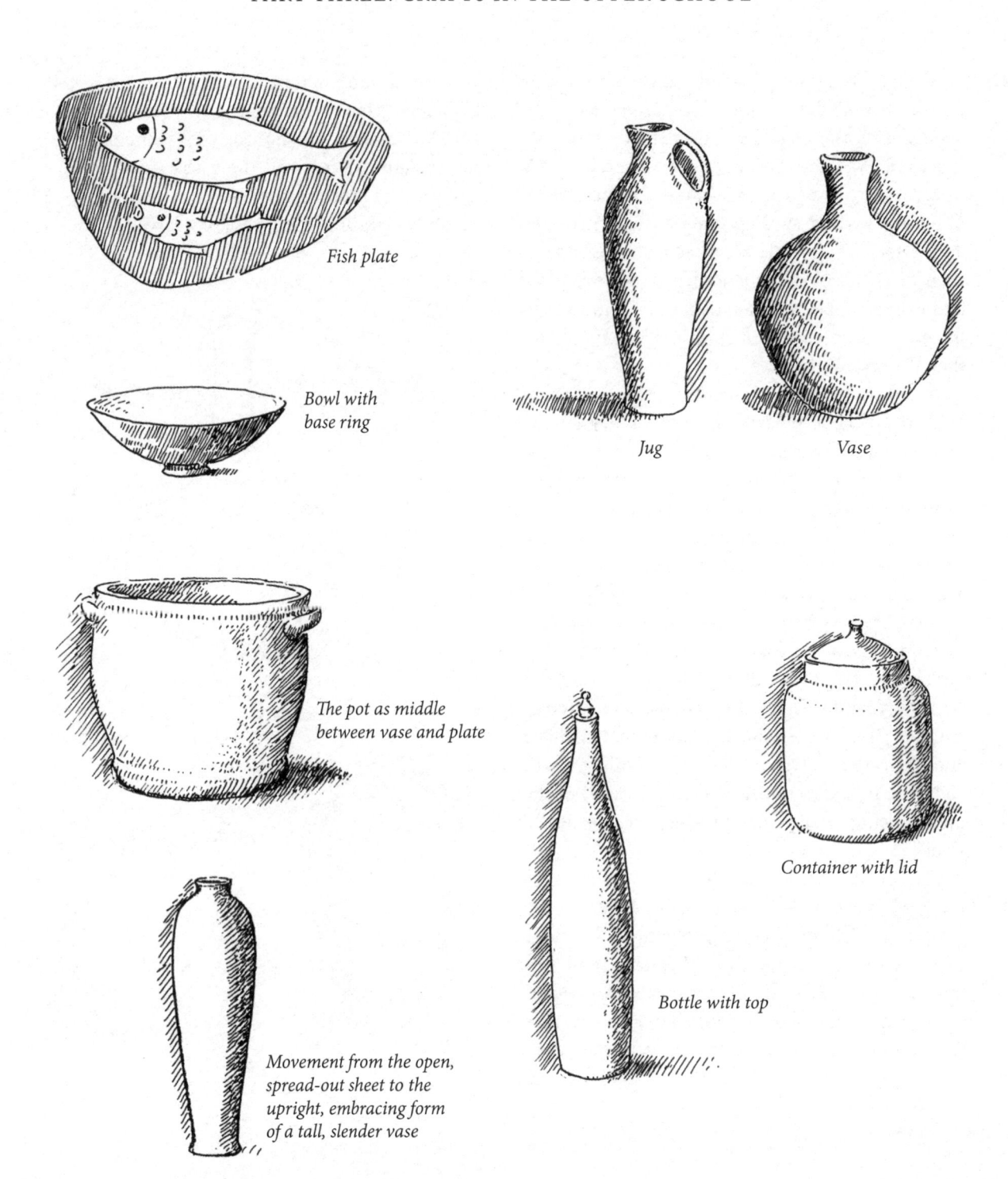

Fish plate

Bowl with base ring

Jug

Vase

The pot as middle between vase and plate

Bottle with top

Container with lid

Movement from the open, spread-out sheet to the upright, embracing form of a tall, slender vase

14. POTTERY LESSONS (CLASSES 9–12)

In determining on a shape it is very important for the pupil to know and have a feel for what happens to clay as it dries, as it is fired for the first time, when it is glazed and when it is given the glaze firing. All the elements – earth, water, air and fire – take part in the process. We must take into account the occurrence of shrinkage and the strains that result from the clay drying unevenly. The moisture escapes from the clay as it dries. The walls become thinner, the whole vessel shrinks. At this time, poorly worked humps, hollows, bumps and additions of coils begin to reappear even if they had been virtually lost to sight previously. The entire 'skin' seems less taut, appearing somewhat 'aged'. If more powerful tensions arise, splits can come about very easily, especially in the base where the foot ring may already have dried out while the base itself remains moist. During the first firing, the bisque firing, the clay shrinks little or not at all; it takes on a different colour however and becomes a stony 'biscuit' which no longer dissolves in water. It still remains porous enough to soak up the watery glaze. During the second firing, the glaze firing, everything in the oven glows brightly as the glaze melts into a liquid state. The clay softens as well, however, and begins to warp somewhat if special measures are not taken to prevent this (e.g. grog, special kinds of clay or a comparable additive having been mixed in with the clay). The pot shrinks again and the whole mass has a tendency to sag where it is not well supported. Heavy parts droop and press down (handles, candelabra arms). It is therefore necessary to 'think big' already during the design process, shaping everything more generously than actually feels right at the time. The whole sequence of shrinkage and sag begins already as the clay is first drying.

All contact with work-a-day utensils should be accompanied by a feeling of respect for what can and should be an image of a higher, humanly significant reality. During the time of life in which the young people find themselves their bodies are undergoing a hardening process. Their bodily sheath has reached a certain culmination of its development; it encompasses a new life of soul. This is not only a transitory passageway for experience, learning and discovery – an enduring inward space is created. This can apply to larger contexts as well; if human beings work properly together out of a spiritual standpoint, they form a vessel where their common striving assembles. In olden days a lovingly formed vessel accompanied the human soul into the after-life as a burial gift.

Throwing pottery on the wheel

The potter's wheel stands amongst the most original and ancient inventions of the human creative spirit. In no other craft is there anything remotely approaching the activity of throwing on the wheel. Neither wood nor metal, neither glass nor any other material appeals so directly to the human being as does the contact with clay.[4]

These are the words of a well-known and experienced potter. His experience may be of interest even though the feeling of a craftsman or artist for his or her material is highly individual. Since throwing pottery on a wheel is not a mass-production technique as is, e.g. casting, we still have all the creative possibilities of shaping by hand. Putting aside for a moment the difference between pure art and artistic craftsmanship, we can compare the potter's wheel to a musical instrument.

PART THREE: CRAFTS IN THE UPPER SCHOOL

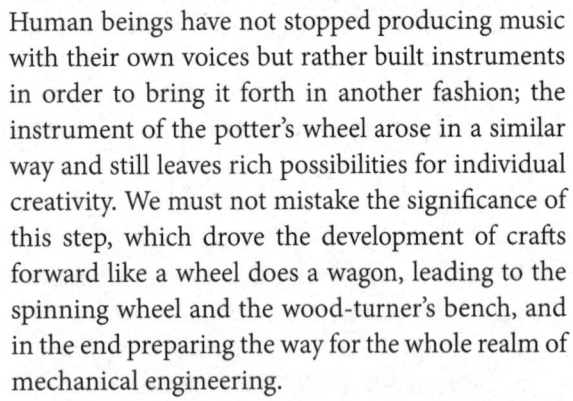

Teapots and cups

Jug with beakers

Human beings have not stopped producing music with their own voices but rather built instruments in order to bring it forth in another fashion; the instrument of the potter's wheel arose in a similar way and still leaves rich possibilities for individual creativity. We must not mistake the significance of this step, which drove the development of crafts forward like a wheel does a wagon, leading to the spinning wheel and the wood-turner's bench, and in the end preparing the way for the whole realm of mechanical engineering.

To the extent that the potter's wheel found acceptance in the profession, production by hand ceased, being no longer competitive. Something similar happened when industrial production began. Despite this, artistic craftsmanship is sustainable again today on a smaller scale, for many people are not finding what they seek in machine-made, mass-produced goods. It is not only the lack of such things as warmth, life, spontaneity and the connection to nature. Perhaps it is not even just the shape and colouring, though these play an important role as well. It comes down to delicate nuances, intuitively grasped and not easy to fasten in words. The value – above all the subjective value – that an object has for the people involved with it is all-important. We

like to have a personal connection with the objects we live with. We want them to be appealing and to have an aesthetic element. It is a question of *which* means serve the same end here. The product is affected by the process of production with all that this involves. This is well worth reflecting on. It is questionable if this apparently necessary process of industrial development hasn't reached its zenith or has perhaps even gone beyond the limits of what is tolerable. There are various Steiner-Waldorf schools which have integrated commercial production techniques right through into full apprenticeship programs leading to work in social fields as part of their curriculum.

When a young school first begins an Upper School, questions and deliberations will arise for the college of teachers and council about the goals of such an institution in the light of the expanded need for educational diversity. There are monolingual and polylingual pupils; there are on the one hand practical and artistic subjects, on the other hand academic and scientific subjects; and the exams cast their shadow years ahead of their actual arrival. The question as to the value of pottery in the curriculum can arise again here. Aside from the prerequisite that there is somebody

14. POTTERY LESSONS (CLASSES 9–12)

who can actually teach the subject, the question of whether it makes sense for the particular school to do commercial pottery in this way and to set up a specialised craft room for this should be carefully considered. Experiences of other schools with pottery on the wheel can also be looked into.

However fascinating it is to watch a potter turning clay on the wheel, however quickly it goes, however delightfully easy it looks to be, however much fun it might be for ourselves (if we are capable and can turn something already) – all this still does not justify spontaneously introducing it into the curriculum.

Those for whom free artistic creativity is all-important and who are less than enthusiastic about a commercial style of doing pottery will ask: Whatever could move us to set up such a terribly complicated and technically and spatially exorbitant activity as pottery on the wheel in the school? Building up and modelling clay by hand offers far freer creative possibilities which reach to great depths of artistic involvement. The latter are also less tied to vertical symmetry, need no expensive machines and lessons are easily co-ordinated with the work in sculpture. In view of the already excessively technological world of the industrialised nations, in which aesthetic sensibility is withering away fast, such an additional technological field of activity could be readily dispensed with!

But let us not be too hasty! Have all the points of view and facts needed for a well-rounded judgement been considered? The question of a pedagogical justification certainly will and should be raised. All-important for Steiner in founding the Waldorf School was that 'life' should be brought into the school; that all the instincts for life be awakened, especially in the Upper School; that a sense for practical matters on the one hand and for an artistic sensibility on the other be nurtured.

Seen from this point of view, the pottery wheel is part of 'practical life' or, better said, practical life-experience, and can therefore be exemplary for all pupils. Ideally, every pupil should undergo such fundamental studies of life and for life – specialised, individualised, dependent on the school's individual situation.[5]

Let us observe and experience the Upper School pupils working on the wheel, comparing this with hand-built pottery as an activity.

In a school which had a well-conducted choir and a competent orchestra it could be observed that pupils who voluntarily took part in these were generally less burdened with problems and appeared freer than other pupils even though the additional activities created extra demands at home and at school. Weaker pupils with difficulties in languages or mathematics were also present in the group. But the musical pupils were generally more active (naturally there were exceptions), joined in more and were less at risk. They had to practise regularly and that helped them in other areas as well.

Now, all lessons cannot be made voluntary. But from Class 10 onwards a limited possibility can be created in crafts lessons, which are, after all, given in blocks. One group does pottery, another works at the same time with wood or metal; thus free choice by the pupil can be incorporated within clearly defined limits. This almost always has a positive effect as long as no disappointments occur. There is also an element of practice which can be brought in with the potter's wheel, indeed which it demands, just as a musical instrument does.

In alternating turning on the wheel with modelling by hand the following observations were made. Even though some pupils had a certain reluctance to try the wheel, it none the less exercised a powerful attraction. It was clear to the pupils that pottery on the wheel is significantly more difficult to learn and demands much more of them. It is fair to say that the enhanced dynamic resulting from the (still modern) technology of the wheel mechanism generates this fascination.

The difference between modelling and turning on the wheel is approximately the same as that between walking and riding a bicycle, between spinning with a spindle and spinning with a spinning wheel. The encounter with technology signifies a step forward, a step into an increased evolutionary speed, demanding correspondingly greater wakefulness. Because of the wheel's demands (the legs must be active as well), the pupils' will is more fully engaged and they must also be more attentive.

A further difference: through modelling relatively few vessels can be made during a block. Even though the creative process is more important than the result, the joy taken in the activity is dampened should the attempt to shape a few vessels well and attractively not succeed.

The possibility of not being distracted by conversations or of not being fully involved in the process, to be thinking about all sorts of other things, is far, far greater for modelling.

At the beginning, the emphasis in turning on the wheel lies not with the creative process but rather with the learning process, the development of skill with the hands, practising and practising again and again until the clay becomes a vessel.

The creative process comes second and slowly. Learning to play a musical instrument is similar; a great deal of practice precedes the moment when music first sounds. Once the basics are mastered, vessels can be completed on the wheel much faster than by hand. 'Production' techniques begin to come into play. We stand in the midst of a real-life, contemporary development. The pupils become truly active and increasingly engaged with the work.

In the long term, working simultaneously with hand-built methods and the wheel is pedagogically poor. It can play a transitional role when there are too few wheels available. The two kinds of pottery work should be separated as soon as possible. They are completely different in their effects upon the pupils.

The actual installation of pottery wheels will depend upon what space is available in the school. In the Stuttgart Uhlandhöhe School, the pupils sit at the wheels facing the wall. To some this may seem odd at first, but it has proved its worth and has never been objected to. The pupils can concentrate better on their work this way.

To begin each block we always gather around the large table in the modelling room. After a general introduction, each pupil makes a little bowl by hand, as described above. This bowl should fit into both hands cupped together. This preliminary activity exemplifies and clarifies the process of turning a pot on the wheel. In the next lesson, work then begins on the wheels.

We have here readily understandable technology: a round wheel-head on which the clay is turned by hand is fixed onto a vertical axle mounted so as to revolve freely both below, at floor level, and above, at table height. A large fly-wheel, the foot-wheel, is attached to the bottom of the axle. The foot-wheel's inertia ensures that the wheel-head will continue turning for a good long time once set rotating through the action of the right foot. The hands now come into play. If the platter slows down too much it is sped up again using the foot; hands and foot thus continue to work alternately. (For work with pupils, electric wheels are unnecessary and in my own judgement inadvisable.) The machinery must of course be properly maintained so that it turns freely.

As with modelling by hand, we begin on the

14. POTTERY LESSONS (CLASSES 9–12)

wheel by forming a ball of moist clay. This ball is without spatial orientation, seeming to float weightlessly. It is thrown forcefully onto the middle of the platter. It must cling firmly to this just as a sprouting seed must first take root before it can begin to grow upwards against the force of gravity. The disc of the wheel is like the earth turning in relation to the sun and stars. This is an incarnation event and must be seized courageously and energetically.

Considering ourselves as a micro-cosmos – compared to the macro-cosmos – around us, it could be said that the idea or imagination of what we want to create must enter the sculptural reality about to be shaped by our hands (the lump of clay). Our forehead and our eyes hover over the activity like sun and stars, wandering over the rotating earth, observing and examining it. Our will enters into what is taking shape on the wheel-head through our sculpting hands, just as in a marionette theatre our will enters into the puppets through the medium of the strings. We must enter into this new activity fully; it is an eternal recapitulation of the birth process itself, an awakening of formative forces and life. Water appears: our hands and the lump of clay are thoroughly wetted. The whole process of turning takes place amidst the element of water, for the clay must be kept slippery. Hands and clay both must be continually moistened, for the clay should never encounter friction from the hands, braking its spinning.

This series of steps should be followed by each individual pupil:

1. The lump of clay must be centred on the quickly turning disc. It is vital to first achieve a state of complete inner peace and concentration. The peaceful centre within must be found; for sanguines especially this is a goal which needs perpetual practice. The upper arms should rest alongside the body, whose weight gives power and resistance to the turning mass on the wheel-head.

2. Only when the clay is completely centred can the next step follow: the clay is to be opened up. Its centre is opened out into a funnel shape by the thumbs, freeing space within, the polar opposite of the preceding step. When everything is turning calmly and smoothly again and the funnel opening reaches down to the final thickness of the base (6–8 mm / ¼–⁵⁄₁₆ in), the next step is ready.

3. The base is formed out and carefully regulated to be level right out to where the wall begins. After the walls are again turning smoothly, they can be.

4. Raised up, forming the actual interior of the vessel; this is the most difficult step so far, to raise the weight of clay against the force of gravity. This work takes place while the clay is in a fluid, extremely unstable state. It must be accomplished calmly and carefully but also quickly, always holding the image of a peaceful, upright centre emanating down into the vessel and around which everything spirals. This lifting process can be repeated up to three times. The final form must be given using the fine sensitivity of the fingers and fingertips. A somewhat thicker edge should remain at the top, giving the vessel stability.

After all of these steps and the corresponding techniques – which cannot be described in detail here – are fully mastered, the pupil can begin to narrow the neck of or even fully close the vessel, creating a hollow interior space. (A pot and its lid are turned together; the lid is then sliced off using a wire and worked on further.) Except for flat bowls and plates, the cylinder is the starting point for all vessels. We must be perfectly secure in turning this before trying more complicated shapes.

After all this practice, it is always a lovely experience for the pupil when he or she manages to turn a jar and lid together in a single piece, cutting it open when it has reached a leather-like consistency and fitting the parts back together. The top always fits and the pupil has really learned and achieved something which offers strength and confidence for the rest of their life.

It is important that the teacher does not simply let the pupils experiment at random. It is easier to acquire than to overcome bad habits! The teacher must pay attention that the various steps are followed consistently. The teacher must observe each pupil precisely, keeping a sharp eye out for when help is required and not letting up until each technique is really mastered. He or she must clarify and demonstrate why one technique is done in one way and another in a different way as well as the effects of the various methods. Pupils must also be able to comprehend all this clearly. A new step may only be introduced after the previous one is brought to completion.

The pupils with the greatest difficulties must be given the most attention: we must repeatedly and patiently watch over their work, demonstrating techniques and offering praise to get them going. With ten or more pupils it is no easy task, especially at the beginning. But their progress, joy and enthusiasm will reward us well for our pains.

In shaping the pieces, what was said above about hand-built pots remains valid: shrinkage must be taken into account. Two special techniques remain to be learnt: the turning of the base or foot-ring on the partly dried, already leather-hard vessel and the mounting of a handle. Both of these must be practised just as intensively as the turning itself.

To turn the base, the leather-hard vessel must be centred upside-down on the wheel with the base up. This is no easier than the original centring and demands full attention and concentration. The process of turning is to lift off curls of clay with a specially formed turning tool, fully analogous to turning wood or metal on a lathe.

Mounting a handle is done with clay as moist as that used for turning. The handle is attached to the turned vessel above, squeezed into shape in its moist state (as if milking) and pressed on to attach it below.

The glazes are critical factors in the vessels' appearance. The pupils can run trials with them, using various glazes mixed together or over-laid. They are as yet unable to develop their own glazes.

Pottery blocks work quite well for Classes 10, 11 and 12. Pottery fits in beautifully with the emphasis on life-experience. In our experience, it is inadvisable to do pottery on the wheel in larger groups.

On-going practice is an absolute prerequisite for facility on the wheel. The intervals should not be excessively long, i.e. pupils should have no less than three double lessons per week. If this is impossible, it is better to do without the work on the wheel unless the pupils have the opportunity to practise in between. The blocks should also not be too short – eight weeks at a minimum, ten weeks or more being better still.

In Classes 11 and 12, some pupils will achieve a production rate sufficient that they may be very willing to give part of their work to be sold at the Christmas Market, possibly even helping run a stall themselves.

Pottery can be a particular help and even have a liberating effect on pupils suffering from the intellectual pressures of the Upper School. When done seriously with full engagement, its

14. POTTERY LESSONS (CLASSES 9–12)

archetypal qualities and formative character are revealed:

- First the pupils learn to concentrate (to centre the clay).
- They learn to open up to a higher reality, the contents (hollowing out the clay).
- They create a foundation for the contents (forming the base).
- They shape the vessels to suit the contents (raising up the wall and shaping it).

Clay

Upon entering the craft room of a Steiner-Waldorf school, its unique atmosphere will be noticed immediately. The woodwork room, the metalwork shop, the modelling or clay room and the pottery workshop: each has its own fully individual character corresponding to the materials used in the various spaces. Even more important than the material, however, is the relationship of the teacher responsible for the space to their environment: how they perceive their medium, how they care for and guard over what is entrusted to them by way of the space, medium and tools. The pupils partake of the room's atmosphere with an immediacy that allows them to experience all this quite deeply.

As used in pottery, clay neither reveals the processes of growth and development that it has been through nor does it show an identifiable structure, in contrast with solid wood and hard stone. It is precisely as if the clay has given up or sacrificed all that it once was in order to serve that which it may yet be. Originally, extremely fine siliceous clay was formed from primeval rock. Together with the coarser loam, sand and humus this provides the basis for plant growth on earth.

At the same time, clay is an ideal raw material for sculpture, pottery and the modern ceramics industry. Like wood, it both offers extraordinary creative potential and also possesses qualities which must be felt to be disadvantageous, especially if we have not taken them into account sufficiently in our work. Wood warps, shrinks and splits while drying. It is primarily active across the yearly rings. Clay shrinks approximately equally in all directions as long as it has been properly kneaded or pugged and can also dry out evenly. Good quality clay is a prerequisite for successful work and strongly influences the overall character of the finished product. Its most important and unique quality is its plasticity, its capacity to take the impress of the slightest pressure of hand or finger and then to maintain the finished form throughout the processes of drying and firing and beyond.

Now, all clays are not equal. There is coarse brick-makers' clay and the finest porcelain clay as well as a great variety of naturally occurring types in between. Of these, the best and most easily accessible are used industrially: they are dug up, processed and marketed commercially. Much of their natural character is unfortunately lost in modern processing. A completely different relationship to clay can be found by going in search of it ourselves. Even a fine loam is often very usable for modelling if first crumbled and put through a sieve through which the finest sand just passes. Mole heaps, river banks and flood plains of streams and rivers, defiles, building pits and large gravel pits all offer possibilities of discovering clay beds. Attention must be paid that there are no particles or bits of chalk in the clay and that no plaster bits are absorbed while the clay is drying on plaster boards. Clay or loam that can be picked up from brickyards is usually quite usable for sculpture and for modelling clay pots.

Renowned British potter Bernard Leach recognised the benefits of naturally found clay in comparison to that which has been processed: 'Rural potters used to dig for a single clean, usable clay located near to their ovens'. These early potters still sensed the whole elemental connection to nature, which bears unseen within it the primeval process by which clay arose. They were usually content with their direct experience of the clay, not seeking out a geological, mineralogical or particularly a chemical understanding of their raw material. In any case, there was little to be known, for science began to interest itself in this specialised field quite late. Even today there are only uncertain insights into it; huge questions remain. If a deeper interest develops for what is passing through our hands almost daily in the way of clays and glazes then the following may be discovered, broadly speaking:

Almost all clays arise from a transformation, crumbling and erosion of feldspar-bearing primary rock (granite and related stone); the causes are many and various. In the process of breaking up, quartz, feldspar and mica or hornblende separate out and disintegrate further. From the feldspar, only the mica-bearing kaolin remains behind at the original location, close to the mother lode. This pure and almost white 'primary clay' withstands high temperatures but is in itself unusable, having too little plasticity. The actual malleable clay used as a raw material by both potters and ourselves is termed 'secondary clay' and is generally found far from the mother rock. It is also called sedimentary clay. This has usually been washed away and carried quite far by the force of water. Further fine mineral and organic material became mixed in – partly at intermediate points of settlement – until the clay was deposited in its final location. Its characteristics are extremely dependent on the various possible processes involved in its origin and formation. Most common is iron-bearing clay which fires yellow to red, or at higher temperatures brown (brick and clinker clay). All colours, including those of the glazes, are produced by various metals and metal-oxides present. South of approximately the 49° of latitude almost all clay contains lime and cannot withstand high temperatures. Above 1100°C (2012°F) it suddenly melts.

The principal components of clay are:
- Quartz (siliceous acid) circa 50–70%
- Aluminium-oxide circa 20–30%

The remainder consists of minute quantities of oxides of iron, lime, titanium, magnesium and alkalies.

Generally, a 'richer' clay contains comparatively more aluminium-oxide and correspondingly less quartz; a lean clay the reverse, more quartz and less aluminium-oxide. Potters' clays are generally moderately rich and can absorb a considerable amount of water, giving them plasticity and malleability. A good clay takes time to mature; this is connected with its plasticity. It must lie wet and become saturated with water – this is called maturing – preferably out in the open where it can freeze in the winter and be rained upon in the summer. Before being shaped it must be thoroughly kneaded or pugged; this also applies to the moist, ready to use 'de-aired' clay marketed in plastic sacks.

Kneading must be learned as well; the most effective technique is spiral kneading. It is much more difficult than commonly supposed, for no air may be allowed into the clay. Should there be air bubbles in clay, they must be eliminated through kneading. The following is a guaranteed method of pugging the clay and eliminating any air: Take a block of clay and cut it with a thin wire

14. POTTERY LESSONS (CLASSES 9–12)

into two approximately equal parts. Slam the one half down onto the other so that edge meets edge or curved surface meets curved surface. Repeat about twenty times.

In the course of drying, a substantial reduction in volume occurs through evaporation; the 'richer' the clay is, the more it will shrink. It can easily happen that it warps or even cracks. To prevent this, the clay can be made leaner by adding ground shards, grog, sand or chalk. Clay shrinks as a result of losing its water content, becoming stable and hard but not yet durable. Sufficient water will dissolve it completely again, breaking it up and softening it, thus reconstituting it for re-use in modelling.

In the kiln the water – which is still chemically bound to the clay (water of crystallisation) – evaporates. The clay loses its malleability irrevocably, becoming stable in shape and durable. Its texture and colour change as well. Properly fired, clay becomes porous, relatively light, insulating, solid, weatherproof and heat-retentive. It feels pleasant to the touch. These are all treasured qualities, especially for building houses or (tile) ovens but also for common pottery or earthenware. Potters call fired clay 'biscuit'. Usually there are two firings. After the first firing, the so-called bisque or biscuit firing (circa 850–950°C/1560–1740°F) the pot is glazed. The second firing, the glaze firing, is done according to the glaze's melting point: earthenware at circa 1020–1080°C (1870–1975°F), stoneware at circa 1150–1300°C (2100–2370°F). At higher firing temperatures the clay begins to sinter (become a solid mass), shrinks further, becomes denser and extremely hard and absorbs virtually no more moisture. It loses a high degree of its insulating value and porosity (stoneware, clinker, porcelain). The shrinkage reaches circa 10% for brick clay or earthenware and up to 14% for stoneware.

Decoration and glazing should be briefly mentioned here. While still in a moist, leather-hard condition, a piece can be covered or painted with white or coloured clays (engobe) made into a thick mud (slipware). It can be decorated using sculptural tools, stamps and cutters. But it is the glaze, actually a layer of glass covering the piece, which really gives a piece a splendid beauty and colour. It smoothes, densifies and hardens the surface, making it considerably more useful through being much easier to clean. Large, built-up pots (e.g. floor vases) can also be waxed like wood or clay tiles.

In principle, a glaze has a similar constitution to the pot itself. It is thus irrevocably bonded to the underlying layer of clay. Malleable oxides are added to it to enable it to melt at low firing temperatures; lead is a familiar agent here, melting easily but poisonous in glazes. Nowadays, pre-melted glass, called frit, is usually used; this contains various finely ground liquefying agents in an insoluble form.

If you want to avoid bought-in glazes, study and above all trial and error will open up a rich, varied, very interesting and artistically stimulating realm. To enter into this here would lead us too far afield.

Until now we have described simple phenomena and experiences which are intended to help less-experienced practitioners to understand the medium and to avoid gross errors. This should be sufficient to make a start with the pupils, leading them into artistic activity and simple practical work with clay. For further help personal contacts, pottery and glazing courses and magazines and books on the subject are all to be recommended.

I would like to close with an observation from another point of view. Perhaps this will throw some light on the origin of the earth itself and the original formation of clays.

It is commonly thought that the minerals which make up clay and the raw materials of a glaze are inorganic, lifeless material. Through our artistic activity we try to let the form come alive and the material speak by sculpting and colouring the clay. When dry, clay no longer reveals the life which is natural to it in its moist state. We entrust our vessels to the kiln's burning heat, hoping for the best.

Honest self-observation reveals the child-like expectation that awaits the opening of the kiln after the glaze firing. Each successful piece arrives like an unexpected gift and is received, still warm in our hands, with unalloyed joy! We look with wonder at the often-surprising unity of form, colour, and surface. Previously, this was all lifeless earthly matter. Now beauty meets the eye! Disappointment is common enough, as well, but it hardly matters in the face of a single life-imbued success! We have contributed to this through our skill and perhaps a lucky touch, but we have by no means done it all. What lies hidden in the world of the 'lifeless' minerals, e.g. in quartz and metal? What lies hidden in fire?

To approach this question, it might be valuable to take a look at various descriptions of potters' mature life experience with pottery:

Slowly I began to comprehend why potters – as in my own case – search for years to find their raw materials outside in nature instead of using standardised, dependable and good quality clays. There is an archetypal instinct at work here that longs to find its way back to the source: not only to the source of the clay and glaze materials but also to the source of our inspiration, the potter's invisible material.[6]

We have arrived at a significant juncture leading us into spiritual realms: to Goethe's artistic genius and Rudolf Steiner's spiritual science.

In his geological research, Goethe recognised the ideal scientific 'system' as not originating with the researcher but with nature itself. Reality contains an order implicit in it. This order is not accidental. Where does it come from?

In his cosmology, Rudolf Steiner presents the principles underlying the formation of the mineral kingdom of the earth in such a way that the earth's mineral deposits appear as the metamorphosed remains of earlier life-forms.

It is obvious that life cannot arise from inorganic, lifeless substance were these not themselves originally imbued with life. Nowhere can life be observed to arise directly from lifeless matter. The reverse process is completely different; living forms can die and leave dead material behind. Thus Steiner describes earthly substances as arising out of originally living matter which then undergoes death processes. We can thus understand the enormous mass of chalk mountains which have come into being through animal life. We can understand how coal and oil exist thanks to mighty, hardly imaginable organic processes. We can truly envisage how the earth had to undergo many metamorphoses before the human being could set foot on solid ground.

Let us look more carefully at our malleable clay. Just as all life must go through death in order not to become fixed and frozen, so that which should serve life of a higher order must give up its old established structure and be renewed.

The forms of creation's work ever renewing,
All armouring growth's rigidity strewing:
Eternally active, life-imbuing doing!

14. POTTERY LESSONS (CLASSES 9–12)

Primeval rock crumbles and erodes down to fine mineral particles. Water converts these particles from a crystalline into a colloidal state; the latter is highly unstable, however, and can easily revert to its original condition (primary clay or kaolin). Colloid solutions play a role primarily in living organisms, e.g. in protein combinations.

In secondary clay formations (malleable clay), a process begins under particular conditions enabling completely new minerals with a very finely layered mica structure to arise out of the colloidal particles mentioned above. (Humus arises in a similar way.) These extremely fine, leaf-like layers are not in crystalline form (which mica is); they are thus capable of binding large quantities of water. This water is what makes the clay malleable. This is, in contrast to unyielding rock, a new development, a life process of the earth not following the usual chemical laws. Inherent in it is something of the natural laws of the primeval mineral-plant world which preceded the formation of primary rock in earth's evolution.

Recall that this formative process does not end with the settlement of the clay, that clay through maturing in the open air – through a rhythmic process of getting wet, drying out, freezing and thawing, of summer and winter and day and night – is becoming ever more malleable. We can also see this as a preparation for new life processes; it is as if the clay would speak: 'Come, shape me, work with me!'

We can ask how it has come about that in the German language the word for malleable earth (*Ton*, clay) is the same word as that for a musical 'tone'. Perhaps an explanation lies in what Steiner says about musical tones:

> *The evolution of form in matter can be properly compared with the formation of form through tones (Chladny figures). Archetypal processes are revealed here. All form is frozen music. The sounding tones must first battle their way through primeval fires. The mineral and animal kingdoms: actually everything is music which has fought its way through fire.*[7]

15

Pottery workshops and modelling rooms
Michael Martin

Pottery and sculpture appear to be closely related activities when the medium and tools are considered on their own. However, there are fundamental differences between them.

The potter's starting point for shaping a piece is the interior space. The original ball of clay is hollowed out, and a cavity which is isolated from the expanses of surrounding space is established. This cavity is made to receive something which it should hold safely and protect. If the vessel has a narrow neck, the interior space is more sensed than seen. The sense of touch working together with the senses of movement and balance are used to create the form. These 'dark senses' are independent of light and the eye and can be active even in total darkness through the hands.

While sculpting, forms are either built up from the inside outwards or else are opened up to embrace the surrounding space. It doesn't matter whether a sculpture is solid or hollow beneath the outer surface. Light and shadow play on it, bringing the surface to life. The relationship of the sculpture to space around is vitally important; changing light and viewing distance affect how the form is perceived. The senses of touch, movement and balance are more active by way of the eyes when viewing it, for a sculpture is usually viewed at a distance. It is important to occasionally step back from the piece while working on it for this reason.

The pottery vessel is experienced in relation to its own interior, its centre, while sculpture is experienced in relation to the periphery. Thus, the potter begins forming his work from the centre outwards, the sculptor from the periphery inwards. Motifs for the architecture of the corresponding craft rooms can be found here.

The pottery workshop is connected with the earth. In our school, an old laundry was used for this. The entrance led a few steps down from the garden; a moist, earthy odour greeted the entering pupils. Copper washbasins served to mix and soak the clay, which came from the immediate surroundings. The pupils experienced the processes involved in preparing the clay for use. This created a well-grounded atmosphere which harmonised with the nature of the work.

When firing pots, even the flame does not leap up freely into the sky, but must be thrown back by the kiln's heavy stone enclosure and inwardly concentrated. Finally, glazing is a kind of science concerned with earth and minerals, just as pottery is tied to the earth by the nature of the medium.

15. POTTERY WORKSHOPS AND MODELLING ROOMS

The flowing silhouettes of the fat-bellied vessels on the shelves reflect the watery element out of which they arise. Wall shelves displaying colourfully painted plates, mugs and jugs once made up the decorative centrepiece of the kitchen of town house or farmhouse. Centuries-old barrel-vaulted ceilings would give the proper character to a pottery space; even a slightly vaulted wooden ceiling would do much. The floor should be able to be wet-mopped in order to pick up the dry clay dust, glazing's worst enemy. A separate room should definitely be provided for the glazing.

The modelling or sculpture room, on the contrary, needs light and space; clerestories can provide this from above. Shadows must be thrown, though; the form dissolves in light alone. Sculpture lifts us into expanses of life-imbued space. It is important that pupils stand while modelling; the upright of one's own body stimulates the creative powers of the hands to give form to the clay. Tables can be high and supplemented by modelling stands. The elasticity of the floor is important while standing; this should be taken into account: a wooden floor laid on joists is one good solution.

Cups, bowls and dishes are well-suited to group arrangements, perhaps grouped around a jug; they are by their nature sociable. Sculpture is rarely shown grouped together, for every sculpture requires its own space in which it sits comfortably and which suits it. Jugs, vases and bowls are shaped by the hand in a mechanical fashion and are therefore reproducible, even in various sizes, with sufficient practice. When rotated on their own axis they maintain the same appearance (the handle and lip of the jug are added later). It is striking that the usual styles today can mostly be traced back to basic shapes which originated as far back as prehistoric times. This reveals the extremely slow development and almost tentative rate of change which characterises the craft. A sculpture, on the other hand, shows a new face with every slight rotation. The art of sculpture has continually evolved over the course of the centuries. A piece is created by the living organisation and free movements of the limbs; each is unique.

Sculpture is also liberated from the necessity to serve a particular use, which a potter is always duty-bound to consider. A jug that is unusable is reduced to a purely decorative function. Pottery has this aspect in common with architecture; both are tied to the necessities of the human body. The former thus approaches that archetypal mother of all the arts. Pottery, like architecture, actively creates space.

In sculpture, what is important is the presentation of forces, the dynamic of either the human body, an animal form or just a movement between surfaces. This is expressed through forms which are either free-standing in space or contribute to shape the space as relief. Sculpture takes hold of and renews the life-bearing, formative forces of the human being.

The completely different starting points for sculpture and pottery thus become clear. Naturally, these have a living interplay and indeed are often consciously exchanged. Above all, no relative value judgement is implied by this (somewhat sketchy) presentation.

16

The shoemaking block (Class 9)
Gerard Locher

Hundreds of years of mystery surround cobblers and their craft. Stories, fables and legends testify to people's interest in shoemakers and their work over many centuries. There are also the stories told by the shoemakers themselves, thought of during their work. The shoemakers' guild, one of the oldest and first mentioned in Trier in 1104, was highly respected, even though they were considered as 'yarn-spinning folk'. This provides proof of the shoemaker's lively, creative spirit, in addition to their trained eye, skilled hands and the thorough knowledge of their trade that is shared with other craftsmen. They were considered to be eccentric and fond of philosophising. No other trade or craft has produced as many important individuals – such as Hans Sachs, Hans von Sagan and Jakob Boehme.

It would not be amiss to connect these qualities to the part of the body and its covering, foot and shoe, which is the cobbler's business. The workshop itself had an extraordinary attraction for people; they liked to congregate there. Leather, too, has a special quality. It is cured from animal skins, an organic material familiar to people. All of which led to the saying: 'Cobbler, stick to your last!'

Although, or perhaps because, the cobbler's craft is a basic one, we do not indulge in nostalgia during our shoemaking block. What we are dealing with are highly topical problems, a subject whose importance will be fully acknowledged in future.

Rudolf Steiner mentioned shoemaking, among other subjects, during a lecture on education and the curriculum of the Stuttgart Waldorf School, soon after its opening:

I should have liked, if it were possible, to have employed a shoemaker as one of the teachers. Current requirements do not permit this. But it would be good for the children to learn how to make shoes – not theoretically, but actually making them, experiencing every detailed skill. It was impossible to persuade the authorities to allow a shoemaker to be employed as a teacher. But it would benefit the children immensely.[1]

On another occasion he said: 'A real philosopher ought to have made at least one pair of boots'.[2] Rudolf Steiner's fondness of shoemaking is obvious. He gave it a special dimension that can indeed be experienced in the doing. His most important statement is undoubtedly, that one should experience every single detailed skill in the making of shoes.

16. THE SHOEMAKING BLOCK (CLASS 9)

When making shoes we are continuously concentrating on the foot, the organ most intimately related to the earth. Our feet are adapted directly to the earth, as well as to the weight they must support. Through pressure and counter-pressure, their mature form is developed during the third seven-year period. In addition, they are of immense significance for the energies connected with the upright posture and for the developing self. The causes for many a foot problem in adult life can be found during puberty. This shows that special attention must be given to the feet during this time.

At the same time these considerations allow us to understand why the shoemaking block is given in Class 9. It is the time of puberty and the beginning of the development of the personality emerging through the young person's own inner life.

The inner processes that occur during puberty are often mysterious and difficult to see, because of the adolescent's reluctance to speak about his or her experiences. He holds something back for his private life, because he tentatively opens up a new inner space that can begin to receive and work with the problems he encounters.[3]

Here, too, Rudolf Steiner is helping us with his indication that the quite personal destiny of the young is now beginning to make itself felt. The light-filled time of early childhood is over, the newly developing inner space is still dark – but it contains a spark that can, through the adolescent's own strength and effort, kindle a new light, at first within this space and, later more and more raying out into the environment.[4]

Ultimately, the making of shoes is nothing else but the forming of an inner space! Imagine the inner space of a shoe not correctly shaped! Most of us have at one time suffered the consequences.

A shoe may be described as a convex-concave hollow body without an axis of symmetry. Examining it more closely, we shall see that there is a left and a right, and that the axis of symmetry lies between both feet. This means: the students are not working, as they do in the other main-lesson blocks, with one object, but must occupy themselves continuously and simultaneously with two, left as well as right, and this homologously as well.

The outer shape of the shoe is, according to this view, of secondary importance. It is sad to see the unfortunate impact of fashions on our young, even when damage to health is the consequence. It is frequently only at the end of a block, when the students put on their shoes (even though they are not pointed enough!) that they have the striking experience of the shaped inner space and, with it, the enjoyment of the work. What they recognise is a universally valid law – be it in shoemaking or architecture – that a well formed inner space makes at the same time for timeless beauty of outer form.

In order to do justice to Rudolf Steiner's indications, it seems to be important that the structure of the shoemaking block corresponds to that of the traditional 'archetypal' craft. This means a clear sequence of the single work stages and material from the flat leather to the upright standing product (the shoe).

The following essay of such a block can do no more than give a faint impression of the work. The soft, tough leather with its typical smell, the unfamiliar tools and work processes engender their very own atmosphere that is further underlined by the initially quite strangely sounding vocabulary used in the trade.

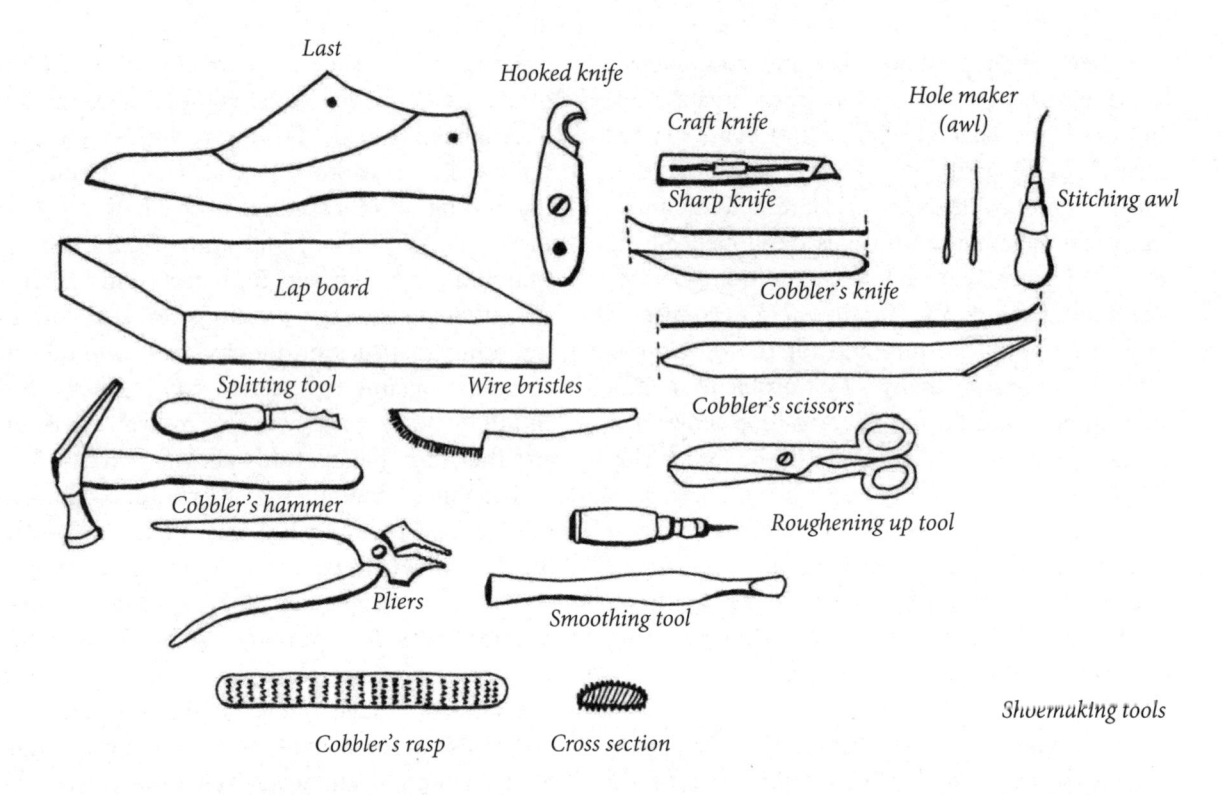

Shoemaking tools: Last, Hooked knife, Craft knife, Hole maker (awl), Sharp knife, Stitching awl, Lap board, Cobbler's knife, Splitting tool, Wire bristles, Cobbler's scissors, Cobbler's hammer, Roughening up tool, Pliers, Smoothing tool, Cobbler's rasp, Cross section

The strict logic behind the processes demands strict discipline of the students if the work is to be successful, i.e. if the shoes are to fit. But they are in the position of fully understanding each step of the work and thus able to follow the 'master's' instructions. And this is, from a pedagogical point of view, especially important at this age.

All the students in Class 9 participate in a four weeks block of shoemaking. The groups do not exceed ten students. About thirty-five lessons are required for the making of a pair of shoes. The work is supported by subjects dealing with the materials used, the history of shoemaking and anatomical aspects.

It will be noted that the work sequences are such that the students can become ever more familiar with the materials and that the different procedures keep repeating themselves in an ever more delicate way until the work is completed. This means that there is hardly any work done that is not later applied to the different parts of the shoes. The many different working steps and tools, when exactly observed, also appear to be logical and comprehensible.

Illustrated (above) is an adequate assortment of shoemaking tools for our work. More specialised tools are usually added to the collection during the years.

Day one

The students learn about different methods of tanning leather. The differences between chrome and vegetative leather is shown; and hygienic and technological issues connected

16. THE SHOEMAKING BLOCK (CLASS 9)

with tanning are studied. The size of an average cow hide (6–8 m²/7–9½ yd²), as well as the qualities of leather in the different parts of the skin, is demonstrated.

The students then measure each other's feet; eighteen measurements are taken. This establishes a direct contact with the feet of another person. The student doing the measuring is also responsible for the fitting of the shoes someone else will make. Thus the necessity of exact workmanship develops by itself.

Since the Class 9 curriculum includes the study of the human skeleton (in the biology main-lesson), the exact study of the bony structure of the foot connects nicely with this block. This allows for a discussion on healthy and harmful footwear. The students frequently bring some of their shoes to school on the following day.

With the help of the eighteen measurements, the teacher then selects the corresponding lasts for each student. They serve as models for the feet on which the shoes are shaped.

Day two

The inner sole is fitted to the bottom of the last. It is described as the sole of the shoe and, because of its direct contact with the foot, the best leather ought to be used for it. It participates to a high degree in the breathing of the foot. The leather must be fulled up on the last in a wet condition, so that it may adapt to the curves of the sole on the last. This demands some degree of skill, as last, tools and leather must be held on the lapboard. In this way, one literally 'grasps' the complicated shape of the last that, during the course of the work, becomes more and more hidden behind the leather and yet provides the measurements for the correct shaping of the shoe. In the fulling process we have the first,

Profile of a foot:

1. the line of the sole
2. line of the circumference
3. measure of the forefoot
4. measure of the ball of the foot
5. measure of the widest part of the foot
6. measure of the instep
7. measure of the bend of the heel, I
8. measure of the bend of the heel, II
9. measure of the ankle
10. point of the bend of the heel
11. measure of the joint

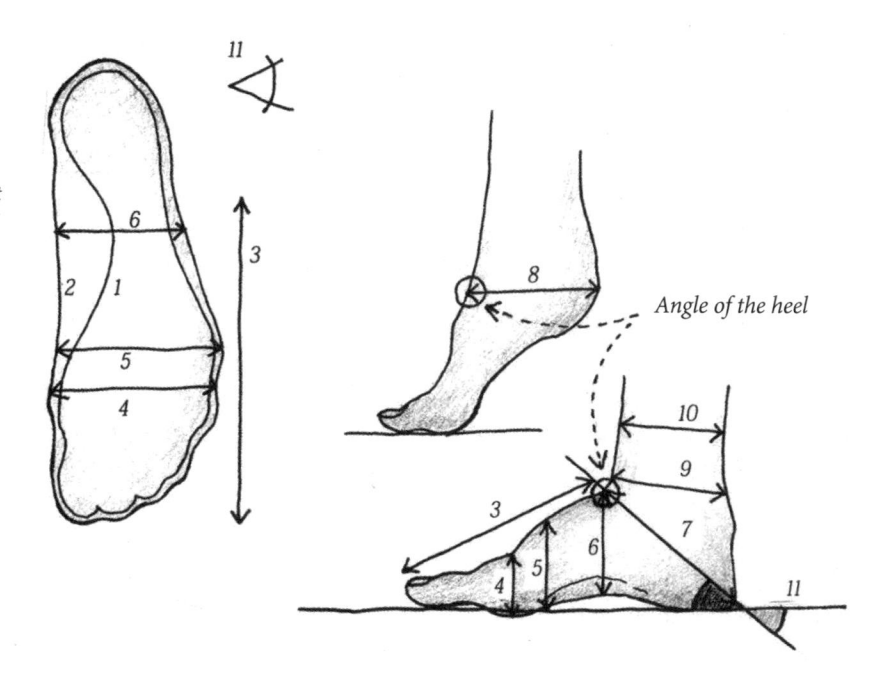

Measurements of the foot

still rather crude, contact with the leather; but many of the working steps are already included which will, in a more refined form, be repeated later on.

Day three

The curved form of the sole is cut from the inner sole leather that has in the meantime dried.

The next stage is the drawing of the outline on the upper leather for which a paper stencil was prepared. The different parts are then cut out, not an easy task considering the tough, elastic nature of the material. It demands the greatest concentration. The leather tends to pull away from the knife, and the attempt at correcting the matter afterwards through cutting away the excess only worsens it and the student has to start again. It is only a courageous approach that will be immediately successful.

The next stage has proved to be the most difficult for students: the thinning (sharpening) of the leather at the edges where two pieces have to be joined. It requires a strong feeling for the material and takes a whole day of practising before daring to attack it.

Days four and five

The different parts are sewn together, using the saddle stitching method. The sewing is done simultaneously at the two threads ending with two bristles (the 'pins'). As they sew, the students quickly get into an individual rhythm. They are obviously enjoying the work – as they see the shoe visibly growing under their hands; indeed, the time simply rushes by!

Day six

The single parts are connected on the last. Except for the actual removal of the shoe from the last, this is really the most exciting day of the block. The lower and upper parts are joined! This means the leather is thrashed from above over the last as, before, the inner sole was fastened to the last from below.

Days seven and eight

Inner and outer soles are accurately glued together. The subsequent work also is a more delicate confrontation with the shape of the last. It is only when the 'frame' (a strip of leather fixed to the edge of the sole) harmoniously meets the overall shape of the shoe that the usable interplay between sole and upper leather is guaranteed. The student here is once again directly confronted with left and right, as the shapes of the soles must obviously be as similar as possible.

Days nine and ten

The sustaining lower part of the shoe is glued on and the holes punched for the nails. The wooden nails are then driven in. The control of the cobbler's hammer is here put to the test! It is only then that the nails can be driven in (with three blows), securely joining the several layers.

16. THE SHOEMAKING BLOCK (CLASS 9)

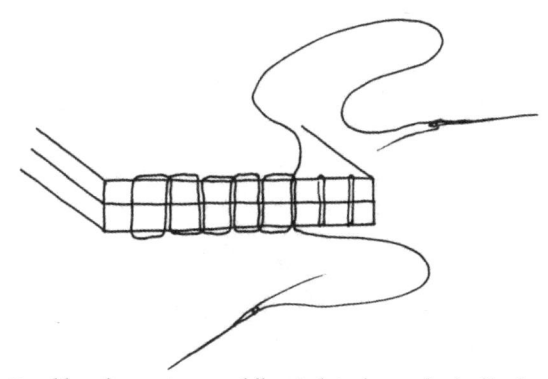

Double soling using a saddle stitch is the method of both shoemaker and saddler: 'Doubly sewn lasts longer!'

Hammering the inner sole on the lapboard

Fulled-up inner sole

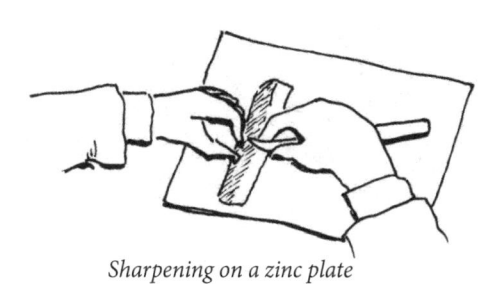

Sharpening on a zinc plate

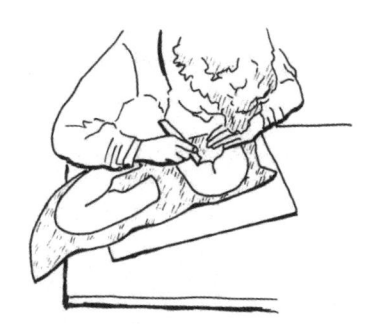

Stitching awl

Upper thread

Shaft

Lower thread

Cutting and flaying the parts of the shoe on a zinc plate

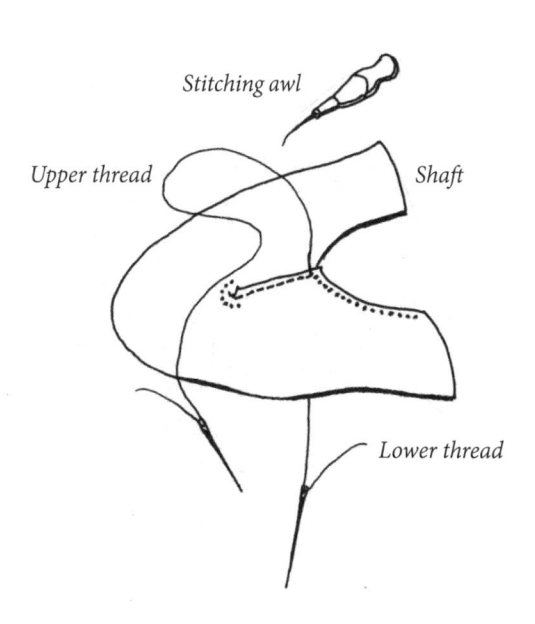

153

PART THREE: CRAFTS IN THE UPPER SCHOOL

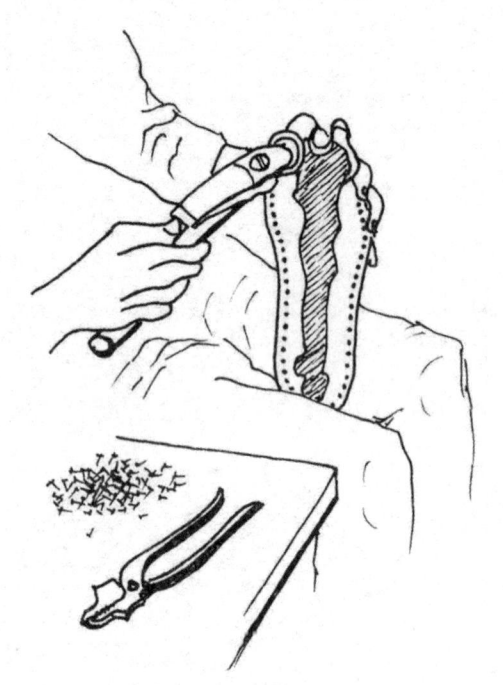

Tacking of the leather

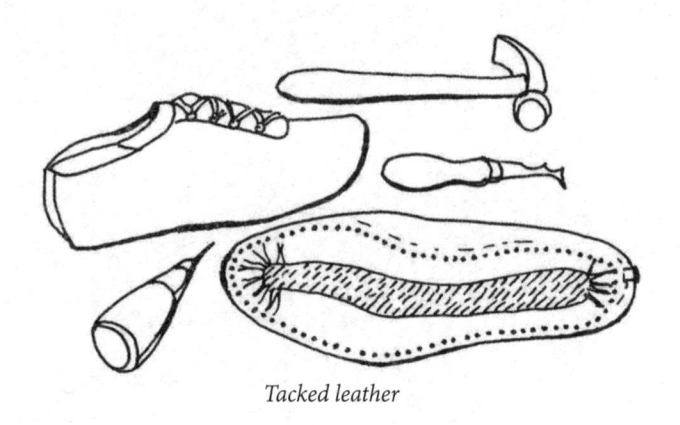

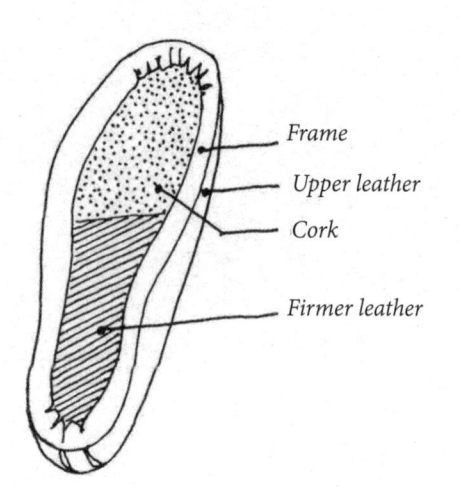

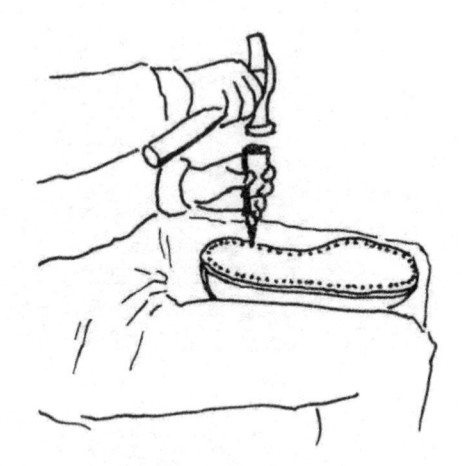

Frame
Upper leather
Cork
Firmer leather

Punching holes for the wooden nails

Tacked leather

16. THE SHOEMAKING BLOCK (CLASS 9)

Day eleven

The heel is built up from leather off-cuts and fastened with wooden nails.

Day twelve

The final touches are given. If wished, the shoes may be dyed. The sole edges are smoothed and waxed. The shoes are then rubbed with a fatty substance, removed from the last, and the inside rasped and smoothed.

The culmination, the high point, of our project is the moment when the shoes are actually put on; it is something to be experienced! The students who jokingly referred to the lessons as 'torture' now see the fulfilment of their struggles, i.e. the inner space they themselves created. They are proud of their achievement, often surprised at their skills.

In spite of its brevity, this essay, may, perhaps, show that it is possible in a relatively short time to produce excellent shoes, provided that everything has been thoroughly prepared by the teacher.

The total process – measuring, making the several parts, fitting them together – is similar to tailoring, but concentrates on the foot, a matter of importance for the development of the students during puberty.

Due to the lack of suitable teachers the shoemaking block is relatively new in our schools. The growing interest in it, however, seems to be proof of its necessary place in Steiner-Waldorf schools.

17

Working with metals (Classes 9 and 10)
Herbert Seufert

The development of the hands and the materials used

Craftspeople create a new world with their hands, supplementing nature at a higher level while the hands themselves have remained at an early stage of evolution. Moles have paws that have evolved into digging tools, fish have fins for swimming and squirrels have claws for climbing. Our human hands can do all the things that animals have perfected in their specialised ways, although less ably, in a universal way. We assign all the very specialised uses to the tools we construct, through which we conquer the nature of the various materials. These tools obey the laws of mechanics which we experience in our skeleton, especially when it is a matter of dealing with hard materials.

Rudolf Steiner tells us how the child's skeleton, after the twelfth year, adapts to the world outside. It submits to the laws of mechanics and dynamics we find to be working independently of the human being.[1] Before this age, the skeleton is more elastic, more in keeping with the static and moving impulses emanating from children's inner beings. It now receives an objective characteristic as though it were no longer part of the human organism, because of its submission to the general laws of mechanics.

If, for example, I hit a nail with a hammer, the effect is identical with that produced by a mechanically driven hammer. The work I can do through the mechanics of my bones corresponds to an activity that can be carried out without me. Unconsciously, a connection arises between my own physical mechanism and the laws of mechanics of the world outside. This development enables children to construct logical trains of thought and to perceive cause and effect in the processes, which are always present in craftwork. I immediately experience why a nail bends when I drive it in badly; my observation teaches me, and the outer reality makes me correct my mistake. This knowledge leads directly to the introduction of the specialised crafts at this age. It should not be done prematurely, because the limbs, the hands with their knuckle bones still retain a remnant of their child nature until twelve to fifteen years old. It is only then that they develop their final form.[2] This physiological fact is the reason why we only now expect the hands to be ready for their corresponding manual activities. They can and should now become the full and complete bearers of will.

17. WORKING WITH METALS (CLASSES 9 AND 10)

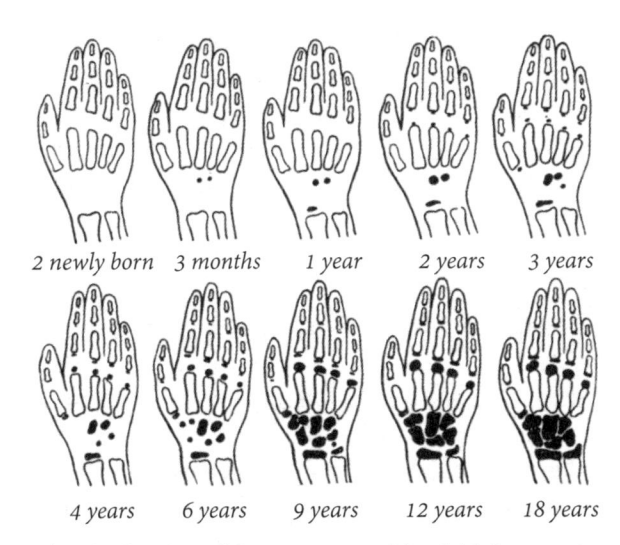

2 newly born   3 months   1 year   2 years   3 years

4 years   6 years   9 years   12 years   18 years

The development of the wrist joints of the child, from:
A. Kipp, *Evolution of the Human Being*

During the craft and handwork lessons the students are made familiar with the quite different methods of work, determined by the material used. Every material requires its own corresponding way of handling, as well as the special, appropriate tools. If we survey the origin of our materials, we shall see a long line reaching as far as to the inorganic kingdom. Wool, wax, silk and leather come from animals. Wood, willow, cotton, hemp and paper are gifts from the plant world. From the mineral kingdom we receive our clay, the metals and stones we dig from holes, quarries and mines.

The young children begin to work with wool. Soft, warm and pliant it feels good to the hands in whose warmth wax also becomes pliable. Wood already demands the stronger hands of children in the Middle School during the woodcarving and basket-weaving lessons.

The challenges increase in the Upper School when metalwork and stone masonry are introduced. The increasing hardness of the materials, their resistance to being shaped, corresponds to the developmental stages of the students and to the possibilities arising from them. Step by step children and adolescents are thus introduced to the really practical and material life.

Thoughts on metalwork

Metals lie secluded beneath the surface of the earth across which we are moving and on which we realise our destiny. We find the mineral veins, containing the ores, enclosed and rigid in the cracks and clefts of the rocks, colourfully sparkling, frequently as magnificent crystals. Often such rocks are permeated by delicately distributed metals whose presence is revealed only by its noticeable weight. With their main ingredients of oxides, silica and carbons, the metals participate in the formation of rocks without actually being recognisable as such.

It is only on rare occasions that we find a metal in its pure, unmixed state – 'true and genuine' in the language of the miner. It is the precious metals, gold and silver, that are found in their pure state and that were consequently used by craftspeople and artists in ancient times. Copper also is often found in its 'true and genuine' forms. It was the most used metal during the copper/bronze age. Only much later did iron come into its own, and later still the other metals whose extraction and production proved to be highly technical.

It is almost impossible to imagine our daily life without metals. Despite the increased use of artificial materials, metals still play a decisive role everywhere in our lives. How did people manage without them in ancient times?

Successive epochs have been named after the minerals/metals associated with them: the Stone Age, Copper/Bronze Age, Iron Age. The metals were also represented in mythology: the golden, silver and brass ages.

Children recapitulate these ages. We may observe something akin to the ancient Greeks in our Class 5 children, or to the Romans in Class 6. The teaching of history is brought up to the present in Class 8. Class 9 concentrates on technological achievements: the steam engine, the telephone etc. Each of these ages depends on the advancing extraction use of metals.

In the mythological past, the sons of Cain gave us the crafts and the arts: Jubal – house building and the breeding of domestic animals; Jabal – music, and the smith Tubulcain – the crafts. Like Prometheus, he brought fire from heaven and gave it to his people. Their sister Naemi is frequently forgotten. Like her primal mother Eve, she gave humankind the knowledge of spinning and weaving.

Giotto, in the Campanile next to the Cathedral of Florence, painted the activities of the children of Cain. Reproductions of these pictures in our workshops provide the rooms with their special character and happily complement the practical work of the students.

Copper and iron have proved to be the best metals from a pedagogical and technological point of view. They are, after all, the most commonly used metals. Three of their basic characteristics are as follows:

Metals can be cut: by sawing, chiselling, filing, drilling, cutting, grinding etc. This they share with other materials, such as wood.

Metals can be melted. We know the custom of lead-melting on New Year's Eve, and we might have visited a smelting plant. Metals allow themselves to be changed from a solid to a liquid state, which enables them to be poured into moulds, cooled and rigidified in the required shape. They also mix with other metals in their liquid state, forming the various alloys. We already know about melting in candle making. This property of melting is typical of metals.

Metals can be stretched and compressed: a dent

Tubulcain: blacksmith

Adam delving and Eve spinning

Andrea Pisano, Campanile of the Cathedral in Florence, 1348/49

17. WORKING WITH METALS (CLASSES 9 AND 10)

in a tin surface is such a process of mis-formation. Consciously placing dent beside dent will force the stretched tin into the desired shape. Or, vice versa, in compression – not unlike the kneading of clay – the shape is produced by pressing the metal. Bending, for example, results in the stretching of the outer surface of a metal plate and in the compression of the inner.

Rolling and pulling are part of the process. A bar of metal is made thinner by being forced through two rollers. In the manufacture of wire, the cross section is reduced by driving the metal through conic holes, stretching the metal longitudinally. Quite special shapes may be rolled and pushed in this way. It is fascinating to watch the brightly glowing iron bars being stretched and shaped into the required rods in a manufacturing plant. Or to see the gold stretched to such a degree that 1 g (0.04 oz) of it can be made into a 2 km (1¼ miles) long wire. We know that it is possible to beat a piece of leaf gold, the size of the point of a needle, into a 10 cm² (4 in²) area so that it is transparent to light, thus giving it a quite wonderful, greeny/blue colouring.

Metals have the property of cohesion. They differ in their qualities of brittleness or pliancy, and the ways of working with them will have to correspond to their properties. But they all share the three basic elements known in metallurgy as divisibility, malleability and elasticity. The students are to perceive all these processes and, if possible, execute them themselves.

In copper work a piece is cut out, filed and polished with emery paper. Here we have the first element, i.e. the divisibility – cutting up. The metal is beaten on a special board and, through the resulting stretching, the required form is produced. A goblet that gets its shape through being drawn, belongs to the category of compression. The handle receives its required form through bending – we here experience the stretchability.

If they wish to connect parts of the metal – e.g. the handle with the pot, the hanger with the wall lamp, the spout with the watering can – the students will learn the art of soldering, a process made possible through the malleability of the metal. The parts to be joined are heated until the melting temperature of the solder is reached. The liquid solder flows into the cracks and binds the parts after cooling and hardening.

The students experience malleability in a much more impressive way during the pouring of metals when they relinquish their previous form, melt, showing an even, mirror-like surface, and then fill the desired hollow form. Really uplifting and at the same time demanding respect, is the experience of seeing metals like brass or bronze (which are hard to melt) being made liquid in graphite containers, glowing white at extremely high temperatures, and then poured – a dangerous procedure! – into the moulds. Schiller's poem *The Bell* reflects something of the mood of this greatest of all concentration, caution and the tense moment of watching for the success of this procedure – waiting for the cooling process, the opening of the mould and the joy on seeing that the metal has indeed filled every single corner of the mould. The steaming, hot sand is then brushed off and the finished product lies there, shining before one's eyes! We watch the original form of the metal dissolve, see its liquid condition, its brightness, experience the heat, the smoke, the pouring from the container, the re-solidifying and the assumption of the new form. These processes are pictures of processes that are unconsciously working in human beings: dying and becoming, purification in fire, re-birth at a higher level.

Everybody should have this experience of watching the pouring of metals. Seeing the flow of melted, white glowing iron, raying out in the almost unbearable heat, affects us deeply. We feel as though taken to the beginning of a new creation. We sense will-forces in the process of creation. In the liquid metal, matter itself becomes warmth-giving light, prior to the assumption of a new form.

Divisibility, melting ability, elasticity are those special properties of metals that distinguish them from other materials. On the one hand, their brittleness and hardness resist the attempts of man; on the other hand, they allow themselves to be dissolved as far as the liquid state and to be remoulded. Extreme hardness (as in steel) and extreme dissolution stand next to each other. The human being has conquered them and put them to his service. In between are the possibilities of stretching and compressing that we utilise in the work with copper and iron. In all this, the participation of heat is the prerequisite.

We now also become aware of the important role of the watery element during the Class 8 craft lessons, especially in the form-giving processes in pottery, but also to a lesser extent in basketmaking. The work with iron in Class 10 is undoubtedly the high point of the immediate experience of the intense heat; and the connection between these and the upward surging will-forces of the adolescents, so often referred to is clear: inner warmth processes are challenged and called forth through the activity with the outer forces of fire!

The work with copper may be seen as a transition, as stretching and compression occur in a cold condition (as with clay), heat merely making the material easier to work with, without actually affecting the shape. The heat of the flame loosens, softens what had become too rigid and hard through the use of the hammer. Thickening and loosening are as in- and out-breathing and, indeed, we shall discover the clenching and stretching of the hand we know so well in eurythmy in a transformed way related to the work with metals, i.e. stretching through hammering and the cooling down process. Working with copper is a harmonising activity between the work with very rigid and liquid materials.

We must draw attention to a quite different relation to the forces of the centre. In copper work are brought into play the different, even opposing functions of the right and left hands that, despite their independence, must harmonise in a precise way.

This constitutes an essential moment during the 'slipping into' the working process. The students separate themselves from their subjective nature and are compelled to pay heed – quite objectively – to every necessary step of the work. They must be fully awake and think of what they are doing. The more complex the exercise, the stronger must be the strength of the ego to hold things together.

Working with copper

Copper work is introduced in our school in Class 9, with at least fifteen to eighteen double lessons. To begin with, the students are made familiar with the room and the tools – the hammers that require careful handling, the cutting tools, files and tongues. They are told of the sources of danger and, last but not least, they are shown the material.

Copper is stored in the form of sheets, pipes, wire and thick rods. When a sheet of copper is held before them they invariably exclaim: 'Isn't it beautiful!' and 'Just look – what a great red!' The question of its monetary worth also arises. The answer increases their respect. The properties of the

17. WORKING WITH METALS (CLASSES 9 AND 10)

metal are then enumerated: it warms quickly when held in the hand – this they can immediately put to the test and confirm. This property is utilised in the copper cable as the ideal conduit of electricity.

A well-rolled sheet is then heated and cooled down. Again the amazement at the softness and pliancy that results from it; and at the restored hardness after it has been worked with. Heating results in loss of colour – the metal turns black and oxidises. But the blue flame of the burner suddenly turns into a beautiful green, the dark surface of the copper shimmers in yellow, green and blue colour hues. What a pity the colours disappear during the cooling!

The students now hear about the origin of copper. It is not only found in the form of copper ore, but also as reddish-golden shimmering metal, without the foreign particles that would class it as an ore. What a wealth of pure copper exists in North America, in Africa where the most beautifully coloured copper ores are to be found in the depths of the mines, especially malachite and azurite.

In Europe we frequently find the golden shimmering copper pyrites and the black copper oxide ores. The students are deeply interested in the mysterious formations and colour of these treasures the earth harbours.

Where did people in ancient times find this metal and how did it get its name? Cyprus was known as the Copper Island. The name 'cuprum' derives from *Kypros*, the ancient name of the island on whose shores – according to Greek mythology – Aphrodite, the goddess of beauty, landed from a shell. Remember the now justified exclamation of one of the students on seeing the copper sheet: 'How beautiful!'

A rather pale girl is now looking at the mirror-like sheet and sees her fresh complexion reflected in the red copper. Indeed, the goddesses had well polished copper mirrors! We can fully understand why the Greeks were looking for the birthplace of the goddess of beauty in the vicinity of the copper island – especially as copper was used for the making of ornaments and vessels rather than for weapons. For a long time, this goddess was known to be connected with the planet Venus. Her beauty radiated, as it were, in the copper whose qualities were attributed to what emanated from this planet. Today the attempt is made to investigate scientifically such connections between planets and metals.[3] Amazing results are already documented and could be discussed with the students in an appropriate way, without relapsing into old astrological views.

The way from ore to metal is now described. Occasionally it is possible to refer to the processes taking place in the furnace of an ironworks – harking back to the main-lesson in Class 8 – where the purified metal is produced, liquidified, poured into the bars, rolled and given the shape we see in our workshop.

But how was this done in olden times? How did the ancient Egyptians produce the sheet of tin we see, beautifully crafted, at a burial site? They had no rollers. The smiths beat the poured bars with hammers, stretching the metal until it reached the required thickness. The master craftsman pointed to the right place and the journeymen or helpers beat the sheet – in rhythmical alternations[4] – stretching it to an ever larger size. When hardening, the metal had to be heated to make it pliant again. This is how the thickness used to be reduced to its required thinness – less than 1 mm ($1/32$ in) in the case of tomb stones. It was skill at its highest: controlled technology.

The word 'technology' was then unknown. Its meaning, translated from the Greek, is 'art', 'skill', 'inspired idea', 'bringing about', even 'giving birth', 'inventing' and, at the same time, 'manufacturing'. A uniquely universal term for the way technology, the crafts and arts used to be understood in those times!

One of the students happened to look at a brass plate. This gave us the opportunity of talking about alloys. By mixing different metals, we can change their properties, make them harder, lower the melting point or, as in this instance, influence the colouring. We add silver-white zinc to the molten copper, transforming the red into a golden-yellow. The tone becomes audible when the mixture of copper and zinc is shaped into a bell.

The particular alloy we call bronze begs the question of how the idea arose of mixing just these metals in their liquid state, in spite of the fact that they are nowhere found together. Even today this puzzle is occupying the minds of our scientists. In ancient times zinc was obtained in the mines of Tintagel, Cornwall, in order to be alloyed with copper (from Cyprus) into bronze; during the processes in the foundry the zinc and lead (frequently found in copper ores) were cleanly separated. In the face of such mysteries even our most vociferous 'know-alls' fall silent and become thoughtful.

We begin our work with the cutting out of round or oval shapes from the copper sheet. The edges are filed and finely polished, because of their dangerous sharpness. Now the beating begins that is to make the flat surface into a bowl. The copper is curved on a wooden base with the hammer, proceeding from the outside to the inside in spiral fashion, or radiating from the edges, beating back any of the creases that may occur. The form gradually grows, round upon round, through 'deepening up' – as the process is called. The students here learn to understand the basic property of metals, i.e. their stretchability.

When the students succeeded in giving the copper a satisfactory form, the process of planishing (smoothing) begins. Here it is not the hefty hammer blows, but the sensitively felt fine hammering that is essential. The smoothing, planishing process requires a uniform, loose, continuous and patient hammering, demanding full concentration, as not even a square millimetre must be overlooked. Too strong a hit may cause new unevenness.

The left hand must guide the object to steady the part that is worked with on the supporting base. Again great sensitivity of the fingers is essential and a constant alertness is needed. The work is done on a clean, even and finely polished iron surface, called a fist or pin anvil.

We also practise other methods, working on a wooden base, e.g. stretching the copper and shaping it into a bowl, in which the planishing process is included.

The bowl – already the subject in woodwork in Class 7[5] – has an inner and outer space. The students in Class 9 can be expected to work at it alternately from within and without. This one task – the making of a bowl, but in two different materials – goes hand in glove with the beginning and ending developmental stages of 'earth maturity'.

The students are shown the different basic techniques of working with copper. The uniform, unbroken hammering of a simple area (such as a bracelet or bookends) teaches them to be exact; the accurate bending of the material develops a feeling for form and symmetry.

The soft, pliable copper makes it possible for the yet inexperienced hands of the student to shape the article simultaneously in convex and concave forms. Working in clay intensifies this feeling for giving form to things. A capacity for giving form is developed, based on the skills that are now

17. WORKING WITH METALS (CLASSES 9 AND 10)

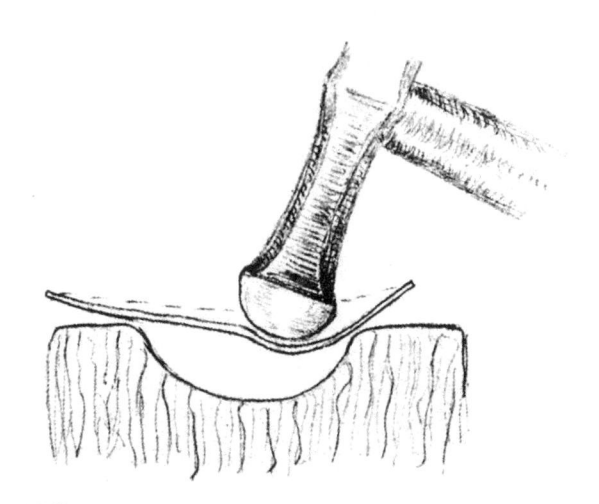

Hollowing out

Planishing

Working in concave and convex forms

PART THREE: CRAFTS IN THE UPPER SCHOOL

Planishing

Examples of metalwork

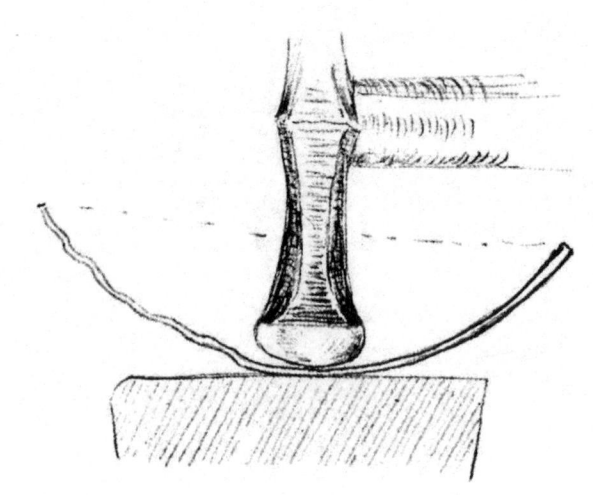

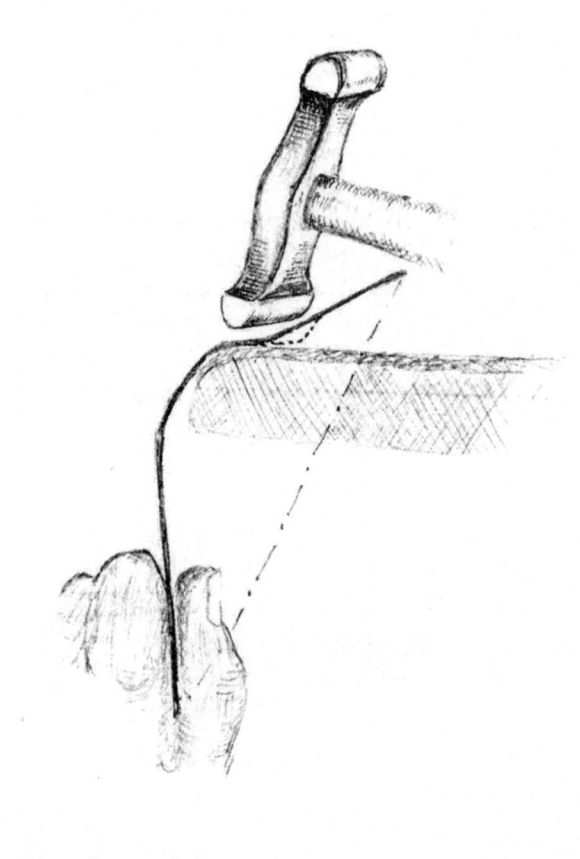

The technique of raising

acquired and on the experience gained during the modelling with clay.

It goes without saying that the accompanying techniques, such as drilling, filing, riveting, soldering, punching, polishing etc., are also utilised so that the students become familiar with many aspects of metal work. The relatively quick production of an article often encourages the making of very imaginative and beautiful objects. Candlesticks, napkin rings, wall lights, teapot warmers, containers etc. are the result. The pliant copper teases forth, as it were, the formative forces of the young, and the joy and pride in their achievements influence and flow into the other blocks.

After the work described so far, in which the stretching of the metal was essential for getting the required shape, where the material became thinner at the places it was worked at, the opposite to stretching, i.e. compressing, will be learnt during the next block. An inner space is to be formed from a round base with a thickness of 1–1.2 mm (1/32 in) – a jug, mug, pot, vase or bell. From the edges, we start by beating radiating creases into the plate. The bowl-like shape almost forms itself during the process.

From the outside it is now worked at on a wooden (later also on an iron) base; the creases are hammered down, beat upon beat, the metal pressing inwards, round upon round from the centre outwards to the edges until an obtuse cone is formed. Here too, the copper is shaped in cold condition, but this allows only for a limited degree of change. The hard, beaten metal must then be heated and this means the practising of the skills connected with the handling of the Bunsen burner.

The heated object is then cooled down in water and loses most of the resulting copper oxide in the process. This is followed by pickling off in diluted sulphuric acid. After rinsing with water, the beating is continued from the outside, leaving the bottom untouched, the sides, however, growing ever steeper. Much concentrated thinking is essential. The students need help and explanations, such as gradually bringing the fingers of the outstretched hand together in order to show the narrowing of the sides. Or one could compare the copper mass to be compressed with a clay form that is to be narrowed towards the top. Here too, the clay must be pushed together in order to avoid creases. The clay thickens, because of its bulk having to find somewhere to go. However quickly one may imagine this process in clay, it is difficult to effect the narrowing with the blows of a hammer. The technique of raising demands quite a lot of strength.

This strength does not come from the muscles, but from the swing of the hammer that has to find its mark securely and accurately, exactly at the place that pressed the material to the inside. The hand holding the object supports it on the supporting base in such a way that the force of the hit is diverted from the already deepened part to benefit the part that is pulled to the inside.

By utilising the laws of leverage, the work of the left hand, undoubtedly the more difficult part of the process, where it is more a matter of comprehension than strength and perseverance, is made easier. With individual attention, each success or failure of a hammer blow must be judged, possibly corrected, and continued.

The necessary alertness, the 'slipping' into a work process, the 'thinking with the fingers' are the things that cause the problems, and not the brute strength. This may explain why a 'dainty' girl can achieve as much or more than a strong boy when working at a vase or some other project, measuring the high and low points of their successes. We can see how the shape here narrows, the bulk of the material compresses, and we watch with astonishment how the material increased its thickness by 30–50% of its original. When the form has been perfected the smoothing and polishing begins. With a thicker kind of material it is possible to give the shape its final touches with a few hammer blows.

From copper to iron

At the beginning of this article we tried to build a bridge between the developmental stages of the young and the craft materials corresponding to them. We saw that through the ages the metals were used both in the cultural-artistic and the practical areas. Their use and importance in technology will continue.

When our students learn to work with copper and iron, the two prime metals, and if, at the same time, they experience the artistic potential of these metals and really understand their nature and qualities, such work will contribute significantly to the education and culture of humankind.

The students are not yet aware of what we adults continually experience in our encounter with copper. How its beauty, its soft formative quality, its sympathetic warm glow come to meet us. The work itself involves a complete immersion into a thoroughly rhythmical activity, connected with constant, undivided attention, during which the material itself seems to encourage us to continue. We have already mentioned the formative forces copper engenders in us, stimulating us to keep on working at new forms. Such concepts as: meeting us, encouraging, engendering, demonstrating how copper affects us from without, as well as the students' and adults' will-forces and imagination. This encounter with copper is enormously helpful to the students in Class 9, the age of the well-known 'revolutionary changes'.

In Class 10 a significant change occurs: the help from outside is no longer desired. The young man or woman wishes to work from within out, relying on their own initiative and activity. It is no longer a case of 'being met by copper', but the self-willed intervention and doing that is required when working with iron. This urge is characteristic of the time when puberty has been conquered. Working with iron also gives directions in life. Historically speaking, the transition from the bronze to the Iron Age also signifies a tremendous change. The constant use of fire during the work, conditions and forces such qualities and activities of the human being that add to the metal what it cannot do by itself. This unattractive, hard, grey, quickly rusting metal challenges us to change its shape through energetic and determined hammer blows. When cold, it resists any attempt at change. Only when red-hot does it begin to be malleable, does it submit to the hammer. What are the qualities iron demands of us? Exact observation, absolute wakefulness, undivided attention, quickness and courage, to know absolutely what seconds later has to be done and last but not least, the knowledge of the possible dangers and how to avoid them.

In the lessons on world literature, the *Nibelung Saga* is often taught in Class 10. The young Siegfried, like many a lad of that age, wishes to forge a sword for himself. The defending quality of iron – related as it is to Mars – here comes into its own. But iron has also other uses. Its virtue is to join: nails, screws, clamps, chains, a bridge, rail lines that connect places all come to mind. Its other virtue is durability and firmness, i.e. props, bearers, the vice. We also know its ability to separate: the knife, plane, chisel, drill. Through sword and dagger it even separates from life. It can also protect: through armour, helmet and shield. The only thing it cannot do is to protect itself from rusting! In spite of its hardness it cannot resist the onslaught of weather, it succumbs to the ravages of water more easily than the oak or elm or copper that outlasts the centuries.

Hence, other metals must come to its assistance – nickel, chrome, zinc, lead – as additions or coating.

In all its uses, the malleability during heat depends on its solidity. Since the eighteenth century, due to the improvements in the methods of firing with bituminous coal, coke and bellows, its importance has increased by leaps and bounds. It has assumed an important place in our lives. Due to the use of iron, the nineteenth century became an age that was strongly connected to the earth.

Pelikan, in his book *The Secrets of Metals*, draws our attention to many such aspects to which we refer, only too briefly, concerning the polarities between copper and iron. We shall, by considering the properties of these metals and the corresponding methods of working with them, discover how the forces of feeling and will of the adolescent can be addressed and engendered. It is not merely the cognitive and aesthetic grasp of what exists in our world that comprise our educational tasks, but also the actual working with iron, because this metal contains the effective 'active strength that is synonymous with will' (Rudolf Steiner), a fact we fully experience during the work.

18

Working with iron
Wolf von Knoblauch

Those of us who spent our childhood in the country may remember the village blacksmith and the smithy from which the rhythmical sounds of hammer and anvil could be heard. The picture of the smoke-filled workshop, at whose darkest spot the fire burnt, will not have been forgotten, and we can, years later, still evoke the smell of the coal and sulphur fumes.

We wish to let our students experience something of this mood during their work with iron. Such perceptions, apart from the work itself, will impress themselves deeply upon their souls. The sounds themselves are given special importance. The rhythmical swing of the hammer becomes the expression of the healthy creative forces of this craft.

If we wish to introduce our students to the blacksmith's trade it would be good to go beyond the purely practical work into a sphere created by the mood of the workshop: the 'old knowledge', a term used by ancient craftsfolk, should be experienced and the students should be allowed to trace its origin.

Preparation of the workpiece precedes the actual work. The students learn to know the most important tools as well as the properties of iron. The concept 'iron' may be used to include the different steel alloys, as the following descriptions apply to all workable types of alloy. Form, colour and sound should be so experienced that the students can gain an initial picture of the material. During the actual working processes they will become ever more familiar with its qualities. This is one of the aims during this block.

The preparations include becoming familiar with the room itself. The tools to be used must be within easy reach. The fire in the furnace must be attended to attain an even, constant heat. As in surgery, the single stages of the work must be carried out quickly and surely; there is no time for dithering, for searching for a hammer when the iron is glowing red hot. Vice versa, as soon as the iron is in the fire the heating must be given fullest concentration. This does not contradict the possibility that the smith may have one piece in the fire and at the same time be busy with another; whatever else the smith might be doing, they will always be aware of what is going on in the fire and will literally 'hear' when the right temperature is reached.

Can this be achieved in one block? Of course not! An inner training is essential and this takes years. But the students can be given pictures and experiences that may prove to be fruitful for

18. WORKING WITH IRON

their future lives. The phenomenological way of observing, as well as the training, will allow the students to find new ways to understand this craft and the properties of the material.

This calls for a third aspect of preparation: that of the individual themselves. The students must learn to conquer their timidity and even fear, the fear of the effort to guide the hammer accurately, fear of the blazing, open fire close by, the fear of the glowing iron.

The following method has proved itself in our school.

The students are asked to beat notches with the fin of the hammer into one of the edges of a thin piece of cold iron, about 50–60 cm (2 ft) long, 2 cm (1 in) wide and 3 mm (⅛ in) thick.

In this the students learn:

1. To get to know the hammer's two sides. These are the 'track', made point by point, where the forces are distributed in a radiating way and the 'fin' that gives the direction of the distribution of forces;
2. To aim and hit accurately;
3. The way they must face the anvil (posture during work), in order to work without tiring.

They also learn to know 'soft' iron and how hard they must beat it in order to get results. If they work rhythmically, they will experience a harmonising effect that will save strength.

Working in this way, the students will discover their own individual rhythm of hammering.

This rhythm will be tested by hearing, by the sounds of the hammer; one can actually hear if the iron has been hit in a way that it is shaped (a full sound) or if the beat was a timid one, merely touching the surface (a shrill, painful sound).

During these preparatory exercises the students learn to know the processes of movement when working with iron without having to work too quickly; they are able to concentrate fully on these processes. This will be a condition for work with hot iron where quickness is required if success is to be achieved.

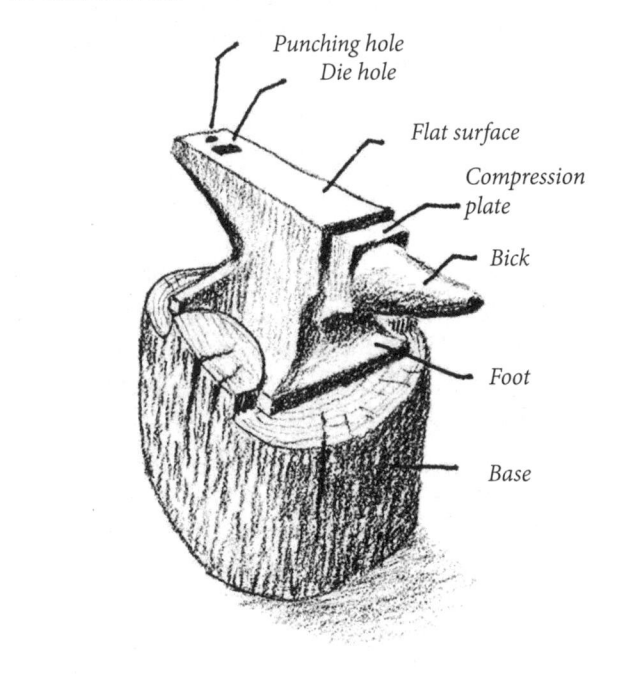

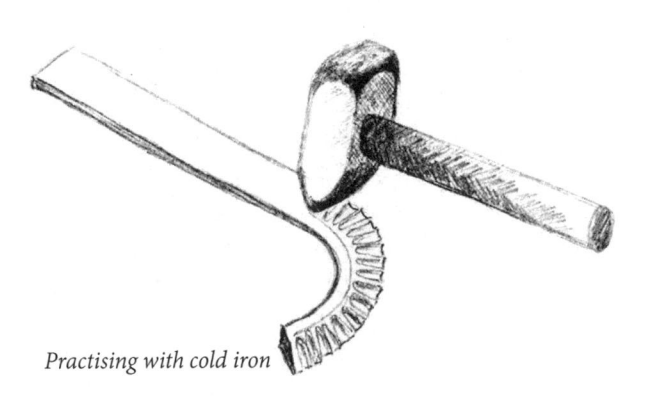

Practising with cold iron

Detail of an iron project

Anvil inserts/dies:

Thorn or cone

Scrape chisel

Round die

In working with hot iron the care of the fire and the right heat of the iron are additional learning stages. The working place and the material will be prepared in the same way as during work with cold iron.

The preparation of the forge is unfamiliar. The students are here offered an entirely new and wide field of hitherto unknown impressions. They must remain fully awake in their observations, and one can easily see how deeply they are affected by these experiences.

The fire is lit with the help of paper, cardboard or sawdust; if available, charcoal is added and then coke.

We shall soon hear strange sizzling and crackling noises, accompanied by the hiss of the wind blown from below by the bellows or a turbine. Dense, yellow-white fumes are rising from the coal, slowly spreading like a thick colour across the furnace. They are so heavy that they drop from the edge of the furnace to the ground, allowing the students carefully to push them up with their hands. The senses of hearing, sight and smell – the fumes and smell of sulphur – simultaneously participate in the process. As soon as the flames rise from the coal the show ceases. It is the eye that is now addressed: the observation of spectacular colours, of the ever brightening glow rising from the dark coal. If the fire is burning well and constantly, the upper layer of the coal may be cooled down (sprinkling with water), an important measure that allows the heat to be conserved and not be torn away by the flames.

All the conditions are now met for the start of our work with heated iron. The students now learn to know another side of iron, i.e. its appearance and qualities in this condition. Watching the colours and feeling the warmth with the palms of their hands makes them more sensitive. Needless to say, this is not the actual touching of the hot iron, but the holding of the hands slightly above the surface, by which they feel the rising warmth.

Why do we emphasise this? Because iron reacts most sensitively when heated to the blue colour stage, one should stop working when it is red hot, lest it snap at a place where it has been overheated.

The students experience the different grades of softness of the iron, dependent on the colour produced by the heat. The ease with which it can be worked corresponds to the degree of softness. If one wants to save one's energy, work must

18. WORKING WITH IRON

proceed swiftly before the temperature changes. To succeed in this the students must know every stage of the work before they begin; they must know in what way they wish to make use of the 'warmth' when it reaches the required temperature.

A decisive factor here is courage. They already had to show some courage during the work with cold iron. It is not easy to use enough force on the hammer and at the same time aim accurately. To do this with the hot iron is an even greater challenge – the greatest concentration and strength of will are necessary if every hammer blow is to find its mark.

Watching a student at this work, we can see transformations: from the initially timid and hesitating youngster to an independently practising apprentice. He or she is gripped by this craft, loses all sense of time and keeps on working, hour after hour. The skill in the handling of tools increases, as well as the control of the fire.

If, due to lack of concentration, the iron should be overheated to the white-glowing stage, it will have reached the melting point (welding heat) and, beginning at the surface, will turn liquid. Sharply contoured stars spark from the heap. If the students withdraw their piece of work from the fire they will have a glistening, white-sparking 'torch' – the shape and inner structure of the iron are dissolved. This brings many a student close to tears. The iron has actually burnt; it has become victim of the fire.

One of the students described the ways iron reacts to the different temperatures in this way:

The cold, black-grey iron is as though dead. Fire awakens it to life – as we can see in the changing colours. If it actually burns, its colours change to white and 'stars' become visible. Iron then dissolves into a 'spiritual condition'.

He experienced, quite consciously, this picture from black (death) via the other colours to white (spirit) and was able to express this in words. It would be difficult to imagine a more beautifully expressive account of this experience.

If the iron has burnt, the students must begin afresh. They will, however, realise – perhaps helped by the sympathetic, consoling teacher – that the new work will have to be done differently. Their experience and the skills they have gained will strengthen their self-confidence; the new work

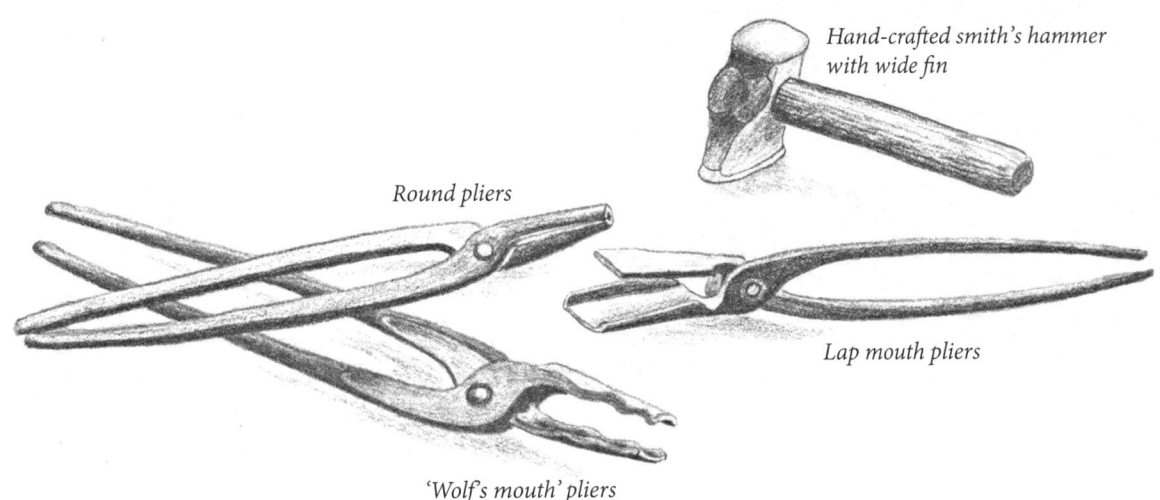

Hand-crafted smith's hammer with wide fin

Round pliers

Lap mouth pliers

'Wolf's mouth' pliers

will be better and more quickly achieved. Such an experience not only strengthens their self-confidence, observation and concentration, but also the actual skills involved.

Once the work is finished, an important educational aspect is added: with hindsight, the students can perceive their ability to persevere with the original idea – its design and execution – until the successful completion of the work. Surveying their experiences, they are able to evaluate the different stages of the work as well as the quality of the end product. A further perception is that of economy. Cleverly chosen projects allow for the practising of economy and social interaction – economy in the sense that the students are to make do with as few tools as possible, as in olden times.

They may, for example, work with objects that can be produced with one hammer without relinquishing their necessary functions and form.

Harness smithy
Copper print by A, Trost, J. Koch (1689)
from: Schmithals/Klemm, Crafts and Technology

Imagination and fantasy here come into their own, replacing the so frequently heard current demands for 'specialised tools' for each stage of the work. Instead, the students embark on a 'journey of discovery' with their simple tools, experiencing their potential. This strengthens the frequent lack of strength in imagination and the students realise the 'maturity' of a simple tool as, for example, the smith's hammer, and know how to use it meaningfully. The same applies to other such simple tools.

Working with iron is a modelling, sculpturing craft. It is not only the material itself but also the students who are formed. This is quite clear already during the preparatory work with a group of several students. The social work is especially cultivated when they are asked to shape a larger piece of iron. As in olden times also, without the use of machines, the smith had to shape the iron together with his apprentices and journeymen, so now the students can learn this working together with small groups. The student, whose workpiece is to be shaped, not only indicates with their hammer the rhythmical beat, but also points to the places where the iron is to be hit. Their helpers swing their hammers in a truly wonderful rhythm, working in unison on one piece. So that everybody may experience this, each student gets a turn.

The sequence of movements

We have several times referred to this in our essay. We shall now show how it affects the students.

Generally speaking, the students face the anvil in a way that the arm holding the hammer may beat the material, moving along the side of the body. The length of the anvil is parallel to the handle of the hammer. The left hand guides the workpiece

18. WORKING WITH IRON

(the form-giving hand) and the right hand guides the hammer (the strength-giving hand).[1]

If the beat is slowed down it becomes clear that the hammer is raised on the body as far as the individual angular point (opposite the height of the head) and then led, in a swinging downward movement, vertically to the part of the material under consideration. This circular movement corresponds time-wise to the rhythms of breathing and the pulse beat.

Within this outwardly visible circular movement that, because of its speed appears to be merely an up and down one, is a further inner movement triggered by what Rudolf Steiner called: 'Will is idea understood as strength (force)...'

'Figure of eight' movement

If we wish to make anything useful from this tough material we must, with all our available inner and outer strength, so swing the hammer as if we wanted to beat the anvil right 'into the ground'. It is a matter of forging into the iron and not, as was made clear in the very first lesson, merely working on its surface. Initially the students beat only as far as to the point they can see when raising the hammer for the next beat. This, after a while, will be experienced as painful, because the hammer, through its weight, is pulled down to the workpiece, while the hand and arm movement is already following the upward impulse. Cramps in the lower arm and pain are the result. This is exacerbated by the realisation that few if any changes are seen in the iron itself. If this should be the case, the student should be made to begin by beating slowly and more consciously. The hammer must rest on the workpiece after each beat before being raised for the next one.

If the necessary will-forces accompany the movements of the hammer, one will experience how the iron willingly submits to them, allowing itself to be shaped quite easily. The anvil supports this process; the smith refers to it as: 'it pulls'. We could see in the anvil the 'tool of the earth' and in the hammer the 'tool of the creator', between them shaping of iron. By further observing the course of the will-forces, we can perceive how these forces, directed by the iron and, through the anvil, to the earth, return in a transformed way. The giving and returning forces and energies cross at exactly the spot where the shaping of the iron takes place. If this were not so, the material would merely bend or resist any attempt at giving it the required form.

The form of the hand and arm movement is a lemniscate. The crossing point is in the workpiece. One half leads through the left hand and arm which holds the piece, passing through the respiratory area, in order to give the right arm and hand its new impulse to return to the crossing point. It continues – in the other half – through the earth, streaming back again transformed as physically perceptible energy, from below through the anvil towards the worker.

The students experience how, through the giving right and the receiving left hand, they are placed into the harmony of the forces of the 'governing will'[2] and the earth. The impulses for form rising from spiritual inspiration can thus, with the help of the harmonious-rhythmical breathing, the beat of the hammer and the individual will-forces, become visible in the iron.

The elements

The fire in the furnace must be perceived as an essential helper. It joins the elements earth (coal), air and fire (light/warmth) in order to melt the ore, to heat the workpiece. In the hardening process, water is added. The students here meet anew and in unexpected ways the picture of the earth that will accompany them throughout their lives.

In conclusion we may say, speaking from experience: in working with the age old craft of the blacksmith, the students are taken hold of in their totality and inwardly formed. The forces of concentration, of awareness, the physical movements, the aim-directed actions, and particularly the soul-widening experiences, constitute a healthy balance to today's predominantly academically orientated subjects. The necessary corrections during the work lead the students to experiences that awaken and engender their will impulses. The fact that the work with iron can also stimulate the moral forces is beautifully described by Abraham a Sancta Clara in a report written in 1699:

Because of the hardness of the horseshoe the blacksmith cannot be 'polite' when shaping it. These people, working long hours, have little time for fun in front of the fire. It is a miracle that so few get burnt by the sparks hitting their faces. The fact that they are black and sooty does not harm their honour, as it is a sign of their industry and, hidden behind their black shirts, is a white conscience. They can also learn many beautiful things in their sooty workshops as, for example, gratitude to the bellows because, when their bellies are filled, they thank the blacksmith by blowing and kindling their fire...[3]

19

Copper and iron workshops
Michael Martin

Although the name 'smithy' is used for both copper and iron workshops, the methods used are so fundamentally different that the appearance and mood of the rooms cannot but affect the person entering them in their special way.

Copperwork needs many tools, finely honed and polished where they touch and form the material. A mark in the hammer immediately impresses itself on the copper – just as a tuck in the edge of a carving chisel would on the final touches on the wood.

This is why the steel must not be allowed to rust, that is, the air must be dry and the floor ought to be made of hard wood that does not harm a tool or workpiece should it drop. The acoustics should be such that the noise of the hammering does not become unbearable. This is something the teacher should be able to deduce from the sound of the hammer beats or the screech of a file whenever a student is handling their tools in the right way. It is essential that the ceiling and walls are soundproofed. It is also important that the daylight is not too bright and that it is entering the room obliquely. It is impossible to see the delicate traces made by the hammer on copper if the light is too bright. All this may perhaps indicate the strong effect of the work processes on the outer form of the room.

A soft twilight in the copper smithy from which the red and golden glistening metal shines forth is ideal. This makes for an almost mysterious mood, intensified by the colourful copper minerals in a cabinet, by the jugs, bowls, lamps, goblets and boxes on the shelves, as well as by the reflected light of the wall lamps. This effect can be increased by the conscious use of the colours of the metal in connection with light.

In contrast to this delicate, sensitive mood in the copper smithy, the iron smithy appears to be crude, uncouth, elementary. In the centre, the fire asks for a quite different environment; it not only has to be stoked, but must be kept going and controlled. This requires the firmness of the fireproof stone, the hardness of the floor, the lining of the furnace with iron, and much more. The master smith cares for the air, water and smoke and controls them. Darkness, heat and soot are as much part of this typical atmosphere as the characteristic smells and powerful hammer beats that can be heard far and wide. The utensils and tools appear to the layman to be uncouth and heavy. Everywhere one senses the necessary application of tamed energy.

The natural, hearty freshness emanating from the finished articles round about immediately appeals to our sense of life.

The Austrian writer Peter Rosegger remembers how, as a boy, he experienced a visit to a smithy where scythes used to be made. The mood Rosegger managed to evoke could well be the basis for the way blacksmith shops might be installed in our schools. The following is an abridged version:

What I saw first was a sparkling piece of the sun that was taken from the howling furnace and thrown on the anvil, soundless as though it were a piece of dough. And then, as the hammer raised itself on a massive lever-beam and dropped down on this soft lump, a whole ocean of sparks shot through the room. Frightened to death, I quickly hid behind my father's back, but the sparks had already hit my shirt and I was surprised that it did not burst into flames and that my hands didn't hurt when these fiery gnats hit them. The second and third beat of the hammer again chased a whole army of sparks into the room but the flatter the lump of iron became, and the quicker the beats fell, the less did the sparks fly. The blacksmith stood there, holding the iron with long-handled pliers, turning it this way and that, until all the cinder was hammered away. The white glow turned red and then quite dull and finally just looked like iron does: grey. The man threw it to the floor and the hammer stopped.

I plucked up some courage and took a good look at all the things, although the room was quite dark without the fire. Above all else I noticed a large leather box that 'breathed'.

It was the bellows that, filled with air – through hydraulic power – blew through pipes into the furnace. All sorts of pieces of iron were lying on the floor. Rows and rows of tongues, hammers, mallets, files, axes and things I didn't know were along the walls. I now also noticed the blacksmiths themselves whose faces and bare chests were covered with sweat. We continued our investigations and saw other furnaces where the men shovelled coal with large iron shovels and threw them on the fire where they immediately started to burn in a dull, blue flame…

But it was the smiths that fascinated me the most. 'Why do they hit the anvil again after the scythes have already been removed?' I asked my father. He answered: 'They always do it. The beat on the anvil strengthens the chain that holds the dragon in place; else it would snap and the evil fiend would break free…'[1]

Darkness, fire, soot, glowing sparks and noise leave us in no doubt as to our connection with the dark spheres of the earth during our work with iron. Will-permeated energies are urging upwards. We already know that, in the visual arts, light can only arise in the correct handling of darkness. This is a quite objective experience in black and white shaded drawing. The smithy gives us the outer picture of this, or better, a true image of this fact. Light, warmth and strength here unite into the deed, conquering dead matter. The darkness constitutes the necessary opposition.

19. COPPER AND IRON WORKSHOPS

Yes, I know from where I came!
Unsatiated, like the flame
Do I glow, exhaust my being.
Into light turns what I'm grasping,
Into coal what I leave gasping:
Yes, a flame I, no denying!

Ja! Ich weiss, woher ich stamme!
Ungesättigt gleich der Flamme
glühe and verzehr' ich mich.
Licht wird alles, was ich fasse,
Kohle allse, was ich lasse:
Flame bin ich sicherlich!

FRIEDRICH NIETZSCHE

20

The joinery main-lesson blocks (Classes 9 and 10)
Friedrich Weidler

So far, children have carved and worked with blocks of wood, shaping them into useful and beautiful objects. The joiner, as the word indicates, puts the parts of wood together in order to create things people need in their homes – cabinets, closets, shelves, storage boxes in which the many household articles may be stored or displayed and tables and chairs to allow us to eat our meals in a dignified way. It is important and interesting to learn how a method of work has developed by which the several parts are perfectly joined. We may say that certain rules have come about by which the single stages of work can be mastered and, provided the students obey these rules, they will succeed in their work as well as any professional. Both the tailor's cloth and the joiner's boards are only semi-finished materials, likewise, the task of going beyond the mere usefulness of the articles in making them also beautiful is common to both crafts.

We shall take our starting point from the basic material 'wood' and not immediately from the artificial materials developed during the age of machinery veneers, plywood etc.

For the work with wood, the joining of boards to larger sizes, it is necessary to apply three techniques that have been developed long ago and are still in use today:

1. Dovetailing
2. Joints
3. Slotting and pegging

Those who haves mastered these basic joinery skills can build a piece of furniture. I show my students what they are to make during the block: a small carrying box, a wooden suitcase, a toolbox, a dovetailed stool or a storage trunk.[1] The basic form of all of them is the dovetailed box that can be modified according to the use of the article.

The blocks themselves take five or six weeks, three double lessons each week, 22 to 29 actual hours when we take into account that a lesson is no longer than 45 minutes. This relatively short time means careful planning by the teacher if they wish to complete the course and if each student is to finish his or her piece of work. When the students have chosen their projects and the corresponding size has been determined, the dimensions of the boards to be glued together are worked out. We then turn to the first stage of work, i.e. cutting out the rough wood.

Lesson one – cutting out the wood

In front of us is a heap of timber resting on slats to allow the air to circulate. On the sides of the 24 mm (15/16 in) thick boards, bark can still be seen. I make sure that the timber is dry (6–8%). Many an unpleasant surprise (warping) is thereby avoided.

I generally use pine, a native timber, whose resinous quality makes for easy work. It also smells good, is relatively inexpensive and has a living graining: the sapwood bright and the heartwood reddish-brown.

The students now lay several boards on the planing benches.

I now measure the correct lengths, adding 3–4 cm (1–1½ in), and taking into consideration the graining, colouring, knots and cracks. The measurements are drawn with a piece of marking chalk and ready to be manually sawn by the students.

We use the frame saw, a typical joiner's tool and very different from any other kind of saw. I demonstrate its use: the blade is guided along the thumb of the left hand; once the initial incision is made, we continue sawing along the marked line, never pressing the saw downwards, and always using the entire length of the blade. Before finishing the cut, I stop and ask the students if they had noticed anything special in the blade. 'It is straight, but at an angle. Why?' 'So that the carpenter may always see the line!' The students will notice later that this also creates a space between the plank and the saw, allowing enough room for the sawn off pieces to drop down.

What do the students notice in the teeth of the blade? They are filed in the direction of the 'thrust' movement. The emphasis during sawing is towards the front. The teeth also alternate from left to right. Why? They widen the cut, making it easier for the blade to pass along without getting stuck. I then give further hints about such things as holding the saw correctly and finishing the cut cleanly, without damaging the board.

I always use the terminology of the trade, giving the work a professional touch. The saws are now shared out and the work begins. The students try their best, some are better, some a little clumsy. I assist and encourage. The lesson soon ends, the floor is swept and the students are told that they will start with the squaring of the boards in the following session.

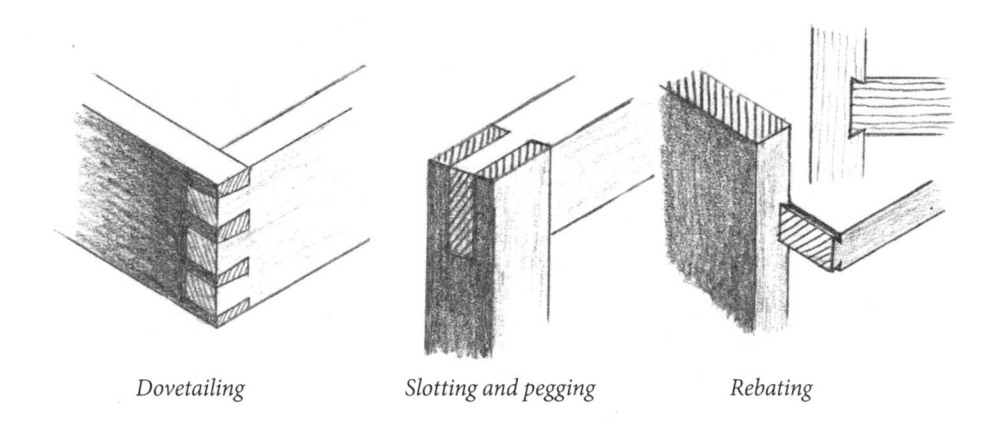

Dovetailing   *Slotting and pegging*   *Rebating*

Division of the board with bark

Frame saw

Direction of thrust

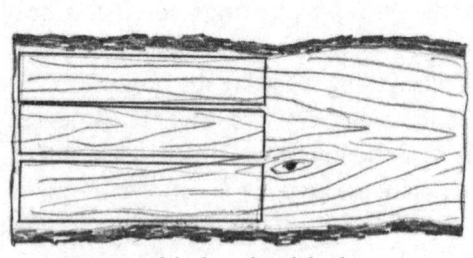

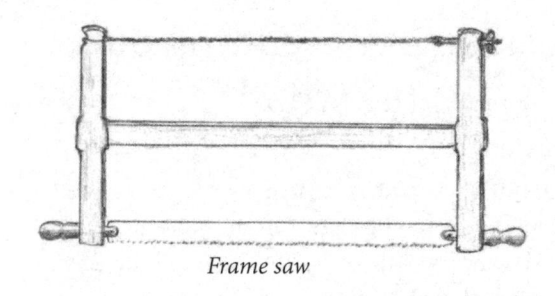

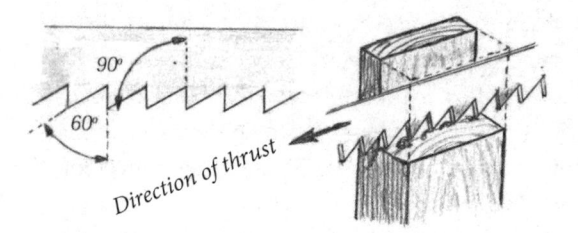

Lesson two – squaring and cutting the timber

The boards, cut to the right lengths, are now ready for the next stage. I place a board on the planing bench, narrow side uppermost. Next to the bark, I draw a straight line along the entire length. Since most of the boards are slightly warped and cracked, the damaged parts must be removed – another line is drawn.

For squaring the board it is clamped vertically into the vice, and I repeat what I have already said in the previous lesson. Success is conditional upon the cut being made accurately along the drawn line. I insist on this and also on an even, determined movement of the saw.

The students begin their work with enthusiasm. It is a joy to watch them, every one of them fully occupied. If the teacher observes accurately, they will see where to intervene and help. Some students still hold their saws incorrectly, although

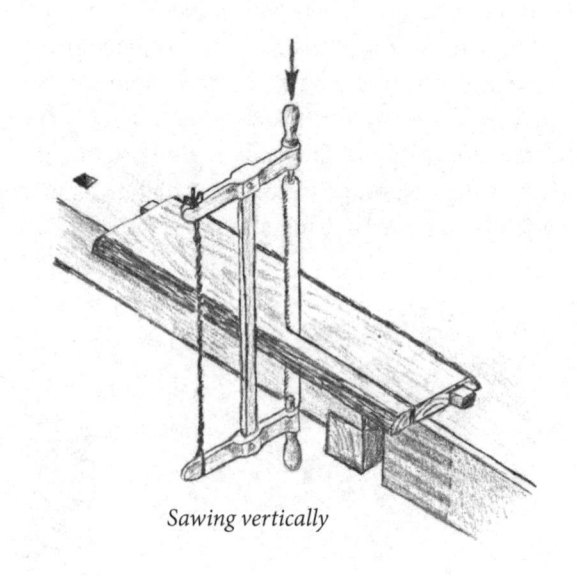

Sawing vertically

this has been taught and discussed in the previous lesson. They must first learn to use their tools and understand their logic. Here the saw is not guided along the straight line, there it wobbles or gets jammed. Some students have problems in starting the cut.

The challenge for the teacher is to guide their students in the right direction and to insist on professional work and accuracy.

The students are fully engrossed in their activities, but must learn, for the sake of the matter in hand, to control their bodies.

Beginning with the placing of the feet, with the posture and arm movements to the head, including the alert eye. Cutting vertically already touches their limits. Although we have only just begun, they have already learnt to respect their work and the skills of their teacher.

Occasionally a student is working too fast. I notice this on hearing the unrhythmical, machine-like noise of the blade. This impatience results in breathlessness and rapid exhaustion.

The teacher explains that the secret of good workmanship lies in the rhythmical movements that prevent tiredness and assure perseverance.

For the separation of the boards in the centre, I show the students another way of sawing, as practised earlier on by the joiner. The board is fastened to the bench, one half extending over the edge. The blade of the saw is turned at right angles to the frame. This is then held by both fists and moved vertically. This allows for the greatest possible space between blade and the centre bar of the frame. Again the students are challenged to guide the saw vertically with the greatest of skill. As soon as one dithers, the blade gets jammed. I now show them how this can be done without effort, even when the saw is only held by the fingers instead of the fists. The vertical direction is decisive.

Lesson three – arranging the parts

The boards are now ready to be joined and put on three or four benches. We look at them and I select several for our first project, i.e. like side to like side (heart or sapwood), with the correct side on top. We also pay attention to colour and graining. Correct joining means a knowledge of the qualities of the wood, and I take the opportunity of telling my students a little of this. I might draw the cross section, reminding them that the most living part of the tree is at its periphery. In the younger sapwood the sap rises as far as into the crown, streaming down again in the bast fibres between wood and bark. The consolidation of the wood takes place within the cambium – the 'living' layer, a quite mysterious process. During spring we get the 'early wood', the result of quick, loose cell growth, and during summer the far denser 'late wood'. Together they form the annual rings. In the annual rings of our cross section we read the tree's biography in picture form. It is really a miracle to see how the woods of different trees produce their characteristic graining, colour and smell.

My diagram of the cross section shows how the centre is significantly denser than the periphery, resulting in the different drying times of the boards. The 'right' side, i.e. the side directed to the centre is drying in a slightly convex way; that directed to the bark (the 'left' side) in a concave way. This must be taken into account in the joining.

When all the parts have been put together (adding a little for each joint) we have completed our preparation for the actual joining (gluing).

PART THREE: CRAFTS IN THE UPPER SCHOOL

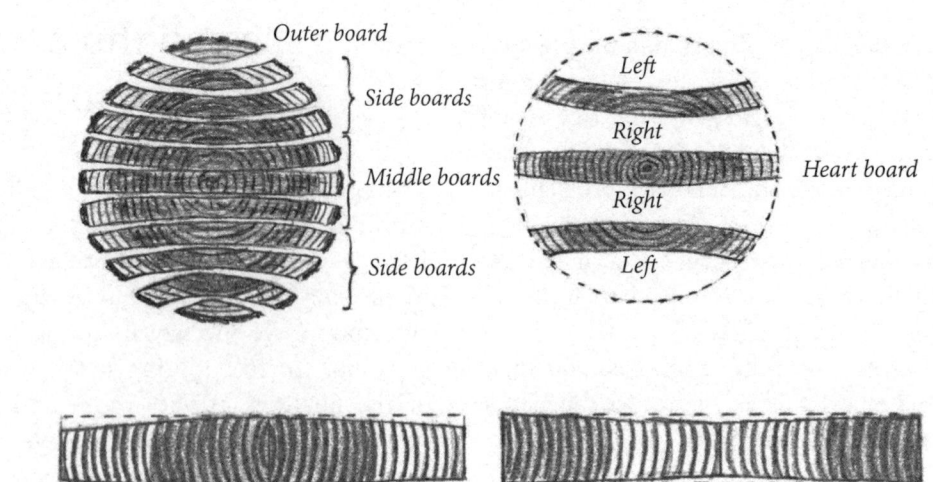

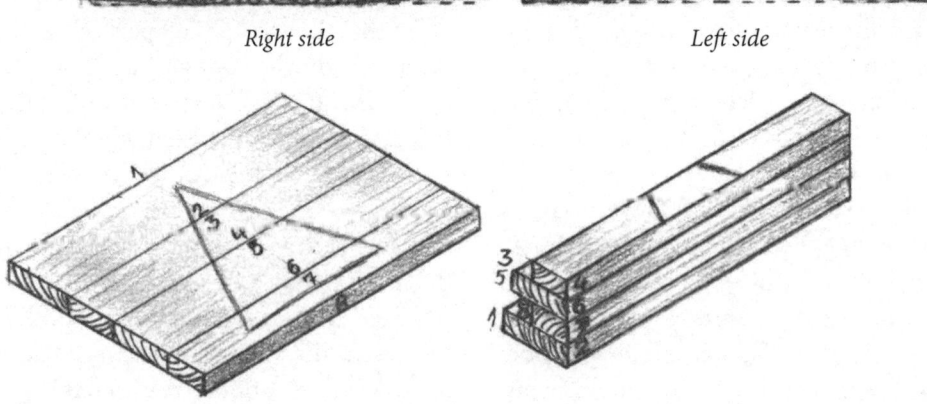

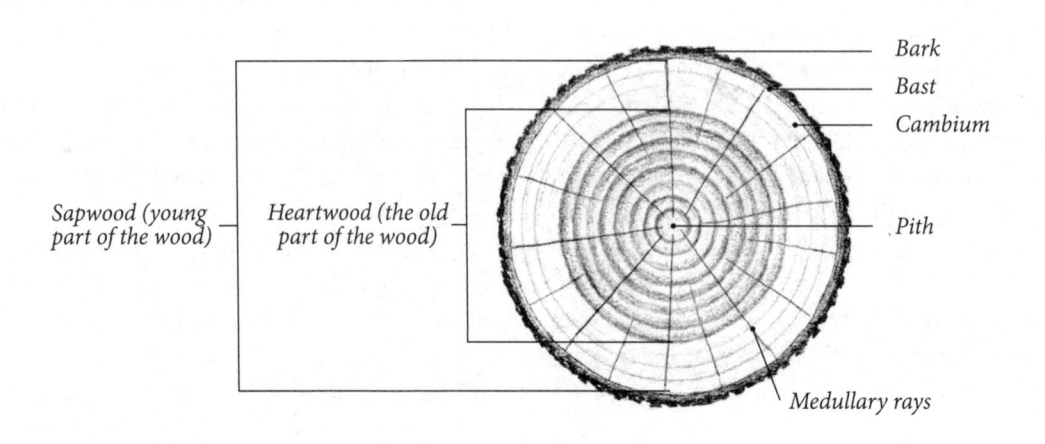

Outer board
Side boards
Middle boards
Side boards

Left
Right
Right
Left
Heart board

Right side

Left side

Bark
Bast
Cambium
Pith
Medullary rays

Sapwood (young part of the wood)
Heartwood (the old part of the wood)

182

20. THE JOINERY MAIN-LESSON BLOCKS (CLASSES 9 AND 10)

Lesson four – joining the boards

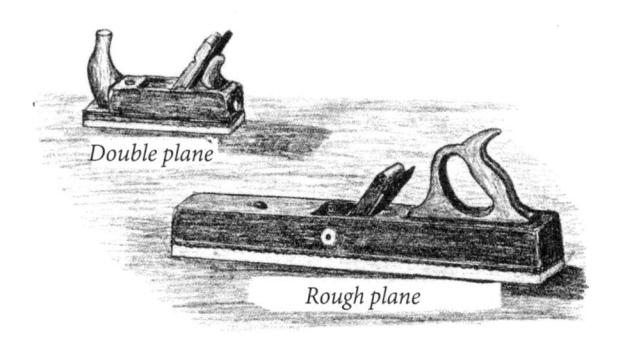

Each student begins by inserting the so-called 'joining board' into the vice. And each one of them makes sure that they have a well-sharpened double plane, a rough plane and a square close by.

They now watch me placing the several boards, all facing in the same direction, on the joining board, pushing them into the metal spikes by allowing the edge to be joined to protrude about 1 cm (½ in). Any inaccuracies that might have occurred when sawing can be corrected with the double plane – the straighter the original line sawn, the better. Using the rough plane, I straighten the first edge. The board is then turned around and the opposite edge is treated in the same way. Corresponding to the square, the other boards follow the same procedure.

I demonstrate how the rough plane is guided along in a lateral way on the bench and, during the work, pressed against the boards, so that the edge tends to be slightly concave. The final thrust of the plane should ideally result in a piece of shaving that extends to the entire length of the edge.

We test our work by holding it against the light, pressing two of the joint edges together. When the two ends are close together, the light may shine through a hairpin crack in the centre.

Now the time has come for the students to try their own hands in this joining process. They have, as yet, no idea of the precision demanded of them, but the success of the work will depend on it.

This lesson is especially taxing. It demands the full engagement of skills and strength. I must point to the differences in the displacement of pressures during the planing. If the work is to succeed the students must be able to muster enough concentration at each thrust of the plane, in order to carry out the movements correctly, to get 'the feel of it'. Repeated practice will help win the day.

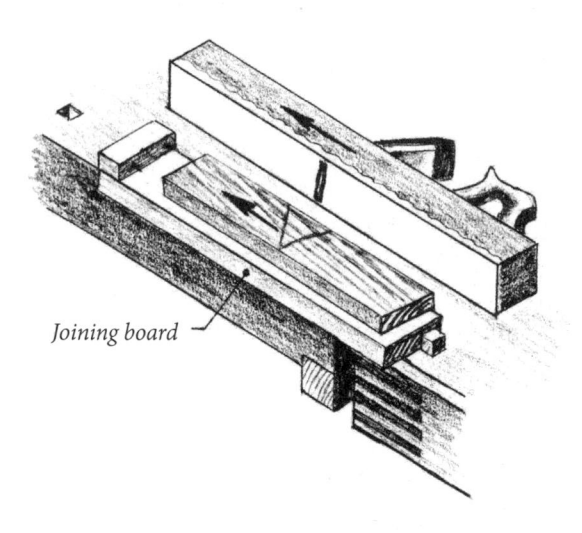

Double plane

Rough plane

Joining board

Lesson five – gluing the boards

The joining must be completed by the end of the first half of the fifth lesson. I help whenever necessary by correcting inaccurate work. Everything is then prepared for the gluing: clamps, gluing planks, the glue itself, hammer and a few nails. I show the group the necessary skills, the correct placement of the parts, the right amount of glue, the use of the square, the exact pressure of the clamps, the use of the hammer in evening out the joints and the measures taken against warping during the drying time by the use of one or two nails in the right place. Keen observation is essential.

After a period of practising, the students begin gluing their boards. No one is allowed to be idle. They work as a team, helping each other. Only when the last board is completed are they allowed to tidy up and leave.

Lesson six – planing (I)

I prepare the work by cutting the glued boards with the circular to a size of approx. 85 x 35 cm (2½ ft x 14 in). Each student will be supplied with a double plane, a rough plane and two alignment rods, a few supporting wedges and a pencil.

I now show that the glued board is by no means absolutely even and that we must achieve complete evenness by planing it straight. We place the board between two clamps on the bench, the 'right' side uppermost, the air cracks at the edges supported by wedges. Parallel to the front and back I place the alignment rods, controlling the extent the boards have warped. This must now be corrected by planing it.

Working diagonally across the board with the double plane, the irregularities are roughly corrected. As soon as a semblance of evenness is apparent, the delicate work with the acutely sharp rough plane begins.

I work along the length of the grain. The straight 'direction-giving plank' allows for accuracy. This plank must always touch the board at every part, be it lying lengthwise, diagonally or straight across. There must be a constant alternating of planing, measuring, correcting, controlling, skill in handling the tools and clear observation. The work is rhythmical; the main direction is horizontal.

The students are now ready to plane their individual boards. It is interesting to see the harmonious work within the group, always relevant to the work. Even though effort is needed and difficulties encountered, they seem to feel the need to reach their aim i.e. to have a perfectly even board. When at last they sweep up the shavings, the sound reminds us of the rustle of leaves in autumn – and the smell of the pine resin wafts through the room.

Lesson seven – planing (II)

Our lessons often overlap. The recapitulation and repetition of the work consolidates what has been learnt.

The board must be perfect even before the work can be passed as finished. The students are encouraged to help each other.

I now show them how the joiner marks the desired thickness of the boards along the edges, using a special tool, proceeding from the planed area.

I am continually surprised and even despair when I see the problems our students have with this stage of work that seems so easy. Many of them just cannot guide the marking tool evenly and at the same time trace the line into the wood with the metal point. I must keep a wary eye on every student to avoid inexact work. I have to repeat showing and helping them.

20. THE JOINERY MAIN-LESSON BLOCKS (CLASSES 9 AND 10)

Marking tool

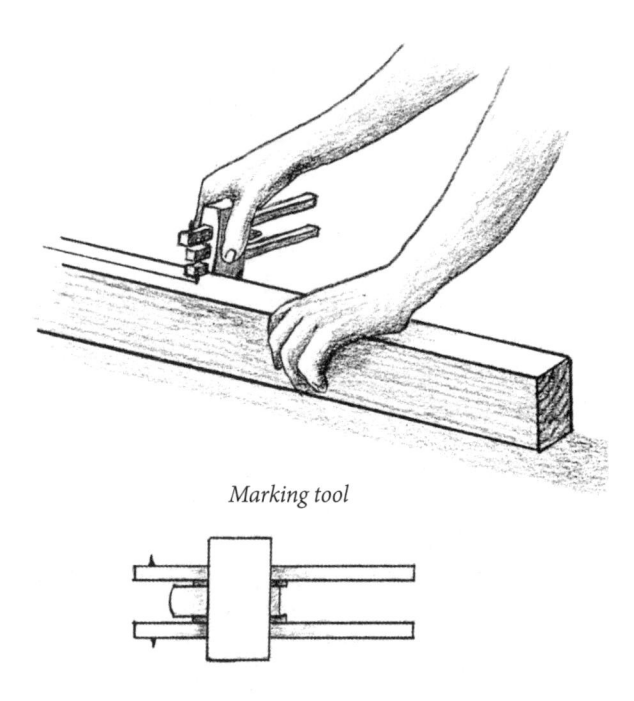

The great challenge here is the will to persevere, and I do my best to develop this faculty in them.

Planing begins with an 'inclined' phase on all the edges, up to the marked line. The rough parts can be cleaned off. Shortly before the desired thickness is reached I use the rough plane that allows me to reach the correct thickness without going beyond it. We then control the evenness with the alignment rod. If it lies completely flat on the board our target is reached and the work completed.

Lesson eight – dovetailing practice

The first thing the students are required to do when entering the room is to get their tools ready for work: two chisels (10 and 16 mm/⅜–⅝ in), a wooden mallet, saw, clamps, small supporting boards, hardboard (to protect the bench surface), square, sharp pencil and alignment tool.

Again I demonstrate by taking apart the dovetailed joint. On one board we can see the teeth, on the other the dovetails. The students can easily see the usefulness of this very practical method of joining.

I continue my demonstration by going through all the stages of this work. The boards are put vertically at the right angle on the bench, the good side to the outside. I draw the joiner's triangle sign at the edges, fixing the right order. The places where the teeth and dovetails are to be cut out are now exactly traced out.

I now put the board vertically into the vice and start sawing along the pencil line, alternating between the left and right side of it, so that exactly half of this line can be seen. This is the greatest challenge for the students.

For the chiselling out of the teeth, I put the boards horizontally between the clamps. With chisel and mallet the in-between spaces are cautiously removed. In order not to overdo the passive thinking/observing part, I let the students practise this work, not easy for many of them. They keep coming to me for help, or they help one another.

Once they start with the sawing and chiselling, I must be careful not to overlook any mishap, and immediately correct mistakes. The rules of the craft must be strictly obeyed; each deviation has negative consequences that become clearly visible later.

When the work on the practice board is complete, the process is repeated on the actual project. Again, I demonstrate and the students watch. The important moment arrives: I hammer the teeth into the dovetails, which fit without any gaps – proving to the students that the meticulous attention to detail is worth it.

It is best to refrain from criticising the students during the preparatory exercises, but rather to let them learn through their mistakes. This increases their attention to detail in the succeeding work. Each of them is working as well as he or she can, showing me the results.

Opportunity is given for a second and independent practice, and I draw their attention to possible mistakes.

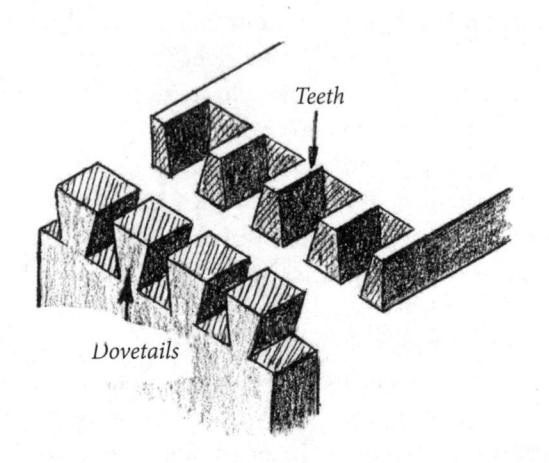

Teeth

Dovetails

Lesson nine – completion of the joining practice

The practical exercises in joining should be completed halfway through this lesson. It is time to proceed to the actual projects. The students must be quite clear about the aims of their work. I retrace the stages of work from the first lesson to the present one. Each of them is described: the fitting of the metal parts, lacquering, priming, grinding and polishing, gluing of the joints. Everybody is aware of the need for determination – time must not be wasted. I fully rely on each student's will to do his or her best.

The repetition of the work at the four ends means additional practice and, with it, improvement. The students develop 'a feel' for their work.

Lessons ten to twelve – joining skills in the students' chosen projects

Two double lessons are devoted to the joining of the students' chosen projects. They all know now how to do it and all I must do is to advise and, perhaps lend a hand. I tell them that they have to finish this stage of the work in the third lesson, that the cuts must be perfectly polished and the boxes glued together (via teamwork). Only then, when every box is finished, are the students allowed to tidy up and leave.

Lessons thirteen and fourteen – final touches and surface priming

During the third year of apprenticeship, the apprentice learns to use the polishing plane. Our students get an idea of this skill when they try their hand at smoothing the joints with this very delicately adjusted and sharp bladed plane. Should the graining be too rough, I must come to the rescue. At last, the surface is polished and primed. It must be allowed to dry, ready for the next lesson.

Lesson fifteen – varnishing

The surface is smoothed with fine emery paper. We place a piece of carpet under the boxes – the delicate surface must not be allowed to get damaged. Feeling the boards with the palms of their hands, the students can test their smoothness. When they are satisfied with their work, i.e. when it is beautifully polished and all dust removed, they may begin with the varnishing. At this stage it is necessary to tell them about such things as staining, waxing, oiling and working with natural varnishes.

Lesson sixteen – completion and fitting metal parts

Many of the projects are now completed, the surfaces varnished, rubbed with fine steel wool and finally with horsehair. They shine like silk.

Some of them have to be fitted with metal hinges, a handle (on a carrying box) or some kind of catch or lock. The use of a screwdriver needs practice. Time flies during this last lesson. Those finishing early spend the remaining time in smoothing out even the slightest unevenness. They all look relieved at having actually succeeded and they proudly take their projects home to show their families.

The work done was beneficial to both head and limbs. Vague thinking and wrong mental picturing immediately showed in the work; an understanding for causal connections awakened. In this way, joinery also serves other subjects, as the faculties gained – skills, exactitude, social interaction etc. – are qualities that apply also to other areas.

The students' horizon was enlarged and it became quite clear during the work what a student could or could not do, and that good will alone is not enough. Thinking and doing met in the processes, leading to self-knowledge – very therapeutic and also sobering at this age. Neither is feeling neglected: each tool demands a delicate feeling touch in order to do justice to the material, wood.

Continuation of joinery lessons in Class 10 and later

During the joinery lessons in Class 10, I always noticed the quite different awareness and active readiness in the students – the result of their experiences in Class 9. It is now possible to introduce the more demanding methods of joining, such as even – with the best students – slotting and pegging, and to apply them to the making of a simple piece of furniture.

To begin with, I let the students recapitulate – without my help – the dovetail joint they learnt in Class 9. This is a quiet lesson for the teacher, during which they can spend all their time observing; at all cost they should refrain from intervening.

My demonstrations in Class 10 are, as a rule, always attentively observed by the students, and the work they do afterwards is carried out professionally.

The work in Class 10 is thus consolidated through recapitulation and taken further and enhanced by practising new methods. One could say that it is only during this second block that the students develop proper faculties: the more superficial processes in Class 9 now gain the necessary depth.

Students opting for individual projects concentrate on the stylistic side of the work. They are allowed to choose any one of the crafts available

PART THREE: CRAFTS IN THE UPPER SCHOOL

at the school, as well as the possibilities within that craft. In the case of carpentry they might prefer working with wood, inlaid wood or veneers.

Our illustrations are of work resulting from suggestions made by smaller groups at the end of this second block. It corresponds to a year's work.[2]

Sideboard

Bedside table

Drawers

Various projects

Writing desk, front and back view

Hanging cupboard with shelves

Desk

21

Wood and carpentry workshops
Michael Martin

The question may be asked: why a special room for carpentry? Wood is, after all, wood, be it for carving or planing. Seen from without, this is indeed so. However, the character of carpentry and its effect on us are absolutely different from those of carving; they represent two quite different worlds.

In a carpentry room we have neatly stacked boards (rough at first, later planed) of exactly the same length, width and thickness. We may add to them if we wish. The colour and graining of the surface is even more important than in the wood we use for carving. Otherwise there is little that reminds us of the original trees they come from. It is doubtful whether someone who had never seen a tree would be able to imagine one just by looking at the boards? The annual rings might, perhaps, provide a clue... The split, massive, curved natural wood chunks are in sharp contrast to the evenness of the boards. They are unique, original, individual, the other repeatable; machines may be used to produce them better and more efficiently than our hands. The task of our hands is to create original objects. Exact repetitions have to be learnt, a skill taking years of practice. It makes far greater sense to mass produce with machines.

The board, the joiner's material, challenges the carpenter to develop ever better methods of joining. Thousands of years of experience are utilised. The right angle plays an almost exclusive role in this work.

Might we assume that the people living in the Middle Ages were actually afraid of the straight line, the exact even surface as they fitted the uneven boards into their half-timbered houses, that made them construct the streets of their towns in gently curved lines? Were they afraid of the sobering coldness of right-angled constructions? Did they have a premonition of the steel structures of our present time? Were they worried about the necessity of developing the ad infinitum repeatable sameness at the expense of losing the elementary/natural qualities? Le Corbusier said: 'In the history of form the straight line is a late product'. He brings it into connection with the rectangle as the culmination of our era.

These reflections are meant to stimulate questions that do not concern themselves with value judgements, but are meant as a help for characterising the mood of a carpentry workshop in contrast to a room in which woodcarving is done. In the former we can feel a direct stream leading from nature into the human sphere; in the latter we enter a highly delicate stage of human creativity that enables us to establish a truly artistic and spiritual culture, as soon as the merely constructive element, justifiable whenever it is in the right place, is overcome.

In the carpentry workshop the pictures on the walls may include diagrams of construction, reproductions of antique furniture and old tools, large photographs of forests, the felling of trees and the milling of timber, attempts at new styles in furniture that liberate them from their straight lines and thus meet our human needs again. It is also desirable to fix panels of different woods or rare veneers from distant countries to the walls.

The mood in a woodcarving room might be engendered by pictures of trees and forest animals, bugs, cones and fruit, by cross sections of stems with their original growth forms and all the things the teacher might bring into the room as the result of their discoveries in the forest about which they speak to their class. Illustrations of old carvings and everyday wooden utensils are also suitable wall decorations – while the humorous touch should never be forgotten.

The reality of a school will not often allow for a strict separation of the two. But we might agree on principles, on the ideal. What is important is the ability to perceive the mood and attitude of the teacher on entering his workshop. And this opens up inexhaustible opportunities.

Who is an apprentice?	*Wer ist Lehrling?*
Every man.	*Jedermann.*
Who is a journeyman?	*Wer ist Geselle?*
He who can.	*Der was kann.*
Who is a master?	*Wer ist Meister?*
The inventive man.	*Der' ersann.*

GOETHE

Part Four

Formative Artistic Lessons in the Upper School

22

Lessons in modelling and shaded drawing
Michael Martin

'It is our destiny and task to recognise polarities accurately, initially as polarities, but later as poles of a totality' (Herman Hesse). Once aware of this truth, one cannot let go of it: we continually discover in all the phenomena surrounding us their underlying contrasting elements that not only dramatically interact with each other but also determine both the life around us and the way we express our innate soul and spiritual nature.

We touch here on a deep mystery of the world, familiar to ancient cultures. In Genesis we read how God created light from chaos as his first deed, bringing about the separation from darkness, and how he placed these archetypal polarities in their measured rhythms as the basis of all subsequent creative acts.

The quote from Hesse points, however, to a far greater and more difficult task than the mere recognition of the world's polarities, that is, where can we find their union?

We see our young people living in the extremes of their soul life during the time of 'earth maturity' – from heavenly ecstasy to the deepest depression. We all know their delicate feeling for justice while, in the next moment, being shocked by their pitiless dismissal of someone whose offence may really be no greater than anyone else's. We observe, at the one end of the scale, a deep laziness, while, at the other end, the fullest commitment to a recognised goal that takes them to the point of self-sacrifice. We may despair at the lethargy of their limbs and yet be surprised at their untiring endurance in sport.

The fresh and living movements during early childhood seem to have vanished during puberty, being replaced by a frequently alarming clumsiness and resistance to activity. The previous gracefulness, with its appealing childlike innocence, visible in the physiognomy, becomes withdrawn and completely transformed. Between joy and pain, sympathy and antipathy, arrogance and depression, we observe the beginning of a world of feelings that provides the soul with all her colouring, manifoldness and inner breadth.

All these tensions in body and soul are caused by the emergence of 'urges, desires and passions' in the individual soul – not negative qualities, but quite generally stimulating, desiring, enthusing energies that engender inner activity and mobility, and kindle liveliness if taken up and directed towards the proper channels.

To create the necessary inner space, however, is only possible through defining boundaries, through separating.

Unavoidably, this makes for a new relation with the world outside; a distancing by which the environment can be perceived as though through new, different eyes, objectively, soberly and factually. The inner as well as the outer world opens up to adolescents; they are trying to find a new connection to both, to discover themselves in them.

In order to develop this inner life, it is necessary to become separated from wider and greater connections. Hand in glove with this process go the dangers of egotism and loneliness. With loneliness comes introspection, causing the world around to descend into darkness. The young person's consciousness of this submerging into darkness may be expressed in words such as the following:

Darkness is a cloud, a dark cloud that rises within us. We are living in a world of darkness.
Michael B. (Fifteen years old)

Night, night – can a human being conquer it or live with it throughout his whole life? Some love it, some hate it. Some are born in it and some die in it. I know that I could not live in the night. To strike a match in the mouth of this monster means to kindle a new sun...
Robert S. (Fifteen years old)

We know that at this age black is a favourite colour. At no other age does it attain such importance.

Every separation or distancing by forming sheaths around oneself needs a firm physical basis – the liquid element does not really allow inner space to develop and every attempt to do so would immediately fail. Hence, we can see the 'consolidation' of adolescents' bodies as corresponding to their soul development.

Loneliness, darkness, heaviness – a depressing condition? Again, Rudolf Steiner has given us a clue to understand it: 'What makes the will mobile? The fact that the soul experiences heaviness through the body.'[1]

The heaviness of the body must first be there; the soul has first to feel it in order to set the will in motion to counter it. Development of will is always a matter of meeting resistance! Heaviness and lightness, darkness and light, death and resurrection – these are primal motifs shining behind the age of adolescence. Is the young person able to 'kindle' that 'sun' which engenders new inner forces, or will they drown in the temptations of a merely materialistic world? This is the decisive question.

This points to a most significant and important educational aim. Does the world in which the young find themselves exhaust itself in purely materially comprehensible events, or is it permeated by elemental formative processes – processes in which spiritual creative forces can come to expression, that can be, if not consciously experienced, at least sensed. Is it possible, by immersing oneself in the polarities evident in the phenomena of form, colour and movement, to become oneself a creator, to bring about, through harmonising such polarities in a work of art into a new unity? Or, more simply expressed, can we discover the first steps that lead our students in this direction? If so, the integration of which Hesse speaks must be present internally, and the hope of attaining it must be entrusted to our responsibility.

Neither explaining these things to the students, nor discussing them, will be as effective as actually creating! Words could all too easily result in either acceptance or rejection, belief or disbelief. In the actual activity they become, if successful, convincing experience. Then it may happen that during the twenties one will again be received by the world from which one was expelled during puberty. One must be received again, one must find the connection, because without it one cannot master life. This connection must be found by each of us, independently. Against this background, the necessity of the formative/artistic subjects will become obvious, as well as the reason why these subjects are allotted so much space in the Upper School.

Principles arising from a knowledge of the human being

There are only scant indications by Rudolf Steiner concerning the curriculum of the formative/artistic subjects in the Upper School. Shaded drawing was to be done in Classes 9 and 10, as well as modelling in clay. Simple carpentry and painting were to be added in Classes 11 and 12.

We shall, however, discover a meaningful structure by again looking at the developmental stages of children's organism of movement. We shall, therefore, briefly recapitulate how these processes in movement during the first seven years are principally caused by the life of the soul that is literally poured across the whole of the organism, and how these inner processes are reflected in the physical body. At the age of seven, the movements are formed more strongly by the rhythm of breathing and the blood. At around age nine it is the expansion and contraction of the muscles that express themselves in the movements.

At age twelve, the muscles incline to the bone structure, grasping and moving this hard system forcefully, heavily, obeying the laws of mechanics.

Bearing these developmental stages in mind, a new subject is introduced at the correct time that supports these processes and intends to help develop them in a healthy way. In an inner picture we can follow children's organisms passing through the elements, a descent from the warm sphere of the soul via the airy and watery as far as its connection with the rigid, the earthy: a densification process. We can observe how

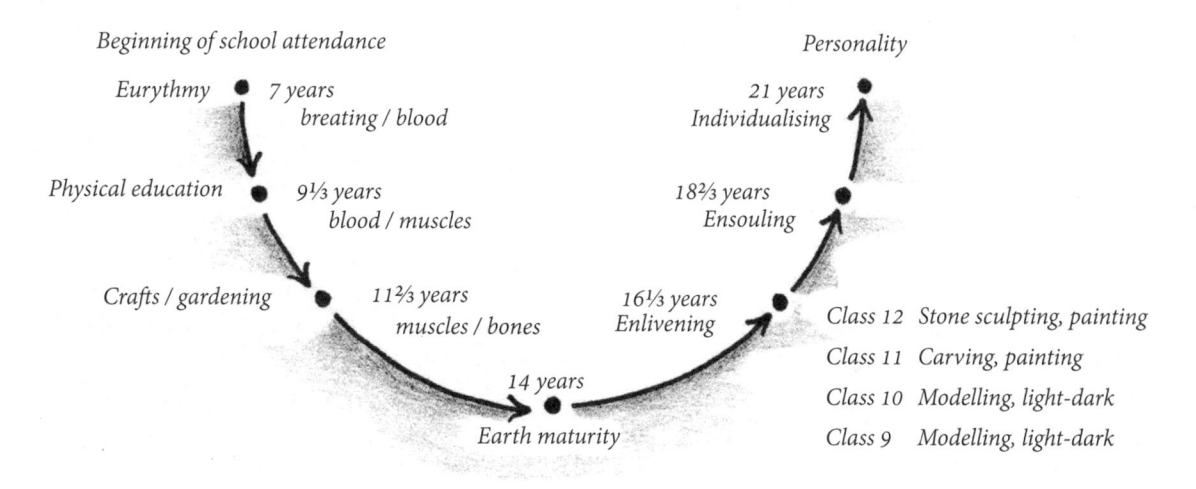

Beginning of school attendance

Eurythmy • 7 years
breating / blood

Physical education • 9⅓ years
blood / muscles

Crafts / gardening • 11⅔ years
muscles / bones

14 years
Earth maturity

Personality

21 years
Individualising

18⅔ years
Ensouling

16⅓ years
Enlivening

Class 12 Stone sculpting, painting
Class 11 Carving, painting
Class 10 Modelling, light-dark
Class 9   Modelling, light-dark

the externally perceptible changes in children's posture and movements directly correspond to their inner development and how this is accurately met in the curriculum.

Adolescents, after having passed through the experience of the earth's gravity, may now, through an inner effort, enliven the course of their movements and formative development. During this work, the muscles can, after their slack phase, begin to make the movements more delicate and flexible. Later, as the germinating soul-forces become stronger, they will en-soul the movements and individualise them through their own will.

We need not stress the fact that our description of the course of development is an ideal one and that it may be coloured and altered in all directions by life situations, such as the environment. A sensitive observer will, however, already see the opposite path in the Upper School students to that of children in the Lower School, in that the bodies of the former separate ever more from their tie to gravity and mechanics, and pass via a moved, enlivened element to an en-souled one, but without losing the ground under their feet, i.e. the connection with the earth on which they are to find their earthly tasks and do justice to them. A diagram of the above should not only show the ascending path of the 'personality' but also and simultaneously retain the horizontal connection with the earth (see diagram on p. 195).

Modelling with clay

This subject is taught in Class 9. The forces of enlivening are active here, as long as it is not a matter of copying nature forms, but rather an attempt at tracing the processes of becoming that eventually lead to a form.

Clay is a substance that lies heavy and cool in the hand. Our first exercise may be to shape a ball from it, as the hands can directly hold and enclose it. The yet shapeless material responds to the most sensitive pressure. Gradually the skin on the surface of the ball develops through the sense of touch by which the form comes about. It is not really possible to place a spherical object on a table – it is not suited to it.

Spherical objects and plane are strong opposites, in need of a mediator, such as a bowl in which a spherical object can be placed. Yet this is still not satisfactory: in order to make its roundness valid to all sides we would have to suspend it from a hook. Even this does not go far enough, because it does not let itself be imparted into our spatial dimensions: it has neither a left nor a right, an above nor below, and is therefore, a stranger to our three dimensional space. Instead, it turns its only plane towards its own centre. It would, in fact, hover or move freely in space – like the heavenly bodies. Are there purely spherical objects in nature? And where are they to be found? We might think of fruit, tubers, water drops, seeds, buds, eggs or of the shape of the human head. These always occur where new life is to arise, still undifferentiated, coming to rest in themselves.

1st exercise   *2nd exercise*   *3rd exercise*

22. LESSONS IN MODELLING AND SHADED DRAWING

Series of curved and animal forms in clay

In our second exercise we now alter the even roundness, stretching it a little flatter, curving it a little more so that a form with several curved planes is produced, but still remaining within the convex, hill-like arched sphere. A third exercise may stretch the initial spherical shape at one end, leaving the other absolutely round. When we have completed all these exercises and displayed our work in three groups we can experience how the spherical objects come to rest side by side, each perfect in itself. We can relate the shapes of the second group to each other – they are livelier and can communicate with each other. The third group seems to point outside itself, seems to show an interest in the environment.

An unexpected polarity arises: there are forms that come to rest in themselves, as spheres; and there are forms that tend to stretch, becoming awake for their surroundings.

If we continue these exercises in a way that rounding off and stretching out arise in rhythmical sequences (longer here, pressed together there), we see animal forms arise that can easily be developed into more realistic forms by adding a mouth or ears. But what is real?

It is the animal's urges and instincts that determine its movements and behaviour. This is different in each species. It is because of this that their shapes also differ. If an urge is excited by some outer happening – the weather, a noise or any other perception – the whole of the animal responds, it becomes eye, ear or smell; its whole organism trembles. Suddenly it speeds off or slinks away – the perception becomes movement as though sucked in by a target a long distance away, outside itself. All these lurking or instinctively moving animals do not stretch – if seen in this way, they have their point of calm or gravity outside themselves.

Another animal is produced, one that changes into a shape that expresses calm – that appears to be rolling into a ball, turning inwards, sleeping. Observers assure us that a cat stretching out on the floor is not sleeping as deeply as the one that contracts into a round form. A wealth of new observations! By doing such exercises, if our students can experience (or at least sense that processes of calmness principally employ rounded forms, whereas movements in the organic world caused by urges and instincts can show these only in outstretched forms), a direct bridge will be built to the manifold mysteries in our world. Namely, that within its infinite wealth of forms, it expresses such laws that testify everywhere to effective formative forces.

Whilst the qualities of calm and mobility essentially determine the physical form of the animal, the human being stretches in its entire form, without allowing itself to be formatively determined by any one urge or instinct, but by bringing its growth to a close in the round, calming form of the head.

Simultaneously, in the human being we have forms of both calm and movement – in the head and limbs – being alternating activities, always in a reserved balance, either in the movement of the limbs to the outside or in the inwardly turned functions of the sense organs. These are mainly concentrated in the head, leading us into the sphere of thinking and reflection.

Physical and spiritual/mental activities of the human being express themselves in quite different physical postures and gestures. This can take us to as many different projects: a person, for example, carrying a heavy load will brace themselves against the weight – the overcoming of weight here becomes visible. Someone who is reading will remain in a resting posture; they will be either sitting on a chair or, perhaps, squatting on the floor. It must, however, be obvious that they are not asleep; their posture must indicate an inner preoccupation with reading. The gesture of a parent's hand resting on their child will be quite different again; their whole posture will express their love and affection. Such inner stirrings can be shown especially in the gestures of arms and hands, determining the movements of head and body. It doesn't do any harm to draw the students' attention to such matters – they are, after all, to become aware of the relation between body, soul and spirit or, in other words, to discover in the outer phenomena the expression of inner processes. At the end of the block we frequently choose the theme: 'Two people' or 'Human and Animal' where the students should in an independent, individual way express the harmony between the opposing emotions and the movements of two or more figures.

If the polarities of calmness and movement are the subject in Class 9, a stronger inwardness is experienced in Class 10 through concave and convex forms. Calmness and movement manifest in the human form as a contrast between above and below: concavity and convexity are localised in the sphere of the soul – in the middle part – and receive their life from the opposites of within and without. In this they are connected with breathing and with all rhythmical human activities. Ancient cultures knew of this and expressed them in human forms considered 'abstract' today.

Rudolf Steiner made us conscious of these laws through his blackboard drawings during lectures. He described in detail the threefold nature of the human form in head, chest and limbs.[2]

The polarity of concave and convex forms will be the topic for Class 10. To begin with, we shape a form whose energies surge as though from within, showing themselves exclusively in convex surfaces and curving to the outside; this is followed by a second form whose surfaces are as though pressed inwards from without, showing themselves as concave, hollow surfaces.

We then observe the effect these two forms have on us: the first seems to be softer, more living, still flexible, as though dreaming; the second, in contrast, seems hard, rigid, determined as though dead – but yet more awake. This effect is due to the edges between the single concave surfaces, separating them. In the first form the edges retreat, giving way to the prominence of the convex surfaces.

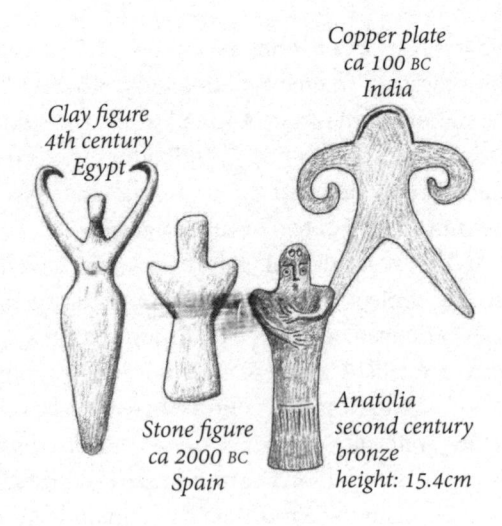

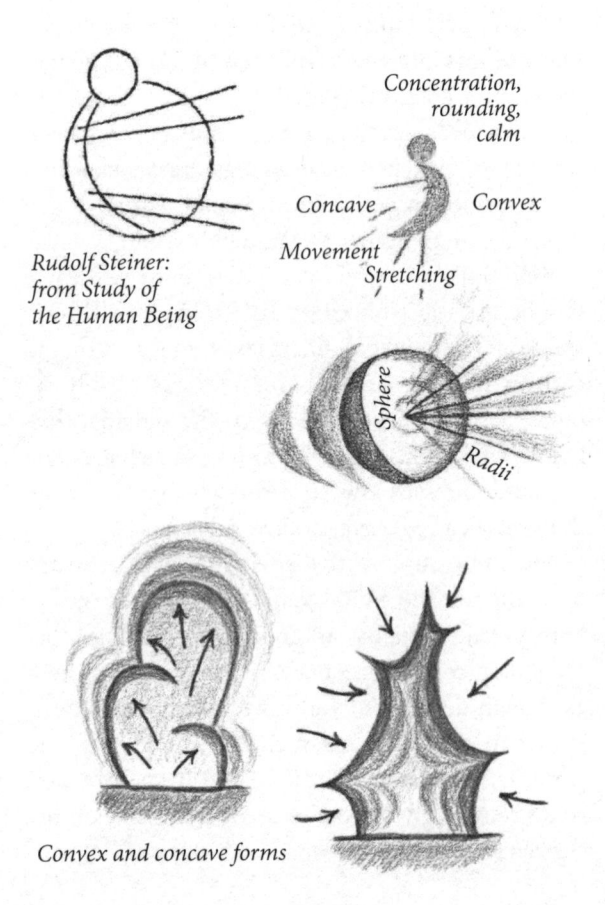

PART FOUR: FORMATIVE ARTISTIC LESSONS IN THE UPPER SCHOOL

Clay figure 4th century Egypt

Copper plate ca 100 BC India

Stone figure ca 2000 BC Spain

Anatolia second century bronze height: 15.4cm

Rudolf Steiner: from Study of the Human Being

Concentration, rounding, calm

Concave *Convex*
Movement *Stretching*

Sphere *Radii*

Convex and concave forms

These exercises do not claim to be artistic. This is of secondary consideration here, in spite of the fact that the students can, although firmly tied to the theme of the subject, invent an incredible wealth of forms. The important thing is to understand that the forms themselves are speaking a language that emanates from inside and can be learnt. In their concavities and convexities they express a 'mood', just as a definite and objective mood is created by red or blue, major or minor that can be described in words.

We now attempt to shape two human faces, each from these same form elements, each one-sidedly. Here, too, we recognise the same effects emanating from either concave or convex forms. But quite unexpected new effects are added. One is not only softer, more living and dreaming, but seems also to be younger, happier, freer and inclined to female features. The other appears to be older, morose, serious and decidedly male. We experience with astonishment the connections between the whole range of feelings; between joy and pain, the life conditions between old and young and the polarity of male–female with the concave and convex form elements.

The whole thing becomes even more exciting when we transfer our experiences of these extreme formative experiments to nature. We already are familiar with the round, flowing forms so strongly related to the watery element. We know the use nature makes of them for allowing all living beings a time of calm, of rest during the embryonic period that may last as long as a year, as in the leaf buds of trees.

We can further experience how the spherical forms break open, differentiate and spread in order, finally, to assume the characteristic of hollowed out and exhausted forms in the shape of dried up leaves, cracked cones, gnawed wood, bony skeletons etc.

22. LESSONS IN MODELLING AND SHADED DRAWING

The forces in 'consuming forms' are, indeed, ageing forces that often come to expression at the end of a sequence of developmental stages in living beings.

We become especially aware of the fact that the ageing process in a human face is synonymous with a 'becoming awake'. This allows us to understand that the development of consciousness necessitates the diminishing of life forces: 'Consciousness is a small and partial death; death is a great and total consciousness, an awakening of the whole being in its innermost depths.'[3]

Leaf buds of oak

Wilted leaves of topinambar

Old olive tree

201

PART FOUR: FORMATIVE ARTISTIC LESSONS IN THE UPPER SCHOOL

A look at contemporary sculptures makes it clear that the 'form-consuming' forces dominate, frequently to the point of destruction, or show merely some traces of matter. What would be the effect of such a sculpture in a school playground? The fact that other attempts at form are made comforts us a little. Far more convincing is the harmonising of the polarities in the 'opening' of the form without losing itself in space.

It goes without saying that we are trying on the one hand to utilise our experiences and knowledge gained, and on the other hand to look for a balance between the polarities and, through it, to arrive at a heightening of our formative work.

We may (and should) happily forget what we have so far learnt, in order to immerse our work into a really artistic-creative element. If, in the course of our work, a student might be unhappy about their failure to make a child's head they are modelling look young enough, the teacher would explain that there are not enough convex forms or that the eyes are too deeply pressed into the head, resulting in a grown up, awake, conscious expression. And if the student understands and responds with an 'Oh yes', the teacher's efforts will not have been in vain.

Our hands, as the only human organs, combine to a great degree of perfection both the rounding and stretching, as well as the concave and arching elements, i.e. a balance between them. There is no animal that comes close to this. To be directed to such an 'open mystery' can be significant for the students.

Forms can be felt and touched by the hands. Beyond their direct reach, the eyes take over this function. Light and shadow, the light and dark of a surface and form, here play an essential role. Through these phenomena of light and dark in nature, a new world arises for us that is of the greatest significance for our eyes, albeit unconsciously

Francesco Somaini (b. 1926) – 'Iron 5925'

Barbara Hepworth (b. 1903) – 'Two Forms' marble, height: 65cm

Henry Moore (b. 1898) – 'Inner and Outer Forms', clay, height: 190cm

perceived. It is not only the Old Testament that begins by speaking of the creation of light from darkness, but also the Gospel of St John. In pointing to the creation of a future world, it begins with light working into darkness – synonymous

22. LESSONS IN MODELLING AND SHADED DRAWING

with the life that Christ brings to human beings for the re-vitalisation of the dying earth. Here we find an immediate concord between the stirrings of the new, inner force during puberty that is to permeate and re-vitalise the bodies that have now 'arrived' on the earth, and the content of the opening verses of the Gospel of St John. A divine-spiritual spark takes hold of the physical-material; will this light be able to shine in the darkness? The confrontation with light and darkness in shaded drawing can express this battle dramatically and become a sustaining element during this age.

Shaded drawing

A group of Class 9 pupils are sitting in front of me. They ask: 'Drawing…? Whatever for…?'

Let us discover the polarities. We shall find the most intense darkness in a cave 'deep down' where the light of day does not penetrate. If we are standing absolutely still in darkness the experience of space is lost. Unless we are familiar with the cave, without light we cannot perceive its width and proportions. And if complete silence surrounds us, uninterrupted by even the sound of dripping water, consciousness of time also is more or less extinguished. Darkness removes us from time and space. The source of light, the sun, cannot be directly perceived by our eyes; we may look at it only through a piece of darkened glass. And yet we have experiences of light, of immeasurable degrees of brightness that correspond to our opposite experiences of deepest darkness.

People whose souls have been loosened from their bodies during an accident, a fall from a rock, a near drowning etc., speak of an indescribably wonderful brightness that does not blind, but is experienced as comforting, as enveloping and sustaining – similar to the experience of falling asleep, but without losing consciousness, a fact which allowed them to speak about it.

Darkness and light exist at the threshold of a different consciousness that takes us from our daily life to another region bordering on it. We now begin to understand why it is easier for us to fall asleep in a dark room: in our sleep we also cross over to another stage of consciousness beyond space and time. The fear many people have of darkness also becomes understandable: they dimly sense the threatening loss of their ego-consciousness through the loss of light, unable to replace it with something else. We begin to pay attention to the *Hymns of the Night* by Novalis who found in the vanishing of the outer world the seed of a new, supersensible consciousness. Twilight also, with all its shades of grey, is seen as a transition from one form of life to another. Goethe's Faust wakes up with the words: 'Life's pulses beat afresh, alive, to greet etheric dawn with gentler mood'. Everywhere, in connection with light and darkness, we find the motif of refreshment and revitalisation; we can extend our vision and become attentive to these every day, although they are unconscious and unnoticed phenomena around us. We are always led to processes of transition, not of actual being, but a becoming of origins and progression.

As in modelling, here we can also meet with an infinite wealth of phenomena with which the students of Class 9 can easily identify, and it is not difficult for the teacher to set them the task of observing well during their walk from school to home, and of reporting their discoveries the following day.

I have found it helpful to begin the lesson with a simple exercise: drawing with a piece of black charcoal so that the brightness at the top of a piece of white paper gradually passes into densifying darkness towards the lower half, descending and experienced as heaviness as it does so. During this work we discover that if we overdo it, the darkness will shut out the light. The darkness must be restrained and assume a receptive form or else the light cannot participate in the process. In a second exercise the same theme is repeated, but in definite stages of grey, so that the light can really be received by the darkness.

Looking at the pictures – all of them displayed on the wall – we realise that the dark seems to press forward and that the light enters the drawing from the depth of the background. We have, added to the opposites above/below from which we began, a new one: distance and nearness. A third dimension, depth and space has arisen. In those drawings where especially delicate transitions from light to darkness is achieved, one can have the impression of light shining into darkness: light is created! Light and space are our first 'achievements', in addition to ever darker graduations. This now becomes the basis for a new theme: e.g. 'light shining across mountains'. A brooding student or one driven by their unconscious will-forces will produce a 'night' picture; a reserved or wakeful student will draw a picture with a delicate mood of light. All of them stimulated by the variety of experiences of the world of mountains.

Very few, if any, of the students would find an answer to the question; what else can you see in these pictures besides mountains, night, light and perhaps clouds?

It is the air – seen here as clear, there as misty, that is the result of either sharp or indistinct contours of the mountains. We discover that the fading of the hills into the background is again one of the effects of air. Near and distance take us, unconsciously, into our breathing processes: nearness, with its clearly recognisable and separated objects, with the contrast of light and shade, asks also for a clear, objective, logical consciousness. In the distance, the single objects seem diffused into a more general element; the sharpness of shadows blurs; the contours merge into the sky at the horizon; we are inclined to look dreamily at them.

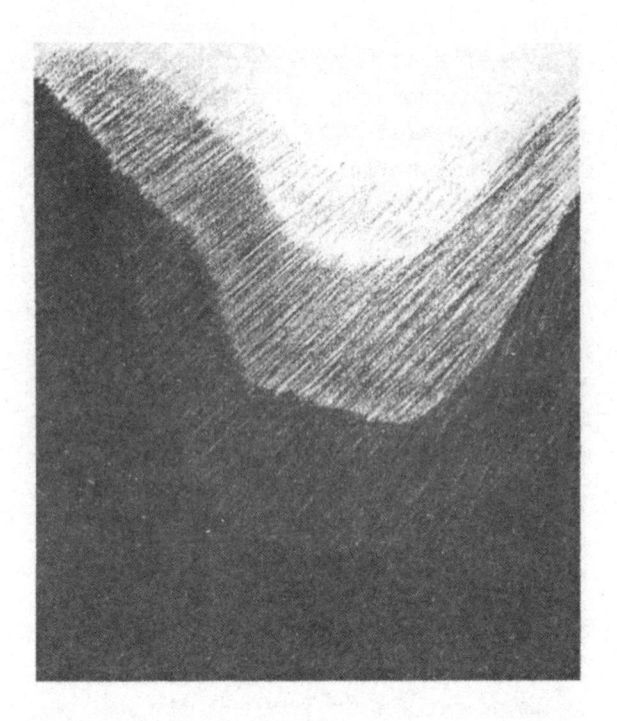

As we draw our pictures we become aware of the air that seems to play a significant part in them as the producer of 'light-perspective'. A space-like impression is produced without linear perspective, which we take great pains to avoid in this technique. As a result our drawings appear to be lifted above the merely natural, embedded as though in a primal creative process, often by an elemental force.

Attentive students will soon notice that they will be more successful if standing in a posture that supports their body. This assures a calm,

22. LESSONS IN MODELLING AND SHADED DRAWING

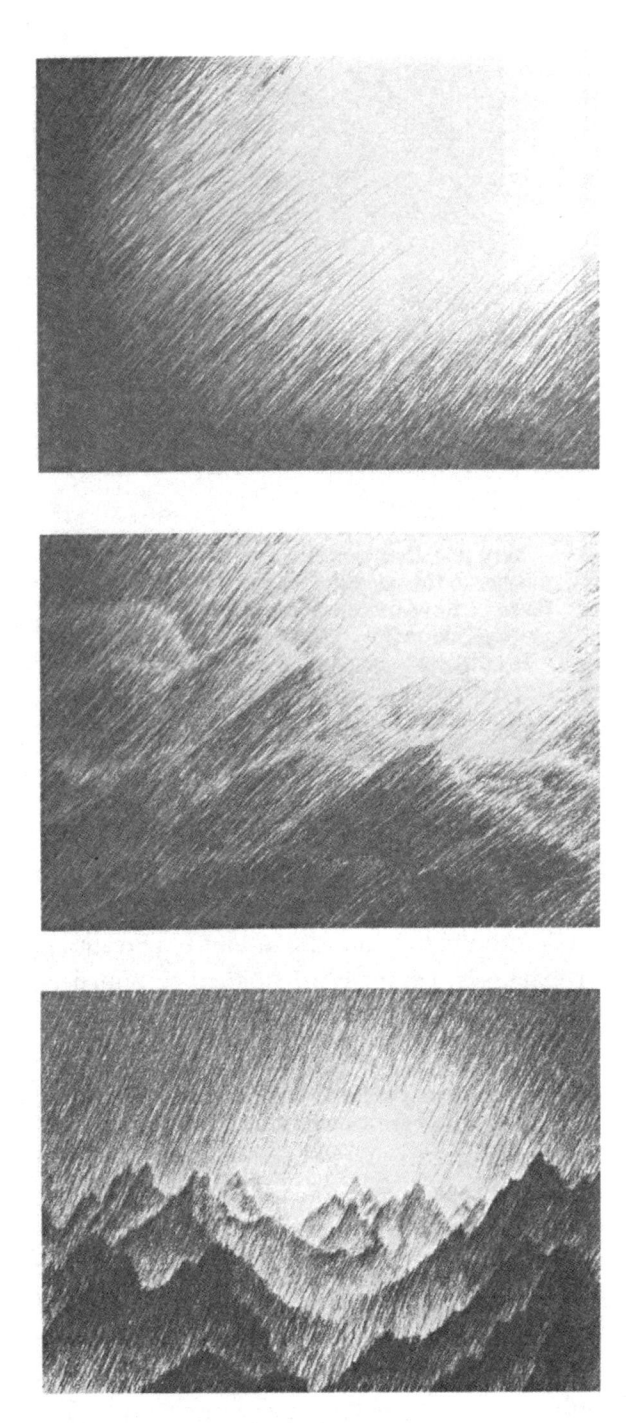

Students' drawings in charcoal

rhythmical breathing during the work. The arm holding the pencil becomes looser when sustained by the vertical spinal column. This allows the breath to flow more freely. This 'taut looseness' during the drawing is combined with the activity of the eyes following the sequences of the strokes; white, black and grey tones are sobering, clarifying, often dramatic experiences. The drawing, as it progresses, constitutes a unity of eye, hand and breathing that, once achieved, effects again the soul of the students, calming and activating them simultaneously.

Indeed, breathing and soul activity are intimately interwoven. Excitement influences our breathing, and our breathing can create an inner mood. The Greek word *pneuma* means breath, a 'whiff, airy substance' as well as 'spirit of God'. The Old Testament tells of the Creator breathing the living breath into Adam, making him into a 'living soul', while the dying man or woman exhales the soul with their last breath. The soul lives within the rhythmical in-and-out breathing; it expresses it directly in singing, sustained by the breath.

During the time of earth-maturity (puberty), shaded drawing is therapeutic. During the process the breathing grows intimately together with the more delicate, reserved, almost mechanical movements of arms and hands. This allows the soul, with the help of the rhythmical-airy element, to permeate and vitalise the middle system of the body. An almost identical process can be observed in a person playing the piano when the soul, through the artist's hands, is induced to express itself in music by means of a most delicate, albeit lifeless mechanism.

22. LESSONS IN MODELLING AND SHADED DRAWING

If the teacher is able to progress to such knowledge, based on their own experience, they will attain the inner conviction that allows them to draw meaningfully with this age group.

Now, let us return to our drawings!

Via the light, air and mountains, we have entered, almost by chance, the realm of the elements that are now to be enlarged step by step by adding trees, clouds, etc. Water is also added, the technique having already been acquired. It lends a new attraction through the mirroring, reflecting effect. The important aspect, however, will always be the way light and air weave around the objects, giving the landscape, as simply as can be represented, its characteristic mood. This mood comes about through the looseness and liveliness of the strokes, through full attention to the formative processes and through the faculty of inventiveness and patient practice.

We arrive at a new stage in our work when we succeed in producing a definite and enclosed space and in drawing the light entering an inner space through a window. Here we become aware of the fact that the light and shade are themselves invisible, until falling on the walls and other objects – just as the soul remains invisible, until perceived together with our sense expressions.

We have taken a path that led from the wide expanse of landscape to an inner space; that constitutes the transition to Class 10. While, in Class 9, we confronted the light coming from the cosmos, which determined the great rhythmical temporal situations on earth, we now turn our eyes to the light that belongs to the physical world: we draw a square lit up by lamps, the inner reflection of light in a crystal, the light shed by fire, or by a candle; a snowy landscape may be included, because the earth covered with snow shines brighter than the sky itself. The theme of our work also leads us from the distance to what is close at hand, from the cosmos to the earth – in tune with the developmental stages of the young.

Shading is the formative means for representing not only light, air and water, but also rigidity and sharpness. If our concern is with the representation of an object, we ought to make use of the line, since this gives us a clearly contoured and unmistakable picture of it. But the object, if so represented, will be standing in an airless and abstract space. Contoured outlines cannot represent day or night, summer or winter. The play of light and darkness in air and clouds opens up the surface that, during the process of densification and loosening, and through bordering and transition, leads us into elemental processes. As A. Turgieneff quotes Rudolf Steiner in her essay on shaded drawing, 'We ought to look for what surrounds the object, for the things that lead to the etheric element...'

What surrounds and vitalises the object

Linear

Shaded

Shading, always done from the top right corner to the left bottom, was a new artistic means developed by Rudolf Steiner during the etching of the glass windows of the first Goetheanum. Max Wolffhügel reports that the method of shaded drawing was 'introduced in the main-lesson as an exercise in Class 9 and beyond (the age of physiological puberty), following Rudolf Steiner's indication on the diagonal direction of the strokes.'[4]

Through the way the lines are drawn – by not flowing into each other, but by remaining strictly side by side – a strong black and white contrast is produced between them. The effect of this method is a very active one, in contrast to the gently formed surface drawn with the side of a piece of chalk, that gives the impression of relaxed outbreathing. By using the rectangular drawing chalk (medium-hard and hard) one can produce the most delicate and deepest black colour tones (through 'veiling').

There are art teachers working with many techniques who assert that shaded drawing does not allow for individual expression, in that all drawings look alike. I could respond by saying that when a hundred people are playing the piano it will still sound like a piano. It is ultimately the choice of music one plays – Mozart or Chopin – and especially how one plays it. The teacher will certainly soon identify the drawing with the student – the characteristic strokes and the manner in which they form their pictures are different even though they 'only' use this method.

Behind the artistic subjects we have briefly outlined, Herman Hesse's words, quoted at the beginning of this article assume an special significance. We become aware of the contrasts of enclosing and stretching out, of concavity and convexity; we discover them in our own physical form, as well as in the objects around us. Do light and darkness also apply to human beings? We can experience them in the contrast of spirit and body – not merely as contrast, but evident in the radiating, elucidating quality we experience in our physical bodies. Similarly we can discover light and darkness in the inner contrast of thinking and willing, whenever we earnestly make the effort to enter into these experiences deeply. We here confront the contrast of head and limb that our thinking and willing produced for themselves as organs for their activities. We may comprehend how the forms and light/darkness emanate from the same roots, shaping the formative forces externally, through what in the sphere of the soul is active within.

Nothing is within, nothing is without
For what's in, is also outside.

Nichts ist drinnen, nichts ist draussen:
Denn was innen, das ist aussen.

GOETHE

Of course, this is not the way to discuss these things with the students themselves; how far one can go in such matters will always depend on the mood, the situation and the human beings themselves. What is important is for the teacher to discover such connections between the human being and the world – it is this that will provide the sustaining foundation for the lessons.

Polarity and unity

Let us consider again the polarity of black and white. Where do we find their unity? By mixing them we lose the polarity and, with it, the fruitful tension between them: what we get is grey. Grey is the outer expression of a static situation, corresponding to a sitting position: heavy, burdensome, inert, lazy. If the poles are attracted by the centre and shaped in grey tones, including black and white, a living,

22. LESSONS IN MODELLING AND SHADED DRAWING

stimulating process will arise, ever changeable, ever progressing in the forming of new spaces. In shaded drawing there is no mixing, the contrast is retained through dark strokes on a white background using strong tension but, at the same time, producing a permeable loosening.

If the concave and convex surfaces are balanced, a flat plane arises, without tension and losing the plastic quality, having only an indeterminate expansion on all sides. The unity in which the poles are grasped and melted into a form without losing their character comes about through stimulating that 'force at the centre' that may lead to an intensification through the artistic taming of the poles. The life of our soul is principally directed to two sides, not only during puberty. But adults have a different access to the 'force at the centre', provided they have developed it in themselves! It reaches maturity at the age of twenty-one.

At the beginning of the third seven-year period, the educator must, therefore, be attentive to two necessary aspects. On the one hand, they must try to tease forth the new, delicate, seed-like soul-forces, hidden behind a still brittle shell, to give them nourishment by which they may unfold. On the other hand, 'the force at the centre', the individual ego of the young man or woman, must become ever more effective, so that, at twenty-one, they have attained sufficient sovereignty to determine their own life. There is wisdom in the fact that the 'coming of age' used to be identified with the twenty-first year.

But both these processes – the unfolding of soul-forces and the emergence of the ego – are parallel. This is because the ego can only become active when placed in the midst of polarity and when challenged by it. It is born from an inner situation of tension that the human being actively addresses itself to. The ego as such is not as yet present, it is in *status nascendi* – a state of continuous becoming through inner effort, energy and the will to be active. It dies, as it were, in inner lassitude. As such it is living within an extremely unstable state, with the possibility of intensifying and heightening, or extinguishing itself, a state that may appropriately be characterised as 'presence of mind'.

Let us try to become more conscious of this process by observing how the human being moves. Walking is a special expression of the ego. Here we can accurately follow and experience in the physical body how the centre is sustained by the polarity.

When we walk, in every step we take, the weight of the body is alternately moved to the left and right – and the spinal column between them quietly moves ahead. Added to this is the fact that each foot is doing exactly the opposite of the other: when the right foot separates from the ground the left surrenders to the weight; when the left foot is carrying the weight of the body, the right foot is free of it. If one steps forward, the other remains behind. The arms are balancing this rhythm by moving in the opposite direction to the feet. Through this rhythmical interaction of polar processes, taking place in the alternation of right/left, backwards/forwards, walking is an unstable process between the surrendering to weight and the overcoming of it. There is no animal that is endowed with such a tense and yet freely balanced relation between heaven and earth as is the human being when he or she walks.

It arises from an impulse of the centre towards the vertical.

When sitting, the polarity working in movement is cancelled, the labile, active condition that continuously arises anew is changed into a stable, inert one. Once we have grasped the significance and meaning of our physical processes, we shall not find it difficult to understand that inner movements arise in the sphere of our soul that challenge the centre.

If, my friend, within you dwell
Forces that oppose each other,
Keep them all! Just fuse them well!
Neither break them, Neither smother.

Hast du, Freund, in deiner Natur
Kräfte, die sich widersprechen,
Wolle sie nicht aneinander brechen!
Behalte sie alle! Verschmelze sie nur!

CONRAD FERDINAND MEYER

Symmetry and asymmetry

During moving (walking), a state of balance is brought about that can only be produced by a continuous balancing of the physical weight and its corresponding physical energies. This happens in movement. When standing, this balance approaches the ideal. The top of our skull and the soles of our feet are above one another along the line of gravity that passes through the human being and is directed towards the centre of the earth. In this state of rest, the body is placed into absolute symmetry. If we wish to take a step, movement can only arise by disturbing this relation. As we push one foot forward, everything begins to enter into the flow of a wealth of asymmetries that 'contradict' themselves in their polarities, as described earlier. Only this makes our movements possible.

The decisive factor is the centre that, invisibly, carries the asymmetrical processes in a rhythmical way. Rhythm here appears to provide the opportunity of saving the asymmetries from falling apart; the inner sustaining force of the centre makes use of the rhythm in order to transfer its forward striving will to the physical a-symmetrical corporal processes. Walking thus becomes the physical realisation of the human ego.

If, now, our moving ahead in walking is possible only because of asymmetry, its tools must also be asymmetrical. One foot by itself cannot do it; without the complement of its mirror image it remains helpless. Organically they are connected to each other in a way that their complement, once mastered during early childhood, seems to be happening as though by itself. If we had to bring about this unity of asymmetry consciously every time we take a step, we should have no time for other things, such as the enjoyment of a landscape, or for the execution of a job that requires the movements of our limbs.

If we consider our middle system with our arms and hands, we meet with a quite different organisation. Our hands are capable of carrying

22. LESSONS IN MODELLING AND SHADED DRAWING

out a task, independently of each other. One hand can do the job of the other if this should be warranted – even though each hand is formed asymmetrically. Continuing with our observation, we are amazed at the freedom of movement given us purely organically for our activities. This high degree of freedom is due to the strongly pronounced, yet restraining centre of our spinal column. Through its strictly symmetrically formed structure – towards left and right – it sustains and carries our most mobile and free organs, that is, our hands.

Our hands have also emancipated themselves from any rhythmical sequence of movements, and yet they are connected to our breathing and blood circulation, the quintessentially rhythmical system.

We have already spoken of the soul expressing itself organically in our breathing. Inner stirrings can, however, also live in physical movements – spontaneously in little children, instinctively in the animal. Here they enter the body more strongly, albeit more externally. Breath is a soul activity tied to the body; the movements of our arms and hands are at its disposal.

What is essential for us is that the soul is physically active in our organisation of rhythm and movement; the soul is active everywhere in asymmetrical forms. This means that, in the sphere of the soul, there is the possibility of turbulence and instability, because of the 'centre' biding its time, waiting behind the scenes until it is either called upon to enter the battle or be ignored, i.e. if the person concerned prefers to be driven by the contrasts of instincts and desires, wishes and antipathies. The more powerful the confrontation, inner mobility and drama, the stronger will the asymmetry appears. The harmonising centre will be challenged – as in the activity of walking. This can become sense-perceptible in the arts:

the light, diminishing in brightness, vanishing into the distance – the dark, encompassing itself, confining, surrendering to weight; the force in a sculpture, urging from within outwards, dissolving the form; the radiating freshness of yellow, the mysteriously enveloping coolness of blue; the forward urging and restraining elements in movement – we can discover ever new creative polarities in the world and in the human being! They permeate all the processes in space and time as though with a great cosmic breath, but they, too, are sustained and borne by a hidden, mysterious law of unshakeable harmony.

Who are the beings that manifest through such forces? Rudolf Steiner pictured them in the sculptures and paintings of the first Goetheanum, showing their reciprocal effectiveness, between the figure moving forward, bearing within itself the spiritual centre in order to keep the two opposing forces in their places. We can clearly see their a-symmetrical form, their polar structure, the interflow of forces in the central figure that shows itself to the onlooker in its asymmetrical posture, powerfully producing the centre in the viewer.

Because of our participation in these cosmic powers, we carry these contrasts and polarities within our inner organisation. From there they radiate through our physical form. We have convinced ourselves of their necessity for, without them, we could not take a step forward. They provide our soul life with inner tension and breadth. All they require is the master who controls them. Overcoming them does not mean destroying them, but rather to muster the strength to hold them in place, to harness and subdue them.

How else could we make a drawing if there were neither black nor white, how else could we live without either day nor night, thinking and willing?

A girl aged sixteen and three quarters wrote about her ego experience in her diary:

A new world has been opened for me, into which I am occasionally allowed to take a look, into which I am allowed to enter. It is an infinite depth into which one is allowed to immerse oneself. It was on a Sunday when I experienced this the first time. I saw it quite clearly in the picture of the golden staff with the black and white serpents. A wonderful great light was in one of them. Before this I was asleep, now I have woken up.

Heightening – intensification

In the art subjects of Classes 11 and 12, the previously learnt skills are now deepened and applied more freely by the students in painting, carving and stone masonry.

If one has the opportunity of seeing black and white drawings side by side with colourful paintings, one will experience the tremendous step from the sobering, yet life-filled severity and restraint, of the light/dark shaded drawings to the breadth and liberating openness of colours. Goethe referred to them as 'the deeds and suffering of light', ranging from the mysterious blue to the radiating quality of yellow.

The subject of painting is dealt with thoroughly in other books.[5] We shall, therefore, only briefly sketch the way it fits into the structure of the curriculum. After they have been made familiar with the basic colour exercises, the theme takes the students via the painting of trees, landscapes, nature moods and flowers, to the painting of the human countenance in Class 12. Without noticing it, we passed through the whole of Goethe's colour circle, beginning with yellow/blue, by which green is naturally produced through their mixing, providing the general basis for all plant life. The experience of light and darkness in yellow and blue provides the immediate continuation of the shaded drawing in previous blocks. The added red densifies the green to brown and effects the firmness of the trunks of the trees. Gradually there unfolds a differentiated range of colours in the trees during the seasons, during sunrise and in the moods created by the moon. The wealth of colour tones then begins to live in the flowers and blossoms as though in an intoxicated forest.

Purple, opposite yellow in the colour circle, is the basis for the 'incarnation' colour of human Caucasian skin. This colour is produced, not by mixing, but by an intensification, a heightened interaction of both colour streams in the careful and correct veiling (layering) of the wet colours. Again this is a path leading across polarities and their natural mixture, right up to a heightening; from the breadth of light and space to the features in a human face in which the individuality finds its most manifest expression.

At the same time, as we painted we passed through the plant cycle: the green lets us experience the sprouting of leaves. A new impulse manifests in the great variety of blossoms that bring the cosmic forces of light to the earth, pushing back the green in leaves and stems, transforming it. Outer growth appears to be most vigorously restrained in the seed, made inward, containing the whole energy of a new plant. Connected with this state of 'individuation', the retreat into oneself, is the frequent glimmer of purple of the early spring buds, the bursting shoots, the unfolding leaves. Friedrich Schiller challenges us to take consciously such steps that live unconsciously within the plant's growth:

22. LESSONS IN MODELLING AND SHADED DRAWING

growth – blossom – seed. They correspond with the progression from body to soul and spirit. Schiller saw in the external step by step development of the plant what can be made inward by the human being and can, thereby, be of the greatest significance:

Are you searching for the greatest, the highest?
The plant can teach it to you, –
In order to achieve your aim,
What it does without willing,
you should do with a will!

Suchst du das Grösste, das Höchste,
Die Pflanze kann es dir lehren, –
Was sie willenslos ist,
Sei du es vollends, – das ist's!

Why is it important to indulge in such theoretical digressions? Quite apart from the fact that botany and cell structures are important subjects in Class 11, and that all areas of natural science lead to a comprehension of the human being in Class 12, we can see how, in the art subjects, the world emerges from the ocean of forms – light/dark, the colour phenomena, how the world in which we live, with which we are interwoven, shapes and forms, reaching into the deepest levels of life.

We may see from this that there is more to art than its aesthetic nature, that it wishes and is able to lead us into the mysterious processes of development, of becoming, processes out of which our world even today creates itself anew and by which it is maintained. Paul Klee said: 'Art does not reproduce the visible – it makes visible'. Through the creative artist, forces and processes are made visible that would otherwise remain invisible, hidden. If we see the encouragement of a comprehensive interest in the phenomena of

PART FOUR: FORMATIVE ARTISTIC LESSONS IN THE UPPER SCHOOL

the world as our educational task in the Upper School, it will be clear that this can be awakened by artistic activities.

The flow of work in the plastic, three-dimensional arts is continued in Class 11 (wood carving) and brought to a close in Class 12 (stone sculpture). The projects concentrate on the human form or abstract work, form for form's sake, not copied from nature. This intensification of the work arises from the material itself as well as from the young students' will to create forms.

Referring to clay, Rudolf Steiner said that the condition for an understanding of the formative forces of life as such, is provided by the way this soft, flexible substance is handled through the sense of touch. Indeed, it is not only water that makes clay malleable, but also the processes that bring it close to an organic substance. Wood is more closely related to the sphere of the soul; this is the reason why older cultures, concerned with giving expression to the soul, preferred wood for their sculptures, frequently in a coloured setting or mounting, or they worked in stone in the way one does with wood as, for example, during the late Middle Ages in Europe. The colour, smell, grain, rhythm of the annual rings, and even the degree of hardness are all expressions of soul-forces.

More than any other material, stone challenges the will and commitment of the personality. Nothing but clear, unequivocal structures rule the day, structures hewn from this lifeless, hard

22. LESSONS IN MODELLING AND SHADED DRAWING

substance with a heavy miner's hammer in order to give it shape. Inexorably the stone will break if the chisel is wrongly placed or if a layer has not been recognised correctly. In ancient Egypt and elsewhere masses of workers submitted to the will of one man, the Pharaoh who acted out of divine inspiration, in order to create a temple with its statues from stone. These days the young men and women are to test their strength and energies, show what they have learnt and what is living in them by independent, formative work.

During the transition to the Upper School, the laws of the plastic-visual arts are first discovered and developed. The students are now led ever more to individual creations. Every single work arising from the will-forces of the students is unique and new in the world.

As the basis of our modern, scientifically orientated consciousness, mathematical laws take us in a general way to the thought connections in the world. However, the laws of form, colour, sound, movement, rhythm etc. of an object or process connect us to the activities and life in everything that immediately surrounds us. Both complement each other; what matters is their correct harmonising. This points to the task a Steiner-Waldorf school must set itself:

In our work, our task will be always to call upon the whole of the human being. We could not do this without paying attention to the development of artistic feeling slumbering in all of us. By doing this we shall encourage our students to have a real and deep interest in the whole world, an interest they will retain and carry into later life.[6]

This is how Rudolf Steiner expressed it in 1919. Only by devoting oneself to the world can one act responsibly, i.e. from knowledge, and take one's assigned place in a positive, meaningful way. By endeavouring to combine the polarities of the world in their unity, ultimately we may discover our centre of gravity in the spiritual strength of our ego.

Comments on the following essays

All the dovetailed wooden boxes made by different people will be identical if correctly and carefully made. The making of the joints follows definite long-established rules. The traditional techniques of the craft are generally valid and form the basic elements of all work.

This is different in the artistic field, where the setting out and methods used can vary considerably. The latter are not tied to general techniques but emanate from the interest and experience of the individual. This applies, of course, to the teachers in the Upper School with their individually developed artistic intentions, else they could not teach with the necessary enthusiasm, and the kindling spark would not reach their students. This is the reason that while we include here only one essay from each craft, there are three descriptions of stone carving and modelling. In the section on working with clay the subject was treated as a kind of 'knowledge of forms' that led to the artistic. In Anna-Sophia Gross's contribution *Metamorphosis and modelling lessons*, the metamorphosis of form up to Class 12 is given special prominence. Modelling will again come to the fore in close connection with drawing and stone carving in the article on *Stone carving in the Upper School*.

PART FOUR: FORMATIVE ARTISTIC LESSONS IN THE UPPER SCHOOL

This will provide ever different ways of understanding the principal elements of the plastic arts. They will be found in each contribution in specific ways. What is important is the attempt to find the formative, changing, vitalising elements in education during the third seven-year period, especially during puberty. Our contributions are intended as stimuli for this.

We have included the article on shaded drawing because of its close relation to the plastic arts. Both have their roots in the etheric-elementary world: modelling in the watery-moist, shaded drawing in the airy-light element. Forms cannot be separated from light and shade; light and dark not from the formative and dissolving processes.

23

Metamorphosis and modelling lessons
Anna-Sophia Gross

When the onslaught of destructive forces in our time constitutes a real threat, it is especially important to have recourse to the forces that revitalise nature. Destructive forces must be confronted with an increased understanding of the mysterious laws of formative forces in nature and in the human being. This alone will make it possible for us to influence the dying life forces in a positive way. This task is well begun with a study of natural science as shown by Goethe. Exact observation of the plants led him to a knowledge of the fundamental principles of plant growth: his idea of the archetypal plant. His descriptions of the single stages in plant life allow us to recognise the metamorphoses and sense the active being of the plant in its continuous transformations.[1]

Rudolf Steiner extended the idea of metamorphosis to all living nature processes, including the human soul in its step-by-step transformation. He described the development of children, with changes occurring not only in their bodies but also in their souls. Body and soul are closely linked during childhood. Educational measures that affect children's souls via the body (food, daily rhythm, meaningful activities and medical treatment) and those that affect the body via soul and spirit (pre-occupation with mental images, thoughts appropriate to the age and artistic activities) all contribute to children's harmonious development. It is only adults who are able to educate themselves through the strength of their ego, in which case they will continue to transform their inner life in old age, not, however, by virtue of natural conditions, but through the strength of their own spiritual striving.

Art and metamorphosis

Art connects these two sides of human development, nature and soul/spirit. Rudolf Steiner applied the idea of metamorphosis to the arts as a new impulse. He graphically demonstrated the way this can be done in the sphere of sculpture in the first Goetheanum. Even today, through studying the models of the large auditorium, we can see how the motifs of the pedestals transformed step by step from the first to the second pillar, intensified and connected by the mighty architrave. And so on, every one of the seven pillars, with its characteristic form, being an intrinsic part of the whole.

During the second decade of the century, when art, through the advent of abstraction and realism, was under threat of losing its original life, Rudolf

Steiner gave us the opportunity to develop an art of sculpture that connected again to active life forces in nature and the human being. An organic sculpture is, according to him, neither a copy nor a simplification of outer nature – as practised e.g., during the 'Jugendstil' period (at the turn of the century, and continued by anthroposophists, as the critics would have it) – but is developed out of the experience of formative forces in the world. Rudolf Steiner put Goethe's words as motto for a future aesthetic: 'Beauty as manifestation of mysterious natural laws that would, without it, remain hidden'. According to Goethe, the artist's task is to make the hidden spiritual tendencies in nature perceptible to the senses, allowing the totality to emerge from the formative possibilities of a single part. He or she must try to break the spell of what is mysteriously enchanted in nature, unable to unfold in it. 'Only that will be experienced as beautiful which appears to be more perfect than nature, where the object grows beyond itself on the basis of what is hidden behind it.'[2]

Rudolf Steiner gave us an example of this: he described the form tendencies to be discovered in the human being, that can be developed in an artistic process – where asymmetry could come to the fore to a greater degree than is made visible by nature. The ossifying form of the head could, in accordance with its tendencies, develop a head with strong, mobile elements. The form-creating forces, active in human nature either as hardening, rigidifying or as mobile, volatile elements are to be brought out as 'spiritual forms'. Rudolf Steiner attempted this in his wooden sculpture for the Dornach Goetheanum building.

We may dimly sense the creative possibilities of this artistic impulse. We stand at a new beginning. What Rudolf Steiner wrote in connection with the plastic forms of the Goetheanum applies to this new approach of the art of sculpture:

The natural, wherever it unfolds in a living way, works in forms that grow from each other. In artistic work one may get close to the work of nature, if one devotedly and emphatically grasps the way nature lives in metamorphoses.[3]

This artistic impulse gives us the opportunity to develop a series of exercises that culminate in the study of metamorphosis. I shall show, by using a number of examples, the basic experiences in modelling that seem important to me. These experiences will always need to be encompassed, albeit more or less consciously.

Modelling

Modelling in the Lower School is mostly connected with the main-lessons. The so-called 'Man and Animal' block (Class 4) is a prime example: when penguins have been discussed, children will joyfully shape these birds, even several weeks later. The experience will still live in them, becoming the motivation for shaping the animals. We see the most diverse shapes of penguins formed – fat ones, skinny ones, large and small headed. Some of them seem to look about with curiosity, others appear to be quite calm and phlegmatic. We see a wealth of possibilities of movements and expressions. Exceptionally quick workers might add one or two chicks – the given subject is differently and individually addressed.

All children are still (in their minds) in the workshop even though they may have gone to do something else.

23. METAMORPHOSIS AND MODELLING LESSONS

In one class, the question was repeatedly asked: 'When can we make swans?' I did not initially respond because of the difficulty for the beginners to succeed in shaping the thin necks. But they insisted. When I found out that swans had been the subject of a lesson the previous year, I at last gave in and they were satisfied. I clearly experienced the children's need to actually shape what had been learnt and seen, and this at a definite time after the event.

Vice versa, modelling has a tremendously enlivening and en-souling effect on physical sight – through watching the hands' activities. By perceiving the forms produced, children take a greater interest in the things around them if they were introduced at the right age and in the right way to the forming of three-dimensional objects.

If one wishes to put this effect on physical sight to the test one could try and model a form with closed eyes or feel an unknown object with the fingers. One will discover one's strong wish to visualise what the hands are doing. In this experiment, the will impulses one can feel in the eyes, allow us, afterwards, to look at the world with greater wakefulness. Our interest in everything we do increases.

Anyone who has experienced the connection between seeing and modelling can, out of true understanding, motivate children to model. The only question is whether we notice and support the events that are important for our children's development. A happy incident gave me an example furnished by daily life.

We were in the mountains and a heavy downpour kept us indoors. As soon as the rain stopped we went outside and looked at the black mud that had washed down from the pine wood further up. As soon as the seven-year-old boy saw it, to his mother's horror, he knelt down in the wet grass and put both his hands in the mud. 'Look!' he cried jubilantly, 'You can make things with it. All you have to do is to mix it with some dry earth!' The fact that the mud would crack when dry did not bother him. The joy in shaping was the decisive factor.

Building sand castles at the beach or in the sand box is an important experience for young children. They have to get the sand moist enough for their castles, mountains, roads, tunnels, caves and lakes. Children's formative forces wish to be used and, if nothing else is available, they will make do with the mud in puddles. The result is of secondary importance; the doing is all.

Water plays an essential part in getting the consistency right. Be it in nature or in the modelling room, it makes it possible for the living formative forces to enter the otherwise lifeless substance. Unformed matter, clay, is given shape through water; it lets itself be kneaded, is enclosed in a skin. Yet it is only the human being who can give it a 'taut' surface; it never just happens by itself. The formative penetration of matter engenders children's growing into the world.

Rudolf Steiner suggested that clay modelling should begin at about the nineth or tenth year. Before that, beeswax is preferable. Children's inner relation to the environment changes considerably during this time. Up to now they did not experience themselves strongly as being separated from the world around them; whereas now it is possible for them to feel apart from it and they must find new ways to relate to their families, homes and nature.

The new subjects of nature study and history are a great help for this, as well as artistic/practical activities.

Woodcarving is introduced in the Middle School and complemented by formative exercises. The work with wood should not exhaust itself in the practical doing, but appeal to children's sense of form. They should be brought to the point where they only like useful articles if they are beautifully shaped. While we need tools for the work we do, the uniqueness in modelling lies in the fact that we can shape the material directly and exclusively with our hands. During the work, the faculties of these most human of all organs are unfolded in differentiated ways. It does not make any sense, therefore, to use modelling sticks in this subject. Children gradually learn to appreciate the truly wonderful structure of their hands. Arched forms are shaped with the palms: with the pronounced arched and muscular balls of our hands, we transform the shapes and are able to produce slightly hollowed surfaces. The wealth of angular forms is already there in the bony structure of the fingers. Just as the complementary copy of the colourful environment arises in our eyes, so do form and hands complement each other to a unity during modelling. With our concave palms we experience the convex form, feel its wish to expand, and we retreat from it. With the balls of our hands and with our fingers we enter actively into the material, force it back. Through this, the form assumes a receptive character. Out of the reciprocal interplay of polar active forces the apparently living plastic form arises.

Modelling animals and people

Our first exercises in the practical/artistic lessons in Classes 5 and 6 are animals and people, just big enough to be enclosed by the hands. Within this space of our warm hands, from the enclosed ball of clay, rounded animals emerge: sitting birds, frogs, hedgehogs, rabbits, baby sheep are all suitable subjects, their simplified shapes especially allowing the expression of convex forms.

During the transforming process the beautifully stretched surface of the ball of clay should not be destroyed. If the surface is roughly handled by inserting the fingernails in it, there will be problems in restoring the broken 'skin' afterwards. Less haste, more speed is a sound principle. We can already see in this exercise how a form differentiates itself as it develops. A little help will encourage children to test themselves again. Without concentration, without being engrossed in the hands' activities, an enclosed surface will not come about. Any hectic state must be avoided. A pleasant and calm working mood is produced when children immerse themselves into the process of feeling by touch.

Not all children find modelling easy. It is important to ensure that their joy does not wane, and that they do not despair by the all too common 'I can't do it!' The essential thing is not what one can do, but what one can develop through practice.

We progress from the rounded animal forms to the stretched ones. The fish has always proved itself as a transition. The fish is formed through the wavy movements of its surroundings; it speeds ahead through the beat of its lateral fins. We get a clear picture of the archetypal movements of the fish, a horizontally forward striving right/left movement. And children can directly see how the movements we give to our animals also express their very soul. A little bird may look sadly downwards or cheekily upwards, can look to the front as it greedily reaches for food or have a critical, sideways expression; every child shapes his or her very own little bird.

The children are learning much by comparing their work at the end of the session that closes with the attempt to make a small upright human figure.

This initial theme can be further developed during the next block by making small groups of animals. If we decide on turtles we begin with

23. METAMORPHOSIS AND MODELLING LESSONS

the shaping of a generous Mediterranean-like landscape. From this the turtles will emerge quite naturally – they look like walking hills. Their armour-like backs are convex and have to be lovingly sensed by the fingers during the work. When making cats we start with the semi-spherical backs that gradually develop into playing kittens. Their movements must be carefully harmonised if a cohesive group is to be the result. In a fox or bear emerging from a cave the forms complement each other in an ideal way; as the cave is modelled the animal's body almost happens to arise from it. It is not only the plastic forms that meet in a harmonious unison, but animal and surroundings can also be experienced in their close connection.

Developing our work further to include human figures – simple at first – we may suggest the modelling of a shepherd with a few sheep, or a man or woman and dog. This allows children to give individual expression to their relation to animals. We get shepherds who caringly bend down to their sheep, shepherds who hold a sheep in their arms, or shepherds standing upright, watching over their flock. Phlegmatic children might insist on their shepherd having a rest.

As soon as we model upright standing figures we must find the balance within the form that corresponds to the balance in walking or standing. In modelling we intensively use those senses Rudolf Steiner called the 'unconscious night senses' or 'will sense' – the sense of touch, movement and balance. We are hardly ever conscious of them and yet we could not take a step without their continuous presence. As we touch an object or exert pressure on it from within our bodies, the sense of touch lets us perceive the surface of the skin. We knock, as it were, against the world outside. Our sense of movement tells us of the movements carried out by our body, our limbs, of changes in the space around us. The sense of balance provides us with the possibility of relating to the directions in space, especially to the vertical.[4] These experiences of the energy relationships are a pre-condition for the ability to perceive them also in sculpting and architecture. Fluctuating movements within us are brought to a static condition in a sculpture. When the main-lesson in Class 8 deals with the study of anatomy it is appropriate and stimulating to model bones. We try to shape the flat top of the skull, a vertebra and tubular bone. We shall easily discover the formative forces in the chest vertebrae finding the balance between these opposite tendencies.

PART FOUR: FORMATIVE ARTISTIC LESSONS IN THE UPPER SCHOOL

One of our students once brought a vertebra bone to school to keep us from making a mistake. It proved to be a bonus as we were able to study exactly how the small bones beautifully interlock.

In order to avoid mere copying I tried to lead to the natural forms by a gradual, developing process. We began with the basic form of a lemniscate, densifying it towards the inner part of the body, resulting in supporting vertebrae. At the same time, the protecting cavity of the hole in the vertebra formed itself. Added to this arrangement in the horizontal are the vertical connections of the bordering vertebrae and the right/left transitions to the ribs through the appendices of the vertebrae. The polar opposites of form, most clearly manifested in the enclosed concave shape of the head and the tubular bones of the legs as vertical props, are only brought together in the vertebra – and at the same time connected with the three spatial directions.

This experience will not be forgotten. How a part adapts to the whole, how, not immediately, but in its form it is in tune with and related to all the other parts, are questions the students in the Upper School carry with them also as inner problems: how can I adapt, with my individual possibilities, to the social life in a harmonious way? Can I learn to control the polar soul-forces in myself, the rising sympathies and antipathies?

The soul's experiences are reflected in the form processes. The subject of metamorphosis of bones is therefore not only an essential basis for free, formative exercises in the Upper School, but is also of assistance in mastering life.

At the beginning of puberty the students ask for more concrete projects. The free forces of imagination give way to the forces of reasoning and intelligence that now develop as independent entities. It is our task during this time, when thinking is assuming a realistic and analytical character, when the video culture either threatens to extinguish the remnants of the forces of imagination or turns them into an unhealthy, fantastic world of pictures, to develop the appropriate forces of imagination through the arts. With few exceptions, the students are unable to respond to a free, individual theme. Past experiences are of no use; we must begin anew. But this offers a great opportunity. The individual students now show us quite new aspects of their personality. During the course of the Upper School, the teacher is continuously surprised by the students. Very slowly, new formative forces keep emerging from the chrysalis of formlessness. The images throughout this essay demonstrate what I attempted to achieve with my Upper School students in the plastic arts. Every teacher will, of course, find his or her individual methods, depending on the point of departure. Experience with students, study of the human being and personal artistic formative abilities will provide the basis on which lessons will be founded and sustained.

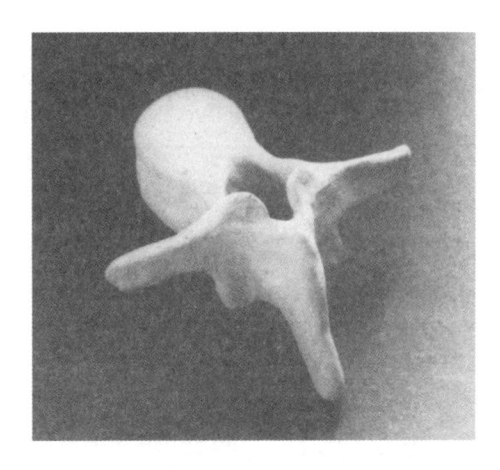

Modelling forms and surfaces

The previous exercises of 'feeling by touch' in the earlier classes are now raised to a higher level in Class 10 – to a free shaping of forms arising from a number of transformations of the sphere. The shaping of surfaces, their stretching as far as to the production of edges, are exactly observed and practised. Art, too, is based on craftsmanship. Rounded forms with their qualities of growth and expansion radiate strength and life.

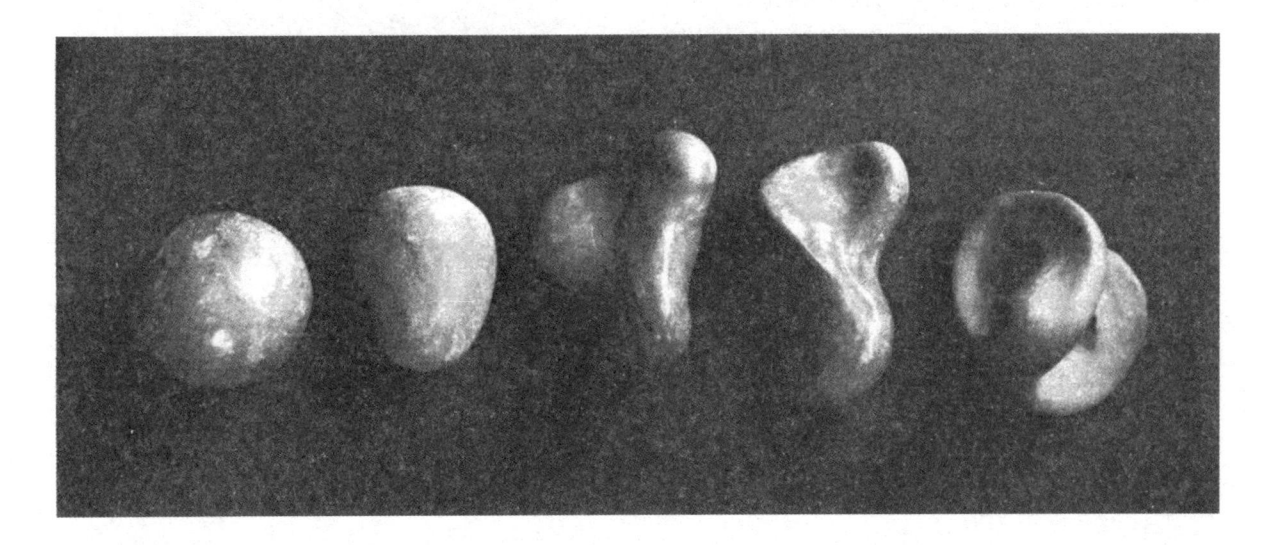

Hollow, concave forms with their enveloping and receptive qualities 'breathe' definite soul moods. Both of them through a wealth of reciprocal interplay shape the plastic forms. We begin to pay attention to the transitions joining the single forms. What kind of curve are we dealing with here? Is it convex? Is it concave? It is both: doubly curved. Convex and concave curves lead, through their working together, to a heightening of the polar formation of surfaces. The moving element, the process of becoming in a form is most clearly visible in the doubly curved surface. Everywhere where forms are continuously passing into each other, be it in organic nature or in a sculpture, this is happening through the doubly curved lines (for instance, as in the surface of a saddle).

If one has not yet observed such a surface accurately, one should take a look at one's outstretched arms, at the transition at elbow and wrist, and one will discover many such places. Contraction, connected with stretching and turning, allows the development of living, active formations of surfaces in the world of organic forms. Movement here is flowing; rhythmical balance is established. The eyes do not here come to rest, cannot be fixed. They are compelled to move from concave to convex forms. We are, as it were, asked to see through the sense of touch. We feel changes taking place, with the pulse of life in them. The simpler the basic exercises, the stronger will be the faculty to observe. A more difficult exercise would be counter-productive to the learning of the basic phenomena in the formative arts.

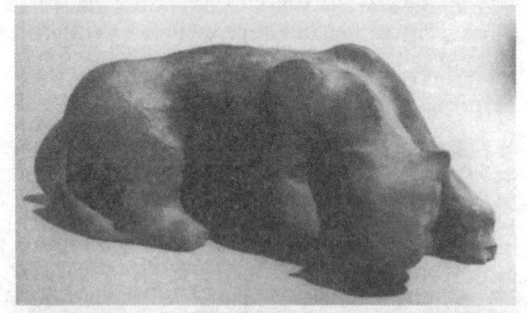

Modelling proportions and movement

During the second half of the block I work in the opposite way. After the main-lesson on the history of art, we practise observing and experiencing proportions.

We derive the sitting figure of an Egyptian scribe from the totality of the form of a pyramid. Afterwards we model a standing figure, allowing ourselves to be stimulated by ancient Greek culture. In the process, the geometrical rigidity of the sitting Egyptian figure with its clearly perceptible forces of gravity must give way to a harmoniously living uprightness. A truly wonderful levity is present in the Greek Korea. As present day students have problems with the attempt at rising to the vertical, at lifting the heaviness and penetrating it with formative strength, the making of an upright figure is therapeutic for them.

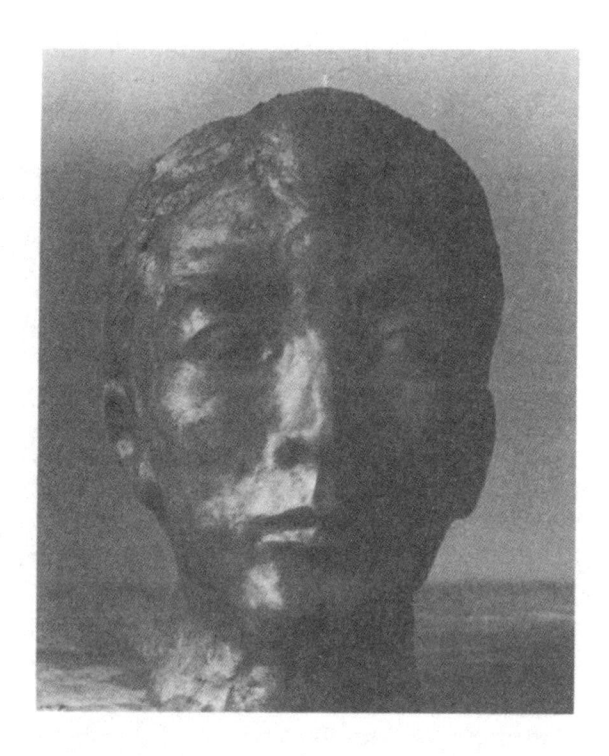

In Class 10 I ask the students to model animals once again, shapes in which soul-forces come to expression. What are the movements by which the animal's soul expresses itself? We refer to Franz Marc's art. In our first free exercise we show the forward movement. We usually get the most amazing variety of quite ancient primal animal gestures. It is now interesting to discover the specific animals that can be developed from them. What we get to begin with are animals that are more closely connected to the ground: a fish, a whale, a beaver, a weasel; imagination is kindled. Later, during the modelling of a wild animal, much will become clear. Looking from above, we can see the symmetrical-rhythmical arrangements. Expanding and contracting parts of the body alternate with each other. In the play of forms, the organisation of each part of the body becomes visible, shared by all animals, but different in their proportions. The rhythm of the spatial animal body (seen from the side) is intensified by the line along its back. It clearly expresses the way the animal moves. Think of a squirrel, a deer or hippopotamus. A third element is added by the right/left movement, still rhythmically-harmoniously swinging during a peaceful walk, but changing to an arhythmical and asymmetrical movement at the slightest inner disturbance; all it needs is a sideways glance, or coming to a halt. During a fight vehement, passionate movements can take place in space. It is a most difficult task to show an animal in a typical movement, most of all the harmonising of all the possible different movements in a group of horses.

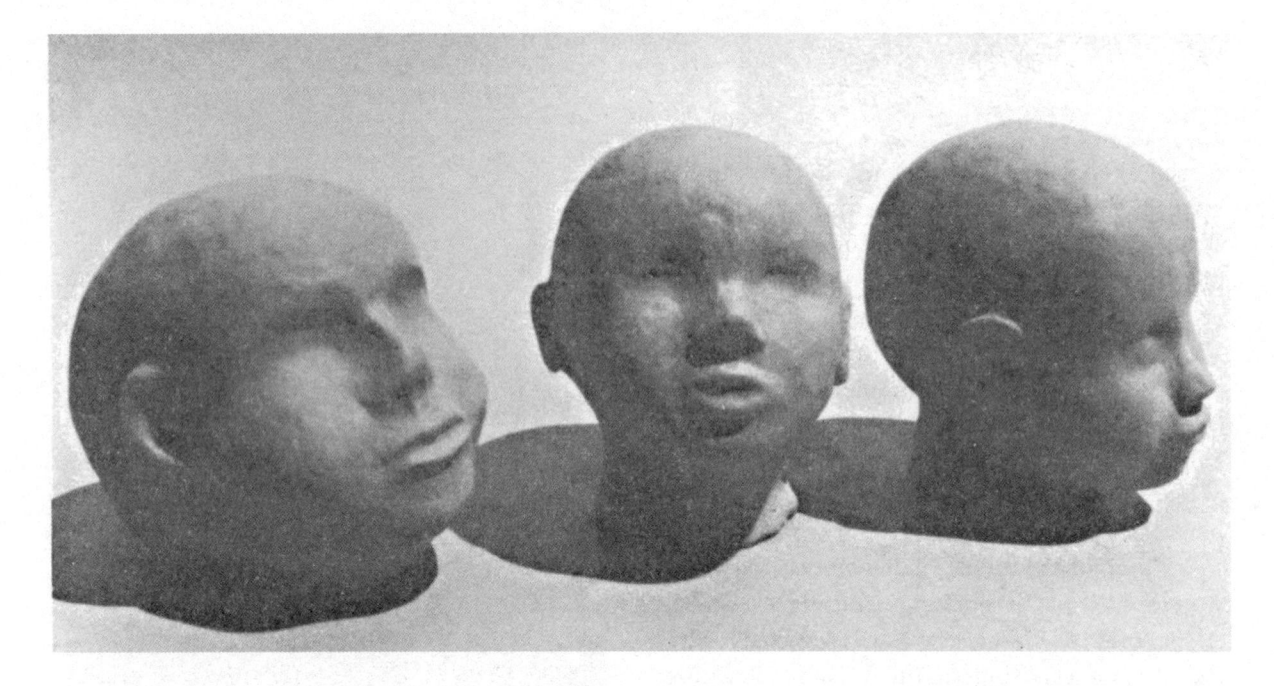

Our last exercise is the modelling of a large, bulky animal of the students' choice – a hippopotamus, rhinoceros or elephant, animals which do not experience movement as much as their massive form impressed on them by strong, vital processes.

The wishes of the students should be responded to. In times when our inner connection to nature is almost non-existent, where animals have been reduced to mere economic units, it seems to me ever more important in the context of artistic subjects in the Upper School to occupy ourselves with the animal as a living and en-souled being.

Our Class 10 students are working with the two aspects of the human head. The quite wonderfully rounded head of a little child expresses most strongly the growth forces active in building the physical body. Future formative faculties lie hidden in the faces of young children. We must proceed caringly and cautiously when modelling them. Indications are sufficient.

As foundation for the head of an adult we begin with a concave form. The very first steps already indicate the temperament, giving direction towards the next stage. We always work with one hand from within and the other from without. Only then can the reciprocal interaction of forces be grasped.

The enclosed and protective inner space is felt by the hand's touch, and gradually urges beyond the arched skull to the outside. The effect of the form is as though filled with life but as yet asleep. Effective energies from outside now intervene, pressing the curved forehead back, flattening it a little, working into the sphere of the eyes, differentiating the shape of the nose, awakening a definite physiognomy.

The physiognomy reflects the ego's confrontation with the world. The emphasis of curves and clear transitions between forms will result in an expression of youthfulness and liveliness. In restrained and reserved forms we get increasing individual and ageing features.

During the process of becoming, of developing, the artist's own formative forces in the head are gently vibrating along as they work; there is a delicate feeling by touch of them, be it consciously or subconsciously experienced. No wonder, then, when the first freely shaped head turns out to be almost a self-portrait.

In most cases, we shall perceive in the sculptures the inner mood corresponding to their creators. For me it is important that the students only learn to see, in their first attempt, the proportions, the two asymmetrical halves of the face, without trying to express soul conditions such as joy and pain that show themselves not so much in the physiognomy, but in gestures and mimicry. There will, of course, always be an expression, but it is of secondary importance; it would tax the students too much. If, as a result of the work, the students tell me that they had observed the faces of fellow travellers on the bus more attentively, a healthy basis has been established for independent work. The students experience this block as the culmination of their modelling lessons.

Modelling metamorphoses

The project in Class 12 consists of the forming of a threefold series of metamorphoses. Taking a number of examples from nature or from lessons during previous years, we try to understand what this means. Before actually starting, the whole of the process must be known and understood. Not the single steps of the work – they will only develop during the creative process itself, from the basic idea. One can get quite excited about the way a single form arises, as this will usually be very different from what one had expected.

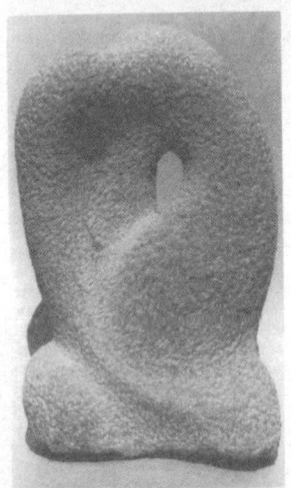

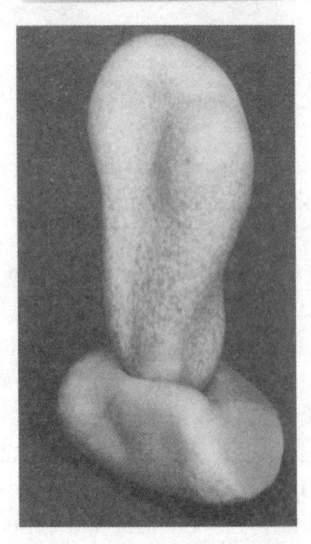

PART FOUR: FORMATIVE ARTISTIC LESSONS IN THE UPPER SCHOOL

The student who remains faithful to the basic idea will recognise it again and perceive it as the moving, driving force capable of developing a wealth of forms from itself.

A number of possibilities were considered and put to the test: movement leading from weight to lightness. A pronouncedly voluminous, seed-like round form develops into a bud-like one, grows upwards and unfolds into its surroundings. This we connect to the plant world. A round form can then be gradually changed into a concave one; this will lead to forms that allow us to think of the development of inner human organs.

Another example: a pronounced voluminous form stretches in a horizontal movement. The freely formed shape will express the animal's nature. Depending on the degree of mobility in mental picturing, the single parts may be lying close together, or the transformation may be so strong that the onlooker is asked to bring movement into their imagination.

And it is just this that makes the work so valuable, because it is here that one begins to feel what nature is accomplishing, when for example, it metamorphoses the petals of the poppy blossoms into the seed capsules.

I consider the exercises in metamorphosis to be a good preparation for stone sculpting. During stone sculpting – if done with the pointed chisel in the classical Greek tradition – one will experience in a truly wonderful way the closing of the circle of our exercises: an undifferentiated round or upright figure, depending on the shape of the stone, gradually transforms, becomes open to a variety of forms and yet retains its organic wholeness.

Again we experience growth forces. The work at a surface, point after point with a pointed chisel, so that one can no longer see any arbitrariness, demands the greatest attention of the students.

23. METAMORPHOSIS AND MODELLING LESSONS

If, during the previous years, they had not noticed what constitutes a stretched, formed surface – and this can happen in spite of the teacher's efforts – they certainly will now. The weaving softness given to the form by the 'pointed' surface produces the semblance of life, and this more intensively as one would expect.

Modelling in clay is, on the one hand, practice and stimulation for the life-building forces of children and, on the other hand, preparation for the work in durable materials. A world of form, closely connected with human nature, is opened up. The need may, perhaps, arise from this to harmonise the things around us in our homes with the human being. They should, in future, not only radiate a geometrical objectivity that excludes us or leaves us cold, but have a vitalising effect on human beings of all ages, especially children. If our children do not get the opportunity of relating their souls to the things around them, they will lack social faculties later in life: insufficient soul development during childhood leads to isolation, to an inability to relate and connect to the world. In this sense we can see in the modelling lessons of the Steiner-Waldorf school more than just a balancing of the predominating intellectual demands made on the students.

24

Working with stone (Classes 10–12)
Rainer Lechler

Michelangelo spoke of stone sculpting as the 'difficult art of taking away without the possibility of adding to it'. And in spite of our excellent modern adhesives that allow 'adding to the stone' a true sculptor will agree with Michelangelo and do without them.

This means, of course, that the stone carver may have to change the original plan if a piece of stone breaks off and they still adhere to Michelangelo's dictum.

It further means – and this can easily be confirmed if we watch a stonemason or sculptor at work – that fullest concentration must be directed to the point of the chisel. The sculptor must quickly discover the way the layers are lying and how the stone can be chiselled without cracking or breaking them. Presence of mind and clear consciousness are asked for. It is only practice and experience that will lead to the necessary knowledge of the material. Every kind of stone reacts differently to the chisel, but all of them directly and inexorably, be it to the crude, hard blows of the hammer or the delicate work on the 'skin' of the surface.

Preparing for stone carving

But how may a student succeed in this art without the necessary preparatory training? Our observations during the years show that Steiner-Waldorf students do, in fact, meet the conditions for working in stone. Their previous work in the crafts develops the faculty of seeing the consequences of each activity, and stone carving demands this faculty. Stone carving disciplines and concentrates through itself.

Added to this is the entirely new experience for our students that induces them to set to work with caution, even with a certain reverence for the stone. These two aspects may be sufficient to point to the pedagogical significance of stone carving. They clearly show that the students are given the means to educate themselves. For this they are ready only in Classes 11 and 12.

Stonemasonry can be understood as merely a craft or trade. As such it can be taught already in Class 10 when craftsmanship receives a dominant place. A project could be the making of a base from a piece of rock taken from a quarry.

The first aim is for the students to make themselves familiar with the typical methods used in masonry. Their task is to change a rough surface into a smooth one. This involves thought: where is the lowest point that determines the level surface? On which side should the first edge be started in order to get a level surface. How do I transfer this edge to the other side of the rock? What must I do in order to achieve this perfectly smooth surface. How can I get rid of the bumps? What must be taken into account so that the edges are not higher than the enclosed area?

The first complete project is now to be undertaken. This allows the students to gain experience, to discover the properties of his or her rock, its degree of hardness, its structure, layers etc. It does not matter too much if this first project – the rectangular or square base – is not exactly smooth and accurate, as it may later be re-worked into an animal shape.

Classes 10 and 11

This is again a new way of dealing with animal shapes. The students have modelled animals from clay in Class 9; they were supposed to express the characteristic qualities of an animal. Modelling in clay is not appropriate to Class 10 students. The detour via the stone allows them to gain a new relation to this task.

They get excited as they see the animal develop in the stone, and their enthusiasm gives life to this otherwise lifeless substance. The animals rise as though liberated from the rock, leaving all heaviness behind, seeming to enter the light of day with wonder and amazement. This immediacy in the outer appearance is due to the students' inability to perceive and reproduce the correct anatomical structure of their animals, as well as to their loving devotion to their new activity. The initially merely technical preoccupation is passing into a new artistic confrontation.

Class 12

In Class 12 the approach is quite different, even if the students have not worked in stone before. Their first project will be the shaping of a head. In Class 11 they had modelled heads in clay, studied the corresponding laws of proportions etc. Doing so in stone necessitates a different 'coming to grips' with their task. The clay head was made by adding clay; in stone it is a subtracting process. The single forms, their effect on each other and the effect of the whole must be consciously considered before the work begins. It is the clear, three-dimensional mental picture of space that determines the shape and not, as in clay modelling, the forming and shaping from immediate observation. What is the form I give to an eye looking about? What is the necessary depth for the lips or chin? Where are the directions of the forehead, the back of the head, and how must they be connected? Such considerations kindle an intensive interest in the shape of the heads or faces of their classmates and lead to keen observation of the people they face in a bus or car. This indicates that, next to the formal aspects, new artistic formative questions are beginning to occupy the students.

The next project is the students' own choice. They usually decide on the human figure, such as Mother and Child, a kneeling person, somebody walking or sitting, an athlete, a male or female torso etc. They may also choose the type of stone they prefer, ranging from sandstone, via chalk, travertine and marble to granite, basalt and syenite.

The time allotted to stone carving in Class 12 – half a year with two hours a week in three blocks –

PART FOUR: FORMATIVE ARTISTIC LESSONS IN THE UPPER SCHOOL

allows enough scope, after the completion of the first life-size project – for attempting even larger tasks. Individual figures, pairs and groupings are created of fine artistic quality, the result of the students' intense preoccupation with their work.

Tools and methods

The handling of the necessary tools and the ability of working with the stone are relatively quickly learnt and the students will easily discover their personal, individual way of working by:

1. The correct handling of the chisel
2. A suitable rhythm of hammering
3. The necessity of making the intensity of the hammer beat correspond with the form and structure of the surface of the stone

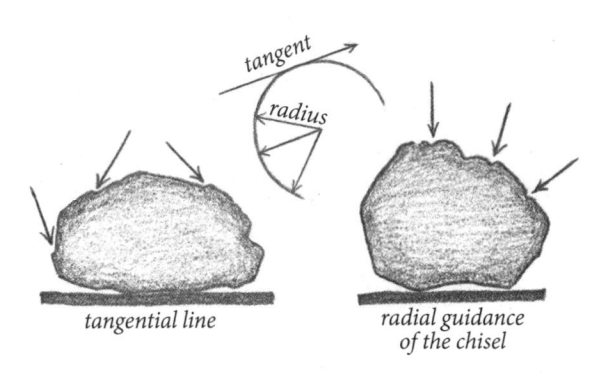

tangential line

radial guidance of the chisel

Regarding the guidance of the chisel we differentiate between the radial and tangential method. The tangential way is suited for the hewing out of a form quickly; the chisel will shape the form the artist has in mind. Using the radial method, changes will always be possible. The chisel is always pointed to the centre of the form, is held vertically to it and must not penetrate deeply into the material.

The disadvantage of the tangential method is the difficulty of making corrections or improvements because of the quicker and definite emergence of the single forms. In using radial strokes, the students could lose themselves in their tasks temporally as well as in the forms themselves.

The students always work without a diagram or model, i.e. the heads emerge from the stone – neither previously modelled in clay nor sketched in a drawing – but purely out of the moment. In doing so it is obvious that they must immediately follow this process with their wide-awake consciousness. The observation of the positive or negative effect of a hit is not enough – they must activate a mental picture of what is to be done ahead of time. By comparing the work done with what is still to be achieved, and by attempting to harmonise the two, the real creative process is effected.

Every hammer beat relates to what has gone before as well as to the planned end product. It is the path towards the realisation of the idea.[1]

25

Stone carving in the Upper School (Classes 11 and 12)
Winifred Stuhlmann

Working with stone, copper and iron does not feature in the original Waldorf School curriculum. It was added after the necessary conditions were met and the teachers found. They all have a connection with modelling, albeit under special conditions; and they are all a tremendous challenge of the students' skills.

In stone carving the emphasis is on method and a clear idea of the aims, based on rules that can always be followed. We shall indicate the extent to which the work can be guided, the point where the sphere of freedom (independent work) begins and how the handling of freedom without arbitrariness can be heightened to independence. Since artistic work must never be a copy of a model, we shall pay special attention to the free artistic activities in this subject.

A successful course will start from the conditions of the craft, as well as from the given themes. We begin with the technical methods corresponding to the material and the correct use of the tools, and point out the fact that these methods were also used by Michelangelo.

In our school, stone carving precedes the architecture main-lesson in Class 12, ending with a trip to places such as Tuscany. We visit the quarry at Carrara, where the students take small pieces of marble and work with them afterwards in the hostel where we are staying. We have already done some preparatory exercises in school. Exercises in drawing and modelling are connected with stone carving. This work, supplemented by short talks and trips to cultural places, such as Florence and Siena, helps the students to get a lively picture of these places and their significance for occidental culture. We are here working in a practical artistic way in a place from which our modern, natural-scientifically formed life style emerged. Stone carving is thus directly connected to modelling and drawing and constitutes the final work in the arts and crafts before the students leave school at the end of Class 12, in order to either find a job or study further.

The material

Stone is available practically everywhere. Many of the natural stone industries, especially when they own their own quarries, have offcuts that can be used in our work. Their depots often include stones from many parts of the world, including pieces from restored churches that make for truly beautiful exhibits. By taking a good look at the immediate environment of the school one will probably find enough usable material. There are parts of Germany

25. STONE CARVING IN THE UPPER SCHOOL (CLASSES 11 AND 12)

where volcanic rock, such as tuff (or tufa), is found. Its softness is especially suited to early work. Delicate, 'soft' sandstone or chalk are also popular.

Although stone has no grain, unlike wood, it does have layers. It is advisable to keep these layers horizontal during the work, since the stone cracks or breaks more easily along the layers than against or across them. It is a pity if, for that reason, pieces 'happen' to drop off. There are, of course, harder rocks close to being homogenous where this doesn't happen. If stone is exposed to weather and the layers happen to be vertical, it disintegrates more quickly while, if the layers are running horizontally, the effect is not unlike that of roof shingles: they oppose the weather and water and snow do not penetrate as much.

We usually begin with a softer stone, like tuff, to get used to the methods. Sandstone is next, as preparation for the much harder marble. The teacher should, of course, be familiar with the different rocks and be at home with the geological features of the environment.

The tools

Figure 1.1 is the pointed chisel used by stonemasons. Figure 1.2 is the same chisel, but flattened at the top, the corners pointed. It used to be called the 'buffer chisel' and is hardly known today. Its history goes back to Ancient Greece and it allows the layers of stone to be removed rather quickly. The flat chisel, as sold in shops, is not suited to our work (2.1) as it is used for smoothing out the rough surface made by the pointed chisel. In any case, three different kinds would be needed; their basic form is similar to a fish's tail. They are known as flat chisels (2.2), toothed chisels (2.3) and curved flat chisels (2.4), the latter for chiselling concave forms.

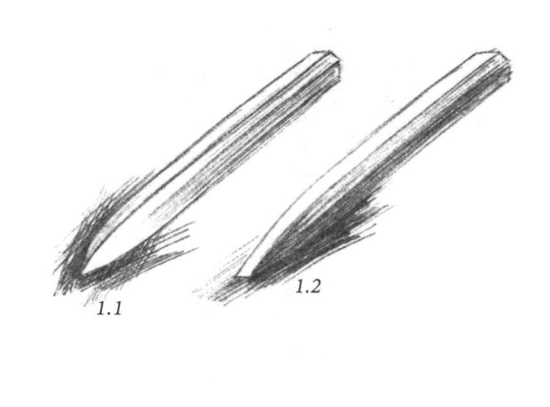

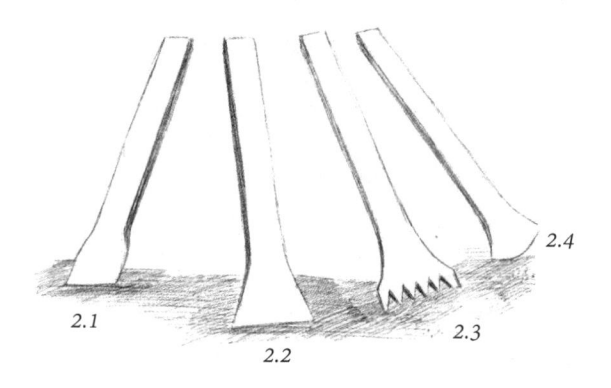

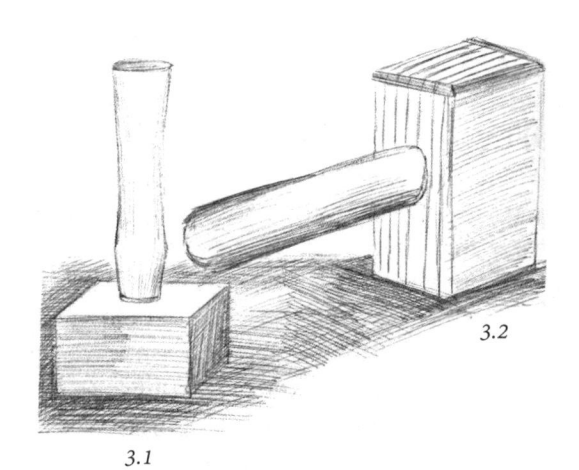

235

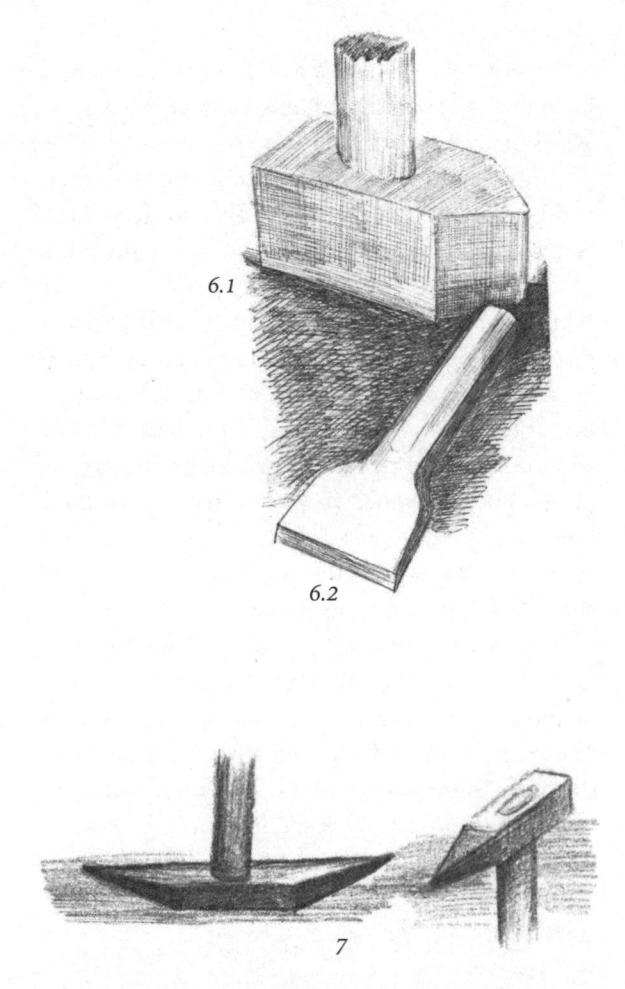

Wood and iron mallets are best; each has advantages and disadvantages. If an iron mallet is used (1 kg/2 lb) (3.1) the handle should be removed and the iron head softened by heating it. The rule is: soft hammer, hard head, so that, for reasons of safety, the surface need not be continuously re-polished. An edge soon forms, and splinters may easily break off, causing injury (4).

Figure 3.2 is of a wooden mallet that can easily be made from red or white beech. Its advantage is that it does not widen the head of the chisel and form sharp edges. Its beat is softer, its weight lighter – but its bulk is greater, making it clumsy.

The jack on which the work is done (5) comes from an old Italian tradition. It consists of three tubular sticks of an arm's thickness and is made from hard wood. They are tied together at the top with rope or wire. The bottom ends are opened up in the form of an equilateral triangle and connected with a rope. It can, if so wished, be folded and put away. A sandbag, not too full, is placed on top so that it can lie easily and the stone rest safely on it.

Occasionally it must be fluffed up – like a cushion – since the sand tends to solidify towards the bottom, like concrete. Fine gravel would, therefore, be a better material.

The splitting hammer should have a weight of 3–5 kg (6–12 lb). It is fitted with a vertical fin and a handle as used in a sledgehammer. In the quarry it is used for breaking off unwanted pieces in order to facilitate transportation (6.1).

The cracking chisel (6.2) should have an edge of 40–60 mm (1½–2½ in). It is used to chip out the rough form of the stone.

When working with soft stones we use kitchen cleavers and have found them to be very good indeed.

We have found no use for the basic hammer – often the only one used in the trade. It hinders the craftsmanship-like work and does little else but systematically grind up the stone.

For soft stones and smaller marble work the one- or two-pointed axe is suitable. The former can easily be made from a 350 g (12 oz), heavy locksmith's hammer (7).

The number of tools can, of course, be increased, but certainly not be reduced if one wishes to produce work of a professional standard. It is most valuable for the students to know that they can make tools themselves during the blacksmith's block. They will then have a more intimate connection to them and use them with care and enthusiasm.

Stone carving in Class 11

Experience has taught us to develop the work in the plastic arts in several stages. Modelling allows the students to familiarise themselves with the theme of the work, without having to worry about technical aspects of the craft. They can concentrate fully on the given project.

Drawing what has been modelled gives the possibility of perceiving soberly what has been done. There are two ways of doing this:

1. Students draw the sculpture with its natural light and shadow effects, which are heightened if the light is shown as coming from the observer. We refer to this as 'thinking drawing'. Since, as a rule, the light shines quite differently on the object drawn, the form itself must first be comprehended, before it is drawn. The position of the light is changed so that what is closest to us is made brightest (e.g. figures 10, 11, 13, 15, etc, p. 240f)

2. In their drawings the students go beyond what appears in their sculptures; do not merely copy, but improve on the original. In practice this may result in the drawings differing considerably from the original. Therefore in order to increase their confidence, the students concentrate on their drawings rather than on the original, improving them by emphasising the three dimensional effect.

This exercise shows them the disadvantage of drawing contours – that it is far better to start in a painting-like, two-dimensional way from the centre towards the periphery, allowing the outer contours to arise in this way. Practice strengthens observation; the basic form will become more accurate.

Modelling with clay is the preparation for stone carving. The artistic process, started with clay is then transferred to the stone. Very soon the stone will show its inexorable character, as everything chipped off is inevitably lost. Corrections are possible only by altering the shape of the whole. Since there is no definite or specific end result, as in architecture, such corrections on an artistic level are possible. The definitive element in stone carving, its finality, can thus only be overcome through the faculty of imagination.

8

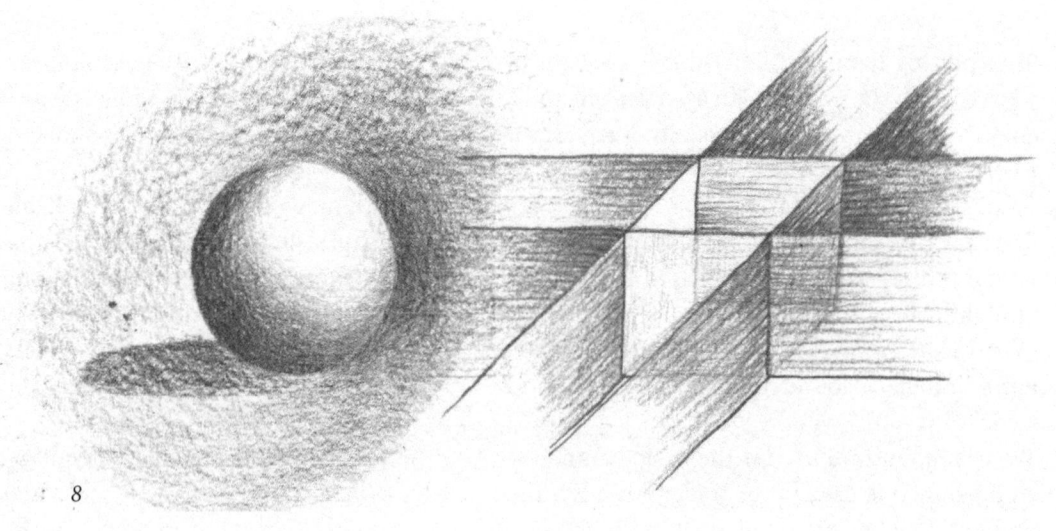

The theme: pointed and rounded forms

The basis for all forms is the straight and curved line with their infinite possibilities of connecting, interpenetrating and blending into each other, following Rudolf Steiner's indications for the first lesson in Class 1 that children begin by drawing straight and curved lines. The lines they draw are the principle behind all cosmic structuring to which everything that is physically-materially formed can be traced.

Modelling can proceed from the same principle. The difference lies in the fact that, while in the drawn line we have a trace of movement, when I model a specific object I am dealing with surfaces that are placed into space. The sphere, representing everything that is round, has but one surface; the tetrahedron, consisting of the finest straight surfaces, has four. The one extreme pole is the sphere, the other the tetrahedron, cube, etc., are always characterised by consisting of sections needed by the centre as its sheath. The sheath becomes visible if we lengthen the surfaces of a cube (8).

The surfaces interpenetrate, thereby determining edges and corners. It makes sense to begin from this primal polarity in three-dimensional bodies.

A perfectly round sphere is possible only as an idea, by realising that every point on the surface is equidistant from the centre. Correspondingly, the precision of the cube's form lies in the number and distances of its corners, the length of its edges, its angles, etc.

Preparatory modelling

It is the teacher's intention, aims and the children themselves that will determine how this subject is introduced. Pointed forms tend to engender order and concentration in the students. Curved forms have a liberating effect; they loosen and create mobility. We practise both – without copying anything – with the intention of stimulating the students' sense of form. To begin with we recapitulate what was learnt previously. It is the same method that was practised in painting during the first three school years in Steiner-Waldorf schools, when colour moods are cultivated

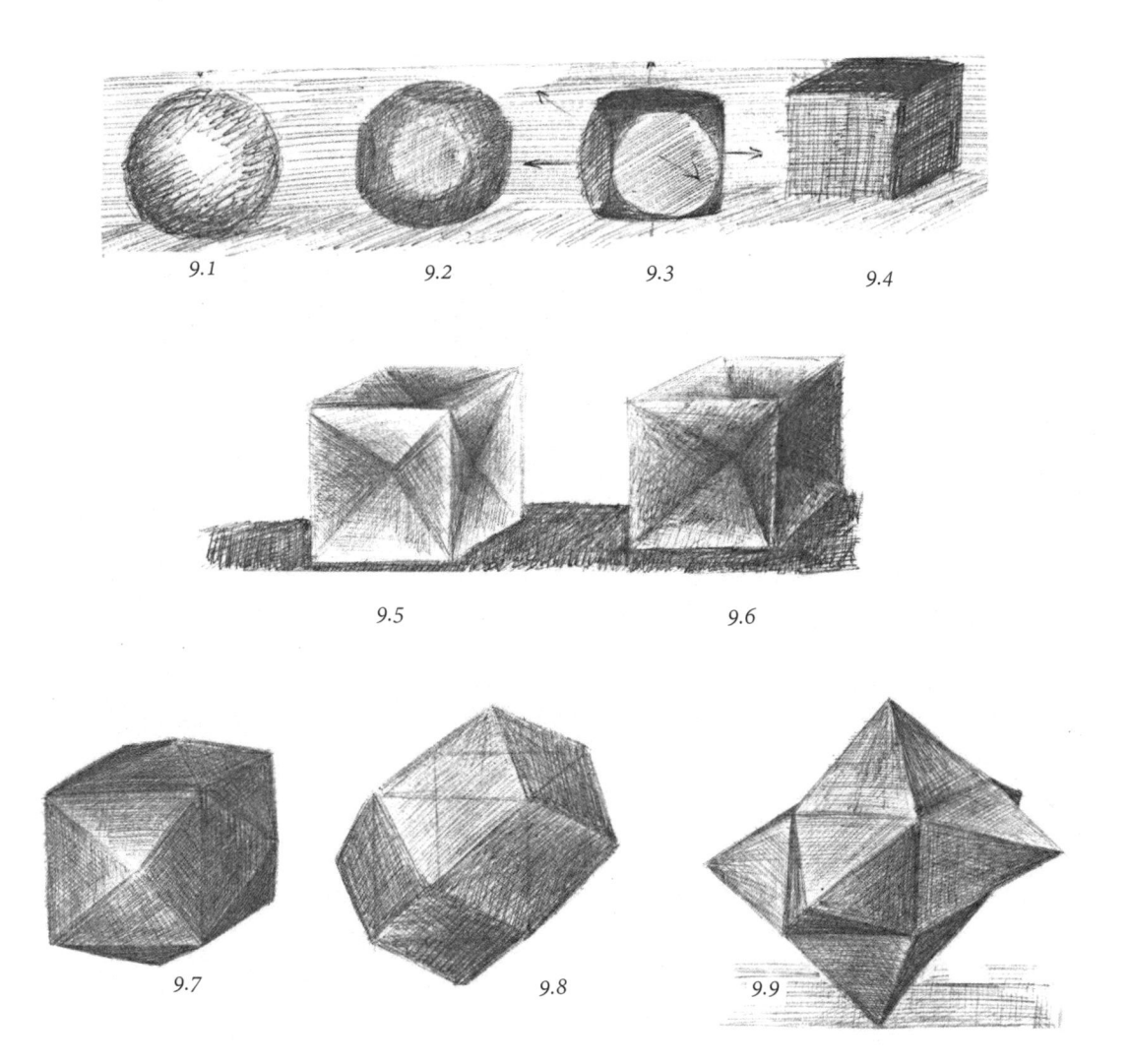

25. STONE CARVING IN THE UPPER SCHOOL (CLASSES 11 AND 12)

9.1 *9.2* *9.3* *9.4*

9.5 *9.6*

9.7 *9.8* *9.9*

through 'colour stories', in order to produce the greatest possible conscious colour experience in children.

This approach allows the students to become familiar with the techniques before trying their hand on the difficult task of creating something that is recognisable as a 'concrete reality'.

Pointed forms may be applied either regularly or irregularly. One can start from a spherical form leading to points and corners. It is a rigidifying, paralysing process we can experience at the soft, apparently vanishing surface of the sphere, in contrast to the straight surfaces, against whose edges one, as it were, collides.

Figures 9.1–4 show the metamorphoses from a sphere to a cube. Similar stages are possible for all the Platonic solids. In modelling them, without turning the work-piece, one will experience most vividly the three directions in space: up-down, front-back, right-left. When one turns the clay

239

these directions will be as though extinguished; all one experiences is surfaces and edges.

It is possible to think of other, quite freely shaped forms consisting of straight surfaces and edges. One of these could be the interpenetration of freely formed architectural and sculptural objects. The characteristic feature of these forms corresponds to the regular bodies that are formed towards the outside (figures 9.7–9). It is possible to reverse this: from out to inside (9.5, 9.6 and 10). This will allow us to experience quite strongly the scaffold-like, lifeless nature of such forms. However interesting the composition may be, its nature will not be changed by it.

Rounded forms can be modelled by proceeding from a spherical object, a cube or an irregular polygon. Such exercises need a general rule for the correct method, since rounded forms, as we have learnt, tend towards formlessness and disintegration. The freedom hidden and slumbering in rounded forms must first be conquered by the students if they are not to degenerate into arbitrariness. They must develop a much greater measure of the will underlying the formative processes than during the work with pointed forms that already incline towards order. Following a rule – and there are several – makes for a kind of binding objectivity that can be tested at all times. And yet we shall never see two identical forms. The progression would be: take a rule to be followed as starting point and, in the process, develop one's own idea.

The rounded archetypal form, our second starting point, is to stimulate an idea as basis for further structures. One of these ideas could be the division of a round form. This can gradually transform it so thoroughly that a form with the characteristics of growth is the result. What matters is the emphasis on the vertical and, through it, the overcoming of gravity. In figure 11.1 we see the line of division that is executed in 11.2. It could, of course, also take a different direction. It leads to a division of the form in the direction up-down and left-right. In figure 11.3 we have another line of division at any desired angle to the first one that brings the whole of the form into motion, resulting in the emphasis on the vertical. The last of the rules states that all the forms are to stream into another without making edges. This example offers inexhaustible opportunities that lead to ever new tasks. Clay allows itself to be stretched and compressed without difficulty, so that such forms can result.

The students must be told that, despite these rules, the forms cannot be predicted; all one can do is to persevere and await the outcome. The truth of this amazes them every time.

12.1

12.2

Drawing

The students could be asked to draw either stages of the work or the completed clay model. Its purpose is to advance the artistic process, hitherto only partly conscious, by creating the form anew through exact observation. The ideal is the expression of something the sculpture cannot do by itself. We recommend four views of the modelling, so that the students can perceive the transformation of the form at one glance – something that is otherwise only perceptible as the work progresses: the development of a form from one movement to the next. The students are often surprised at the differences of the four views that might lead one to assume that they are of four different pieces of modelling.

We could, indeed, say that the greater the differences in the individual drawings of the same object, the richer and more living it is. An even more objective experience will result from the students drawing each other's work. Again they are surprised at the way somebody else sees it.

After these reflections on drawing and modelling as preparation for stone carving we can now take a look at this activity.

Carving in stone

The conditions for this work will be different if we use tuff or soapstone rather than sandstone or marble.

Tuff is best used when taken straight from its place of origin, still damp. Problems are always caused by the sand and basalt grains, as the sand tends to drop out, leaving holes, and the harder basalt does not let itself be ground and polished. Dried tuff becomes very light, increasing its hardness by 40%. It can quickly be made soft again and acquire its original 'freshness' by immersing it in a basin of water. An added advantage is that there is no dust during the work. Its degree of hardness is comparable with that of one day-old concrete.

We begin by removing the rough edges with a kitchen cleaver. Guiding it tangentially and obliquely across the stone and away from the centre, a rough, rounded surface is produced. This will prevent the stone from cracking as the result of too violent vibrations (12.1). Once the corners and edges have been roughly removed, the surface tension can be produced through quick, light beats from the wrist in a radial direction towards the centre. This will result in a quite beautiful form, even if the surface itself remains rather rough. (12.2).

The stone will be lying on the sandbag on top of the three-legged jack, as previously described. A siliceous-like initial form emerges – not unlike that formed by a stream. We have to discover the possibilities in this basic form that must now be newly divided and shaped according to a 'rule of forming' that arises almost naturally. We draw a line with a wax crayon – indicating the idea – on the stone as a kind of boundary.

We already know this process from our modelling lessons. The students, familiar with this way of developing forms, can therefore begin their work with some confidence. The unyielding quality of the stone demands thinking ahead – what is done cannot be undone, as in clay, but only altered. This means self-discipline and clear thinking through concrete forces of imagination: What will the form look like if I chip off this piece? The students must be told that what applies to all life also applies to the arts: transformation is essential for the creation of something new. The form of the siliceous stone must be transformed, must differentiate itself; one must be able to relinquish it, in order to chisel from it an idea and making it visible. In the same way, youth cannot remain where it is, but must leave it behind and pass into maturer years. A blossom must progress to fruit: as it fades and the seed ripens, it reaches a higher stage of life. If such things are discussed before the work begins, there will be few problems.

In figures 13.1 and 2 we see the path of the line of idea whose beginning and end should not meet. Figures 13.3 and 4 show the side views. What inclines to the onlooker from the top left is turned in the opposite direction at the bottom right. The other side is done in the opposite way (13.4). In addition, a turning form arose in both parts. The direction of the dividing line on the bottom of the stone produces a very mobile play of forms that can affect the whole of the work if it is transferred to the top surface as impulse of movement (13.5 and 6).

The final touches are carried out with the toothed chisel. The surfaces are made smooth, all unnecessary protuberances and dents removed, until the surfaces appear to be stretched and tensed. When polished, the extremely hard basalt particles look pimply – not at all beautiful. With patience this can be corrected. Before the very last touches, the tuff should be allowed to dry, so that a fresh-looking surface can be achieved, rather than a greasy-looking one. This also helps to retain the basalt particles better.

The next project in tuff (14) is better suited to Class 12, as it necessitates greater independence and challenges the students' full initiative if it is to be successful. It also presupposes some experience in both clay modelling and stone carving. The raw piece of stone (14.1) without any previous planning is shaped, with the help of a hatchet, into a composition of straight edges and surfaces. It is the stone itself that will stimulate the students and suggest each step to be taken (14.2–4). The final touches are again made with the toothed and flat chisels.

The climax of such an exercise is, at the same time, a culmination of the subject, where everything that has been learnt can be freely applied: the straight, the curved in concave and convex formation (15.1–4). The basic formative principle in this exercise is momentum, animated motion and counter motion. This is quite sufficient for our theme and rules, as long as the students' imagination has been trained to the point where they can work with it. The final form (15.4) takes them to the limits possible and meaningful in stone carving. Since today it can no longer be taken for granted that students actually experience anything meaningful in work, they must be made aware of

25. STONE CARVING IN THE UPPER SCHOOL (CLASSES 11 AND 12)

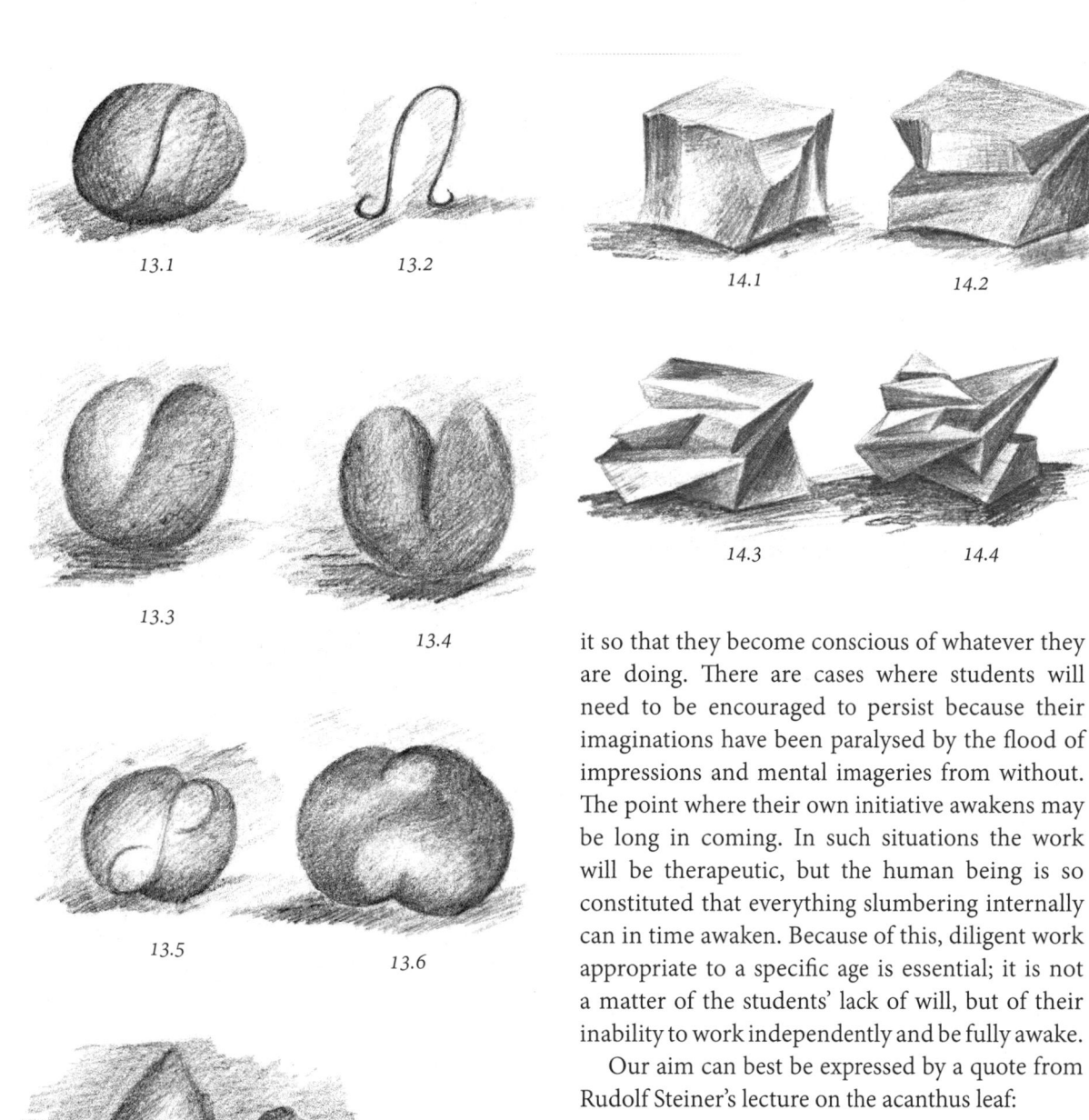

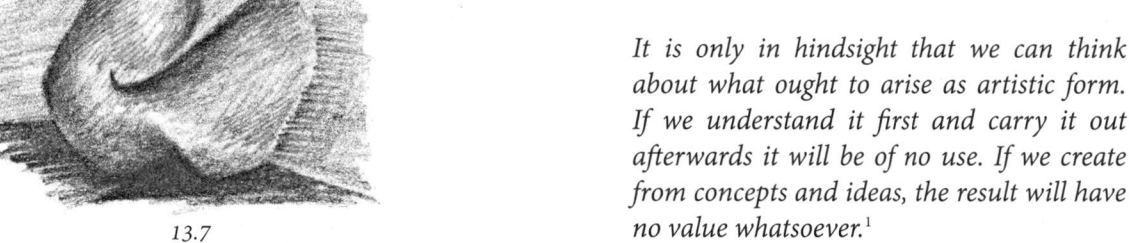

13.1

13.2

13.3

13.4

13.5

13.6

13.7

14.1

14.2

14.3

14.4

it so that they become conscious of whatever they are doing. There are cases where students will need to be encouraged to persist because their imaginations have been paralysed by the flood of impressions and mental imageries from without. The point where their own initiative awakens may be long in coming. In such situations the work will be therapeutic, but the human being is so constituted that everything slumbering internally can in time awaken. Because of this, diligent work appropriate to a specific age is essential; it is not a matter of the students' lack of will, but of their inability to work independently and be fully awake.

Our aim can best be expressed by a quote from Rudolf Steiner's lecture on the acanthus leaf:

> *It is only in hindsight that we can think about what ought to arise as artistic form. If we understand it first and carry it out afterwards it will be of no use. If we create from concepts and ideas, the result will have no value whatsoever.*[1]

15.1   15.2

15.4   15.3

us of the hammer used by geologists, but it is easier to use. It allows us, for instance, to work concave shapes into surfaces that are clearly distinguished from the roundly ground edges and, if we so wish, increase their convexity to the point where they pass to the other side (16.1–3). Another possibility would be to start from the roundly ground edges, so that a new form arises (17.1–3), similar to a 'hand flatterer'. It is advisable to protect the hand that holds the stone with a glove. Such forms can be left pointed as the effort of grinding and polishing would be unwarranted. The size of the piece does not allow the use of the toothed or flat chisel. A clearly pointed surface can, because of its softly fading structure, be quite beautiful.

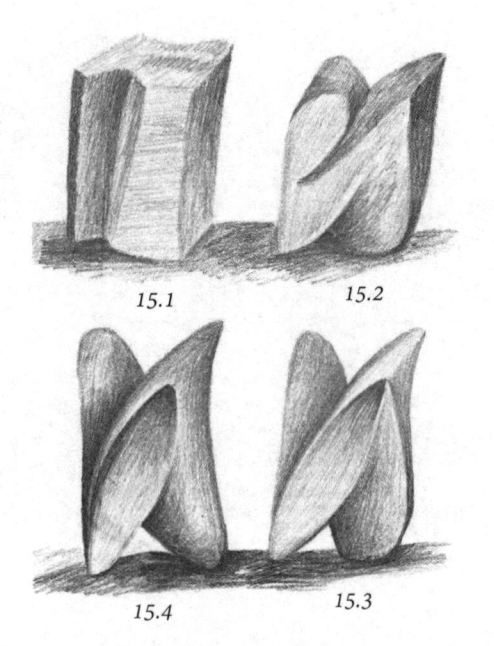

If earlier on we spoke of an introductory idea leading to the artistic process, this idea is no more than the key to the artistic process whose end one cannot pre-think. Hence the reason for doing the drawing at the end, creating the sculpture anew in a two-dimensional picture, and thereby prompting recognition of what has been produced.

Rules and ideas are here merely signals. The process of becoming can thus be made conscious, but only by retracing it afterwards. We may use a rule or idea as help in feeling our way; what actually happens in the process is something we can understand and know only afterwards.

A brief 'interim project' will give rise to further possibilities. It can be done without any complicated technical means, with just one tool held in the hollow of the hand. Even marble can be worked in this way, provided we have the patience. During our trip to Seravezza near Carrara, we collected several polished pieces of marble, the size of a hand, from the riverbed. We shaped them with a one-pointed hammer (figure 7, p. 236). It reminds

Stone carving in Class 12

This course culminates in Class 12 with subjects taken from the world of animals and the human figure. Modelling and stone carving here reach a new level of synthesis.

The students are asked to observe accurately. They can agree on the value of clear observation in all areas of life, not only in sculpting or modelling; it will help them to perceive and understand better.

They must understand at least the rudiments of animal anatomy for this exercise; it is one of the conditions for the work – the other is the ability to translate this knowledge into plastic forms.

An overview of the work will show that we are dealing with an artistic understanding of the four natural kingdoms, something that has to be learnt. To begin with, we get the principal forms in the sharp edges and points. This is then dissolved into the rounded, swelling forms we discover as archetypal gestures in the buds and fruits of plants. These forms then stretch

16.1 *16.2* *16.3*

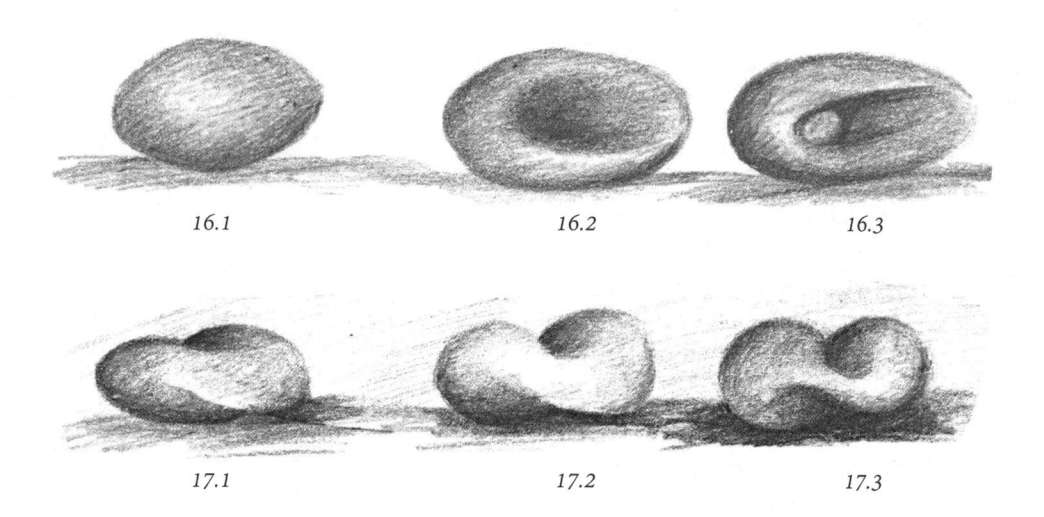

17.1 *17.2* *17.3*

into the vertical to enlivened plant-like shapes. The animal loosens itself through its movements from its ties to the earth; its form structure becomes the expression of an instinctive inner life. Finally, the human being unites within itself the rigid, enlivened, en-souled elements of the three natural kingdoms and expresses its personality in its upright posture, restrained movements and controlled and en-souled gestures.

Animal forms

The work with animal forms is in preparation for the carving of human figures which we do during the three week long art block in Italy.

Animal forms are first modelled in clay. One way is the copying of animals depicted in ancient cultures, in order to get the feel for this subject. I found Inuit sculptures and also modern ones by artists such as Ewald Mataré useful. The students may immediately begin to model in clay. Figure 18 shows a selection of animal forms in the Etruscan museum at Volterra. Similar sculptures can be seen in Greece and elsewhere. We can see the simplicity of the forms without losing the original characteristics of these animals. But the students must understand that such forms are not appropriate for stone sculpting. Figure 19 shows such a development. The last two indicate inner gestures; the animal 'wants' something, it follows its instinct. It is the simplest form of an animal and is modelled in the hand. As preparatory exercises, three types of animals are carved in stone: lying down, crouching and freely moving.

The work can either be quite simple in its elementary gestures or more sophisticated (21).

Figures 19 and 20 clearly show the way this can be done. The forms carved in stone must remain simple, but without losing the essential element. We select one of the clay figures we wish to transfer to stone. It serves as a guide – as did the rules we followed during the modelling of free forms. What is, therefore, necessary is to reduce the animal form to its bare essentials, in order to make this possible.

We select a piece of stone, one-and-a-half to two times larger than the clay sculpture. The layers

PART FOUR: FORMATIVE ARTISTIC LESSONS IN THE UPPER SCHOOL

should lie as horizontal as possible. The stone is then reduced – with a cracking chisel – to the correct basic size and shape. The outline of the clay model is drawn on the side and then generously hewn from the stone.

The next step is the fixing of the animal's movement as it manifests in the spine. This movement can be shaped along the body in the form of an 'S'. Beginning at the head, the main form is then differentiated, layer after layer, all the parts being chiselled out in accordance with this movement.

In order not to lose the overview, it is advisable to draw the line of the spine on the stone. We must be aware that head and pelvis constitute the immovable parts on this line, and that every movement must emanate from the neck, chest and tail. With the clay model we started from the body (sphere and egg) and proceeded to head and limbs. Now we begin with the lateral view of the total figure, determine the gesture of the head and proceed from there to the body.

The final touches can be carried out by alternating the tools used.

The pointed chisel will produce a shaggy pelt; the toothed chisel a pleasant contrast at the base; the flat chisel is especially suitable for carving of a flattish mouth. Animals, such as seals, almost ask to be polished smoothly all over. Under the belly and between the legs the stone should be left as a prop, without being too noticeable, i.e. it is shaped concavely, making it an integral part of the total form.

It is not the naturalistic form we have in mind, but the representation of a typical characteristic feature of the animal. A little mishap can sometimes prove to be a blessing. Some students may feel that their first attempt is enough – only to be surprised at the difficulty one of their friends (who shirked a more complicated project)

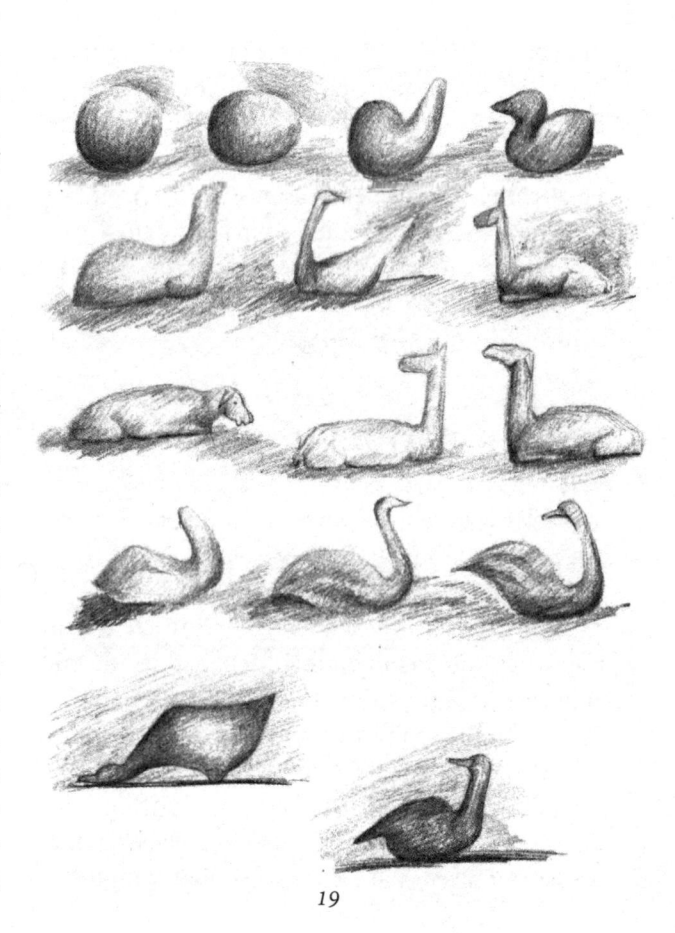

18

19

25. Stone Carving in the Upper School (Classes 11 and 12)

Only experience maketh the master. And it is good for the students to know that their teacher is still learning. They are usually impressed by their teacher's ability to produce two or three animals during the time they are struggling with just one. A great deal is asked of the teacher who dares to touch this subject. But working with the students is so exciting, and the variety and strength of expression so amazing, that it is well worthwhile to give all one can to it. It's hard to imagine more intense work.

The human figure

As with everything done so far, the sculpting of a human figure must also develop gradually.

Speaking sculpturally, the human figure may be understood as the result of gesture. Three of these can be differentiated: the outer physical – somebody stemming themselves against the wind, someone skipping down a hill or resting on the ground. The second gesture may express an inner state: joy, rage, fearlessness, pain. The third is the result of an inner purpose: gestures in work, in eurythmy or dance. Gestures arising from inner stirrings and feelings can be divided into two groups: a person laughing or singing will have a communicating gesture, opening out; a person in despair or a thinker, one of contracting, concentrating. Between these extremes we get a whole range of feelings.

The easiest way of dealing with this problem is to start by expressing a feeling or gesture abstractly, as mere form. This can be done in clay (22).

Louise van Blommestein who was present when Rudolf Steiner sketched the picture *Mother and Child* (pastel, February 28, 1924) described this as starting from a completely free gesture, without people, to the finished sketch. According to her,

experienced in the sculpting of such a simple shape as that of a chicken.

The teacher wishing to make a success of this work is advised to practise as much as possible themselves, because of the unexpected problems encountered by the different group of students.

PART FOUR: FORMATIVE ARTISTIC LESSONS IN THE UPPER SCHOOL

22

Rudolf Steiner started from an abstract colour composition that became the foundation for the subject. This method, applied to stone carving, leads from a general gesture to the human figure – the general gradually becomes specific.

Figure 23 demonstrates this process. It was prepared by chipping out the rough shape with an axe. Figure 24 shows the same method for a crouching figure. One only needs to have a rough idea of what one is aiming for, the rest will develop from the activity itself.

As with animal sculptures, here, too, it is possible to make use of drawing as a preliminary stage. There are many most interesting examples of quite simple sculptures of human beings in the history of art. The drawings shown in figure 25 are the result of studies in the Etruscan Museum in Volterra.

This preparatory work in stone carving can be done in several ways. If we use a wood or clay model as starting point, we must select an appropriately shaped piece of stone. Its size must be such that the steps leading to the gesture can be chiselled out. After the preliminary work it will be a matter of directly teasing forth the required shape from the stone. In this way, the process of becoming can be based on previous experiences, before continuing to the finished product.

We can heighten this approach by trying to discover a piece of stone that almost tells us what we should do with it. This means the faculty of perceiving the hidden possibilities in the stone. We are reminded of Michelangelo who, when asked: 'Master, what is it that enables you to hew this wonderful figure of *Moses* from the rock?' answered: 'Simple. I look at the marble until I see the figure in every detail. All I have to do is to remove the rest.' Tremendous power of imagination is necessary for this, as well as a good memory as it takes time, sometimes months, until such a large sculpture assumes its final contours. In the *Nicodemus Group* (in the museum in the Cathedral of Florence) we can easily recognise at its back the way the master must have proceeded from a free composition of forms, in order gradually to bring out the motif. The *Matthew* sculpture (in the Academy of Florence) has long been the teaching model for generations of sculptors. Tradition has it that, with this sculpture, Michelangelo emphasised the need of keeping the parts of the composition in an unfixed state as long as possible, in order to be able to change them if necessary.

The *Rondanini Pietà* shows that he kept faithful to this principle to the end of his life. It is his last work; he continued to make alterations until shortly before his death, leaving a part of the group – a right arm – without its body. He used yet another method in the sculpture of his *Slave* (Florence Academy) where he chiselled directly the single parts of the body, leaving the viewer the job of arranging them into the whole.

In a lecture given on October 16, 1920 Rudolf Steiner said:

25. STONE CARVING IN THE UPPER SCHOOL (CLASSES 11 AND 12)

23

24

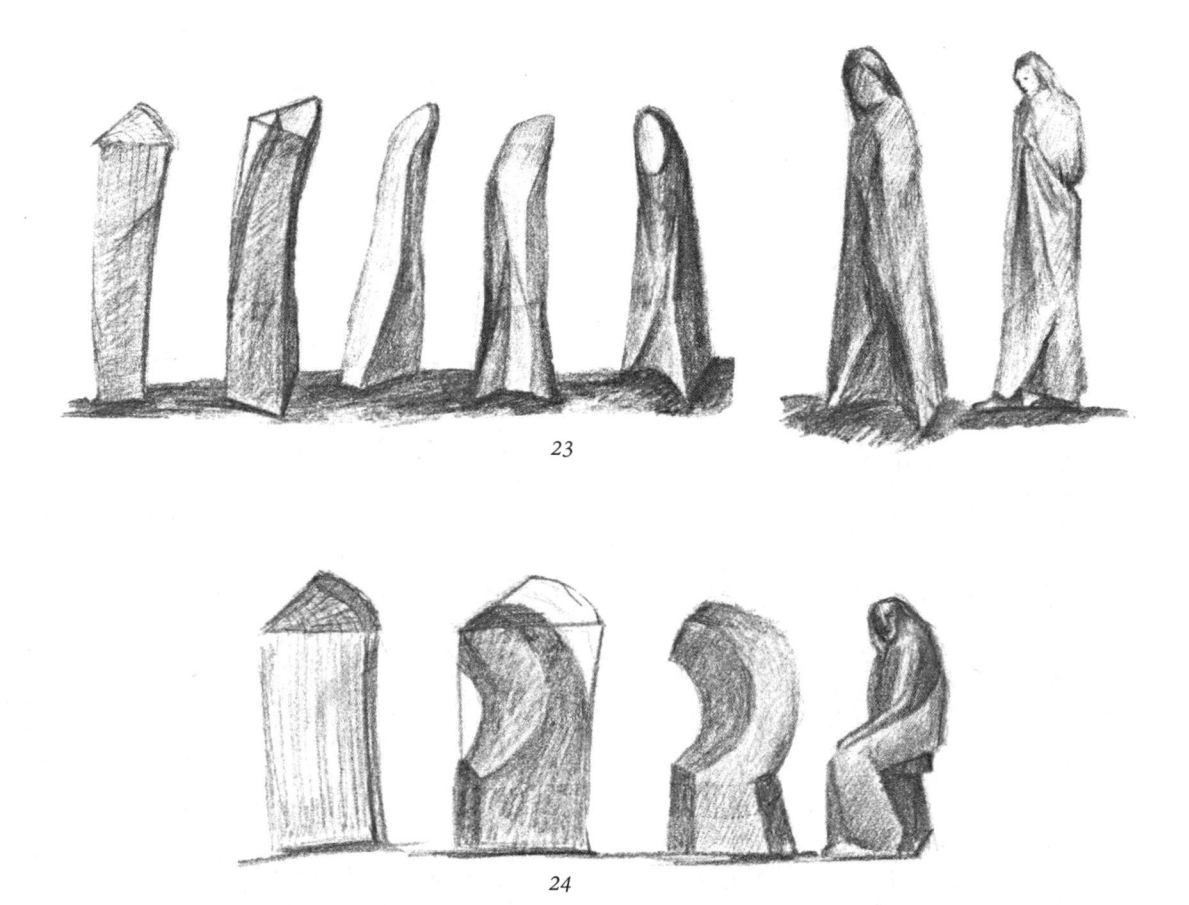

…if one shapes the human figure plastically from stone or similar material, it is necessary to proceed from the face, from the head… and the rest of the figure is, artistically speaking, really no more than an appendix of the head. One must not… sin against the natural forms of the head, and one has to sculpt the whole of the limbs and trunk organism from what is disposed in the head. The marble, the stone demands this of the sculptor.[2]

Experience shows that it is easiest to carve such figures by taking the hand as a starting point – similar to the way a human being develops their body during the first seven years. The essential thing is to remain in the gesture and not to lose oneself in details. We can learn much from Ernst Barlach, in whose sculptures the gestures mature only through face, hands and feet to full expression.

Figure 26 shows the attempt at working with stone by thinking a different form into each of the views. The forms are then further thought out and taken to their final stage, i.e. simple groups of people. The sketches represent merely a series of variations that could be added to and done also in clay. With practice, drawing will prove itself as a much quicker means for experimenting with one's imagination. The possibilities are inexhaustible and it is worthwhile to investigate other areas. For example, the stone may be turned or put upside

25

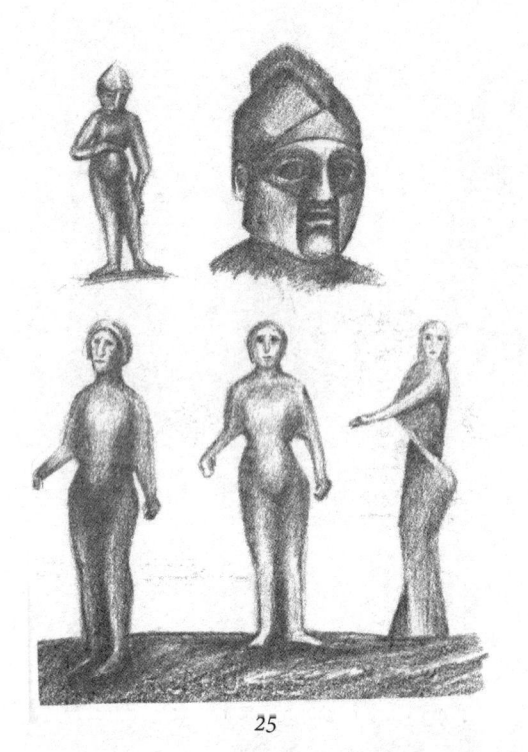

down; it will then 'speak' to us differently. The drawing could be used as a good starting point, giving directions. In order to avoid mistakes, we may model, using the drawing as a guideline. Such drawings, seen together, could be taken as a preparation for carving the stone directly, with a specific drawing or a model, resembling the end result and the wish to wait and see what happens.

Stone carving, in this sense, will be similar to the way a lesson develops: we arrive well prepared, and only discover afterwards the direction the lesson took. This makes it into an artistic process parallel with that of stone sculpting. It is a process that is beyond the possibilities of most of the Class 12 students, but the teacher themselves, again and again, should practise and strive towards it. It is important for them to address not to what their students are, but to what they could be in order to tease forth a heightening, an intensification. This makes it necessary for the teacher to be fully immersed in the artistic process, to try to work in the way Schiller indicated:

> *Just imagine what they could be if you had an effect on them… Wherever you find them, surround them with noble, with large and ingenious forms, enclose them with symbols of excellence until the semblance of the reality and art conquers nature.*[3]

The talents, wishes, inhibitions, joys and worries the students bring into the workshop are mainly hereditary traits, or qualities they brought with them from the spiritual world. It is the school's task to engender and develop personality. We must bring out what is not yet apparent: the spiritual, the 'essential kernel' of the young. This points to the future; is not yet developed; is a higher element than the outer physical form we see before us.

If we work artistically in the way we are attempting, we are superimposing an ideal element upon the material or, better expressed, we develop an ideal element out of the stone, clay or line. Matter is thereby raised to a higher stage, something higher rays from the artistic form. It is the reflection of the process attempted in Steiner-Waldorf education. Rudolf Steiner summarised it as follows:

> *The task of education, spiritually understood, is the harmonising of the soul/spirit with the physical/corporeal body. They have to be attuned to each other, because at the time of birth they are not as yet in harmony. The task of the teacher and of education is to harmonise them.*[4]

25. STONE CARVING IN THE UPPER SCHOOL (CLASSES 11 AND 12)

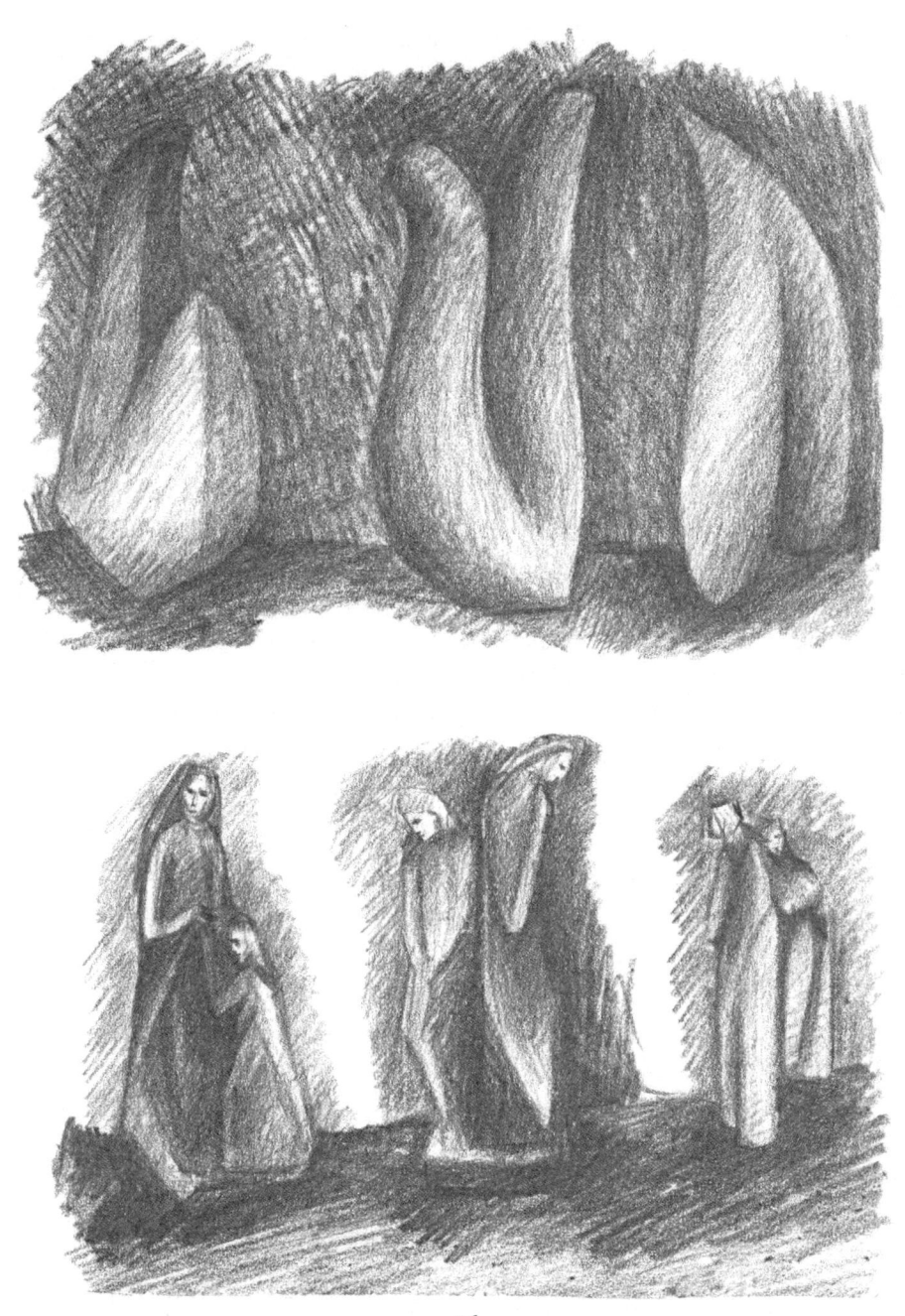

26

26

Woodcarving and art (Class 13)
Uwe Bosse

The students in Class 13 have a choice between painting/drawing and woodcarving. Their previous work in clay, wood and stone is the pre-condition for woodcarving in Class 13. The carving or whittling of a simple figure in Class 6 is the first step in this direction. The time allotted to our course is three quarters of the year, with three lessons a week. The theme of the work is the human figure, carved in vertically grown wood.

The students select their piece of wood and gradually develop the idea of form in its structure and shape; or they start with an idea and look for the piece of wood corresponding to it, and attempt to force the idea on it. Experience will show that both approaches are necessary – as a kind of interplay between them. Carving becomes a tentative conversation (through touch) between the intention and the deed, between the wish and the fact. Rigid ideas and mental pictures become mobile; while vague, indefinite ones assume contours. In the search for the essential elements in carving, successful forms are found and recognised as such. During a reflective conversation, the students learn how the quality of form arises through divisions, proportions and the direction of surfaces, making possible its essential expression in the harmony between idea and wood. Looking at art works and studying the sayings of artists are a great help. Such a quote was used by a student for the following essay. It was the theme for the examination project. The quote is from A. de Saint-Exupéry's *The Little Prince*. In the paragraphs accompanying the illustrations of their sculptures, the students themselves are expressing their thoughts concerning their work.

Attempting to make the heart see

'It is only with the heart that we may see well. The essential remains invisible to the eye'. These are the parting words of the fox to the Little Prince. And, as in this story by Saint-Exupéry, so we too have to leave everything we had done in our school for thirteen years, and I would not be surprised to learn that it was because of this that this specific theme was chosen for our art course. But what was the 'essential element' in the course?

Our main concern was to discover a reasonable relation between our practical activities – the concrete artistic work – and the study of general questions in the world of art, in order to arrive

26. WOODCARVING AND ART (CLASS 13)

at the really important and, for us, essential questions. Again and again we met with this 'essential' element. It became clear already at the beginning when we looked at the blocks of wood and discussed the basic sculptural forms. What, indeed, are edges, surfaces and curves, and where are their points of origin? We learnt that an edge must not arbitrarily be 'pulled' from a surface, but that it arises as though by itself at the meeting of two surfaces, that turned and curved surfaces are far more interesting to the person looking at them or touching them than flat ones. We discovered all this when we looked at organically formed bones, pebbles and stones smoothed by water, as well as the growth forms in wood. A form is essential when it arises consequentially from movement, from the nature of the thing itself underlining it.

During the actual carving we were able to understand that the recognition of what is essential and right is more easily attained through the sense of touch than through sight. To return to Saint-Exupéry: it is perhaps easier for the hands to establish a closer connection to the heart, since the perception of an object through the hands pre-supposes stronger feelings and experience. This faculty is especially strongly developed in blind people.

We agreed that in art the decisive matter is not the outer view of, e.g. a piece of sculpture, but the inner movement and stirrings effected by it; 'it is always with the heart that one sees well'. Through this work, the artist thus must succeed in imparting their ideas, feelings and intentions so that the person looking at it may feel and experience beyond the visual impressions what the artist experienced. In this sense, art becomes connection, communication, language.

This means that we confronted the problem of bringing the form we saw in us as idea together with the demands of the material, the wood. We had to manage, in time, to harmonise the block of wood with its knobs and decayed spots with the intended shape so that the one impressed itself correctly on the other: the matter in the form and the form in matter. The painter Otto Bamberger described this process as: 'Art grows between what we let arise and what we intend'. During our carving, we arrived at the conflict between the principles of form and matter, as stated by Schiller. It was an interesting confirmation of the way Schiller's thoughts can be put concretely into practice. Both these popular urges in the human being – that of matter which characterises the living transitoriness of feelings, the sensuous part in us; and the urge of forms that could perhaps be described as spiritual and moral strength of form – both, according to Schiller, suppress us if one-sidedly developed. The same applies to art: neither a brick nor a lump of rock will be seen as a 'work of art'; only one of these principles dominate in them.

What matters, therefore, during an artistic activity, is to work simultaneously at the whole and the detail, attentive to the moment while at the same time cognisant of the idea, of the inner archetype whose copy one wishes to produce. Only in this way will it be possible to express the essential on the one hand, and the necessary, on the other.

What always matters in art – and in this it will be recognised as such – is the connection between the temporal and the eternal, matter and idea. Art in this sense is uniting.

Schiller extended his thoughts on aesthetics to the social life, the art of living together. Looking about today in, say, either a museum or on the street, we will easily be convinced of the truth of his thoughts. Far too many people see merely with their eyes; they lose themselves in the world of colour and cannot see, perceive the essential. Loss of direction, of purpose, and aimlessness that ensues lead to depression, the dominant illness today – a phenomenon of our time. If we take heed of Saint-Exupéry's idea, and admit the necessity of seeing with our hearts, we shall be enabled to form judgements about the worth and nature of things. How can this be done?

Surely only by training oneself to see and express the important and essential. This is obligatory in art. Is it, therefore, possible to develop social faculties through artistic activities, faculties that open the eyes, so that we may perceive our fellow beings behind the outer physical appearance? I believe so. Schiller would surely nod his head enthusiastically. In this way I understand the art lessons in our school as an attempt, an exercise, to make the heart see. Because of this, this course, often considered of secondary importance during the examination year, is in my opinion an important experience at the end of the school years.

Students' accounts of their work

Joy

I know of two possibilities of looking at things: the everyday one is a disinterested look at a strange object, the other is a perception of the permeating life; it flashes through the whole of the human being as joy. Carving at my sculpture was a continuous wrestling with the second of these possibilities. Because only this, as inner interaction and conversation with the wood, led to its form.

ROMAN R.

Turning away (alienation)

As the work proceeded, it became ever clearer to me that the sense of touch was far more essential than I had thought. By touching the sculpture, its beauty, the interplay of surfaces, the forming and dissolving of edges – all things that constitute the quality of a sculpture – can be recognised and judged. One of the most successful surfaces of my sculpture continues from the back of the right shoulder. I would love to invite people to experience the interplay of form in my sculpture with the sense of touch.

BERNHARD P.

Deep in thought

The translation of my idea into a piece of wood happened in a very naturalistic way that did not satisfy me at all, the less so the more naturalistic it became. Almost by chance I made a discovery. The left arm had the effect of life, even though it consisted only of a shape that turned within itself, very abstract and not at all naturalistic. By building on the experience that edges and surfaces are more important than exact copying, I then attempted to realise this also in various places of my sculpture.

FELICITAS J.

26. WOODCARVING AND ART (CLASS 13)

Joy

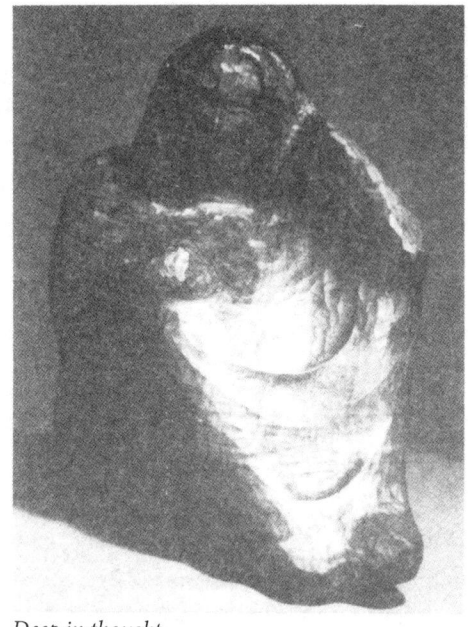

Deep in thought

Turning away (alienation)

Listening Mother

255

Listening mother

During the carving of my piece of elm, a surface soon showed itself at the centre that could be interpreted as 'hands'. It was protective quality that prompted me to think of the name. The surfaces which arose, and my ideas which I found difficult to realise, resulted in a reciprocal interplay, leading to the overall form of the figure.

THOMAS W.

Man giving orders

Originally I intended to carve an abstract sculpture. I imagined that I could satisfactorily represent a commanding gesture in an abstract way – a few surfaces, from which new edges would arise… But I had forgotten one thing. I had never tried my hand at carving a naturalistic form. Questions arose, such as 'What indeed is the essential element of an arm?'

I gradually pushed my first idea aside, with the result that the overall sculpture became 'essential'. In this way I could thoroughly practise the effects of carved and other surfaces.

SONJA T.

Man giving orders

Untitled

I abandoned all attempts at a naturalistic copy by trying to shape my sculpture as an organic structure emanating from the stream of form with all its movements of turning and whirling – as is present in the form of a human being or in an animal bone.

KÄTHE S.

Untitled

Part Five

Further Thinking

27

Work and rhythm
Herbert Seufert

A statement of Rudolf Steiner's during the *Konferenzen* held with the teachers touches on the age-old custom of singing during work:

> *… if you try … and this is an ideal … to bring what is called rhythm into the work, if you try to connect the musical – singing – eurythmy lessons with the craft and handwork lessons. The effect on the children would be extraordinarily beneficial. I recommend Karl Bücher's Work and Rhythm to you.[1] It should be in the school library. All work used to proceed from music, be it threshing, iron forging or laying cobblestones. It is rarely practised today. But if you had gone to the country even a few years ago and heard the people threshing their wheat: you would have noticed the rhythm by which it was done. I believe we could do this again in our lessons. This is what I intended when I said that spirit should again enter our work.*[2]

But is this not backward-looking, mere nostalgia, if we let our children sing during their handwork and craft lessons? Would they indeed wish to enter the spirit of the 'muse', especially today, when the radio often does the entertaining in work places? And if we were to try it out, how would we go about it?

A unifying rhythm

A dozen boys and girls are preoccupied in copper work in Class 9. They are hammering away at their bowls. It is hardly possible to make oneself heard; the cacophony of the hammer blows on the hard metal, the typical ping-ping-ping fills the room. Suddenly we hear two or three children hammering in unison. Others follow and soon all of them are hammering to the same beat. After a while the beat is lost; one student stops, the rest continue and, again, the unison is there.

Then, one of the boys or girls starts whistling a rhythmical melody, and everyone begins to hammer to it. It stimulates, is almost contagious, nobody now stops work; and the mood continues for quite a while.

Every student experiences this in our copper beating blocks, and they are always amazed at the fact that a common work rhythm comes about, positively influencing the work. Soon the questions come. Some of them remember their farming block in Class 3 when they were allowed to thresh the wheat they had sown and harvested. They sang the traditional *Threshers' Song* as they worked with a will until it was all done:

Threshers' Song

Can you hear the threshers,
Their beat as they worked,
Snip-snip-snap
snip-snip-snap
snip-snip-snip-snap!

Hört ihr die Drescher
sie dreschen im Takt,
klipp-klipp-klapp
klipp-klipp-klapp
klipp-klipp-klipp-klapp!

Such memories lead to the discussion of earlier ways of working and – as we shall show – to their value today. Our previous school caretaker learnt his joinery trade at the beginning of the century. During his last years with us he remembered his apprenticeship days and, every time he entered the carpentry shop, he burst into a song, a modification of the well-known *Joiners' Bench Song*:

Joiners' Bench Song

And isn't this a joiner's bench, joiner's bench
Ooh aah you lovely joiner's bench
Short and long
Short and long.

Is des net e Hobelbank, Hobelbank
Ei-ei-ei die scheene Hobelbank
kurz und lang
kurz und lang.

And then he would tell us how, as an apprentice, he was taught to use the plane, to push it forward and draw it back, to the rhythm of this song. They kept singing this and similar songs as they worked. Depending on the type of work they replaced the words 'joiner's bench' with 'garden gate', 'kitchen bench', 'closet', etc. There was good sense behind this singing during work. Why? If I work too fast I tire quickly; if I work too slowly I don't get the necessary momentum needed for a clean shaving. In both cases I get short of breath, and the quality of my work suffers.

Behind it all is the ancient 'law' that maintains the need of all work to harmonise with the pulse beat and the rhythm in breathing: the work will then be good and the worker will not easily be exhausted. Songs animate, engender imagination; many a merry song was written and composed during work.

The same happened in the blacksmith's shop. The master smith led the beat, his two helpers took it up and a three beat rhythm ensued. Most of their songs have this rhythm. Goethe used it in the *Smith's Song* in *Pandora*: 'Light ye the fire, men, fire is burning then' ('*Zündet das Feuer an, Feuer ist oben an…*'). Richard Wagner gives this rhythm to Siegfried to sing: 'Forge, oh my hammer a hard edged sword!' ('*Schmied mein Hammer ein hartes Schwert!*')

C. E. Meyer used the iambic beat for the rhythm in sowing in his poem: 'Take care each step, each move just right, the earth will stay quite fresh and bright, a seed drops here' ('*Bemesst den Schritt, bemesst den Schwung, die Erde bleibt noch lange jung, dort fällt ein Korn*').

The sower puts his hand into the sack of seeds and scatters them across the field. Putting the hand in, scattering evenly, the momentum, the strength is directed to the throwing. In this rhythm he proceeds across the field.

27. WORK AND RHYTHM

The pleasure the Ancient Egyptians, Greeks and Romans took in making pictures and sculptures of their activities allows us to know the methods they used in the construction of their massive buildings. An Egyptian sandstone relief depicts a gigantic statue being pulled on runners by a multitude of workers. A man is standing on a rock, gesturing wildly, with his mouth open – singing! At every accented beat of his song, the workers strain at the rope and pull the massive statue forward. Is our 'gee-up!' the last remnant of this rhythm? Or is there something else that is connected with this rhythmical singing?

In Thor Heyerdahl's *Aku Aku* we read how the Polynesians' work of their rock pictures only succeeded through singing. Another instance is the rock temple Machu Picchu in Peru: how was it possible to move these massive rocks from a quarry in a neighbouring valley up the steep hill? Here, too, the work was accompanied by singing, presumably, in very definite sound sequences.

We don't have to resort to ancient times, however. An example taken from the very recent past shows how topical such things still are, or at least could be! During the building of the Aswan Dam the rock temple of Abu Simbel was removed in its entirety and rebuilt further up the valley. The whole building was sawn into blocks and moved. One day, the mechanical lifts broke down just as one of the blocks was to be moved. The engineers discussed the situation in their tent: to get a replacement or the necessary parts would take at least four days. Outside the tent the workers were singing, in the opinion of the engineers a waste of time. Imagine their surprise when, on leaving the tent, the rock had gone! Just as 4,000 years before, the workers, led by their foreman and 'foresinger' in rhythmical singing and corresponding movements had transported the rock through human strength.

Towing their boats upstream – hard work indeed – the boatmen were helped by their special songs.

They were mostly deeply melancholic and monotonous, sung as they trudged along the towpath. The best known of them is that of the Volga boatmen. Repin's painting shows most impressively and movingly the raggedly dressed,

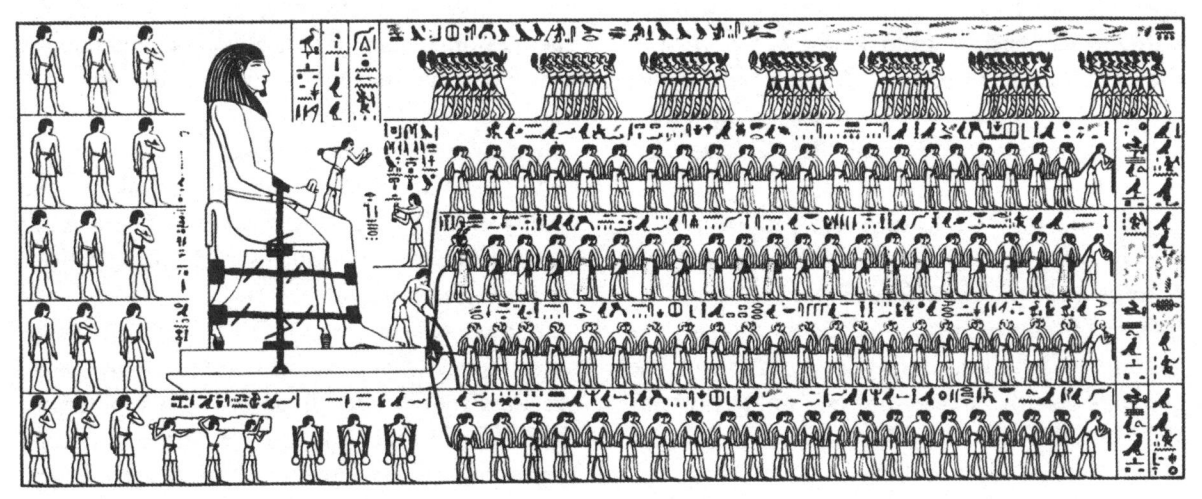

Transporting the statue of Thuthotep, from K. Bücher, Work and Rhythm

PART FIVE: FURTHER THINKING

Why rhythm in work matters

We began by mentioning the students' experience during copper work. It provides the opportunity of telling them about methods used in the past. Occasionally one of them might contribute by recounting something they had read. It is not only an understanding of ancient customs that matters, but a help for their own work. Class 9 students are already concerned with a wish to understand connections, cause and effect; they no longer simply, naively and spontaneously merge with the work processes as did the people of the past.

Reflecting on these examples, the students quickly discover a number of possibilities: a monotonous kind of work I have to do by myself can be made easier and helped along if I sing a song that has a fresh, lively ring to it. Work done by a small or large group needs direction, a given rhythm, in order to establish steady continuity, e.g. in a rowing competition. The latter provides the opportunity of mentioning the galley slaves.

The students also discover that rhythm increases the efficiency of the individual and especially of the group. The concentrated co-operation of all the energies during a rhythmical song or beat makes possible unpredictable achievements that can border on the miraculous – as was obviously the case with the rock figures in *Aku Aku*.

We also notice the effect of rhythm on the quality of the product. This is yet a subject under investigation whose results may deeply affect our life processes.

It is good to mention such things in order to allow the students to understand these processes. We hardly ever find rhythmical work processes today, since most of them have been replaced by the continuous movements of machines. Gadgets are used in drilling, sawing, slicing bread and even

'Baking bread to the accompaniment of flute music'
Greek terracotta
Louvre, Paris

haggard and pitiful men as they pull the heavy cargo boat upstream, harnessed to leather belts, a day's work that would not be possible to endure without the help of singing.

In former times, there was hardly any work done in which singing did not feature. The Greek terracotta group shown in the image above shows several women kneading dough to the rhythm of flute music. It helped to make the consistency of the dough even. Imagine a choleric, phlegmatic, sanguine and melancholic person working side by side without this rhythm! What would have been the result?

All our examples – and many more could be added – show the effect of rhythmical singing. It indicates the best speed for relating the movements necessitated by daily toil to the rhythms in breathing and blood circulation. The students quickly noticed that singing strengthens their perseverance! And it guarantees and even improves the quality of the work.

27. WORK AND RHYTHM

cleaning our teeth. All that's left for us to do is to use and control them; rhythm has no place there. Mechanisation of work paralyses our life, insofar as lungs, blood circulation, our rhythmical organs no longer vibrate along our organism of movement, cannot harmonise with it.

It is our nerve/sense and limb/muscles activities that tire us, never our pulse and breathing that continue to be active throughout our lives. To adapt the working conditions to this rhythm is not only an economical measure, but also a matter of hygiene and therapy.

Every healthy rhythm sustains life. The balanced alternation of day and night, waking and sleeping, movement and rest, in and out breathing, although not often consciously noticed and appreciated, is a vital support for our physical health.

In Steiner-Waldorf schools, rhythmical movements in connection with language and sound are cultivated in a variety of ways. In our workshops, the forging of iron, the planing of wood, hammering and sawing always challenge rhythmical processes, but only in small groups of two, or when working by oneself.

It is already significant for the students, when watching the teacher lightly beating the chisel with the mallet, they learn to hold the mallet correctly in their hand, without gripping it too hard. Rhythm soon shows its effect when they hammer in this way. Another element is added: the chisel is placed on the wood; the first hammer beats are tentative; the depth of the cut, the direction of the chisel along the fibres are estimated; the beats become firmer and fade again as the chisel is removed… only to repeat the process: a rhythmical one! Another example: driving in a nail begins with some caution, to give the nail the necessary hold; the force of the beats increases, the sounds become brighter until the nail is finally driven home, when energy and the effect of the beats must be rhythmically intensified! Quite different from sawing a piece of wood where the to and fro movements have to find their correct measure of time, determined by the breathing and pulse beat of the worker, their physical build, but also by the wood's resistance, the kind of saw used and the arrangement of its teeth.

Many such working situations can be 'translated' into sound by virtue of the inherent rhythm of the process. Craft teachers ought to try to transform each 'mechanical' process into a rhythmical one. The musical influence on work goes further: an entire working group can be led, via the beat in a melody, to rhythm – as we have seen in the work with copper. What does this mean? It is the soul that expresses itself in singing. It flows, as it were, on the waves of air, into the rhythms of movement, and thus into the whole of the work processes. Our work is no longer directed only by an idea, a mental picture, and done by the strength of the muscles, but co-determined by the en-souled rhythm of breathing. The whole of the human being participates in it – and this allows 'spirit to enter', as Rudolf Steiner pointed out. A monotonous, continuous beat tires the worker; rhythm, overcoming this, enlivens, refreshes and liberates us from the possible oppressive burden of work if it is carried out merely mechanically through the strength of our muscles.

28

Methods in the formative lessons
Michael Martin

A look into the world of plants will open our eyes to the inexhaustible wealth of form structures. We can observe the continuous metamorphoses of plant forms, starting from the shoot, via the unfolding of leaves and blossoms, to the mature seed. First are simple, spherical shapes: buds, seeds, tubers, bulbs. Comparative processes take place in animals and human beings. All organic forms emanate often from very tiny, yet undifferentiated and more or less rounded forms, very similar to each other.

Finding form

The basic forms modelled in Class 4 and 5 also look similar due to their being true to the organic formative processes. From the pressure of the ball of the hands, the fingers, the palm, the lump of clay gradually differentiates itself into an archetypal animal shape. There the back compresses into the shoulders, the head inclines threateningly, at the ready; here it slinks away, soundlessly and cautiously; in yet another work, the archetypal form of a fox, bull or dog emerge from the greedy, scenting instincts leading to a pointed, scenting mouth. Such forms emerge through the teacher's guidance. The qualities of movement in crawling or slinking away, or the alert poise in the region of the sense organs are brought to children's attention, who experience and then model them. The shape and form of the animal is already hidden in the human hand and it is, therefore, not at all difficult to discover that it presses and forms at the right places, produces protuberances and indentations, in order to find the characteristic form of an animal.

Guided by their teacher, children set to work out of the movements of the basic gestures (jumping, slinking, lurking, swimming, etc.) and not from the memory of a particular animal. In the process it gradually becomes clear to which animal the activity will lead. It is the inner experience of the way the form develops that leads to the shape, and not the conceptual idea or picture of a specific animal. From the creative variety of the moving (and moved) world of form, the different animals arise, mediated, as it were, through the universal formative forces of the hands. In the process, children also spontaneously express their temperaments and individualities.

In his lectures on the curriculum, Rudolf Steiner encouraged this approach for the drawing lessons, extending it immediately afterwards to painting and crafts.[1]

28. METHODS IN THE FORMATIVE LESSONS

Form, experience and environment

Children should learn to recognise this experience before discovering the corresponding forms in the environment. They are first to draw an angle, to be told afterwards that such an angle can be found in a chair. 'Don't ask the children to copy before having cultivated in them, out of inner experience and feeling, the form as such, independent of where it may be found. Afterwards it is alright to copy...'[2]

We have here a manifest mystery of the greatest importance for children's healthy growing into the world. From a creative enlivening of their own formative forces, a feeling for form within children is stimulated and made visible in their drawings, paintings and modelling. Awakening step by step to their surroundings (at ages nine and eleven and during puberty), they will re-discover these forms, carried within their inner sphere of experiences in their environment.

In their discovery of forms and lines, they salute their environment as something with which they are familiar, something they already know. They experience the world around them, not as a strange, but a familiar intimate one, insofar as it is already present within themselves, albeit in an unconscious way. The objects outside have merely assumed another substantiality, another reality.

Once aware of this motif, we teachers can see our educational tasks having this aspect. Children's individuality is to be led into the objectively visible world of space; personality and world are then no longer polar opposites, but the human being experiences itself in many ways interwoven into the world: both physical and inner (soul) life have their foundation in whatever the world presents. The opposites of subject and object are conditioned

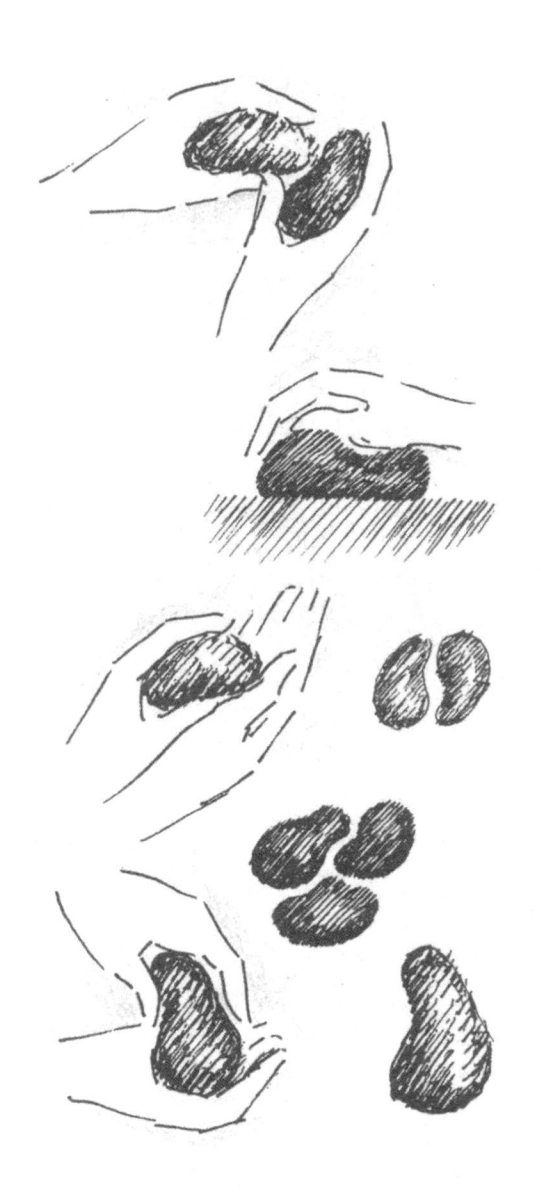

All imaginable form elements should be practised 'out of the form itself' in order to give children the immediate experience of round, concave, pointed, straight and sharp forms. For round, convex forms have a different effect than pointed ones; they come from different formative forces.

by our modern materialistic consciousness that makes it difficult for our children to relate to their environment.³ Adolescents especially run the danger of looking for an understanding of themselves only and not for the connections with the world into which they must grow. A dangerous 'retreating into themselves' can be the result; or they might lose themselves in the materialistic temptations of the environment.

On the other hand, a thirteen-year-old boy described his feelings of complete oneness between himself and the world, causing him the greatest happiness:

> *The fact that a boy was lying on his back amongst heather or somewhere, this interesting situation that – in similar situations – enriches the life of every young person would not have remained in my memory if it had not served as framework for one of the greatest pleasures I have ever experienced.*
>
> *My ordinary and meaningless dreams gradually transformed into an exceptional experience that I can only imagine to be comparable to clairvoyance. It was as though a veil was removed and my eyes began to penetrate the objects in my environment. The blue sky above me with its summer clouds, the trees, bushes, grass, the birds on the branches, the tiny bugs, ants and spiders – all seemed to me endowed with a, for me, new and, until then unthought-of value. The whole of nature had become transparent, had thrown off its mask. Everything that had been dark, dead and material had vanished and things revealed their eternal nature, as living light and life and, indeed, as the very same light and life that was also within myself; it was*

Forms and lines in the environment

the one and the same consciousness, the one and same substance in myself and in them. The one and the same band connected me with them and them with me, there was no longer anything hostile, anything foreign in the whole, large creation. My heart glowed and I experienced something of the joy of someone who suddenly recognises in strangers whom he had learnt to love his very own brothers and sisters...[4]

I must emphasise that this description is of an exceptional change of consciousness.

But it does clearly demonstrate that the duality of the world and the 'I', necessary for the development of the personality, can, at a higher stage, pass into a state of concord and harmony. Can artistic exercises contribute to the bridging of this necessary distance between subject and object, and establish a balance between inner and outer world as condition for every real 'interest'?

Individual and instinctive forces

The theme of the simple animal sculptures, e.g. made in the hollow space of children's hands in Class 4 or 5, is taken up again in the Upper School leading to differentiated projects in which the students can express their individual feelings of forms and show their individual creative ability. As before, they begin with the archetype, the characteristic form; this is brought into movements in which the instinctive life of the animal lives. The students must try to experience this movement in order to find the corresponding form that will be convincing to anyone seeing the sculpture.

PART FIVE: FURTHER THINKING

It is quite easy to distinguish whether the carving is just the animal's physical appearance or one in which the gestures have arisen from its inner instinctive urges.

The consciousness of the sculptor directs their own instinctive nature to the forming of an animal: they separate from themselves, as it were, and become one with the animal's shape. The subjective, instinctive forces then assume objectivity, becoming visible in the animal form. By this, we do not attach a negative meaning to 'instinctive forces'; they indicate merely the personal energies behind the wishes, momentum and motivation that emerge in the young during puberty as soul-forces.

Our example is valid for every theme in modelling. If we conduct our lessons in this way, they will serve the students as a help for 'growing into the world'. They will discover their inner world expressed in the world outside through valid forms. The things rumbling within are not 'taken out', but transformed. The students will not indulge in subjective forms that may impress as 'modern art' or individual fancies. Three guidelines by the sculptor Hans Wimmer will make clear what we mean:

> *Are you thinking of the work,*
> *Or are you looking at yourself in the mirror?*
> *To efface yourself is essential:*
> *Self-assertion through self-renunciation.*[5]

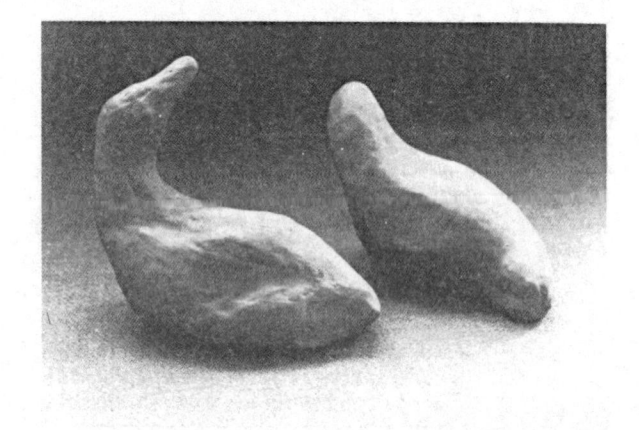

Herein lies a source for misunderstandings. It is not the intention of Steiner-Waldorf education to awaken the young artist's quest for his or her specific forms of expression, just as it does not implant the seed of the future craftsman during the carpentry or blacksmith blocks. Neither are the arts and craft lessons merely taught as a balance for the academic work. They become themselves a method by which a bridge is built for the students, and across which they may pass from their own world to the world in which they will later find their meaningful places.

Little children grow in the same way, through the learning of the alphabet, into the written work of the world. They can do this only by willingly accepting the laws of spelling and grammar, in order to be able to make individual use of them later. And although the letters have objective characteristics, this does not prevent the development of individual handwriting. There are many such examples that show how the starting point of an objective activity, that has to be learnt, becomes the basis for the unfolding of the individual element of the human being.

Methods, material and 'style'

Unlike wood, stone or metal, clay lends itself for free and varied forms. This is mainly due to its substance, which is not tied to any specific form. Because of this, it is a preferred material for modelling. Always changeable because of its flexibility, it submits to every pressure of the hand until the creator has found the final form before relinquishing any further work from his or her hands.

Method, material and hands as the only tools give the work a certain style one finds again and again in Steiner-Waldorf schools, as distinct from that elsewhere. Looking more closely, however, one will discover the individuality of the students' work. It is only the superficial observer, not familiar with the material, who can assert that the individuality of our students is not sufficiently expressed there. True, our schools do not offer the scope of techniques and materials in the art subjects as do other schools. We do not seek the individuation of our students so much in the choice of different techniques, but rather provide the individuality itself free scope within a given theme – and a given technique – as we also do in written work. It is the structuring of form that individualises, and not the technique.

The present contributions may have shown the importance of the described methods and materials for the training and maturing of our students. We chose them according to the principle: how may the developmental stages of the students be meaningfully supported? Tackling too many techniques will be at the expense of thoroughness and may easily lead to the illusion of having mastered something that one has only superficially dabbled in. An intensive connection seems to be more important today than rapid changes; and this conditions the selection of a few basic techniques. Lack of time does not allow for more.

A similar case to that made out here for modelling would apply also to painting and shaded drawing. In all of them, methods are used that allow for changes during the work. As it develops, a process of maturing can take place in the students' imagination that manifests outwardly in the continuing transformations.

A superficial glance at an exhibition of students' work will see much of a sameness, even an 'unmistakable style', already referred to. What is missing are collages or the popular copies of modern schools of art. Everything assembled from single parts, artificial materials, waste products of our culture etc. comes from a world of form derived from technological products. Technological articles must indeed be 'synthesised' from a variety of materials and forms. We meet such methods in the area of handwork – such as basket weaving, metalwork, joinery and tailoring – practised in the Upper School. It is there that the preparatory stages for methods used in technological productions, are to be found.

The organic principle develops its living formation actively from oneness to differentiated forms, without renouncing its inner totality. It does not synthesise from single parts, but forms from the whole. This organic quality in our students' artistic work radiates something of a living harmony and inner calm the onlooker experiences as beneficial and, perhaps, unexpectedly so. There are such critics who maintain that this does not correspond to the tensions of our technological age! We respond: because of this; our understanding of the reality of the organic-living world is in danger of being lost. Our environment and our social life are today largely determined by human beings. Is it not time to work at a new picture of the human being that understands not only the technology around us, but also – and largely through artistic activities – the organic laws in the world?

29

The influence of work on thinking
Michael Martin

A correct way to awaken the intellect would be, as far as possible, through the will. This we can do only by passing via the artistic to the developing of the intellect.

Rudolf Steiner's sentences, spoken during the *Study of Man* lectures,[1] are a kind of milestone for education. Although spoken in 1919, they are hardly understood today by the general public. This is understandablez, seeing that the 'intellectual education' to which Rudolf Steiner refers is practised everywhere and successfully so, without the development and cultivation of children's life of will and without artistic activities in many schools. It is no longer a matter of surprise when a nine-year-old child passes their Upper School leaving certificate or a thirteen-year-old child excels in the study of mathematics.[2] Such faculties can be awakened quite early and systematically heightened. Rudolf Steiner emphatically spoke of the inadvisability of both the premature and the one-sided development of the intellect. It is not easy to prove their negative consequences in individual cases. The following example may show the direction in which such harm can be found. A year before his death in 1882, Charles Darwin (in a self- critical passage) wrote an evaluation of his mental faculties:

I mentioned the change my mental/ spiritual mood underwent during the last twenty or thirty years. Until my thirtieth year or so I took great pleasure in poetry; I enjoyed Shakespeare when a boy, especially his Histories. I used to love paintings and music. And now, during the last years, I cannot bear even a line of poetry. I recently tried to re-read Shakespeare's plays and found them unbearably boring; they almost made me sick. And I also, more or less, lost my enjoyment of paintings and music … it is as though my mind had become a machine that grinds out universal laws from collections of facts. Why this should have been caused by the atrophy of those parts of my brain on which the higher sensations of taste depend I cannot understand. I imagine that somebody endowed with a more highly organised and pre-disposed mind than mine would not have experienced this. And, should I be in a position to re-live my life, I would make it a rule to read some poetry at least once a week, and listen to some music. The atrophied parts of my brain might then perhaps have remained active through their being used. The loss of receptivity for *such things is a loss of happiness and may well be of disadvantage for the intellect, and even more so for the moral life, since it weakens that part of our nature that can be stimulated by the heart-forces.*³

The deeply tragic note overshadowing these sentences has become, one hundred years later, the symbol of our times. The laborious acquisition and application of the intellect not only stunts our forces of will and feelings, as Darwin experienced it, but he was also correct in realising the negative effects on the intellect itself. For, although the pure intellect is able to grasp clearly and astutely the things and facts of our world, it can merely describe their outer physical nature. In this it loses the connection with the environment, from which it separates all objects in order to examine them in their isolated state. Everything of a mere logical nature tends towards clear border lines. This can also be seen in the teaching methods that have developed: already eighteen years ago, on the occasion of the third inter-schools exhibition in Dortmund, one of the exhibits was an egg-shaped plastic cell containing a comfortable chair and all the necessary technological media in use today. The 'swotting egg', as this mobile learning studio is called, is so protected from the outside that the student may learn without being influenced by any outer influences. Learning has become degraded to a process that is removed from life.

The frequently windowless speciality rooms in schools, the insulated lecture halls of our universities are, just as the 'swotting egg', consequent developments of the Town Hall of Laleburg. The *Lalebook*, published in 1597, tells of the windowless building, the forerunner of the *Schildbürger Book* (the wise men of Gotham) published a year later. Both became very popular.

What today is conscious intention, was then a prank: the good burghers of Laleburg had forgotten the windows during the building of their town hall, and afterwards attempted in vain to catch the daylight in sacks and to carry it inside. They finally stuck torches in their hats. Could we imagine a more perfect caricature for the intellect localised purely in the head?

Intellect and spirit

Rudolf Steiner obviously had a different kind of 'intellectual education' in mind. For us the recognition of such connections has become one of the basic questions in Steiner-Waldorf schools. It really is not (only) a matter of balancing mental (head) work – which keeps increasing – with heart and hands. Our concern is the 'awakening of the intellect through the will'. We shall, therefore, take a look at this connection between intellect and will.

In the middle of the *Study of Man*, Rudolf Steiner emphasises and describes the importance of all three elements – intellect, heart-forces and will. Everything depends on their correct cultivation. He then summarises their interaction:

The intellect, to begin with, is the most spiritual element in us. But, if we develop it in a one-sided way, unsupported by feeling and will, we shall always develop the tendency towards thinking materialistically. For though the intellect is the most spiritual element in us during our life on earth, it strives towards materialism. We must not assume that, by developing the intellect, we also develop the spiritual in the human being. As paradoxical as this may sound,

29. THE INFLUENCE OF WORK ON THINKING

it is nevertheless true: in the human being, we only develop the disposition to understand matter by developing the intellect.

It is only when we tastefully and aesthetically develop the heart-forces and feeling that we direct man's intellect to the soul. Furthermore, only by practising an education of the will – even if this is done only through the dexterity of the hands in handwork, – do we lay the foundation to directing the intellect to the spirit. If today there are so few people wishing to direct their intellect to the spirit, this is the result of their will having been wrongly cultivated during their childhood years.[4]

We have here a clear distinction between what is living within the sphere of ideas and mental images as intellect in our heads and the 'spiritual in the human being', developed through the life of will. It is surely more than a coincidence when Rudolf Steiner on the evening after the festive opening of the Waldorf School gave a lecture devoted exclusively to the subject of consciously differentiating between the intellect that speaks to the 'forehead', and the spirit that 'speaks to the heart'. He struggled with his listeners – and we are in the self-same position – for an understanding of this matter. He challenges us to distinguish between the mere words and the spiritual tone, between the logical and the well of truth.

With our feelings, we tend to connect the 'logical', the 'mere words', with the intellect; we know from experience that it is possible to separate from the 'well of truth' with a logical statement without being guilty of being untruthful. The 'spiritual tone', the 'spiritual fluid' from which we draw our striving for truth, and logic need not be identical with this.

Through self-observation we may discover several ways of thinking. The intellect allows us to understand the world as it is, as it has become: a lifeless truth. If we wish to arrive at a living truth we must activate the thinking process to include the deeper-seated forces of feeling and will. Through this concentrated thinking, permeated by will and feeling, we can approach the 'source of truth', the 'spiritual fluid' as Rudolf Steiner called it. There, the whole of the human being must be employed, not only the head.

Many of you have come to despise thinking, because you experienced it merely as being passive. But this only applies to head thinking, where the heart has no part. But give active thinking a chance and you will see how the heart will become engaged. Modern people only strongly connect with the spirit if they succeed in activating their thinking … This is initially a matter of will, a will experienced with feeling.[5]

Thinking, taken hold of by feeling and will, can take us to the spiritual world – while mere intellect tends to become materialistic. Once this difference has become clear to us, the next step will be the question: how can these guidelines be anchored and organised in us, how is the latter related to the limbs? In what ways can artistic and manual activities engender its higher development? We shall address these questions, making use of an exercise in modelling, though this should not be taken as something especially 'artistic'. Its purpose is a more scientific observation and understanding of form conditions, and this will help us to go further in our enquiries.

PART FIVE: FURTHER THINKING

Form conditions

We begin this exercise with the shaping of a clay ball – just big enough to fit comfortably into our hands. As we shape, we try to become aware of the special quality of this form. The idea itself – to confront a three-dimensional form in space with only one infinite surface – is already quite remarkable. All the points on this surface are equidistant from the centre. This may give us the impression that its whole concentration is directed to the centre. In shaping this ball with both hands, the palms turn inwards, enclosing an inner space that can only be seen from outside. This makes clear the in/out relation in a sphere; any other orientation in space is essentially absent. This is the reason why a spherical object cannot really be put on a level surface – it has no 'below' and starts to roll as soon as the surface is not absolutely horizontal. It doesn't really 'belong' in our three-dimensionally structured space. The only thing corresponding to its quality would be gliding freely in space, sustained by energies that again would have to be produced by a balanced inner/outer tension.

We then elongate this clay ball at one end into an egg shape, and flatten a part of the stretched surface: it can now rest securely on the board. This allows it to retain more of its quality of 'free' roundness than if we had simply pressed the original ball to the board, the effect would have been one of weight, heaviness.

The next step is the shaping of an identical ball, but we now alter the surface, by carefully pressing it, making the even roundness uneven, more pronounced here, flatter there.

The original spherical shape is divided; indications of several different surfaces are formed. In our attempt at continuing with these surfaces we

29. THE INFLUENCE OF WORK ON THINKING

touch the clay. Naturally, we are here speaking of formatively active energies and forces.

Our third exercise will be the shaping of a kind of complementary form to the first. We first recapitulate the first two forms. Then we exert stronger pressure from outside, making the surface gradually curve towards the inside. The edges will be much more marked than in the previous exercise. We also notice that we have left the characteristic quality of the sphere behind, and that the effect of the form on us is different. If – in our minds – we continue the concave curves of the surfaces into space, we shall see (invisibly, of course) bowl-like surfaces intersecting and penetrating each other.

In attempting a complementary picture to the spheric one of our first exercise, we shall meet with a problem: against the uniformly curved surface of a sphere, we have a variety of concave ones. And we cannot think of a pure concave form in clay shaped from just one concave surface. To do this we ourselves would have to be within a concave form curving around us as in a perhaps endless space – something only possible in the mind and not in matter.

A law of our being interwoven into the world of matter seems to force us into producing several hollow, concave surfaces as complementary forms to the sphere. We now push harder into the ball-shaped clay: the edges press further to the foreground; the surfaces deepen more and more in the process. It is even more instructive if we use exactly the same amount of clay in these exercises by weighing the quantities. In our last exercise, the matter, during its being pressed inwards, is increasingly pushed to the periphery at the edges, extending at the corners, where three surfaces meet, into elongated points – if we make the effort of shaping really and quite consequentially in a concave way. The form increases; it seems to be

shall see that edges will unavoidably result between them. In spite of this, every surface should be convex, i.e. should remain curved to the outside.

If we draw such a form it will become even clearer that the surfaces actually intersect at the edges and continue invisibly into space. No longer the finite quality of the sphere, the newly produced surfaces are only partly visible – where they

275

growing. This creates the illusion for our eyes and hands: that the larger form is lighter than the more compact sphere. But we had weighed the clay! It is almost impossible to mould their radiating shapes in clay: it dries and crumbles in the process. In our mind we are searching for a more suitable material and discover the metal that can be poured into a mould. It is relatively easy to shape a spherical form with the watery clay; the shape that has now evolved would need the fiery liquid of metal casting. The form before us opens up to space in many ways; it receives it, more or less, depending on the way the bowl-like surfaces are formed

We complete our fourth exercise in the mind. The energies and forces working from the outside are directed to the centre of the earlier sphere; the clay is pressed out, in a radiating way, into the periphery to the point of dissolution. In between there is only space into which the single concave surfaces melt.

If we are fortunate in doing these exercises in a group, we can display all the clay balls side by side, next to the concave forms.

By comparing them we can try to discover what emanates from them (but not by what we wish to see in or deduce from them), to grasp something of their essential nature. We shall see in the spherical shapes that each of them is complete in itself. They do not require space around them; they are cool and calm, as though asleep. The concave shapes, on the other hand, cannot really be too close to each other; they need space around them, else they would get in each other's way. They seem to dissolve, to lose themselves as they ray out, are lively, awake and open to their surrounding.

If we look for the corresponding forms in nature we shall discover the former in the buds, tubers and eggs – everywhere where new life, resting within itself, is prepared. The latter we shall find in the final

stage of life condition, in a plant that, as blossom, streams out into space, or in a pine cone that, in its early stage is still round and later, through the summer's warmth, cracks open, opens up to space. With animals we must see the egg shape in the embryo in relation to the limbs or the overall shape. In the former, we have the effect of the germinating, enclosing, formative forces; in the latter, we have a form dissolving, from consuming energy leading to mobile liveliness, and opening in the development of form. This allows us to experience – with our feeling, and yet concretely – the effect of water and fire in these two different forms.

If we apply these polarities of form to the human face, we shall see in them the same expression we just characterised. This is quite naturally so. But we shall see how in the physiognomy in which the inner (soul) life is reflected, the dreaming, sleeping and the fully awake elements express themselves even more clearly: in sleeping the physical feeling of comfort, a faint smile – in the fully awake an earnestness that can be intensified to pain and sorrow.

At the same time we get the impression that the physical is consumed in this sorrow, it ages. The sleeping face grows younger. What K. Fortlage, the nineteenth century psychologist, discovered, becomes here visible: 'Consciousness is a little and partial death, death a large and total Consciousness, an awakening of the whole being in its innermost depths!'[6] When the soul is consciously present in the body, the latter is consumed, ages and hardens. When the soul provides the body with the necessary rest during sleep it can regenerate itself. We can see how the life conditions of the body depend on the conditions of soul and spirit during waking and sleeping. A higher life of the soul causes the dying away of the physical, although it is the bearer of the soul's life.

Soul and spirit tend to hollow out the form; the forces building the physical body manifest in concave forms.

Form-building and form-consuming forces

The Ancient Greeks at the turn of the sixth century B.C. still lived strongly within the life building forces. Their sculptures are formed as though urging from within, pressing, swelling, convex. At the same time we see the dreaming soul in the body expressed in a happy smile, not yet a radiating of the soul permeated by its individual forces. It is, therefore, correctly referred to as the 'archaic smile'. At the moment when sorrow or joy are actually experienced in the depth of the soul and become manifest in the features of the face, instead in the whole of the posture of the figure, the body appears to be quite consequentially as though consumed, dissolved. This is apparent in the sculptures of the late Middle Ages, when the healthy, physical form behind the fluffed up folds of the gowns that consist of mere concave forms and edges, are hiding in concave, hollow spaces, as though dying.

In its stead the whole of the soul's world of feeling is lighting up not only the faces, but penetrating the whole body from head to toe. This is the reason for the prominence given to the hands during this time (fifteenth century), their impressive, en-souled language – ridge formations, as it were, between concave surfaces, as a result of the soul's deep immersion into the body. Modern sculptures are frequently created by these form-consuming forces: the body gets lost in the process; instead they ray out into space to which they open themselves. They have become 'space' figures.

PART FIVE: FURTHER THINKING

The 'Apollo of Tenea', c. sixth century B.C., marble, Munich Glyptothek

Tilman Riemenschneider, 'Lamenting Maidbronn', c. 1525, sandstone

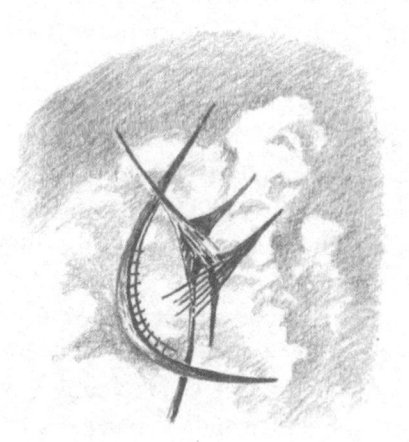

Carmelo Capello, 'Eclipse', 1959, bronze, h. 225 cm

Krumau, 'The Beautiful Mother of God' c. 1400, wood, Kunsthistorisches Museum, Vienna

Copperplates from c. 1000 B.C. Hindu University, Benares, India

29. THE INFLUENCE OF WORK ON THINKING

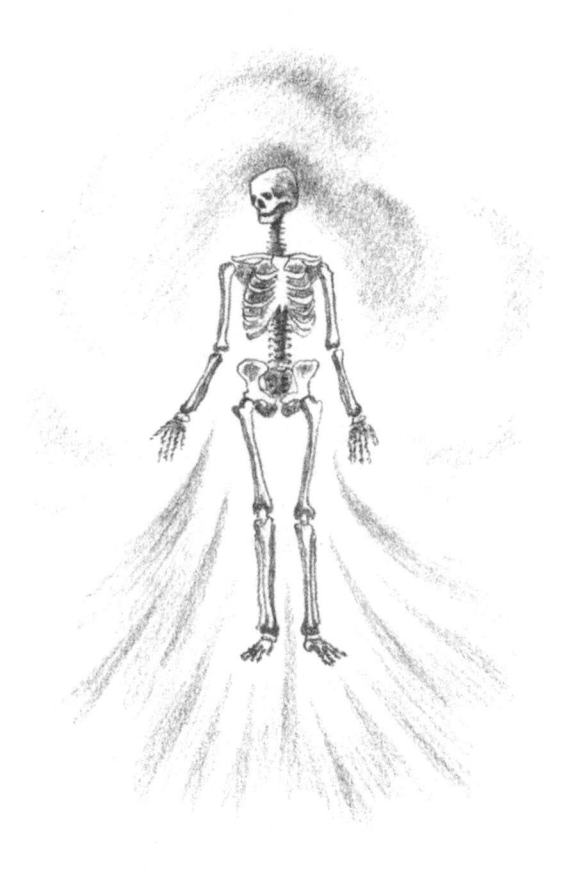

We mentioned the stages of consciousness in sleeping and waking with their alternating effects on the physical body, either form-building or form-consuming. The examples taken from the history of art embrace a long period of time. We shall now consider the human physical form, not from the point of time, but from space. To do this we shall consider an Indian 'Idol' from 1000 B.C. There are seven such copper plates whose purpose is unknown and whose appearance is unique in the history of art. For our study, their form is of special significance, if we do not merely see in them the craftsmanship, but if we include the surroundings from which this obviously primal form of the human being might have arisen. This can be attempted through drawing. We can try to form the figure itself from the stream of forces coming from the environment. Surprisingly quickly it becomes clear to us that we are dealing with an interaction of our first and fourth exercises in clay. What we had formed as sequence, one after the other, is here simultaneously formed as the basis for the human body. From the polarity of the radiating element that streams from below upwards, together with a damming from above by which the convex-round form arises, a form is produced in the middle part that is neither round nor radiating, but a connection or, better, a penetration of both.

Through drawing, we recognise what could not be made clear during our clay exercises: how the opposites of the round and the radiating have a common element in the inward moving spiral at the centre. This means that the opposites are bridged or reconciled.

In a human skeleton we can see the reality of this primal picture translated into real life. It can be seen more clearly in the structure of a bone than in the living human figure. We discover in the fingertips the splintered, consumed element, tamed to the top by the unifying formative forces of the upper pole, coming to rest and rigidifying in the uniformity of the round element. In this vigorous onslaught of the forces of soul and spirit, hidden in the radiating forms, we experience directly the fiery, stimulating warmth and, as we look at the tubular bone, we are reminded of the clay that, in our fourth exercise, was compressed together into thin rays between the energies breaking in from outside. Conversely, in the calm of the skull, we can experience the cooling off, the densification, the form-building elements in matter. The enclosure, the form of our idol is made even more effective through the folding over of the copper at the upper edge of the head.

To summarise: the consuming forces of soul and spirit radiate from without into our limb system, developing warmth through the unfolding of the will in blood and muscle, which we experience during the use of our limbs. Combustion processes take place within our metabolic organism, while the forms of the limbs are as though splintered, torn apart.

Movement comes to rest in the processes of the head, leading to an enclosed, round form that, as skull cover, produces the outer physical basis for our thinking. Physiologically this shows itself in the processes of secretions, in the solidifying of matter. The forces of intelligence in the world manifest coolly and clearly in our heads. We have thus arrived at two different organisations of the spirit and soul nature, localised in the periphery of the limb system and in the head.

In Lecture 13 of the *Study of Man* Rudolf Steiner drew attention to this:

> *A continuous kind of pressure is exerted on the palms of your hands and the soles of your feet that is equal to the pressure exerted from the centre of the head to the forehead, only in the opposite direction. As, therefore, you stretch out the palms of your hands and place your feet on the ground, there streams through the soles of your feet from outside the same that streams from within towards your forehead. This is a most important fact, important, because it enables us to understand the place of soul and spirit in the human being. As you can see, soul and spirit stream, as a current, through the human being. And the human being, what is he in connection with this soul and spirit? Imagine a current of water being arrested by a dam, so that it is thrown back. In this way soul and spirit are whirled back in the human being. The human being is a damming mechanism for soul and spirit. They would like to stream through him without impediment, but he keeps them back, slows them down, allows them to be dammed up in him.*[7]

This 'streaming and damming' can be most clearly seen in the drawing below. Our previous observations and exercises make it quite clear that we are dealing with soul and spirit currents. And we can now understand that, when human beings move their limbs during physical work, they move in the spirit, 'splashing about in it'. The result is that, unconsciously, we connect ourselves with the spirit around us during physical work. 'The spirit flows around us when we are engaged in physical work.'[8]

Streaming and damming

29. THE INFLUENCE OF WORK ON THINKING

Intellect and will

We now have a clear picture of the two polarities of our soul/spiritual nature as found in head and limbs. In his lecture on August 31, 1919, Rudolf Steiner characterised intelligence with its tendency towards materialism.[9] Head thinking comprehends and describes the created things in our world, their outer manifestation, their being here. We can see that the shape of the head, its solidity and hardening process corresponds to this.

This makes it possible to use it as a 'machine' that can – as Darwin characterised his own thinking – 'grind out' universal laws from the great collection of facts.

The use of our limbs counters this; processes of becoming create changes, new structures. These energies are of a spiritual/will nature. They can become active only through the radiating form and the 'splintering' of the limbs. We could never, with rounded, undifferentiated fists, with spherically folded hands or stunted rounded arms handle a tool and carry out sensitive movements in work. All differentiated movements are possible only through the stretching and divisions of our limbs that are as though splintered, as though having become transparent, loosened in their form and grasped by rhythm.

We refer to Rudolf Steiner who was able to investigate spiritually-scientifically these processes, and who indicated the steps to be taken for the development of the intellect: it is essential that we know that children begin to fully connect with their bony system only during the twelfth year. Before this they live – also physically – far more in the rhythm of breathing and blood circulation, in the stretching and contracting of their muscles, i.e. in their 'liquid organisation'. During the twelfth year a 'push' begins, clearly perceptible to the sensitive observer. Through the bony parts becoming more prominent, through the lengthening of the limbs, through a change in the quality of movement and through the whole bearing. In a word, the children have become more earthy; will energies surge upwards, asking to be used. This need is met by the introduction of gardening and crafts, both of which include the earth: in gardening it is the working place itself, in crafts, the necessary resistance during the work that needs the firm support of the floor, as in sawing, hammering, carving etc.

Hand in glove with this, thinking progresses from picture-like, feeling permeated mental images to clear, lucid thought sequences that make it possible to grasp and understand physical and chemical processes. It descends, as it were, from the head and meets the hardness of the skeleton. It also meets the stream of will that radiates into the limbs as new soul-forces. Through the seizing of the organism right into the bones, thinking is endowed with a will-like element. During the Christmas Course, Rudolf Steiner lectured on these processes in detail. We quote verbatim:

As we enter [children's] twelfth year we acquire a way of thinking that, corresponding to its will nature, is rooted in the bones, the dynamics of the skeleton. It marks the important transition from the soft to the quite solid, hard system of the human being, that places itself objectively into the world, as it were, like a system of levers...

During our thinking about physical nature, especially the thinking rooted in the skeleton, the process dominates the entire human being. We place ourselves into our skeleton also with our thinking during the twelfth year...

We must now begin to lead into the intellectual understanding of the inorganic world what was formerly experienced in pictures, what was then extended to the living plants, to the feeling life in animals.[10]

Strong, meaningful use of the limbs can engender the healthy development of the intellect. Nothing can replace the logic hidden in the work processes.

A wrong thought will immediately show in the work, be it in the garden or workshop. In this sense, too, the intellect awakens during the practical work of the hands.

Young children are not yet familiar with their awakening will. They can be amazed – whether it be with joy or disappointment – at the result of work that has turned out differently from what they had expected. Wakefulness of the head and clear reflection that affect the way the tools are handled are now in balance; the subjective will rising from below is controlled and put to good use: the intelligence of the upper pole permeates itself with the will of the lower pole that now, fructifying each other, have become new faculties to be used.

The effect of art and craft work on body and spirit

The processes just described intensify during the next years. Because of this we increase the number of art and craft subjects, beginning in Class 9. It takes time before the full harmony between intellect and will is established, often a taxing time. We must not remain at the purely logical nature of the craft activities. The techniques of sawing, chiselling and planing must be learnt, but should only provide the basis for further work. This brings the merely logical structure of a shelf into movement: support, and stability of the boards receive artistic forms. The rigid framework of the four identical legs of a chair comes to life in the forms of the seat and back. Their sensitively bordering edges and shaped surfaces have a stimulating and educating effect on the perception, the life of ideas and mental images connected with it. Goethe recognised the value of such perceptions on the development of the spirit. The more banal the form, the lazier the spirit! A living form also affects the muscles, making them more sensitive, the muscles that carry out the mechanical movements of the tools in manual work.

The form and material of the workpiece determine the use of the tools and the respective movements of hands and arms. When fastening a nut or driving in a screw, my bone and muscle must adapt to these simple, purely mechanical turning movements demanded by the nut and screw. If I use machines for this work, ever fewer differentiated movements of arms and hands will be employed, due to the machine doing most of the work for me. My organism of movement must fully adapt to the machine. Digging the garden or chopping wood already allows the worker the freedom of including the conditions of their physical body in the work. And even if the aim of the work is the same, a short person will dig differently from a tall one; a strong person will chop wood differently from a weak one.

An artistic way of shaping a piece of material can liberate us still more from purely mechanical and rigid movements. The sensitive rotations of wrist and lower arm that can be felt through the whole body as far down as the soles of the feet, determine the quality of a carving. Working at a clay sculpture depends on the sense of touch with its highly sensitive muscle movements. It is formed effort.

29. THE INFLUENCE OF WORK ON THINKING

We can see how artistic work affects the sensitivity of the whole body in many ways, as well as forming and making more sensitive our will-forces. It is true education of the will. It also works into the sphere of ideas and imagination (in the head), making them more flexible, stimulating, flexible and mobile.

But Rudolf Steiner draws our attention to yet deeper connections between doing and thinking. They are based on the experience that the will is a soul-force that can be active in different parts of the human being. Its most important activity is in the physical energies in movements; but further, it can bring feeling into movement and kindle imagination. And it can stir and make mobile the pictures of our ideas to the point where they are no longer mere copies of outside events, but assume individually creative forms, leading to archetypal forms such as Goethe perceived in the archetypal plant. In a wealth of lectures and books, Rudolf Steiner describes the training of such imaginative creative forces in great detail.[11]

On one such occasion, he speaks of the importance of the effort needed in the use of muscles during adolescence; recalling the benefit such work had on him during his boyhood – chopping wood, harvesting potatoes, digging the garden and sawing. He states that this made it easier for him to develop that imaginative thinking which makes possible access to deeper layers of life. The two are connected. Such efforts of will, stimulating the muscles during physical work, in another situation, affect the thinking process where our equivalent inner effort is required.

Adolescents, too, after having been educated in the strict exactitude of logic (Classes 6–8), must be led during puberty to the beginning of a 'living thinking' able to grasp the phenomena of the world that go beyond the sphere of logic to deeper connections, to a 'living truth', as Rudolf Steiner called it. How are the young man and woman to grow into the world? By being isolated in the 'swotting egg' – or by enriching their intelligence through work and being open for what is in the world?

It was Rudolf Steiner's wish that students in Steiner-Waldorf schools be helped and challenged to access ideas by which they could enter the essential nature of things rather than merely perceive their outer appearance. This presupposes the cultivation of feeling and will. This may explain why Steiner-Waldorf schools make every effort to establish possibilities where 'the intellect is awakened through the will as far as possible'.

If we know that the intellect is not developed through the direct cultivation of the intellect, if we know that clumsy fingers point to a clumsy intellect that will bring forth but few flexible ideas and thoughts, while skilled fingers lead to flexible thoughts and ideas, to an ability of entering the essential nature of things, then we shall not underestimate the significance of developing the 'outer' human being with the aim that the intellect will emerge as one piece from the way the outer human being applies himself to manual work.[12]

Thus intelligence and will interpenetrate during the third seven-year period. Strong polarities characterise this new soul life developing from thinking, feeling and willing. But it is just in this field of polar tension that the 'I' can develop itself as the organ of personality. Being still sustained by the will-forces, it expresses itself as self-willed, because it has not yet fully come into its own. If the will becomes active in work, the 'I' becomes mobile and can unfold. Artistic activity inducts the 'I' into its polar elements. In the formative work, it takes hold of the polarities and, by resolving them, it frees itself from its soul-sheath. At about the twenty-first year it assumes a central place in the personality.

If these will-forces in the field of polar tension within the soul are not activated, the 'I' cannot develop in a healthy way and wilts. This being the case, people with a highly developed intelligence may then become prone to achieving great things in their specialised fields but without being interested in ethical issues, or feeling responsible for the consequences of their actions.

Darwin realised that the stunting of his artistic feelings must have had negative consequences for the 'moral' character. Many a well-known scientist shares his view.

Moral impulses today emanate only from spiritual sources that are deeper seated in the human being than is the intellect. The intellect, centred in the head, cannot produce morality, for these forces can only be awakened by the artistic. If, however, we pass from artistic activities to intellectual development, we will provide the basis for a moral life that is stimulated from the sphere of the spirit. Through our activities, it can 'grow into' our thinking and there be active. This, too, is a consequence of the path that wishes as far as possible to awaken the intellect through the will.

Logic and work

Let us once more turn to the *Lalebook*. The title page on which the author reveals his name in the following way, is most instructive:

With too many letters are we blessed,
Take but a few and throw out the rest;

Then join what is left, a worthwhile game:
It will reveal the author's name.

A quite logical piece of computer thinking, for 1597! Since, however, the key for cracking the code was not provided, its author has remained unknown.

The author's insight into the spiritual current of his time is obvious, as are his concerns about the future, which he expressed in popular language. He recognised the danger of our becoming fools if we do not warm and enliven our cerebral thinking, that can do no more than lead to a materialistic world conception, with the forces of the spirit. In Chapter 17 he writes:

Since all of us have become Lale people by having lost the right wisdom and this in a wanton way – we now follow all foolishness and investigate tomfoolery rather than wisdom.

This 'tomfoolery' consists of our observing the world only at the surface, i.e. superficially. It is significant that the Lale people trace their origin to ancient Greek culture. It was the Greeks who stimulated and developed technological thinking by observing natural physical phenomena, and then correctly applying natural laws.

The effect of the elemental beings in nature faded for man's perception to the same degree that the physical properties of nature were discovered through outer observation. The opening of the temple gates through a mechanical physical device, or the holy water automaton Heron of Alexandria constructed (circa 100 A.D.) deflected the consciousness from the service to God, whose presence disappeared more and more from inner sight; observation, reflection and thinking

29. THE INFLUENCE OF WORK ON THINKING

The Temple Gates at Heron, opened by the sacrifical fire, c.100 A.D. From S. Strandh, The Machine

were directed to the outer appearance of things whereupon processes became superficial.

In this way, Greek thinking freed itself from the old, mythical way of perceiving the world, and passed into a purely logical way of thinking during Roman culture. In doing so, it became abstract.

How can logic in thinking be practised in a living way? By developing it from the activity of the limbs! Crafts and handwork directly link thinking to the hands, which immediately correct each thought that has not originated from the matter in hand. If we wish to work in metal, wood or clay, during the work, we must extract the 'logic' of the material concretely from the material itself. This logic does not come from the head, but from the necessity arising from the task and the material in a consequential way.

The 'logic of life' and not that of the head is practised in crafts, especially where accurate planning must precede the actual work – as in carpentry, shoemaking or bookbinding. Ultimately, the exact fitting of the parts will be the proof of the accuracy of our thinking: my thinking lives within the objective laws of the things and materials as much as in my doing. In crafts and handwork I identify myself with the material, the matter in the world.

Rudolf Steiner frequently and emphatically said that the real, actual life should reign in all the lessons rather than being preoccupied with ancient cultures whose life had ended long before.[13] People who have passed through a training of logic in craft and handwork lessons confront life differently with their thinking than those who can only access a logic of concepts in their heads. Only concrete thoughts can stand the test of life, and have a positive and beneficial effect.

Towards a living thinking

It would be tempting to study the rapid development of factual logic through the arts and crafts since the Middle Ages, which initially was still embedded the forces of pious feeling placed in the service of the supersensible. But, especially since the end of the eighteenth century, logic has concentrated on investigating and researching the earth, resulting in our modern technology. However, this is only one aspect: that same clear consciousness also taught us to turn to the spiritual nature of life. Rudolf Steiner referred to both these (polar) directions that thinking can take today. If thinking concentrates on the world, it will be stimulated, guided, perhaps even determined by the phenomena in the way it should work.

It is different when thinking concentrates on the supersensible. The supersensible is reserved and does not make it easy for us. Effort is required

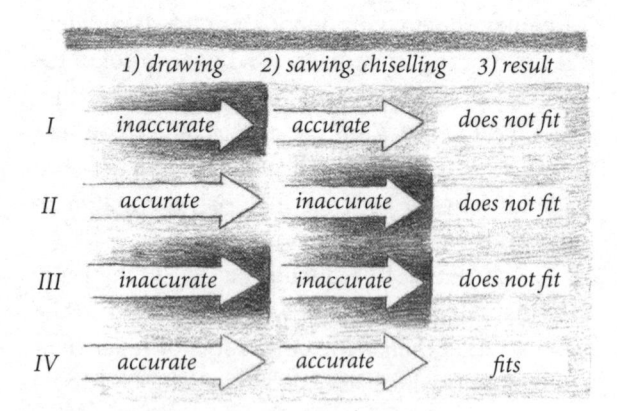

	1) drawing	2) sawing, chiselling	3) result
I	inaccurate →	accurate →	does not fit
II	accurate →	inaccurate →	does not fit
III	inaccurate →	inaccurate →	does not fit
IV	accurate →	accurate →	fits

'Logistics' in the making of a wooden joint in joinery (e.g. dovetailing)

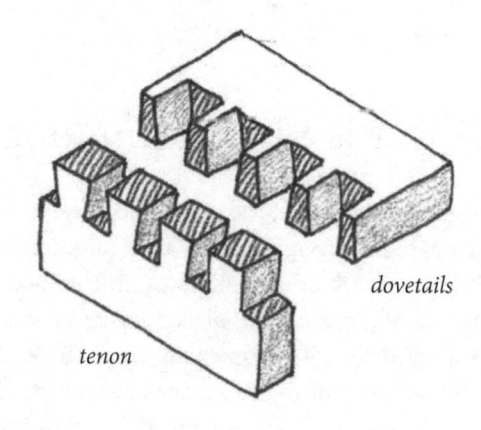

dovetails

tenon

to become conscious of its phenomena and processes.

It is as though we are looking at a mountaintop in the distance. We long to be there, but can only look at it, unless we make the effort and take time to actually go there and climb it without counting the cost. In the same way, our thinking regarding supersensible processes may perceive the target of knowledge, but will only get there if it develops strong inner impulses. These impulses – energies and forces – reside in feeling and will. Without the loving devotion of our feeling to the still unknown – the not yet reached target – the will that is to take our thinking selflessly to it, is helpless, and cannot bestir itself. Our will must trustingly surrender to the guidance of the feeling that lovingly embraces the unknown. Only in this way, i.e. borne by the feeling of love and the selfless devotion of the will, can the thoughts reach the unknown, its target of knowledge. Insofar as this process is consciously taking place within our soul, it is the ego that is the comprehensive force of these three soul activities to which Rudolf Steiner referred as 'consciousness soul'. He described this concord of thinking, feeling and willing, guided by the ego, in connection with the supersensible as the modern human being's attitude to knowledge as such.

We have become accustomed to think of devotion – the word he used in connection with this activity – merely in a religious sense. Rudolf Steiner extended it to the basic mood of soul regarding the perception of all spiritual phenomena. If it is truly stimulated in the soul, not as a mood of feeling, but as a cognitive force, i.e. thinking, borne by feeling and willing, it can make the outer appearance of the phenomena transparent for the effectiveness of the spirit. Through this, the 'spiritual in the human being', mentioned above, can feel its way to the 'fount of truth', where the human being can enter the 'essential nature of things'.

He or she who has followed our considerations will not be surprised when we maintain that the feeling of love and the devotion of the will are soul qualities that can be developed during the arts and crafts lessons in the workshop. Indeed, love and restrained self-will are pre-conditions for such work. Already earlier on, we pointed to the necessary unfolding of the 'love of work'.

29. THE INFLUENCE OF WORK ON THINKING

It is difficult to imagine anything other than indifference resulting from working with machines. Such an attitude is unthinkable in an artistic activity or when making a pair of shoes or in gardening. A lovelessly drawn surface or carved object will immediately be spotted by the practised eye and dismissed as a bungled, clumsy piece of work. Loving attention to detail characterises the artist's devotion to his or her work.

But this is only possible through harnessing the will that streams through the hands. Licentiousness or unbridled will soon reveal itself as techniques not yet mastered, and in the uncontrolled use of tools. Calm and perseverance in practising are essential to achieve technical mastery; without patience, the work cannot improve and grow. Just as important are obedience and submission to the directions given by the teacher or master craftsman who knows the correct way of doing things, who has tested them.

He who uses both hands in driving the chisel into the wood is still a victim to the self-will of his impatience. Bad, uneven cuts will be the result. Only when the left hand soberly guides and controls the pressure of the right will the cuts be accurate and clean. The surface will have a different quality. The same applies to all other work processes carried out with circumspection, guided by astute observation.

Submission of the will and loving, feeling devotion to the world are faculties which, initially put into practice during the craft lessons, can gradually affect the soul, develop further in the artistic work and, finally, affect the thinking. What at first has been active in the body can become the foundation for the unfolding of soul and spirit forces.

Expressed differently, the work in arts and crafts may be seen as a method for the development of feeling and will, which we need for the development of a living thinking. The connection of 'work' with attitude to knowledge which Rudolf Steiner called 'devotion', will now be clear.

Feeling and will combine with the intellect to raise it to a higher condition/plain. The intellect no longer only receives the processes in the world as mirror images, but frees itself through its own creative energies from its inclination towards becoming materialistic. Feeling and will have awakened it to a higher, spiritual world conception.

We have come full circle. The starting point of our reflections was to discover how will and intellect – polar entities, active within us – can melt into each other. In this, special importance is given to hands and arms. They are active in the centre, balancing, linking, melting. Free for work, they are in a position to bring about the transformation. In the crafts they turn more to our daily needs. In the arts they bring to expression what is living within the sphere of soul and spirit in us.

If we make these thoughts mobile, then, within the tensions of the polarities mentioned – polarities that can interweave to a fruitful union – there lights up that spiritual fire that alone can win the battle being waged within the human being: the 'I' that unfolds and develops itself the more it is active in the balancing of its own being. It is only by such an unfolding of the personality that we may pass 'from the artistic to the intellectual culture'.

Steiner-Waldorf education attempts this awakening of the slumbering forces and energies in the human being. Its effect in later life will freely depend on the intentions of each individual and on his or her destiny. All the school can do is to try to give a foundation. What the young man or woman builds on is entirely within their freedom.

30

An integrated approach to craftwork
Aonghus Gordon

Michael Martin's exhaustive research and experience in compiling the previous chapters offers a fresh momentum towards an intensification and reappraisal of craft handwork and technology in Steiner-Waldorf schools. The content of the book reiterates one of the principle tenets of the Steiner-Waldorf approach – that thinking arises out of activity and movement in the early developmental stages of children. His use of Kant's quote, 'The hand is the outer brain of the human being', creates a powerful image for all handwork and craft teachers; an image that needs to be taken more seriously in view of the accelerating decline in opportunities to move actively and appropriately in early childhood.

During recent years society has moved at a disproportionate speed towards a two-dimensional as opposed to a three-dimensional cultural orientation. Increasingly teachers observe restlessness, hyperactivity and above all concentration difficulties as well as a dislocation between point and periphery in children's growing awareness. If unchecked in adolescence, three powerful subcultures are likely to take effect. The intellect that is not incorporated into the world of imagination becomes conceited and arrogant, while the search for the imagination can sometimes lead to dangerous substance experimentation. If the will is not diverted into appropriate skilful activity and endeavour it can become criminalised and search for extreme experiences to compensate for the absence of movement and activity. And if the feeling life of adolescents is aberrant, where feelings of devotion are not cultivated, an overt form of sexualised behaviour can arise. These counter pictures can ensnare adolescents. Practical skilful craftwork within itself has the opportunity of re-embodying thinking, feeling and willing. In thinking, the preplanning of the conceptual framework; in feeling, the sense of purpose in the service of a social context and in willing, the capacity to fashion and execute the form. However, it is becoming increasingly apparent that all this may still not be sufficient. The environmental context, as yet an undiscovered emerging parameter for the later and more mature development of adolescence, offers many challenges to enact a new ethic based around the principles of sustainability, a new craftsmanship of the environment, a living technology.

Craftwork is embedded in the development of human consciousness and has a history of 10,000 years. This history is additionally embedded in the Steiner-Waldorf school, in particular in the main-lesson curriculum, and can be sourced as a further opportunity of extending the range of practical skills that enable the experience of learning to be grounded though the context of the material and the intended purpose of the objects made. Sourcing the materials is essential to enable children to handle at first hand the three kingdoms of nature and engage in the four elements.

Re-animating movement

The remarkable aspect of movement inherent in executing primary craft activities, whether rolling felt or shaping hot metal, is the pre-ordained nature of the movement itself. The movement arcs that are inscribed on the material, and developed by the pupils, resonate in the etheric body of children as a 'cosmic imprint'. True agility of movement in craftsmanship when inscribed on paper even reminds one of the movements of the planetary spheres. Few movement activities are so objective, as the craft movement is defined by the laws inherent in the quality of the material and the purpose of the object. Egotistical movement is limited if the object being undertaken serves a human social world, such as a knife from the Iron Age forge, a chair from green woodwork, slippers from felt.

Reanimating movement in children and adolescents serves to release the etheric body out of the muscular structure, which is so often frozen, even in a state of shock. Releasing the fluidity of movement through a craft activity may be described as accessing a slipstream of movement in which the pupils or adolescents are held.

Children's first movements, gripping, rotating, sliding, lifting, crawling, or more simply put, exploring the three dimensions of space, are available in different measures of intensity in the simple craft activities drawn out of a primary craft curriculum. These can be used as a recapitulation of missed stages of development, which is increasingly common. Similarly to children's early drawings, these movements are primordial and are a prerequisite to achieving a healthy integrated relationship to the world. Where a movement experience becomes rhythmical out of which a skill develops, there is a term often used to describe it: 'I can do it in my sleep'. In observing this state of awareness, something interesting happens. It is as if this awareness comes out of the stream of time. The skill is gained through past experience, but it brings something towards the individual out of the future. It is possible to experience non-time, in other words, a state of presence in which opportunities arise so as to observe oneself in movement. This is a profoundly therapeutic experience and many pupils touch this point when they become more skilful in their movement articulation. This 'presence' can be described as a state of self-healing as it can act as a path towards self-knowledge.

An approach to re-envisioning the school landscape

Goethe required any serious student who wished to understand the environment in which they participated to become conversant with the genius loci, the spirit of the place. Scale is no impediment to this process of re-engaging with the immediate grounds of the school and the context of the school within the landscape. Schools that have researched and entered into this relationship have found a new route of identity and, more importantly, reincorporated the craft skills of the landscape into the craft curriculum. A survey over the course of one year, in which all aspects of the school's grounds and landscape are touched on by each class in the school, brings new ownership and awareness. The gardening curriculum finds a new context; the water takes pride of place in the development and the diversification that is required to re-enliven the etheric sheath of the school. Plants and hedges can be sourced for making Easter nests in the Kindergarten, for providing coppicing and charcoal making for the Iron Age forge. Clay is dug to build a bread oven. So over the year an emerging alchemy of the four elements will become apparent.

New skills and teaching methods are required to take children to often-new experiential frontiers. These frontiers enable new imaginative pictures to take effect, powerful feelings of empathy for the environment and new exercises in the will to emerge. In schools where this process of developing the landscape is taking on an educational imprint, the context becomes child-centred, not recreational or economic, but applied through educational practice and supported by biodynamic principles. The school thereby takes ownership of and responsibility for the landscape, which becomes increasingly transparent to the pupils, particularly as they ascend towards the Upper School and the dawning of their intellectual capacities.

As the pupils ascend in age with newfound intellectual skills, craftwork is gradually replaced by a crafted landscape organism in which sustainable environmental practice is underpinned by an ethic of sustainability, but enacted through the freewill gestures of the pupils. The pupils move from 'point to periphery'. The building of a water-cleansing reed bed system, a practical ecology in working with the kingdoms of nature and the elements to service the growing environmental degradation, offers the older pupils the opportunity for self-judgement. Their highly developed intellectual capacities can be channelled into servicing environmental and human requirements. This may be called a new form of living technology. In this way aspects of the Upper School science curriculum can externalise from the laboratory into the environment and have direct application. One may be even so bold as to call it a new form of practical literacy.

During a Class 12 project in which pupils were placed into an environment in which they had to resource materials and processes to sustain themselves, the pupils encountered a high level of motivation and skill in resolving their requirements; building a baker's oven to cook food, constructing a compost toilet to deal with their personal waste, creating tools and implements. Their level of engagement is testified through the following series of impressions by students Saul Grant and Danielle Radojcin:

Working with the issue of sustainability in mind we acquired hands-on experience of the use of such materials as wood, clay and iron in our activities. The result was that each of the four groups faced its own individual challenges, which the students themselves had to overcome with guidance from the tutors where necessary. Thus the complexities of a sewage system, a bread oven and how to fit a chair together without straight pieces of wood were tackled and overcome.

We soon discovered that the activities were not dissimilar to arts and craft lessons… but with one significant difference: rather than simply watching and then taking part in a craft, which, it seems, is productive only insofar as it provides gifts for one's relatives… we were actually applying what we learned to serve a useful human need. Building a compost toilet requires much physical labour... the idea behind the compost toilet being that, by giving back what we take from the soil, we refrain from disrupting the natural cycle, and simultaneously develop an awareness of being responsible for our own wastage rather than flushing it away and forgetting about it. This pleasing balance of intellectual and practical learning generated a real enthusiasm amongst us... self-sufficiency in a facility devoid field meant that each group became dependent on the other for resources. We were able to develop a consciousness of some of the most pertinent environmental issues today, by way of direct application.

Eighteen-year-olds today will often be found searching through an intellectual framework to test the evidence and correctness of their thoughts and actions placed within the contemporary context of sustainability. These pupils were thirsty to have themselves tested, not solely on an intellectual level, but so as to confront a threshold experience of an inner nature; a test which sustains and contributes long term to human development. Through such activities a school can develop a new and potent resource and an educational framework that incorporates the outdoor classroom as a complement to the existing learning environment.

Curriculum

Activities can be organised in an open and flexible framework around the theme of 'a descent into matter'. This descent follows the incarnation path of children into adolescence and uses the age appropriate practical skill to engage the path of incarnation. The nine ancient crafts of mankind, sourced from the three kingdoms of nature and found at the interface of the four elements, arise from within the inspiration of the Steiner-Waldorf curriculum. By sourcing the primary materials, as is so often done in the Kindergarten, we are in effect starting to reinvigorate children's sensory perception of the world through the hand. The age appropriateness of any activity must arise out of a clear understanding of child development in conjunction with the teacher's observation. With the advent of current lifestyles, teachers are finding that a more fundamental and therapeutic intensification in gestures of movement is increasingly required to cultivate healthy development and limb, hand and eye co-ordination. Fewer children cook, climb trees, play on farms and in forests. The natural world is more and more a foreign experience. The world of play requires an intensification and orientation towards the practical. This practical aspect is more consciously applied to the main-lesson curriculum in Class 3; the awakening to landscape, shelter and buildings. Foundations are laid during this period for the craft curriculum to work on later in the development of thinking skills. By employing empathetic processes and materials at source, appropriate access is granted to what has often been seen as premature experience in the past in developing a handcraft curriculum for the younger children in the school. For example, with regard to blacksmithing, Rudolf Steiner requested that the blacksmith work back to back with the Kindergarten so the rhythm, fire and stature of the blacksmith imprints itself on the senses of the child. But blacksmithing itself is only practised in Class 10. Perceiving the elements of blacksmithing as opposed to executing the function of an item enables children in their Class 4 main-lesson on Norse mythology to become Thor at the anvil in the blacksmith workshop, guided by the element of fire and the rhythm of beating. Children in Kindergarten, whittling with their knives and sticks, are exploring the first qualities of resistance. Incorporating the activity of whittling into the woodwork curriculum is of particular value so as to give the foundations of co-ordination prior to the more sophisticated expectations of cutting and carving.

Looking at the textile curriculum in a similar way, the Kindergarten children on a walk will collect wool from the hedges and hawthorn. This point of contact is a treasured moment as the soft, delicate, warm and ephemeral quality of the material is experienced. Children will invariably return with their pockets full and will compress and form it into nests, figures, animals or a simple wall hanging. This is in fact the start of the textile curriculum. Its emergence and appropriate application will be based on the judgement of the teacher. Rudolf Steiner left the craft teachers in the Study of Man with a remarkable opportunity of fashioning their curriculum based largely upon their own observation of children, their perception and understanding. This meeting of the material from the kingdoms of the earth and the school teacher's understanding of child development is a creative area in the Steiner-Waldorf approach, leaving a free space for development and research as regards curriculum content.

The diagram overleaf is intended to be more of an imagination of the three kingdoms and the four elements. In looking at a broader application of craft and practical skills activities in the lower part of the school, inspiration can be drawn from the earliest human craft activities. An interesting guideline for the application of a particular craft activity is to observe the gesture in the activity and the density of the material required. The denser the material the more appropriate the activity becomes for the development of the adolescents. Encountering the resistance of the material encourages forces of self-judgement and a pragmatic testing of the boundaries of the materials. It is notable that leatherwork, wood turning and metalwork in particular offer the highest levels of resistance in material, whereas papermaking, felt and clay work harmonise more readily with the Lower School curriculum. Negotiating fire is a crucial ingredient in the Upper School experience, as its potentially destructive forces need to be controlled, understood and directed. Activities such as casting metal, where the adolescents prejudge, think and make a model, requires an attitude of complete responsibility for the perfection or imperfection of the crafted item. In the repetition of the item all flaws are revealed. Craft activities that necessitate a high degree of judgement and intellectual rigour support the pupil in the last years of schooling. Challenging the adolescents to place the context of the activity in a sustainable and environmental context where rigour, reflection and prejudgement are required at each step, directs them into new areas of application towards a new ethic of deed, an orientation for the development of the world from the development of self. The descent into matter through animal, plant and mineral thereby becomes a developmental somersault into an ascent into community.

30. AN INTEGRATED APPROACH TO CRAFTWORK

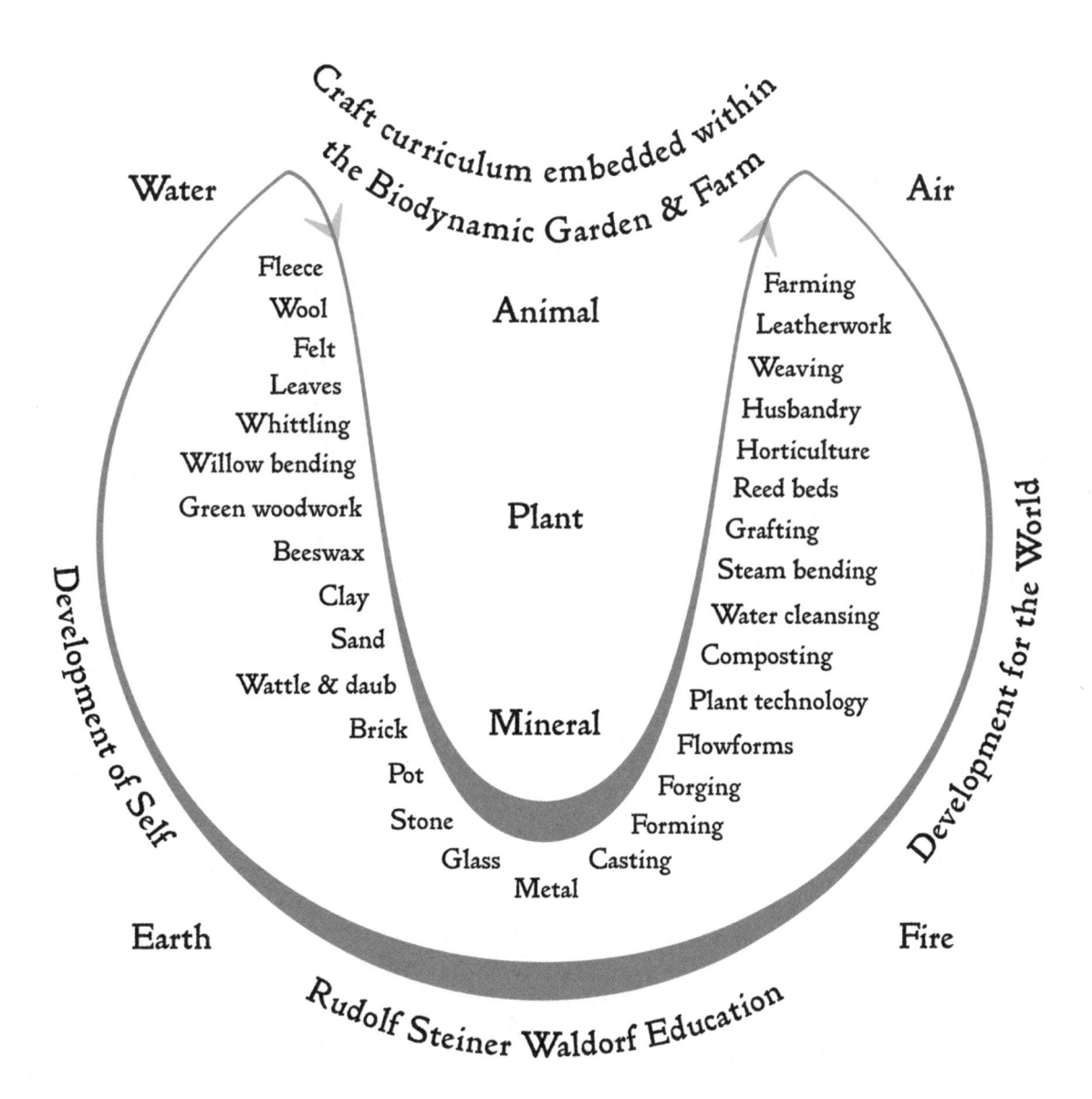

Craft curriculum embedded within the Biodynamic Garden & Farm

Water — Air

Animal
- Fleece
- Wool
- Felt
- Leaves
- Whittling
- Willow bending
- Green woodwork
- Beeswax
- Clay
- Sand
- Wattle & daub
- Brick
- Pot
- Stone
- Glass

Plant

- Farming
- Leatherwork
- Weaving
- Husbandry
- Horticulture
- Reed beds
- Grafting
- Steam bending
- Water cleansing
- Composting
- Plant technology
- Flowforms
- Forging
- Forming
- Casting

Mineral

Metal

Development of Self — *Development for the World*

Earth — Fire

Rudolf Steiner Waldorf Education

Notes

Preface
1. Heydebrand, C. von, *The Curriculum of the First Waldorf School*, Steiner Waldorf Schools Fellowship, UK 1989.

Introduction
1. Steiner, R., *The Foundations of Human Experience* (Study of Man), lecture of Sep 4, 1919, Anthroposophic Press, USA 1996.
2. Stockmeyer, E.A. Karl, *Rudolf Steiner's Curriculum for Steiner-Waldorf Schools*, Floris Books, UK 2015.
3. 'Transition Towns' is a model whereby communities can respond to the twin challenges of peak oil and climate change.
4. Wilson, F.R., *The Hand*, Vintage Books, UK 1999.

1. From play in learning to joy in work
1. Steiner, R., *The Renewal of Education*, Steinerbooks, USA 2001.
2. Steiner, R., *A Modern Art of Education*, Steinerbooks, USA 2004.

2. The age of 'work maturity'
1. Steiner, R., *The Spiritual Ground of Education*, Steinerbooks, USA 2004.
2. Ibid.
3. Ibid.
4. Ibid.
5. Ibid.
6. Steiner, R., *Soul Economy: Body, Soul, and Spirit in Waldorf Education*, Steinerbooks, USA 2003.
7. Steiner, R., *Balance in Teaching*, Steinerbooks, USA 2007.
8. Rudolf Steiner spoke about these processes in most of his lectures to teachers. Basic material can be found in *The Education of the Child*, Anthroposophic Press, USA 1996.
9. Heydebrand, C. von, *The Curriculum of the First Waldorf School*, Steiner Waldorf Schools Fellowship, UK 1989.
10. Steiner, R., *Soul Economy: Body, Soul, and Spirit in Waldorf Education*, Steinerbooks, USA 2003; *The Spiritual Ground of Education*, Steinerbooks, USA 2004.

4. Getting ready for craft lessons
1. The pocket knife must be very sharp. Cutting with blunt blades is both dangerous and pedagogically unsound. Handling carving tools demands the greatest caution and responsibility of the teacher.
2. A 'frow' is used especially as a splitting tool in the manufacture of shingle.

5. Shifting emphasis in craft lessons
1. Steiner, R., *The Spiritual Ground of Education*, lecture of Aug 22, 1922, Steinerbooks, USA 2004. See also 'Part Three: Working with Metals'.
2. Ibid.
3. Steiner, R., *Soul Economy: Body, Soul, and Spirit in Waldorf Education*, lecture of Jan 2, 1922, Steinerbooks, USA 2003.

6. Crafts in the Middle School

1. All illustrations are of work done by children.
2. Steiner, R., *Soul Economy: Body, Soul, and Spirit in Waldorf Education*, lecture of Jan 2, 1922, Steinerbooks, USA 2003.

8. Reflections on moveable toys

1. Wolffhügel, M., in *Erziehungskunst*, 1952, Nos. 5 and 6.
2. Ibid.
3. Steiner, R., *The Spiritual Ground of Education*, Steinerbooks, USA 2004, lecture of Aug 23, 1923 on the occasion of an exhibition of arts and crafts made by Waldorf children.
4. Steiner, R., *Faculty Meetings with Rudolf Steiner*, Sep 22, 1920, Anthroposophic Press, USA 1998.
5. Steiner, R., *Practical Advice to Teachers*, lecture of Sep 2, 1919, Anthroposophic Press, USA 2000.
6. Steiner, R., *The Spiritual Ground of Education*, Aug 22, 1922, Steinerbooks, USA 2004.
7. Steiner, R., *Soul Economy: Body, Soul, and Spirit in Waldorf Education*, lecture of Jan 2, 1922, Steinerbooks, USA 2003.
8. Baravalle, H. von, *On Teaching Physics and Mathematics*, Mercury Press, USA 1993.

9. Investigating the nature of wood

1. Steiner, R., *The Child's Changing Consciousness*, lecture of April 20, 1923, Anthroposophic Press, USA 1996.
2. Steiner, R,. *Architektur, Plastik und Malerei des ersten Goetheanum* lecture of Oct 16, 1920, Rudolf Steiner Verlag, Switzerland 2014 (no English translation).
3. The first Goetheanum was built in Dornach (Switzerland) entirely of wood on a concrete foundation. It was destroyed by fire on Dec 31, 1922.

10. Artistic elements in the crafts

1. Rudolf Steiner referred to these forces as 'etheric formative forces'.
2. Steiner, R., *Faculty Meetings with Rudolf Steiner*, July 30, 1920, Anthroposophic Press, USA 1998.
3. Wolffhügel, M., in *Erziehungskunst*, May/June 1952.
4. Steiner, R., *The Spiritual Ground of Education*, lecture of Aug 23, 1922, Steinerbooks, USA 2004.
5. Steiner, R., *A Modern Art of Education*, Aug 17, 1923, Steinerbooks, USA 2004.

11. Colour in the craft room

1. Stockmeyer, E.A. Karl, trans Everett-Zade, R., *Rudolf Steiner's Curriculum for Steiner-Waldorf Schools – An Attempt to Summarise His Indications*, fifth edition, Floris Books, UK 2015.
2. See original text, ed. Martin, M., Verlag Freies Geistesleben, Stuttgart 1991.
3. Steiner, R., *Colour*, lecture of Jan 1, 1915 Rudolf Steiner Press, UK 1997.
4. Ibid.

12. Arts and crafts and the human being

1. Steiner, R., *Education for Adolescents*, lectures of June 15 and 17, 1921, Anthroposophic Press, USA 1996.
2. Ibid.
3. Steiner, R., *A Modern Art of Education*, lecture of Aug 17, 1923, Steinerbooks, USA 2004.
4. Wolffhügel, M., in *Erziehungskunst*, May/June 1952.
5. Steiner, R., *Education for Adolescents*, lecture of June 16, 1921, Anthroposophic Press, USA 1996.

13. Form-giving elements and techniques

1. Steiner, R., *Soul Economy: Body, Soul and Spirit in Waldorf Education*, lecture of Jan 4, 1922, Steinerbooks 2003.
2. Goethe, J.W., *Über die Spiraltendenz des Vegetativen* (On the Tendency to Spiral Forms in Plants), 1831.
3. Steiner R., *The Kingdom of Childhood*, lecture of Aug 19, 1924, Anthroposophic Press, USA 1995. See also 'The shoemaking block', pp. 148–55.
4. Steiner, R., *Faculty Meetings with Rudolf Steiner*, June 17, 1921, Anthroposophic Press, USA 1998.
5. Steiner, R., *Practical Advice to Teachers*, lecture of Sep 3, 1919, Anthroposophic Press, USA 2000.
6. Steiner, R., *The Child's Changing Consciousness*, April 21, 1923, Anthroposophic Press, USA 1996.
7. Ibid.
8. Steiner, R., *Faculty Meetings with Rudolf Steiner*, April 28, 1922 and June 20, 1922, Anthroposophic Press, USA 1998.
9. Heydebrand, C. von, *The Curriculum of the First Waldorf School*, Steiner Schools Fellowship, UK 1989.

14. Pottery lessons

1. Stockmeyer, E. A. Karl, *The Steiner School Curriculum for Steiner-Waldorf Schools*, fifth edition, Floris Books, UK 2015.
2. Leach, B., *A Potter's Book*, Faber and Faber, UK 1976.
3. The German word *Schale* can mean a dish, bowl or even cup, but also a creature or nut's shell or a fruit or vegetable's skin.
4. Leach, B., *A Potter's Book*, Faber and Faber, UK 1976.
5. Steiner, R., *A Modern Art of Education*, 1923, Rudolf Steiner Press, UK 1981.
6. Carden, M., *Pioneer Pottery*, Prentice Hall Press, USA 1971.
7. Steiner, R., *The Spiritual Hierarchies and the Physical World*, question and answer period to the lecture of April 22, 1909, Steinerbooks, USA 2008.

16. The shoemaking block

1. Steiner, R., *The Kingdom of Childhood*, lecture of Aug 19, 1924, Anthroposophic Press, USA 1995.
2. Steiner, R., *A Modern Art of Education*, lecture of Aug 17, Steinerbooks, USA 2004.
3. All quotations from *Education for Adolescents*, lectures of June 15 and 17, 1921, Anthroposophic Press, USA 1996.
4. Martin, M., in *Erziehungskunst*, October 1985.

17. Working with metals

1. Steiner, R., *The Spiritual Ground of Education*, lecture of Aug 22, 1922, Steinerbooks, USA 2004. See also 'Shifting emphasis in craft lessons', pp. 41–43.
2. Kipp, F. A., *Die Evolution des Menschen*, Verlag Freies Geistesleben, Stuttgart 1991 (no English translation).
3. "Especially important are L. Kolisko's experiments that could justifiably be called: the stars' effects on earth substances. She was able to show a series of reactions of metal solutions upon one another (passing the process through complicated colloidal-chemical changes) that they became sensitive to certain cosmic constellations." – From: Pelikan, W., *The Secrets of Metals*, Steinerbooks, USA 2006.
4. See 'Work and Rhythm', pp. 258–62.
5. See 'Investigating the nature of wood', pp. 77–89.

18. Working with iron

1. Homologous for left-handers who will face the anvil correspondingly.
2. Steiner, R., *The World of the Senses and the World of the Spirit*, lecture of Dec 28, 1911, Rudolf Steiner Press, UK 2014.
3. Santa Clara, A., *Etwas für alle*, Würzburg, 1699.

19. Copper and iron workshops

1. Rosegger, P., *Als ich noch der Waldbauernbub war* (When I was a Peasant Boy in the Forest), 1902.

20. The joinery main-lesson blocks

1. See illustration on p.188.
2. Many Steiner-Waldorf schools encourage individual projects in Class 8 and/or Class 12, chosen by the students. Although supervised by the teacher, the students do most of the work in their spare time. The projects may be in any of the available subjects.

22. Lessons in modelling and shaded drawing

1. Steiner, R., *Theosophy*, Anthroposophic Press, USA 1994.
2. Steiner, R., *Colour*, lecture of Dec 10, 1920, Rudolf Steiner Press, UK 1997.
3. Steiner, R., *Soul Economy: Body, Soul, and Spirit in Waldorf Education*, lecture of Jan 3, 1922, Steinerbooks, USA 2003.
4. Wolffhügel, M., in *Erziehungskunst*, May/June 1952.
5. Wildgruber, T., trans Barton, M., *Painting and Drawing in Waldorf Schools (Classes 1 to 8)*, Floris Books, UK, 2012 and Bruin, D., Lichthart, A., *Painting in Waldorf Education*, second edition, Floris Books, UK 2004.
6. Steiner, R., *Practical Advice to Teachers*, lecture of Aug 21, 1921, Anthroposophic Press, USA 2000.

23. Metamorphosis and modelling lessons

1. Goethe, J. W., *The Metamorphosis of the Plant*, MIT Press, USA 2009 (originally published in German in 1790).
2. Ibid.

3. Steiner, R., *Kunst und Kunsterkenntnis*, lectures of Nov 9, 1888, and Feb 17, 1918, Rudolf Steiner Verlag, Switzerland 1985; *A Modern Art of Education*, lecture of Aug 16, 1923, Steinerbooks, USA 2004.
4. Aeppli, W., *The Care and Development of the Senses*, Floris Books, UK 2013.

24. Working with stone

1. The last image is of a project done for the Technical College Certificate *(Fach-hochschulreife)*.

25. Stone carving in the Upper School

1. Steiner, R., *Architecture as a Synthesis of the Arts*, lecture of June 7, 1914, Rudolf Steiner Press, UK 1999.
2. Steiner, R., *Architektur, Plastik und Malerei des ersten Goetheanum*, lecture of Oct 16, 1920, Rudolf Steiner Verlag, Switzerland 2016.
3. Schiller, F., *On the Aesthetic Education of Man*, Letter 9.
4. Steiner, R., *The Foundations of Human Experience*, lecture of Aug 21, 1919, Anthroposophic Press, USA 1996.

27. Work and rhythm

1. Bücher, K., *Work and Rhythm*.
2. Steiner, R., *Faculty Meetings with Rudolf Steiner*, Anthroposophic Press, USA 1998.

28. Methods in the formative lessons

1. Steiner, R., *Practical Advice to Teachers*, Anthroposophic Press, USA 2000.
2. Ibid.
3. In this connection the following statement by Jaques Lusseyran might be interesting: "Everything happened as though the light were no longer an object of the outer world, no longer this strange shedding of light, no longer this natural phenomenon that may or may not be there, over which we have such little power: but as though this light from now on was enveloping both the outer world and myself with just one grasp. Having no physical sight, I was not able to say whether the light I perceived came from without. Neither could I say whether it came from within. Indeed, inside and outside had become inadequate concepts. When, much later during my studies, I was told of the difference between objective and subjective facts, this did not satisfy me: I saw only too clearly that such a difference rested on an erroneous conception of the way we perceive..." – From Lusseyran, J., in *What One Sees without Eyes: Selected Writings of Jacques Lusseyran*, Floris Books, UK 1999.
4. Wiesenhütter, E., *Blick nach drüben*, Furche 1975, (no English translation).
5. Wimmer, H., *On Sculpting*, publication details not known.

29. The influence of work on thinking

1. Steiner, R., *Foundations of Human Experience*, lecture of Sep 1, 1919, Anthroposophic Press, USA 1996.
2. *Nürnberger Nachrichten*, July 6, 1985.
3. Charles Darwin, *Autobiography*, W. W. Norton & Company, New York, 1993.
4. Steiner, R., *The Spirit of the Waldorf School*, lecture of Aug 31, 1919, Anthroposophic Press, USA 1995.
5. Steiner, R., *Becoming the Archangel Michael's Companions*, lecture of Oct 10, 1922, Steinerbooks, USA 2006.
6. Quoted by Steiner in *Riddles of the Soul*, Mercury Press, USA 1996.
7. Steiner, R., *Foundations of Human Experience*, lecture of Sep 4, 1919, Anthroposophic Press, USA 1996.
8. Ibid.
9. Steiner, R., *The Spirit of the Waldorf School*, lecture of Aug 31, 1919, Anthroposophic Press, USA 1995.
10. Steiner, R., *Soul Economy: Body, Soul, and Spirit in Waldorf Education*, Steinerbooks, USA 2003.
11. Steiner, R., *Theosophy*, Anthroposophic Press, USA 1994; *Knowledge of the Higher Worlds*, Rudolf Steiner Press, UK 2009; *Occult Science*, Rudolf Steiner Press, UK 2013.
12. Steiner, R., *The Renewal of Education*, Steinerbooks, USA 2001.
13. Steiner, R., *Soul Economy: Body, Soul, and Spirit in Waldorf Education*, lecture of Jan 2, 1922, Steinerbooks, USA 2003.

Index of activities and materials

Ceramics and clay
animals 220, 226
bowls 127f, 138
brick-makers 141
ceramics 126
clay 127–30, 139, 141, 144–46, 196, 219, 229, 237, 245, 247, 268
drying 143
firing 135, 143
forms 223
glazing 140, 143
iron-bearing 142
kneading 142
loam 141
modelling 33, 35, 131, 146f, 193, 196, 198, 200, 215, 217–21, 223, 225, 227, 229, 237f, 244, 267, 274
movement 225
people 220, 226
pinch-pot technique 128
porcelain 141
pots 131–33
pottery 109, 126, 146f
proportions 225
pugging 142
sedimentary 142
surfaces 223
throwing 135
vases 133
wheel 136–40

Drawing
shaded drawing 193, 203f, 207, 216

Metalwork
alloys 162
beating 172
copper 157–62, 175
chrome 167
forging 170
gold 159
hammering 169
iron 158, 166–72, 175
— forging 115
lead 167
metalwork 112, 156f, 168, 175
nickel 167
planishing 162
pouring 159
raising 165
rolling 159
zinc 167

Other crafts
basketmaking 110
bookbinding 121
soap manufacture 119

Stone carving
animals 231, 244f
chalk 235
marble 237, 244
people 231, 247
sandstone 235
stone 230, 245f
— carving 230, 234, 237, 245
tuff 235, 241

Textiles
dressmaking 118
leather 150, 152
macramé 111
shoemaking 112, 148–50, 155
spinning 113
tailoring 118
weaving 116

Woodwork
animals 96
apple tree 83
balsa 47
birch 54, 82
bowls 51
cherry tree 83
chiselling 185
dovetailing 178, 185
elm 88
fir tree 54
gluing 183
houses 50
humming toys 36
joinery 119, 178, 181, 189
juniper 47

laburnum 78
lilac 47
lime 38f
maple 86
moveable toys 70, 72
musical instruments 59, 81
nut tree 47
oak 47, 85
pear tree 83
pine 47, 86, 179
planing 184

plum tree 47, 83
polishing 186
reed flutes 36
reeds 36
rope ladder 47
sapwood 181
sawing 37, 179
— wood 37
slotting and pegging 178
splitting wood 37, 80
spoons 48

squaring 180
toolmaking 38, 49
toy boats 61
varnishing 187
waxes and oils 58, 219
wood 36, 37, 78, 189
woodcarving 33, 42, 46f, 190, 219, 252
woodwork 46, 77
yew 78

More books on arts, crafts and Steiner-Waldorf education

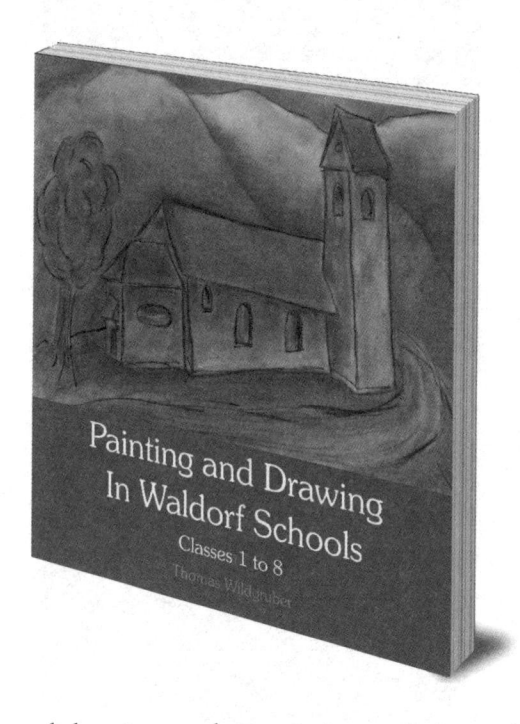

Painting and Drawing In Waldorf Schools, Classes 1 to 8
Thomas Wildgruber

Painting and drawing are key artistic expressions which play an important role in children's physical, emotional and spiritual development. This comprehensive teachers' manual provides a complete artistic curriculum for Classes 1 to 8 in Steiner-Waldorf schools (age six to fourteen).

At each stage, the book demonstrates the skills that teachers can help children to develop. There are 280 practical exercises for teachers to use, and over 800 drawings and paintings as inspiring examples of artistic possibilities. The curriculum moves from free drawing, to guided colour exercises, to precise perspective drawing.

The exercises draw on elements of the Steiner-Waldorf curriculum at appropriate ages, incorporating themes from fables and legends, the Old Testament, Norse mythology, animals, Ancient Greece and botany.

florisbooks.co.uk

The Gnome Craft Book
Thomas and Petra Berger

Earth, Water, Fire and Air
Playful Explorations in the Four Elements
Walter Kraul

Transparent Window Scenes through the Year
Michaela Krohshage and Sylvia Schwartz

Astronomy for Young and Old
A Beginner's Guide to the Visible Sky
Walter Kraul

Woodworking with Children
Anette Grunditz and Ulf Erixon

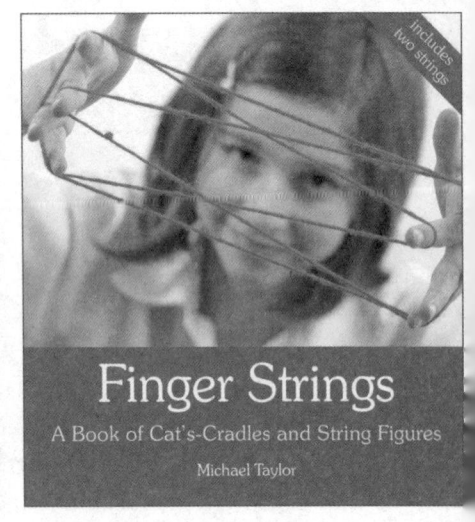

Finger Strings
A Book of Cat's-Cradles and String Figures
Michael Taylor

includes two strings

Spring and Summer Activities Come Rain or Shine
Seasonal Crafts and Games for Children
Edited by Stefanie Pfister

Magical Window Stars
Frédérique Guéret

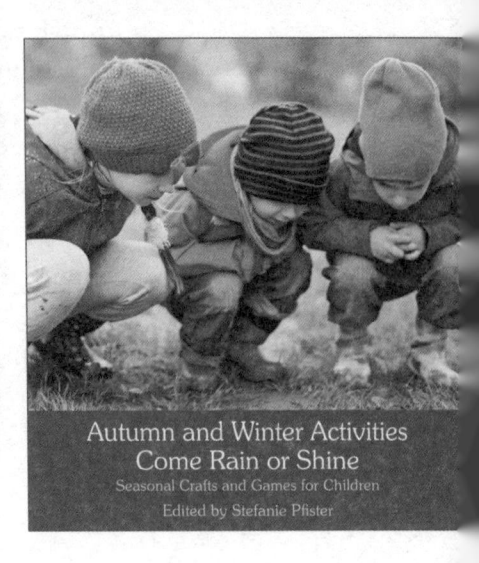

Autumn and Winter Activities Come Rain or Shine
Seasonal Crafts and Games for Children
Edited by Stefanie Pfister

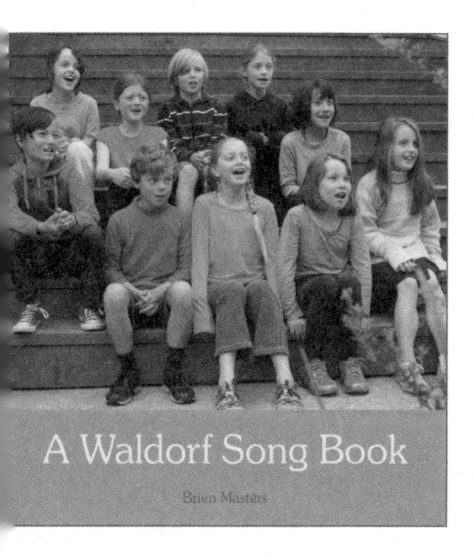

A Waldorf Song Book
Brien Masters

Nativity Plays for Children
Celebrating Christmas through Music and Movement
Wilma Ellersiek

Pumpkin Soup and Cherry Bread
A Steiner-Waldorf Kindergarten Cookbook
Rikke Rosengren and Nana Lyzet

EDUCATING through Art
The Steiner School Approach
Agnes Nobel

Earthwise
Environmental Crafts and Activities with Young Children
CAROL PETRASH

Drama at the Heart
Teaching Drama in Steiner-Waldorf Schools
Neil Smyth

TOWARDS CREATIVE TEACHING
Notes to an Evolving Curriculum for Steiner Waldorf Class Teachers
EDITED BY MARTYN RAWSON AND KEVIN AVISON

A Handbook for Steiner-Waldorf Class Teachers
Written and compiled by Kevin Avison

The Tasks and Content of the Steiner-Waldorf Curriculum
Edited by KEVIN AVISON and MARTYN RAWSON

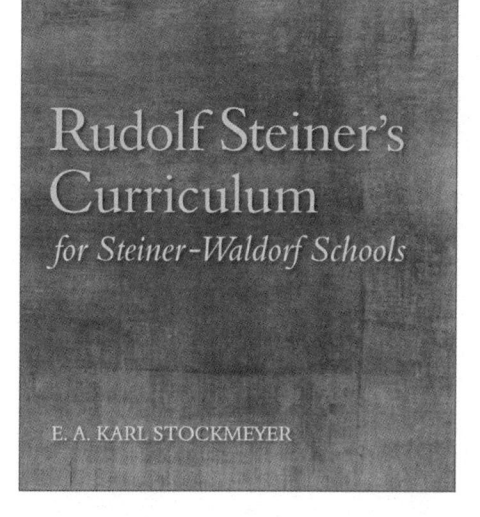

Rudolf Steiner's Curriculum for Steiner-Waldorf Schools
E. A. KARL STOCKMEYER

Floris Books

For news on all our **latest books**,
and to receive **exclusive discounts**,
join our mailing list at:

florisbooks.co.uk

Plus subscribers get a FREE book
with every online order!

We will never pass your details to anyone else.